The Psalms for Everyday Living

The Psalms for Everyday Living

A Year of Devotions with Charles Spurgeon's
Treasury of David

David J. McKinley

Foreword by Ross Purdy

RESOURCE *Publications* · Eugene, Oregon

THE PSALMS FOR EVERYDAY LIVING
A Year of Devotions with Charles Spurgeon's Treasury of David

Resource Publications
An Imprint of Wipf and Stock Publishers
199 W. 8th Ave., Suite 3
Eugene, OR 97401

www.wipfandstock.com

PAPERBACK ISBN: 978-1-6667-0838-7
HARDCOVER ISBN: 978-1-6667-0839-4
EBOOK ISBN: 978-1-6667-0840-0

06/10/21

To Dad and Mom

John and Joyce McKinley

For their love and encouragement

throughout the years and for this project.

We look forward to rejoicing in heaven with Dad

(1928–2020)

Foreword

When David McKinley asked if I would be willing to write a foreword for his work on Charles Spurgeon's commentary on the Psalms, I wondered how anyone could improve on the powerful words of the great nineteenth-century preacher. As soon as I looked at McKinley's writing, I found myself engrossed in a new format of devotional material. I practiced the daily meditations and quickly realized that what McKinley has done is to highlight the Scripture and Spurgeon's wisdom, then to add an explanation of Spurgeon's context and meaning. The daily prayers seal the pieces of truth found on each page. McKinley offers practical advice on how to live in the wisdom of the Psalms, enhanced by the brilliance of Spurgeon.

As a colleague of McKinley's at the International Theological Seminary, I have had the privilege of lecturing in his courses on Spiritual Formation for the Christian Leader. His knowledge of spiritual growth, developed over the years by his studies and meditative practices, has influenced many seminary students in their understanding of the spiritual life. McKinley's passion for meditation inspires people to grow in their faith and to discover what it means to be a person of theological, spiritual, and personal depth.

Both Spurgeon and McKinley show that there is no better place to find insights into what it means to be a person seeking righteousness than in the words of the Psalms. In addition to being a journey toward a holy God, the Psalms are also a collection of the human experience, in all its victories and failures. In sum, the Psalms describe a relationship between the Great Shepherd of King David and our fragile humanity as God's people.

As I began my journey in McKinley's devotional, I expected to find a useful tool to aid my spiritual development. Over the weeks of putting his devotional into practice, what I found was a satisfying surprise: McKinley did not get in the way of Spurgeon's work, thus muddling the great preacher's wisdom on the Psalms. Instead, he reorganized the material to make it more meaningful for the twenty-first-century reader. McKinley provided a context for Spurgeon's words on the Psalms, then offered advice on how to apply it in daily living. His labor of love aptly places the reading of the Psalms into a new context for our time. McKinley has advanced Spurgeon's depth in a way that a modern person will find helpful as they experience the Psalms.

McKinley states that his purpose is to introduce us into the life and thought of Spurgeon and the sound theology of the Psalms. You will find that he does this effectively. He shows us how the great preacher introduces us to layers of depth in the Psalms. He rightly points out that Spurgeon introduces us not only to a biblical and doctrinal level of meditation, but also into a deeply personal one. The devotional takes us on a journey, with each step drawing us into a greater love for the Lord. To me, the highlight of each daily devotional is found in the prayer that completes each page with a useful and effective way to discover spiritual insights for one's daily life. Both the Psalms and Spurgeon's notes on the Psalms create within us a spiritual longing for God while hinting that the worship of the Lord is something to be grasped, not just in this life, but along the journey that leads onward forever into the fullness of God's love.

I have always had a fondness for Spurgeon's works, including *The Treasury of David*. I remember the feeling of reading his *Treasury* for the very first time and being struck by the way Spurgeon helped me grasp deep concepts. In the same way, I suspect I will remember McKinley's impact on me as fondly as I remember Spurgeon's. I know that as a pastor and a professor of Christian history, McKinley's devotional has already had a significant influence on my life.

I believe you will also find McKinley's insights as an aid to growing deeper in your faith and spiritual life. I trust that as you practice the daily devotions, you will discover that the wisdom of Spurgeon's *Treasury*, written more than a century ago, is still very much applicable today. If Spurgeon can be considered a spiritual guide in helping us to understand the Psalms, then McKinley is one of the modern-day guides leading us to enjoy the path of spiritual discovery in these ancient songs.

I think that you will find that this much-needed devotional for our time renews you in your faith journey and in your relationship to a wonderful God, to whom belongs all praise. I believe this was the endeavor of Spurgeon and, as a friend of David McKinley, I know that it is his as well.

Rev. Dr. Ross Purdy
Pastor, First Presbyterian Church of Burbank, California

Preface

I have vivid childhood memories of my maternal grandfather reading the Psalms at the breakfast table when we vacationed at our summer cottage. Since then, I've studied the Psalms in Hebrew at seminary, read about them in popular books, and preached from them numerous times. Most recently, my wife and I spent an entire year reading through the Psalms. Yet, far from having had my fill, I sensed I had only begun to plumb the depths of the psalter. Where else could I turn to satiate my hunger?

The answer was sitting on my library shelf. My paternal grandfather had bequeathed to me *The Treasury of David* by Charles Haddon Spurgeon. Believing "old" to be outdated and inferior to more contemporary scholarly commentaries, I had, to my embarrassment, left the clothbound volumes unopened for years. In so doing, I had overlooked a goldmine of precious insights into the Psalms.

A Unique Devotional

This one-year devotional on the Psalms is the first to harness the wealth of *The Treasury of David*. Spurgeon wrote a multivolume work from 1865 to 1885. It was his *magnum opus,* and has been described as "one of the greatest works on the Psalms ever written."* The sheer breadth of the *Treasury,* with Spurgeon's commentary, accompanying notes by other writers, and sermon outlines, is sufficient reason for this claim. However, it is the depth of the *Treasury* that makes it such an invaluable resource for the reader. A few factors contribute to its richness. One, Spurgeon draws us deep into the exposition of each psalm at a *biblical and doctrinal* level. He wrestles with the various interpretations of each psalm, leaving us with a better understanding of the psalter. Also, he uses the Psalms to teach us the essential doctrines of the Christian faith, including God's sovereignty and providence, salvation through Jesus Christ, and the role of the church.

With his expansive knowledge of and fervent love for the Puritans, Spurgeon wants the biblical and doctrinal knowledge to permeate and percolate in our hearts. Thus, the *Treasury* emphasizes both the mind and heart,

* Dallimore, *Spurgeon,* 197.

providing what he calls an "experimental" (experiential) thrust throughout the commentary. He instructs us that one

> must traverse the territory of the Psalms himself if he would know what a goodly land they are. They flow with milk and honey, but not to strangers; they are only fertile to lovers of their hills and vales. None but the Holy Spirit can give a person the key to the *Treasury* of David; and even he gives it rather to experience than to study. Happy is the one who knows the secret of the Psalms.*

Two, Spurgeon wrote the *Treasury* during his pastoral ministry at the Metropolitan Tabernacle in London. His warm pastoral experience and heart, along with a concern for a commitment to the word of God, spiritual growth, evangelism, personal and corporate worship, global missions, and social issues all mirror what is in the Psalms.

Three, since Spurgeon wrote most of the *Treasury* during severe personal crises, he enables us to read and study the Psalms at a deeper existential level. Throughout the twenty years it took to write the *Treasury*, he suffered painful physical illnesses such as rheumatic gout and kidney disease. In addition, he experienced bouts of chronic depression. Readers of the *Treasury* gain insights into the psalmists' own afflictions.

In Spurgeon's own words:

> In these busy days, it would be greatly to the spiritual profit of Christian men if they were more familiar with the Book of Psalms, in which they would find a complete armoury for life's battles, and a perfect supply for life's needs. Here we have both delight and usefulness, consolation and instruction. For every condition there is a Psalm, suitable and elevating. The Book supplies the babe in grace with penitent cries, and the perfected saint with triumphant songs. Its breadth of experience stretches from the jaws of hell to the gate of heaven. He who is acquainted with the marches of the Psalm country knows that the land flows with milk and honey, and he delights to travel therein. To such I have aspired to be a helpful companion.**

By delving into the *Treasury*, this devotional will contribute to a biblical and doctrinal understanding of the psalter, address vital matters related to the church and its people, and explore a number of personal issues.

---

* Spurgeon, *Treasury of David*, 2:vi.
** Spurgeon, *Treasury of David*, 6:vi.

How to Use This Devotional

Each daily reading begins with a portion of a psalm, for it is Scripture and the most important part of the devotional to be read and meditated upon. A pithy quote by Spurgeon follows, summarizing the theme for the day. The devotional itself is a summary of Spurgeon's writing with quotes from the *Treasury*. Examples from Spurgeon's life are used to illustrate biblical truths within the psalter. At the end, a short prayer is included, which is meant to stimulate further prayer and a desire for personal transformation in line with the day's theme.

There are 366 devotionals, providing the opportunity for morning and evening devotions on February 28 when there is no leap year.

In his commentary on Psalm 1:2, Spurgeon challenges us, "Do not many of you read the Bible in a hurried way—just a little bit and off you go? Do you not forget what you have read, and lose what little effect it seemed to have? How few of you are resolved to get to its soul, its life, its essence, and to drink in its meaning?"

To receive maximum benefit from these devotionals, it is wise to follow Spurgeon's advice to practice the "soul of reading," that is, to read slowly and meditatively while depending on the Holy Spirit to give insight into Scripture and into our own hearts.

Reading the *Treasury* every day for eight months gave me a greater awe for the beauty of the Psalms, a sharper hunger to learn from these ancient writers, and a deeper love for God, the ultimate author. My prayer is that this book would do the same for you.

Acknowledgments

I began this writing journey in relative isolation during the pandemic of 2020, but I am thankful for the many companions who joined me along the way. Without them, this book would not have become a reality.

I am grateful for the opportunity I had to spend one year reading through Timothy and Kathy Keller's *The Songs of Jesus*. This investment of time and thought in the Psalms became a catalyst to explore them further by reading and studying Charles Spurgeon's commentary—*The Treasury of David*. Keller's framework for his devotionals also influenced my work.

My family and numerous friends cheered me along the way. Dad and Mom were such big supporters. Only a few weeks before his passing, Dad told me what an important project I had undertaken and he believed it would touch people's lives. My sister, Brenda, and my brother-in-law, Grant Del Begio, faithfully encouraged me and prayed for me throughout the entire project. The home Bible study groups which I am a part of at Christ Church Sierra Madre supported me with their interest and prayer.

Thank you to Robert Covolo, Steve Daniels, John Murray, Arvid Olson, and Ron Unruh, who read various portions of the draft in its earlier stage. Your helpful recommendations and affirmation motivated me to press on. My faculty colleagues at International Theological Seminary emphasized the value of this project and provided timely suggestions. Thank you to Ross Purdy who wrote the foreword; your love for church history in the Victorian Era offers you a unique perspective on Spurgeon and his ministry.

Ryan Smernoff's publishing expertise steered me in the right direction for publication. Mary Ong's excellent editing skills enhanced the quality of the manuscript. Matthew Wimer, the Editorial Production Manager at Wipf & Stock, and the rest of his team, patiently and wisely guided me along every step of the publication process. A big thanks to each one of you.

I am deeply appreciative for my wife, Laura, who provided a quiet sanctuary for me to write for many months. Her encouragement and prayers kept me going—especially during the challenging moments.

I am most grateful for the grace of the Lord, who turned my daily readings of the *Treasury* into this book. More importantly, I am thankful to God for giving me a deeper love for his word, and for drawing me closer to him.

January 1   Psalm 1

1 Blessed is the man who walks not in the counsel of the wicked, nor stands in the way of sinners, nor sits in the seat of scoffers; 2 but his delight is in the law of the Lord, and on his law he meditates day and night. 3 He is like a tree planted by streams of water that yields its fruit in its season, and its leaf does not wither. In all that he does, he prospers. 4 The wicked are not so, but are like chaff that the wind drives away. 5 Therefore the wicked will not stand in the judgment, nor sinners in the congregation of the righteous; 6 for the Lord knows the way of the righteous, but the way of the wicked will perish. (ESV)

"It is not outward prosperity which the Christian most desires and values; it is soul prosperity which he longs for."

A fruitful life. Charles Spurgeon points out the word "blessed" (v. 1) is plural in Hebrew. It is the follower of Jesus who can experience the "multiplicity of blessings" from God. By delighting in and musing on God's word (v. 2), spiritual fruit is produced in the different seasons of life. For example, there is the fruit of patience during a period of suffering, the fruit of faith in trying times, and the fruit of "holy joy" in seasons of prosperity (v. 3). Such prosperity should not be measured by external standards but by the means which will be good for our "soul's health." Whether it be poverty, bereavement, or strong opposition, Spurgeon wisely reminds us, "Our worst things are often our best things." There is no other viable option for a fruitful life. Those who oppose God are like chaff, with a divine judgment awaiting them.

Prayer. Heavenly Father, you know everything I will experience in this coming year. Whatever may occur, help me to delight in you and your word by daily meditating on it. I long to have my life bear fruit of godly character this year so that you may be honored through me. Amen.

1 Why are the nations restless and the peoples plotting in vain? 2 The kings of the earth take their stand and the rulers conspire together against the Lord and against his Anointed, saying, 3 "Let's tear their shackles apart and throw their ropes away from us!" 4 He who sits in the heavens laughs, the Lord scoffs at them. 5 Then he will speak to them in his anger and terrify them in his fury, saying, 6 "But as for me, I have installed my King upon Zion, my holy mountain." 7 "I will announce the decree of the Lord: he said to me, 'You are my Son, today I have fathered you. 8 Ask *it* of me, and I will certainly give the nations as your inheritance, and the ends of the earth as your possession. 9 You shall break them with a rod of iron, you shall shatter them like earthenware.'" 10 Now then, you kings, use insight; let yourselves be instructed, you judges of the earth. 11 Serve the Lord with reverence and rejoice with trembling. 12 Kiss the Son, that he not be angry and you perish *on* the way, for his wrath may be kindled quickly. How blessed are all who take refuge in him! (NASB)

"O how wise, how infinitely wise is obedience to Jesus, and how dreadful is the folly of those who continue to be his enemies."

A foolish life. Spurgeon gives three reasons why it is futile to oppose God. Rage (v. 1) and "deep-seated hate" toward God lead to the foolish belief that one can be victorious against God. Such thinking amazes the psalmist. Secondly, God laughs at those who oppose him (v. 5). His son, Jesus, is already established on the throne, reigning over the world (vv. 4–6). "He has not taken the trouble to rise up and do battle with them—he despises them, he knows how absurd, how irrational, how futile are their attempts against him—he therefore laughs at them." Finally, Jesus has made his enemies a part of his inheritance (v. 8). "Those who will not bend must break." In light of this, we are called to be wise (v. 10). We can do so by heeding divine warning (v. 10), by humbly serving Jesus, and by praising him (v. 11). Such actions reveal our trust ("refuge") in him who blesses us (v. 12). This is far better than living like useless pieces of broken pottery.

Prayer. Lord, help me to see clearly the foolishness of opposing you. I willingly submit my heart, my ambitions and activities to you, Jesus, who reigns over the world. Reign in my life, for this is the path to living wisely! Amen.

1 O LORD, I have so many enemies; so many are against me. 2 So many are saying, "God will never rescue him!" 3 But you, O LORD, are a shield around me; you are my glory, the one who holds my head high. 4 I cried out to the LORD, and he answered me from his holy mountain. 5 I lay down and slept, yet I woke up in safety, for the LORD was watching over me. 6 I am not afraid of ten thousand enemies who surround me on every side. 7 Arise, O LORD! Rescue me, my God! Slap all my enemies in the face! Shatter the teeth of the wicked! 8 Victory comes from you, O LORD. May you bless your people. (NLT)

"O for grace to see our future glory amid present shame!"

Afflictions and assurance. David's psalm is a realistic reflection on his own life and a sober reminder that we are not immune from struggles and painful experiences. He faced not only the rebellion of his son, Absalom, but also the desertion of many others (2 Sam 15:12). Critics would have us believe there is no hope when God apparently cannot help us in our adversity (v. 2). "It is the most bitter of all afflictions to be led in fear that there is no help for us in God." Yet, David did not give up hope, knowing God would protect him. He could sleep at night knowing God was his deliverer who destroyed his enemies and blesseed those who trusted in him (vv. 5-8). Very early in his pastorate in London, Spurgeon faced vehement criticism from the secular media who regarded him as a charlatan due to his young age and lack of theological training. Religious media also attacked him because of his theological beliefs and his concern to see people come to Christ.* In response, Spurgeon's "strongest reply to them was the glory of the gospel that he preached." We too can rest in God and depend on all the resources of his grace which he avails for us. He has the final word.

Prayer. Lord, I think of your Son, Jesus, who was rejected by his enemies and deserted by his friends. He who suffered so much for my sake trusted you, Father, in the darkest hours. I am thankful for your assurance you are with me—even in my darkest of times. Help me to trust in your great love in my present circumstances! Amen.

---

* Dallimore, *Spurgeon*, 66–71.

1 Answer me when I call to you, my righteous God. Give me relief from my distress; have mercy on me and hear my prayer. 2 How long will you people turn my glory into shame? How long will you love delusions and seek false gods? 3 Know that the LORD has set apart his faithful servant for himself; the LORD hears when I call to him. 4 Tremble and do not sin; when you are on your beds, search your hearts and be silent. 5 Offer the sacrifices of the righteous and trust in the LORD. 6 Many, LORD, are asking, "Who will bring us prosperity?" Let the light of your face shine on us. 7 Fill my heart with joy when their grain and new wine abound. 8 In peace I will lie down and sleep, for you alone, LORD, make me dwell in safety. (NIV)

> "How many of our sleepless hours might be traced to our untrusting and disordered minds."

Peace at night. At nightfall, David could reflect and admit the day had been very challenging. How can a person move from the "sleepless hours" to experience peace at the end of a stressful day? Spurgeon instructs us to appeal to God, who is a righteous judge. He not only hears our distress (vv. 1, 3) but he grants us relief and mercy. "The best of men need mercy as truly as the worst of men. All the deliverances of saints, as well as the pardons of sinners, are the free gifts of heavenly grace." Moreover, those who oppose God are delusional and their mockery will be short-lived (v. 2). It is equally important to experience the intimate presence of Jesus ("your face shine on us") through the indwelling Holy Spirit who gives us "joy unspeakable" (vv. 6–7). With these assurances, one can sleep well with a trusting heart and an ordered mind on him (v. 8). "They slumber sweetly whom faith rocks to sleep. No pillow so soft as a promise; no coverlet so warm as an assured interest in Christ."

Prayer. Father, I confess that I often go to bed with my mind churning and my heart racing because of the day's stresses. I am thankful that you are not only aware of my plight but you are also with me. Help me to trust you more in such times, and to lie down and sleep in peace like David every night. Amen.

January 5   Psalm 5:1–7

1 Listen to my words, Lord, consider my sighing. 2 Listen to the sound of my cry for help, my King and my God, for to you I pray. 3 In the morning, Lord, you will hear my voice; in the morning I will present my prayer to you and be on the watch. 4 For you are not a God who takes pleasure in wickedness; no evil can dwell with you. 5 The boastful will not stand before your eyes; you hate all who do injustice. 6 You destroy those who speak lies; the Lord loathes the person of bloodshed and deceit. 7 But as for me, by your abundant graciousness I will enter your house, at your holy temple I will bow in reverence for you. (NASB)

> "We should be careful to keep the stream of meditation always running; for this is the water to drive the mill of prayer."

Meditative prayer. Spurgeon describes "two sorts of prayers—those expressed in words, and the unuttered longings which abide as silent meditations." This psalm includes both. What David does not verbally express, he asks God to consider his heartfelt lament (v. 1). In great need he calls out to God in the morning (v. 3) for he faces those who oppose him and sin against God (vv. 4–6). However, David's prayer is not an impulsive prayer. Forethought in prayer involves carefully meditating on what we should say before God (v. 1). Then, with thoughtfulness we can either cry out to God (v. 2) or worship in his presence because of his great mercy (v. 7). Spurgeon spent much time reading and meditating on Scripture—we should do likewise.[*]

Prayer. Father, thank you for instructing me on how to approach you in prayer. Teach me to meditate on your word in order that my prayers go beyond my selfishness and shortsightedness. I want to call out to you in worship and with requests that honor your name in a world that opposes you. Amen.

---

[*] Morden, *C.H. Spurgeon*, 87.

January 6   Psalm 5:8–12

8 Lord, lead me in your righteousness because of my enemies; make your way straight before me. 9 For there is nothing trustworthy in their mouth; their inward part is destruction itself. Their throat is an open grave; they flatter with their tongue. 10 Make them pay, God; have them fall by their own schemes! Scatter them in the multitude of their wrongdoings, for they are rebellious against you. 11 But rejoice, all who take refuge in you, sing for joy forever! And may you shelter them, that those who love your name may rejoice in you. 12 For you bless the righteous person, Lord, you surround him with favor as with a shield. (NASB)

> "[W]hen we have learned to give up our own way, and long to walk God's way, it is a happy sign of God's grace."

Living rightly. There are those who strenuously oppose followers of Christ by saying anything to ruin them. It is tempting to retaliate when we have been insulted and hurt, but it is not the way Jesus would want us to respond. Following him means asking God to lead us in our response (v. 8), like a father leads a child. This is not always easy and it requires God's grace. Spurgeon comments, "[W]hen we have learned to give up our own way, and long to walk in God's way, it is a happy sign of grace; and it is no small mercy to see the way of God with clear vision straight before our face." We do this not only for the blessing we might receive from God (v. 12) but as an expression of trust and love for Jesus (v. 11).

Prayer. Lord, it is so tempting to retaliate when I have been insulted because of my association with you. I see how your Son continued to live rightly in a hostile world—enable me to grow in my trust and love for you so that I can live more like Jesus. Amen.

1 O Lord, don't rebuke me in your anger or discipline me in your rage. 2 Have compassion on me, Lord, for I am weak. Heal me, Lord, for my bones are in agony. 3 I am sick at heart. How long, O Lord, until you restore me? 4 Return, O Lord, and rescue me. Save me because of your unfailing love. 5 For the dead do not remember you. Who can praise you from the grave? 6 I am worn out from sobbing. All night I flood my bed with weeping, drenching it with my tears. 7 My vision is blurred by grief; my eyes are worn out because of all my enemies. 8 Go away, all you who do evil, for the Lord has heard my weeping. 9 The Lord has heard my plea; the Lord will answer my prayer. 10 May all my enemies be disgraced and terrified. May they suddenly turn back in shame. (NLT)

"Soul-trouble is the very soul of trouble."

Healing prayers. David prays for healing (v. 2) for "the curing of the wounds" which had afflicted his soul. The spiritual pain is real, expressed with groaning and weeping (vv. 6–7). In such a state we are weak, or, as Spurgeon writes, "I am one who droops." How can we go about experiencing spiritual healing? First, we have to be open to the Lord's rebuke (v. 1) where there might be sin. We also have to confess our weakness and need of healing (v. 2), which may be spiritual and emotional. We should then cry out to God for his mercy (v. 4). We do so not primarily for our sake but for God's sake. Spurgeon writes, "[M]ercy honours God . . . this is true of God, who, when he gives mercy, glorifies himself." We know healing has occurred when we have the renewed strength to face the day's challenges. Spurgeon went through times of "deep spiritual depression" but he persevered in his pastoral ministry by God's grace.[*]

Prayer. Loving Savior, I confess my bruised soul needs healing of resentments and hurts. Jesus, you show mercy to those who cry out to you. I ask you to bring healing to the deep places of my heart and relationships in order that you may be honored. Amen.

---

[*] Dallimore, *Spurgeon*, 74, 187.

January 8   Psalm 7:1–5

1 O LORD my God, in you do I take refuge; save me from all my pursuers and deliver me, 2 lest like a lion they tear my soul apart, rending it in pieces, with none to deliver. 3 O LORD my God, if I have done this, if there is wrong in my hands, 4 if I have repaid my friend with evil or plundered my enemy without cause, 5 let the enemy pursue my soul and overtake it, and let him trample my life to the ground and lay my glory in the dust. *Selah* (ESV)

"It is only at the tree laden with fruit that men throw stones. If we would live without being slandered we must wait until we get to heaven."

Slander. Spurgeon calls this psalm the "Song of the Slandered Saint." Like David, who was accused of conspiring against Saul, followers of Jesus are not spared from being slandered. Spurgeon cautions us, "Let us be very heedful not to believe the flying rumors which are always harassing gracious men." In other words, we should not be surprised when our character is smeared on account of our relationship to Jesus Christ. Even so, slander hurts (v. 2). How then do we turn such pain into a song? David examines his own life (vv. 3–5) and concludes with a "protestation of innocence." Spurgeon reminds us, "He needs not fear the curse [of slander] whose soul is clear of guilt." Once we know we are truly innocent, we place our trust in the character of God and ask him to exonerate us. Spurgeon writes, "What a blessing it would be if we could turn even the most disastrous event into a theme for song, and so turn the tables upon our great enemy." We cannot do this in our strength but by God's grace we can sing to God at such times.

Prayer. Gracious Father, when I am falsely accused and criticized, instead of lashing out with hurtful words, help me to turn to Jesus, who experienced what I am experiencing. Strengthen my trust in you during these painful times. Amen.

6 Arise, O LORD, in anger! Stand up against the fury of my enemies! Wake up, my God, and bring justice! 7 Gather the nations before you. Rule over them from on high. 8 The LORD judges the nations. Declare me righteous, O LORD, for I am innocent, O Most High! 9 End the evil of those who are wicked, and defend the righteous. For you look deep within the mind and heart, O righteous God. 10 God is my shield, saving those whose hearts are true and right. 11 God is an honest judge. He is angry with the wicked every day. 12 If a person does not repent, God will sharpen his sword; he will bend and string his bow. 13 He will prepare his deadly weapons and shoot his flaming arrows. (NLT)

"The judge has heard the cause, has cleared the guiltless, and uttered his voice against the persecutors."

God is Judge. When we have been falsely accused, we take the slander and criticism of others to God who judges fairly (vv. 6, 8). Though he is stirred by anger he still responds with justice, in contrast to the rage of his enemies (v. 6). We are often frustrated with God for his apparent lack of response to the rage of his opponents, hence the psalmist asks God to wake up (v. 6). However, God has his purposes for delaying. In Spurgeon's words, "God's silence is the patience of longsuffering, and if wearisome to the saints, they should bear it cheerfully in the hope that sinners may thereby be led to repentance." The psalmist does go to God because he looks beyond the actions to the mind and heart of each person (v. 9). At the same time, God will also search our lives to ensure integrity (v. 8) both in our heart and our conduct. God hates all forms of wickedness, and one day he will deal with and punish his enemies.

Prayer. Lord, apart from your righteousness in Jesus, I should face death for my own sinful ways. By your Spirit, shape my heart to hate all forms of sin. Grant me the patience to wait on you as you are the only fair judge to deal with all wickedness and evil. Until then, help me to speak truthfully and with love. Amen.

14 Behold, an evil person is pregnant with injustice, and he conceives harm and gives birth to lies. 15 He has dug a pit and hollowed it out, and has fallen into the hole which he made. 16 His harm will return on his own head, and his violence will descend on the top of his own head. 17 I will give thanks to the LORD according to his righteousness and will sing praise to the name of the LORD Most High. (NASB)

"Curses are like young chickens, they always come home to roost. Ashes always fly back in the face of him that throws them."

Imploded accusations. The psalmist uses word pictures to give insight to the nature of slander. Slander is conceived from "the virus of evil" within the person, giving birth to grievous disappointment (v. 14). Like hunters who use cunning methods to trap animals, slander is devious (v. 15). Also, slander is self-destructive (vv. 15–16). The wicked who plan against others discover their schemes have imploded on their own lives. "Men have burned their own fingers when they were hoping to brand their neighbor." Slander is dangerous for it hurts others and one's self. In contrast to the one who speaks maliciously, the Christ-follower praises God for who he is and what he will do (v. 17). "The slandered one is now a singer" because God's purposes are being carried out against those who oppose him.

Prayer. Lord, while I wait for you to judge all forms of sin one day, I know that the self-destructive nature of evil is a form of your judgment. Guard my heart from gloating over those who get what they deserve. Direct my eyes to see you acting according to your standards of righteousness. Help me to wait patiently on you and, in the meantime, to sow good deeds which will bear long-lasting fruit. Amen.

1 LORD, our Lord, how majestic is your name in all the earth! You have set your glory in the heavens. 2 Through the praise of children and infants you have established a stronghold against your enemies, to silence the foe and the avenger. 3 When I consider your heavens, the work of your fingers, the moon and the stars, which you have set in place, 4 what is mankind that you are mindful of them, human beings that you care for them? 5 You have made them a little lower than the angels and crowned them with glory and honor. 6 You made them rulers over the works of your hands; you put everything under their feet: 7 all flocks and herds, and the animals of the wild, 8 the birds in the sky, and the fish in the sea, all that swim the paths of the seas. 9 LORD, our Lord, how majestic is your name in all the earth! (NIV)

"A survey of the solar system has a tendency to moderate the pride of man and to promote humility."

The dignity of creation. The psalmist elevates the value of creation, from naturalistic origins to a supernatural starting point with God, who created both nature and humanity. In nature, the glorious might and power of God is seen (v. 1). When we consider the greatness of the universe, we may wonder about our value as human beings (v. 4). One may seem to be "an insignificant being . . . amidst the immensity of creation." However, the psalmist reminds us that God places a high value on each human being (vv. 5–8). Each one of us "is an object of the paternal care and mercy of the Most High." The dignity of humanity is fully realized in Jesus Christ, who suffered but is now exercising dominion over all creation. And we, in Christ, "are raised to a dominion wider than that of the first Adam." As humans we have dignity because we have been created by God, and one day we will reign with him for eternity.

Prayer. Lord, I confess that it is easy to feel puny and insignificant when I gaze at all the stars. It is also tempting to believe I have the power to do whatever I want. Your creation gives me the right perspective. You value me even though I may feel very small in comparison to the galaxies. I am humbled by your love and I gladly depend on you who created and redeemed me. Amen.

1 I will give thanks to the LORD with all my heart; I will tell of all your wonders. 2 I will rejoice and be jubilant in you; I will sing praise to your name, O Most High. 3 When my enemies turn back, they stumble and perish before you. 4 For you have maintained my just cause; you have sat on the throne judging righteously. 5 You have rebuked the nations, you have eliminated the wicked; you have wiped out their name forever and ever. 6 The enemy has come to an end in everlasting ruins, and you have uprooted the cities; the very memory of them has perished. 7 But the LORD sits as King forever; he has established his throne for judgment, 8 and he will judge the world in righteousness; he will execute judgment for the peoples fairly. 9 The Lord will also be a stronghold for the oppressed, a stronghold in times of trouble; 10 and those who know your name will put their trust in you, for you, LORD, have not abandoned those who seek you. 11 Sing praises to the LORD, who dwells in Zion; declare his deeds among the peoples. 12 For he who requires blood remembers them; he does not forget the cry of the needy. 13 Be gracious to me, LORD; see my oppression from those who hate me, you who lift me up from the gates of death, 14 so that I may tell of all your praises, that in the gates of the daughter of Zion I may rejoice in your salvation. (NASB)

"It is our duty to praise the Lord; let us perform it as a privilege."

Joyful thanks. We do not express "jubilant thanksgiving" to God as if there is no pain and suffering around us. Rather, even though there are "many forms of oppression" heard and seen on a daily basis (vv. 3, 9), the psalmist is teaching us that we must train our minds and hearts not to dwell on the woes of the world which discourage us but on the Lord. For he has done great things (v. 1), his presence is with us (v. 3), his judgment against evil is certain (vv. 7–8), and he tenderly cares for the afflicted (vv. 9–12). These actions are based on God's name or character (v. 10). Experiential knowledge of his character provides us with the "grace of faith" in difficult times. "The humble cry of the poorest saints shall neither be drowned by the voice of the thundering justice nor by the shrieks of the condemned." We can give thanks to God in such times.

Prayer. Almighty God, at times I feel overwhelmed by all the evil in the world. My heart can become skeptical that you are accomplishing your purposes. However, teach my heart to give thanks to you because of your greatness and your tender love for me. Amen.

15 The nations have fallen into the pit they dug for others. Their own feet have been caught in the trap they set. 16 The Lord is known for his justice. The wicked are trapped by their own deeds. 17 The wicked will go down to the grave. This is the fate of all the nations who ignore God. 18 But the needy will not be ignored forever; the hopes of the poor will not always be crushed. 19 Arise, O Lord! Do not let mere mortals defy you! Judge the nations! 20 Make them tremble in fear, O Lord. Let the nations know they are merely human. (NLT)

"Mercy is as ready to her work as ever justice can be."

Mercy and justice. These two seemingly contradictory qualities of God's character are expressed when wickedness is perpetrated against the followers of Jesus. If God overlooks evil, then he violates his own justice; if he is "severely just in judgment" he shows no mercy. However, God can act with both justice and mercy without violating either quality. The wicked are punished by God either by their own deeds or by future judgment (vv. 15–17). Spurgeon points out that there is a "warning to forgetters of God" (v. 17) for they will experience God's justice. Yet, this same God comes with mercy to those who "fear that they are forgotten" by him (v. 18). With this confidence, we can pray with anticipation that God will do what is right among the nations, and at times he will do this through his people. In every century, believers are called upon to show both justice and mercy to others. In Spurgeon's day, the opium trade afflicted the Chinese population and demanded justice among those who were greedy for the profit of opium.* Today, mercy must be shown to those who are afflicted by drugs and racial prejudice, while demanding justice for those who perpetuate the crimes of greed or violence. Showing mercy and concern for justice is the believer's way to honor Christ, who justly dealt with our sin and in mercy granted us eternal salvation.

Prayer. Lord, I get distressed when I feel you are not dealing with those who oppose you. I panic when I feel like you have forgotten me and have not shown me your kindness and mercy. Align my mind to the reality of who you are and change my wrong assumptions about your apparent lack of response in the world. Amen.

---

* Nettles, *Living by Revealed Truth*, 434.

January 14   Psalm 10:1–11

1 Why do you stand far away, Lord? Why do you hide yourself in times of trouble? 2 In arrogance the wicked hotly pursue the needy; let them be caught in the plots which they have devised. 3 For the wicked boasts of his soul's desire, and the greedy person curses and shows disrespect to the Lord. 4 The wicked, in his haughtiness, does not seek him. There is no God in all his schemes. 5 His ways succeed at all times; yet your judgments are on high, out of his sight; as for all his enemies, he snorts at them. 6 He says to himself, "I will not be moved; throughout the generations I will not be in adversity." 7 His mouth is full of cursing, deceit, and oppression; under his tongue is harm and injustice. 8 He sits in the lurking places of the villages; he kills the innocent in the secret places; his eyes surreptitiously watch for the unfortunate. 9 He lurks in secret like a lion in his lair; he lurks to catch the needy; he catches the needy when he pulls him into his net. 10 Then he crushes the needy one, who cowers; and unfortunate people fall by his mighty power. 11 He says to himself, "God has forgotten; he has hidden his face; he will never see it." (NASB)

"The presence of God is the joy of his people, but any suspicion of his absence is distracting beyond measure."

Silent suffering. Spurgeon states that "the character of the oppressor is described in powerful language" in verses 2–11. The troubles we face may be very difficult and even overwhelming. As one who personally experienced dark days in his own life, Spurgeon points out, "It is not the trouble, but the hiding of our Father's face, which cuts us to the quick." When there is a solar eclipse, daylight turns to darkness. Through God's hiddenness, he is accomplishing his purposes in our lives—even when we experience all kinds of animosity and hatred because of our allegiance to Christ. While our antagonists may think God has forgotten us and gone into hiding (v. 11), we know he has not. Believers in Christ are not immune from such dark days, but God is still silently with us.

Prayer. Lord, even in the darkest days I am thankful you have not abandoned me—even though I may feel like you have. I thank you for the indwelling Holy Spirit who is with me by your grace. Even when I cannot feel your presence, help me to face my day with confidence, knowing that you are still walking beside me. Amen.

12 Arise, Lᴏʀᴅ! Lift up your hand, O God. Do not forget the helpless. 13 Why does the wicked man revile God? Why does he say to himself, "He won't call me to account?" 14 But you, God, see the trouble of the afflicted; you consider their grief and take it in hand. The victims commit themselves to you; you are the helper of the fatherless. 15 Break the arm of the wicked man; call the evildoer to account for his wickedness that would not otherwise be found out. 16 The Lᴏʀᴅ is King for ever and ever; the nations will perish from his land. 17 You, Lᴏʀᴅ, hear the desire of the afflicted; you encourage them, and you listen to their cry, 18 defending the fatherless and the oppressed, so that mere earthly mortals will never again strike terror. (NIV)

"To the men who had neither justice nor mercy for the saints, there shall be rendered justice to the full, but not a grain of mercy."

Social injustice. Witnessing many social injustices in his own day,* Spurgeon could relate to this psalm, which he entitles "The cry of the oppressed." he goes on to say, "In these verses the description of the wicked is condensed" and yet the evil is no less here than what the earlier verses described in more detail. Knowing God sees "the trouble of the afflicted" (v. 14) is small comfort when he is seemingly unresponsive. What must God's people do? They must submit to his purposes and trust him to act in due time. "Resigning their judgment to his enlightenment, and their wills to his supremacy, they rest assured that he will order all things for the best." He will act and address social injustices (vv. 15–18). There is good reason to give praise, knowing God will act in his good time.

Prayer. Lord, my heart cries out for those who are oppressed because of the color of their skin, or their ethnicity, economic status, or religious beliefs. While society is filled with hatred and prejudice, guard me from being shaped by our culture. Shape my heart and mind with your love so that I may speak against social injustice and act with compassion. Amen.

---

* Nettles, *Living by Revealed Truth,* 341–43. Employees were paid very little for the work they did. The rich abused the medical system and the poor needlessly suffered in the hospitals.

1 In the LORD I take refuge; how can you say to my soul, "Flee as a bird to your mountain? 2 For, behold, the wicked bend the bow, they have set their arrow on the string to shoot in darkness at the upright in heart. 3 If the foundations are destroyed, what can the righteous do?" 4 The LORD is in his holy temple; the LORD's throne is in heaven; his eyes see, his eyelids test the sons of mankind. 5 The LORD tests the righteous and the wicked, and his soul hates one who loves violence. 6 He will rain coals of fire upon the wicked, and brimstone and burning wind will be the portion of their cup. 7 For the LORD is righteous, he loves righteousness; the upright will see his face. (ESV)

"When Satan cannot overthrow us by presumption, how craftily will he seek to ruin us by distrust!"

Escapism. The temptation to escape from one's personal issues—whether financial, emotional, or career- or marriage-related—is as real to us as it was to David, whose friends encouraged him to flee danger (vv. 1–3). Today's culture offers myriad means of escape to make us feel better. Behind these is Satan, who uses many schemes to destroy us, including distrust. "He will employ our dearest friends to argue us out of our confidence, and he will use such plausible logic, that unless we once for all assert our immovable trust in Jehovah, he will make us like a timid bird which flies to the mountain whenever danger presents itself." How can we resist such temptation and remain steadfast? Spurgeon believes David's unwavering courage comes from knowing the "God of the believer is never far from him . . . the Lord is ever near to us in every state and condition" (v. 4). This is deeply personal, for then "Jehovah's smile shall light us" on the path we should follow (v. 7).

Prayer. Lord, society offers so many "cures" for my troubled soul. I know my heart is prone to wander away from you. Take it and seal it in your love by focusing my attention on your personal presence in my life. By your grace, I will grow to trust you more. Amen.

1 Help, LORD, for the godly person has come to an end, for the faithful have disappeared from the sons of mankind. 2 They speak lies to one another; they speak with flattering lips and a double heart. 3 May the LORD cut off all flattering lips, the tongue that speaks great things; 4 who have said, "With our tongue we will prevail; our lips are our own; who is lord over us?" 5 "Because of the devastation of the poor, because of the groaning of the needy, now I will arise," says the LORD; "I will put him in the safety for which he longs." 6 The words of the LORD are pure words; like silver refined in a furnace on the ground, filtered seven times. 7 You, LORD, will keep them; you will protect him from this generation forever. 8 The wicked strut about on every side when vileness is exalted among the sons of mankind. (NASB)

"It is worthy of observation that flattering lips, and tongues speaking proud things, are classed together . . . in both cases a lie is in their right hands."

Flattery. The psalmist highlights the reality and prevalence of flattery in society—even among neighbors (v. 2). False compliments and "fawning congratulations" are manipulative. Those who are recipients "know that if they take they must give them" to the flatterer. Thus, flattery must be taken seriously for it is a form of lying and deception. This should not surprise us for such words come from a "double heart," by which people show us one side of their heart but the other side is "black with contempt for me, or foul with intent to cheat me." Such deception is opposed by God (v. 3). How can our speech be radically different? One, we need to call on God for his help (v. 1) for we cannot tame the tongue ourselves (Jas 3). Two, we allow God to shape our hearts so our conversations reflect the way God speaks (v. 6). "What God's words are, the words of his children should be. If we would be God-like in conversation, we must watch our language, and maintain the strictest purity of integrity and holiness in all our communications."

Prayer. Lord, I admit it is too easy to couch my words to influence people for my own selfish purposes. Change the duplicity of my heart. Make it purer so that I talk to others with genuine sincerity and truth. May my words honor others, and thereby honor you. Amen.

1 O Lᴏʀᴅ, how long will you forget me? Forever? How long will you look the other way? 2 How long must I struggle with anguish in my soul, with sorrow in my heart every day? How long will my enemy have the upper hand? 3 Turn and answer me, O Lᴏʀᴅ my God! Restore the sparkle to my eyes, or I will die. 4 Don't let my enemies gloat, saying, "We have defeated him!" Don't let them rejoice at my downfall. 5 But I trust in your unfailing love. I will rejoice because you have rescued me. 6 I will sing to the Lᴏʀᴅ because he is good to me. (NLT)

"It is not easy to prevent desire from degenerating into impatience."

Impatience. Four times in verses 1–2 the psalmist asks, "How long?" We are also impatient, for as Spurgeon wrote, "[I]s not this the more true a portrait of our own experience?" Impatience is not easy. Perhaps writing from personal experience,* he figuratively describes the trial of impatience, "A week within prison walls is longer than a month of liberty." For the psalmist, his impatience runs deep in his soul, reflecting a "very intense desire for deliverance, and great anguish of heart." When we see evil triumphing and we feel so overwhelmed, what can we do? At such times, we cry out to God to give us insight to the situation and to foil the plans of those who oppose God (vv. 3–4). Our prayer is not primarily for ourselves but for God's sake. "It is not the Lord's will that the great enemy of our souls should overcome his children. This would dishonor God, and cause the evil one to boast. It is well for us that our salvation and God's honor are so intimately connected, that they stand or fall together." Following prayer expressing confidence in God, we can begin to praise God for his love shown to us (vv. 5–6). "Now will the tide turn, and the weeper shall dry his eyes." Our impatience can be turned into confident waiting on God, who is good to us. "So shall it be with us if we wait awhile."

Prayer. Lord, while I may get impatient with the daily morning rush-hour traffic, other significant issues give me greater anxiety. Open my eyes to your long-term perspective, that I may have growing confidence you are working out your purposes at just the right time. Jesus, I remember your delays with people always resulted in you being glorified. Increase my trust in your timing. Amen.

* Nettles, *Living by Revealed Truth*, 391–92, 611–18.

January 19   Psalm 14

1 The fool says in his heart, "There is no God." They are corrupt, they do abominable deeds; there is none who does good. 2 The LORD looks down from heaven on the children of man, to see if there are any who understand, who seek after God. 3 They have all turned aside; together they have become corrupt; there is none who does good, not even one. 4 Have they no knowledge, all the evildoers who eat up my people as they eat bread and do not call upon the LORD? 5 There they are in great terror, for God is with the generation of the righteous. 6 You would shame the plans of the poor, but the LORD is his refuge. 7 Oh, that salvation for Israel would come out of Zion! When the LORD restores the fortunes of his people, let Jacob rejoice, let Israel be glad. (ESV)

"He would not deny God if he were not a fool by nature, and having denied God it is no marvel that he becomes a fool in practice."

The human condition. While our culture elevates the goodness of humanity, this psalm is a sober reminder of the true human condition. It is a succinct and accurate summary of Paul's description of the heart that needs major spiritual surgery (Rom 3:9–20). Spurgeon notes that the psalmist is speaking of the human "race as a whole, as a totality; and humanity as a whole has become depraved in heart and defiled in life." People who deny there is a God express this belief in a multitude of morally unhealthy ways (v. 1). Thus, Spurgeon suggests this psalm is about "practical atheism," for one's denial of God is revealed in his or her own actions. However, to convince someone of the existence of God requires more than "intellectual enlightenment" because the issue is "an affair of the heart." The only way our hearts can truly be changed is by God's grace, which enters our very being and transforms our hearts to acknowledge God and our sin, which make it possible to love and follow him. This is God's wonderful salvation which restores our lives and our relationship with him (v. 7).

Prayer. Lord, I have had my doubts about you not because of a lack of intellectual answers but because my heart has been far from you and has not been inclined to love you. Do your transformative work in my heart, which I am incapable of doing, so that I can joyfully confess you and lovingly follow you. Amen.

1 LORD, who may dwell in your sacred tent? Who may live on your holy mountain? 2 The one whose walk is blameless, who does what is righteous, who speaks the truth from their heart; 3 whose tongue utters no slander, who does no wrong to a neighbor, and casts no slur on others; 4 who despises a vile person but honors those who fear the LORD; who keeps an oath even when it hurts, and does not change their mind; 5 who lends money to the poor without interest; who does not accept a bribe against the innocent. Whoever does these things will never be shaken. (NIV)

"Saints not only desire to love and speak truth with their lips, but they seek to be true within."

Godly character. The psalmist raises the issue of who can fellowship with God and come into his presence (v. 1). Verse 2 invites us to consider the "walk, work, and word" of a person. Stated negatively, a blameless person's speech and actions will not hurt or take advantage of others (vv. 3, 5). Stated positively, such a person speaks truthfully in love, keeps his or her word, and generously helps others (vv. 2, 4–5). This is more than moralism or good behavior. This righteous behavior (v. 2) is an indication of a faith that is "no dead faith." Spurgeon clearly states this quality of "outward character" is due to the internal working of the Holy Spirit in one's life. When one sees the fruit of the Spirit, "the root may not be seen, but it is surely there." Even then we are still far from being perfect. How then can we approach a holy God? "Without the wedding dress of righteousness in Christ Jesus, we have no right to sit at the banquet of communion." With gratitude for all he has done on the cross for us, we are "the best doers in the world upon gospel principles."

Prayer. Lord, I cannot change myself without your divine work in my life. I invite your Holy Spirit and the word to transform me, not only so that I come into your presence, but so I can become increasingly more like your Son, Jesus, who is the perfection of godly character. I want to change so people can see the Spirit's work in my life, and thereby honor you through my relationships with others. Amen.

January 21   Psalm 16:1–4

1 Keep me safe, O God, for I have come to you for refuge. 2 I said to the LORD, "You are my Master! Every good thing I have comes from you." 3 The godly people in the land are my true heroes! I take pleasure in them! 4 Troubles multiply for those who chase after other gods. I will not take part in their sacrifices of blood or even speak the names of their gods. (NLT)

> "[T]hey count themselves to be less than nothing, yet he makes much of them, and sets his heart toward them."

Delightful love. Due to many factors, it is not uncommon for followers of Jesus to question whether God really loves them. According to Spurgeon, these verses represent Jesus addressing his heavenly Father. Jesus tells him that he takes pleasure in us (v. 3)! When we don't feel worthy of anyone's love, God tells us that he affectionately delights in us. Whatever the cause for our doubts, God mercifully reassures us of his unconditional love for us. When we feel that God does not value us, we need his perspective, which is so different from ours. He thinks far more highly of us than we could ever imagine. But we can surprisingly and tragically give "our heart to idols" or false gods (v. 4). Why does this occur? Spurgeon believes this is due to the root of "self-love." We love our choices and objects of affection, which will ultimately result in sorrow and pain. Far better to accept and embrace the Father's infinite love for us (Rom 8:37–39).

Prayer. Lord, I know my heart can be so easily drawn to misplaced loves which seek to control my life. I also know my attraction to these idols is due to self-love. You have shown the depth and wonder of your love for me through Jesus' death on the cross. Why would I want to wander away from your love? I choose to be secure in your love and trust in you. Amen.

January 22   Psalm 16:5–11

5 LORD, you alone are my portion and my cup; you make my lot secure. 6 The boundary lines have fallen for me in pleasant places; surely I have a delightful inheritance. 7 I will praise the LORD, who counsels me; even at night my heart instructs me. 8 I keep my eyes always on the LORD. With him at my right hand, I will not be shaken. 9 Therefore my heart is glad and my tongue rejoices; my body also will rest secure, 10 because you will not abandon me to the realm of the dead, nor will you let your faithful one see decay. 11 You make known to me the path of life; you will fill me with joy in your presence, with eternal pleasures at your right hand. (NIV)

"Our shallow cup of sorrow we may well drain with resignation, since the deep cup of love stands side by side with it, and will never be empty."

Contentment. When hardships and grief come into our lives it is very easy not to be content. However, Jesus shows us the pathway to contentment. Jesus experienced grief ("my cup") on the cross (v. 5). Yet, while his cup of grief was full, his heart was also full by being content to do the Father's will on the cross. Jesus could experience delight because he knew his Father would give him his inheritance—those who are his followers (v. 6). Similarly, we too will experience grief and pain in life. However, we can find contentment knowing we will receive an inheritance that will allow us to be with God forever. Meanwhile, we can experience this inheritance by God giving us his counsel (v. 7), presence (v. 8), and the hope of the future resurrection (vv. 9–10). Thus, while our joy will be made complete one day in heaven, we can even now be content in this world through our relationship with Jesus Christ.

Prayer. Loving Father, when I think about Jesus' afflictions and grief, culminating in his suffering on the cross, I remember he did so, knowing he would redeem people for your glory. Whatever challenges and grief I may face, empower me to live for your purposes—and with contentment and joy. Amen.

1 Hear a just cause, LORD, give your attention to my cry; listen to my prayer, which is not from deceitful lips. 2 Let my judgment come forth from your presence; let your eyes look with integrity. 3 You have put my heart to the test; you have visited me by night; you have sifted me and you find nothing; my intent is that my mouth will not offend. 4 As for the works of mankind, by the word of your lips I have kept from the ways of the violent. 5 My steps have held to your paths. My feet have not slipped. 6 I have called upon you, for you will answer me, God; incline your ear to me, hear my speech. 7 Show your wonderful faithfulness, Savior of those who take refuge at your right hand from those who rise up against them. 8 Keep me as the apple of the eye; hide me in the shadow of your wings 9 from the wicked who deal violently with me, my deadly enemies who surround me. (NASB)

"David was slandered, as if to show us that the purest innocence will be bemired by malice. There is no sunshine without a shadow, no ripe fruit unpecked by the birds."

Innocence. In the first part of this psalm, David focuses on his own life before asking God to deal with his enemies (vv. 10–15). In prayer, he declares he is innocent of any wrongdoing (v. 3). Is he trying to deceive God? No! "Hypocritical piety is double iniquity . . . he who would deceive God is himself already most grossly deceived." Instead, David knows God has searched his heart and found him to be sincere. In order to maintain his innocence, David knows he has to be very intentional about living (vv. 4–5). Obedience requires God's strength. "Grace alone can hold up our goings in the paths of truth." God will respond to our prayer because he loves us—even though we are not perfect—for we are precious to him (vv. 6–8a).

Prayer. Father, I see the value of a clear conscience when I am accused by those who oppose me. At the same time, I acknowledge I am far from perfect. It is with a thankful heart that I stand innocent before you because of Jesus' righteousness. In gratitude, I want to obey you for I am precious in your sight. Amen.

10 They have closed their unfeeling hearts, with their mouths they speak proudly. 11 They have now surrounded us in our steps; they set their eyes to cast us down to the ground. 12 He is like a lion that is eager to tear, and as a young lion lurking in secret places. 13 Arise, LORD, confront him, make him bow down; save my soul from the wicked with your sword, 14 from people by your hand, LORD, from people of the world, whose portion is in this life, and whose belly you fill with your treasure; they are satisfied with children, and leave their abundance to their babies. 15 As for me, I shall behold your face in righteousness; I shall be satisfied with your likeness when I awake. (NASB)

"When God meets our foe face to face in battle,
the conflict will soon be over."

Facing hopelessness. David had every right to be overwhelmed by the immensity of the threats to see him destroyed, for "they who war against our faith aim at the very life of our life" (vv. 11–12). These enemies "laid his spirit waste," or oppressed him, as they do to us. What can we do when we feel so helpless? First, we begin by asking God to intervene and deal with the situation that is so oppressive (v. 13). In such cases, it is important to remember that God's power is far greater than those who oppose us. Also, we need to keep focused on our relationship to Jesus and live in his presence until we see him one day (v. 15). "To behold God's face and to be changed by that vision into his image . . . this is my noble ambition." Our sense of hopelessness fades in light of our present and future hope in the Savior.

Prayer. Lord, I experience hopelessness due to many factors. I am thankful you not only hear my prayer but you are with me today and forever. Remind me that my present trials are small in comparison to the joy of seeing you one day. In the meantime, I will look to you so that I can be aware of your presence and become increasingly like Jesus. Amen.

January 25   Psalm 18:1–3

1 I love you, LORD; you are my strength. 2 The LORD is my rock, my fortress, and my savior; my God is my rock, in whom I find protection. He is my shield, the power that saves me, and my place of safety. 3 I called on the LORD, who is worthy of praise, and he saved me from my enemies. (NLT)

"Our triune God deserves the warmest love of all our hearts. Father, Son, and Spirit have each a claim upon our love."

Love for God. Spurgeon entitles this psalm "The Grateful Retrospect" because David praises God for past deliverance. Thus, "[W]e too should feel that to God and God alone we owe the greatest debt of honour and thanksgiving." Spurgeon provides us with solid reasons to praise God throughout this psalm. In today's devotional, we remember that our praise for God flows out of our love for him (v. 1). Our affection for the Lord stems from knowing his trustworthiness. Our trust in him is based not only on good theology but from experiencing a deep personal relationship with him ("my" occurs eight times in vv. 2–3). Based on this love relationship and what he has done for us, God is worthy of praise and worship (v. 3). When we look to the future, we can "anticipate new trials with a confidence based upon past experiences of divine love!"

Prayer. Lord, it is quite easy to say "I love you," because the Bible tells me so. However, I have experienced your profound love for me in the past, and now, from the depths of my being, I want to say how much I love you. I am thankful that Jesus Christ, who is my Savior, revealed his great love for me. Amen.

4 The ropes of death encompassed me, and the torrents of destruction terrified me. 5 The ropes of Sheol surrounded me; the snares of death confronted me. 6 In my distress I called upon the LORD, and cried to my God for help; he heard my voice from his temple, and my cry for help before him came into his ears. 7 Then the earth shook and quaked; and the foundations of the mountains were trembling and were shaken, because he was angry. 8 Smoke went up out of his nostrils, and fire from his mouth was devouring; coals burned from it. 9 He also bowed the heavens down low, and came down with thick darkness under his feet. 10 He rode on a cherub and flew; and he sped on the wings of the wind. 11 He made darkness his hiding place, his canopy around him, darkness of waters, thick clouds. 12 From the brightness before him passed his thick clouds, hailstones and coals of fire. 13 The LORD also thundered in the heavens, and the Most High uttered his voice, hailstones and coals of fire. 14 He sent out his arrows, and scattered them, and lightning flashes in abundance, and routed them. 15 Then the channels of water appeared, and the foundations of the world were exposed by your rebuke, LORD, at the blast of the breath of your nostrils. 16 He sent from on high, he took me; he drew me out of many waters. 17 He saved me from my strong enemy, and from those who hated me, for they were too mighty for me. 18 They confronted me in the day of my disaster, but the LORD was my support. 19 He also brought me out into an open place; he rescued me, because he delighted in me. (NASB)

"In most poetical language the psalmist now describes his experience of Jehovah's delivering power."

In retrospect. When we look back at our lives we can have different perspectives. For some people, past difficulties dominate their minds and emotions, leaving them embittered. Others turn a blind eye to hurts and talk about the good old days in idealistic terms. A healthy perspective acknowledges struggles while believing God was at work. Spurgeon reflects on a tragedy in his ministry and comments, "[W]hat mercy was there in it all, and what honey of goodness was extracted by our Lord out of this lion of affliction? God was actively at work in our past situations even though we may have been unaware at the time.

Prayer. Lord, I ask you to turn my pessimism of the past into an increasing confidence in you and your work in the present. Open my eyes to see how you, Sovereign God, were mercifully and powerfully involved in my life, so that my trust in you can continue to grow. Amen.

January 27   Psalm 18:20-28

20 The Lord has rewarded me according to my righteousness; according to the cleanness of my hands he has repaid me. 21 For I have kept the ways of the LORD, and have not acted wickedly against my God. 22 For all his judgments were before me, and I did not put away his statutes from me. 23 I was also blameless with him, and I kept myself from my wrongdoing. 24 Therefore the LORD has repaid me according to my righteousness, according to the cleanness of my hands in his eyes. 25 With the faithful you show yourself faithful; with the blameless you prove yourself blameless; 26 with the pure you show yourself pure, and with the crooked you show yourself astute. 27 For you save an afflicted people, but you humiliate haughty eyes. 28 for you light my lamp; the LORD my God illumines my darkness. (NASB)

"A godly man can see that in divine providence uprightness and truth are in the long run sure to bring their own reward."

The blessing of integrity. David claims he is a person of integrity (vv. 20–23). However, in light of his own personal sin, does such a claim reflect pride on his part? Spurgeon notes that David is responding to false charges by his opponents and that David was a "humble sinner" with a heart for God. In addition, honesty before God is not self-righteousness. For David to deny his integrity would be to violate his consciousness and the work of the Holy Spirit. With such people, God shows his favor (vv. 24–27). "God first gives us holiness, and then rewards us for it." In other words, it is the Holy Spirit who produces godly qualities in us. We do not take the credit for growing in integrity. Instead, God receives the glory for what he has done in our lives. As Spurgeon illustrates, "[T]he child wins the prize from the schoolmaster, but the real honour of his schooling lies with the master, although instead of receiving he gives the reward."

Prayer. Lord, I want to be a person of integrity in my private and public life, and in what I say and do. However, I admit I cannot be this kind of person without your work in my life. Come, Holy Spirit, make me the person you want me to be. Make me a blessing to the people around me. Amen.

29 For by you I can run at a troop of warriors; and by my God I can leap over a wall. 30 As for God, his way is blameless; the word of the LORD is refined; he is a shield to all who take refuge in him. 31 For who is God, but the LORD? And who is a rock, except our God, 32 the God who encircles me with strength, and makes my way blameless? 33 He makes my feet like deer's feet, and sets me up on my high places. 34 He trains my hands for battle, so that my arms can bend a bow of bronze. 35 You have also given me the shield of your salvation, and your right hand upholds me; and your gentleness makes me great. 36 You enlarge my steps under me, and my feet have not slipped. (NASB)

"Let us never wickedly rob the Lord of his due, but faithfully give unto him the glory which is due to his name."

Giving credit. All too often, we like to take the credit for what we have accomplished. While our ego may be fed, God is sidelined. This is not the way God wants us to live. While David is well-known as a great warrior, this passage points out it was God's active participation that gave David victories in battle. "Secret support is administered to us by the preserving grace of God and at the same time Providence kindly yields us manifest aid." How does God do this? He stoops to those who are humble and gives them what they need. Knowing this, David recognizes his greatness is due to God's grace extended to him. Thus, Spurgeon challenges us, "[L]et us ascribe all the glory to him who girt us with his own inexhaustible strength, that we might be unconquered in battle and unwearied in pilgrimage."

Prayer. Lord, it is very tempting to take all the credit for my life's accomplishments. This is wrong for it robs you of the honor you alone deserve. We your people "confess that whatever of goodness or greatness [you] may have put upon us, we must cast our crowns at [your] feet." Recalibrate my heart to give you all the credit. Amen.

37 I pursued my enemies and overtook them, and I did not turn back until they were consumed. 38 I shattered them, so that they were not able to rise; they fell under my feet. 39 For you have encircled me with strength for battle; you have forced those who rose up against me to bow down under me. 40 You have also made my enemies turn their backs to me, and I destroyed those who hated me. 41 They cried for help, but there was no one to save, they cried to the LORD, but he did not answer them. 42 Then I beat them fine like the dust before the wind; I emptied them out like the mud of the streets. 43 You have rescued me from the contentions of the people; you have placed me as head of the nations; a people whom I have not known serve me. 44 As soon as they hear, they obey me; foreigners pretend to obey me. 45 Foreigners lose heart, and come trembling out of their fortresses. (NASB)

"We may exalt over sin, death, and hell, as disarmed and disabled for us by our conquering Lord; may he graciously give them a like defeat within us."

Defeat and victory. We may despair of the wickedness in the world, which prompts us to pray for the defeat of all forms of evil. Followers of Jesus often suffer at the hands of those who embrace violence and hatred. What hope is there? The psalmist reminds us that God is the one who will defeat the nations in his time (v. 42). However, spiritual victory among the nations is also a real possibility (v. 44). Spurgeon writes, "In many cases the gospel is speedily received by hearts apparently unprepared for it." Defeat and spiritual victory on the national level gives hope for us on the personal level. But there are not only external enemies but also internal ones which need to be defeated (v. 38). These "sins which have entrenched themselves in our flesh and blood as in impregnable forts, shall yet be driven forth by the sanctifying energy of the Holy Spirit, and we shall serve the Lord in singleness of heart."

Prayer. Lord, help me to see the sin, not only in the world, but in my own life. I want to rely totally on you to defeat sin in my life, as well as in the world, through the gospel and the power of the Holy Spirit. I cannot do this alone; I need you! Thank you for the victory I will experience by your strength! Amen.

January 30   Psalm 18:46–50

46 The LORD lives, and blessed be my rock; and exalted be the God of my salvation, 47 the God who executes vengeance for me, and subdues peoples under me. 48 He rescues me from my enemies; you indeed lift me above those who rise up against me; you rescue me from a violent man. 49 Therefore I will give thanks to you among the nations, LORD, and I will sing praises to your name. 50 He gives great salvation to his king, and shows faithfulness to his anointed, to David and his descendants forever. (NASB)

"All this mercy is given to us in our King, the Lord's Anointed, and those who are blessed indeed who as his seed may expect mercy to be built up forevermore."

God's lovingkindness. In this section, David praises God for delivering him from his enemies among the surrounding nations (vv. 46–48). Commenting on verse 49, Spurgeon describes David as "an example of a holy soul making its boast in God even in the presence of ungodly men." Spurgeon points to the apostle Paul, who referred to verse 49 in Rom 15:9. Paul proclaims the gospel among the nations so that they might also praise God for his lovingkindness extended to them through Jesus Christ. As God was faithful to David, he shows his love to us, David's spiritual descendants. We can be absolutely certain of God's faithfulness for he is our Rock (v. 46). Our appropriate response should be "the most rapturous delight of gratitude" in all that we do.

Prayer. Gracious Lord, too often petitions occupy much of my time in prayer. Fill my heart with joy for all you have done for me—even as I present my requests in the midst of great challenges. Rather than obeying you out of obligation, help me to live and serve you out of gratitude for all you have done for me, my Rock and my Savior. Amen.

1 The heavens declare the glory of God, and the sky above proclaims his handiwork. 2 Day to day pours out speech, and night to night reveals knowledge. 3 There is no speech, nor are there words, whose voice is not heard. 4 Their voice goes out through all the earth, and their words to the end of the world. In them he has set a tent for the sun, 5 which comes out like a bridegroom leaving his chamber, and, like a strong man, runs its course with joy. 6 Its rising is from the end of the heavens, and its circuit to the end of them, and there is nothing hidden from its heat. (ESV)

"He is wisest who reads both the world-book and the Word-book as two volumes of the same work, and feels concerning them, 'My Father wrote them both.'"

God's glory in creation. From this passage Spurgeon mentions several reasons why we should seriously reflect on the created world. First, nature reflects God's glory (v. 1) for we see his intelligent design. Also, the natural world speaks to us without words. These heavenly bodies speak to our rational minds with biblical insights. "They give forth no literal words, but yet their instruction is clear enough to be so described . . . the heavens speak by their significant actions and operations." Furthermore, both the world and the word are weaved together in one fabric for God's glory. Spurgeon states, "Strange is it that some who love God are yet afraid to study the God-declaring book of nature; the mock-spirituality of some believers, who are too heavenly to consider the heavens." We do well to be lovers of creation, for we learn more about our divine Creator.

Prayer. Lord, help me to increasingly appreciate the created universe, with its galaxies and protons, so I can see more of your glorious wisdom and power. Enable me to respond with care for nature and to honor those who are exploring all of your creation. My soul sings in praise to you! Amen.

February 1   Psalm 19:7–11

7 The law of the LORD is perfect, reviving the soul; the testimony of the Lord is sure, making wise the simple; 8 the precepts of the LORD are right, rejoicing the heart; the commandment of the LORD is pure, enlightening the eyes; 9 the fear of the LORD is clean, enduring forever; the rules of the LORD are true, and righteous altogether. 10 More to be desired are they than gold, even much fine gold; sweeter also than honey and drippings of the honeycomb. 11 Moreover, by them is your servant warned; in keeping them there is great reward. (ESV)

"It is God's Word rather than one's comment on God's Word which is made mighty with souls."

The powerful word. Spurgeon indicates that verses 7–9 contain several descriptive titles, qualities, and spiritual effects of the word. Scripture transforms us and gives insight into spiritual truth (v. 7). Then, "truth which makes the heart right gives joy to the right heart" because the person better discerns life (v. 8). In addition, God's word removes our love for sin (v. 9). Nothing else can change one's life like Scripture! Thus, there is a benefit to both desiring and obeying the word of God (vv. 10–11). Spurgeon's students at the Pastors' College were taught to preach the Bible, which resulted in many people coming to know the Lord.* The word of God is powerful and still changing people's lives today!

Prayer. Lord, thank you for your written word which reveals your grace and has the power to change my life. I want to know more of your revealed truth so I may continue being transformed from the inside out by your Spirit. Amen.

---

* Morden, *C.H. Spurgeon*, 126–29; Dallimore, *Spurgeon*, 107; Nettles, *Living by Revealed Truth*, 361.

12 Who can discern his errors? Declare me innocent from hidden faults. 13 Keep back your servant also from presumptuous sins; let them not have dominion over me! Then I shall be blameless, and innocent of great transgression. 14 Let the words of my mouth and the meditation of my heart be acceptable in your sight, O LORD, my rock and my redeemer. (ESV)

> "If we had eyes like those of God, we should think
> very differently of ourselves."

The searching word. Spurgeon states that David is praying for God's grace in this passage. This is understandable as David becomes keenly aware of his sin through God's word. Thus, "in the presence of divine truth, the psalmist marvels at the number and heinousness of his sins." Spurgeon elaborates on these sins. There are the secret sins that others do not know about and that we may not even be conscious of (v. 12). Then there are the "presumptuous" or willful sins (v. 13) that are more dangerous and serious. Spurgeon reminds us of the pernicious nature of sin in our lives. How can we deal with its power? While verse 14 is often used as a prayer before the sermon, it talks about how intentional meditation on God's word is required to give us the spiritual strength to obey.

Prayer. Father, I confess that all too often I rush through my reading of Scripture. This doesn't allow the word to seep into the dark places of my heart that need to be exposed and changed by your Spirit. Help me to slow down and properly meditate on a biblical truth, to let you search my inner life and do your spiritual surgery. I rest in your mercy for your redemptive purposes. Amen.

1 In times of trouble, may the LORD answer your cry. May the name of the God of Jacob keep you safe from all harm. 2 May he send you help from his sanctuary and strengthen you from Jerusalem. 3 May he remember all your gifts and look favorably on your burnt offerings. 4 May he grant your heart's desires and make all your plans succeed. 5 May we shout for joy when we hear of your victory and raise a victory banner in the name of our God. May the LORD answer all your prayers. 6 Now I know that the LORD rescues his anointed king. He will answer him from his holy heaven and rescue him by his great power. 7 Some nations boast of their chariots and horses, but we boast in the name of the LORD our God. 8 Those nations will fall down and collapse, but we will rise up and stand firm. 9 Give victory to our king, O LORD! Answer our cry for help. (NLT)

"[T]hey shall have their desire, and their plans to glorify their Master shall succeed. We may have our own will when our will is God's will."

Success in conflict. As David faced his military battles, how can we face our own battles? Spurgeon points to how Jesus prayed to his Father, who heard him and gave him strength (vv. 1–2; Ps 22:21) to face his great spiritual battle. However, our cries for help must be matched by aligning our hearts to God's purposes in the same way Jesus submitted to the Father's will. "What need for submission in our case; if it was necessary for him, how much more for us!" When we address our heart's desires, we cannot trust in our own power (v. 7). Rather than getting caught up in the many visible displays of power, we trust more in the name our invisible God (v. 7). He is "the self-existent, independent, immutable, ever-present, all-filling I AM." We also rest in the sacrifice of Jesus (v. 3) whose life and conquest over Satan makes spiritual victory possible for us. "The victory of Jesus is the inheritance of his people."

Prayer. Lord, I want to experience spiritual victories in my life. Forgive me when I trust in my own resources rather than depending on you. Change my heart to lean more into your spiritual resources through Jesus, whose victory is my inheritance. Amen.

February 4   Psalm 21:1–6

1 The king rejoices in your strength, LORD. How great is his joy in the victories you give! 2 You have granted him his heart's desire and have not withheld the request of his lips. 3 You came to greet him with rich blessings and placed a crown of pure gold on his head. 4 He asked you for life, and you gave it to him—length of days, for ever and ever. 5 Through the victories you gave, his glory is great; you have bestowed on him splendor and majesty. 6 Surely you have granted him unending blessings and made him glad with the joy of your presence. (NIV)

"We must crown him with the glory of our salvation; singing of his love, and praising his power."

Praise to the King. Since Psalm 20 anticipates what is realized in Psalm 21, Spurgeon refers to these psalms as companions. In today's devotional, the focus is on a king who ultimately foreshadows Jesus, our King. Spurgeon appropriately entitles this section "Thanksgiving for victory" for we give thanks to God who has not only granted us success, but given us the desires of our hearts (vv. 1–2). While God gave David a number of years, "the length of days for ever and ever can only refer to the King Messiah" (v. 4). While David had his moment of glory, it paled in comparison to the glory of Jesus, who overcame death on the cross (v. 5). Now Jesus is "an overflowing wellspring of blessings to others" which gives Jesus great joy (v. 6). How shall we respond? Spurgeon says, "Let us shout and sing with them, for Jesus is our King, and in his triumphs we share a part."

Prayer. Almighty God, fill our minds and hearts with your greatness so that we, your redeemed people, may praise you as our King. Salvation with all of its blessings have come to us through Jesus Christ. Amen!

February 5   Psalm 21:7–13

7 For the king trusts in the LORD; through the unfailing love of the Most High he will not be shaken. 8 Your hand will lay hold on all your enemies; your right hand will seize your foes. 9 When you appear for battle, you will burn them up as in a blazing furnace. The LORD will swallow them up in his wrath, and his fire will consume them. 10 You will destroy their descendants from the earth, their posterity from mankind. 11 Though they plot evil against you and devise wicked schemes, they cannot succeed. 12 You will make them turn their backs when you aim at them with drawn bow. 13 Be exalted in your strength, LORD; we will sing and praise your might. (NIV)

"When he appears to judge the world hard hearts will be subdued into terror, and proud spirits humbled into shame."

Judgment of sin. At a quick glance, praise to the King and judgment of sin seem so unrelated. However, Spurgeon points out these verses give "confidence of further success" when we look at how God responds to the evil in society. For those who are our enemies and enemies of Christ, the Lord will expose those who thought they could hide from him (v. 8). Apart from evil actions, God even knows the hearts of all for he notes the intentions of those "who have the wickedness to imagine, and the cunning to devise, and the malice to plot mischief" (v. 11). God will judge their hearts at the appointed time (vv. 9–10). Meanwhile, we trust Jesus, who "was not moved from his purpose, nor in his sufferings, nor by his enemies, nor shall he be moved from the completion of his designs." In response, we worship God for it is "always right to praise the Lord when we call to remembrance his goodness to his Son, and the overthrow of his foes."

Prayer. Eternal King, while I enjoy worshipping you with your people, I cannot hide from the cruel reality of our world. I admit being shaken by the apparent advances of evil. Deepen my trust that you will deal with acts of injustice and the hearts of people who oppose you. Even seeing all the wrongdoing in this world, I place my trust in you. Amen.

February 6   Psalm 22:1–10

1 My God, my God, why have you abandoned me? Why are you so far away when I groan for help? 2 Every day I call to you, my God, but you do not answer. Every night I lift my voice, but I find no relief. 3 Yet you are holy, enthroned on the praises of Israel. 4 Our ancestors trusted in you, and you rescued them. 5 They cried out to you and were saved. They trusted in you and were never disgraced. 6 But I am a worm and not a man. I am scorned and despised by all! 7 Everyone who sees me mocks me. They sneer and shake their heads, saying, 8 "Is this the one who relies on the LORD? Then let the LORD save him! If the LORD loves him so much, let the LORD rescue him!" 9 Yet you brought me safely from my mother's womb and led me to trust you at my mother's breast. 10 I was thrust into your arms at my birth. You have been my God from the moment I was born. (NLT)

"We may remind the Lord of his former lovingkindness to his people, and beseech him to be still the same. This is true wrestling; let us learn the art."

Dark days. Jesus' use of this psalm on the cross is a powerful reminder of the suffering he experienced. In addition to physical suffering, he endured the abandonment of the Father (v. 1). Spurgeon writes, "It [this psalm] is the photograph of our Lord's saddest hours." While any sense of rejection we might experience pales in comparison, it is nevertheless quite real and profound. Dark days drown us when we feel helpless, powerless, and totally overwhelmed (v. 6). We can feel confused by the ways of God who "delights in him [Jesus], and yet bruises him; is well pleased, and yet slays him" (vv. 7–8). How can we get through our dark days? It is essential to remind ourselves that the Lord is "my God" from birth and through dark days until I see him (vv. 1, 10). Spurgeon points out that the word "trust" is used various times in verses 4–5. Reflecting on God's loving faithfulness to past generations should encourage us that he will be with us in the darkest days.

Prayer. Lord, I confess that I have felt darkness blanket me, creating the sense that you have abandoned me. Remind me once again to rely on your unfailing character and my covenant relationship with you through Jesus, your Son. Amen.

11 Do not be far from me, for trouble is near and there is no one to help. 12 Many bulls surround me; strong bulls of Bashan encircle me. 13 Roaring lions that tear their prey open their mouths wide against me. 14 I am poured out like water, and all my bones are out of joint. My heart has turned to wax; it has melted within me. 15 My mouth is dried up like a potsherd, and my tongue sticks to the roof of my mouth; you lay me in the dust of death. 16 Dogs surround me, a pack of villains encircles me; they pierce my hands and my feet. 17 All my bones are on display; people stare and gloat over me. 18 They divide my clothes among them and cast lots for my garment. 19 But you, LORD, do not be far from me. You are my strength; come quickly to help me. 20 Deliver me from the sword, my precious life from the power of the dogs. 21 Rescue me from the mouth of the lions; save me from the horns of the wild oxen. (NIV)

"We need much grace that while reading we may have fellowship with his [Jesus'] sufferings. May the blessed Spirit conduct us into a most clear and affecting sight of our Redeemer's woes."

Fellowship of suffering. Spurgeon mentions many aspects of Jesus' suffering before and on the cross. The cry, "Do not be far from me" (v. 11), is a painful reminder that all the disciples had deserted him. "There is an awfulness about absolute friendlessness which is crushing to the human mind, for man was not made to be alone, and is like a dismembered limb when he has to endure heart-loneliness." There is also the anger and hatred of those around him (vv. 12–13, 17–18). "They could not vomit forth their anger fast enough through the ordinary aperture of their mouths, and therefore set the doors of their lips wide open like those who gape. Like roaring lions they howled out their fury, and longed to tear the Saviour in pieces, as wild beasts raven over their prey." Finally, Jesus suffered physically on the cross (vv. 14–16). Spurgeon, with his many physical ailments, could probably identify with Paul's willingness to participate in Jesus' sufferings (Phil 3:10).

Prayer. Lord, I am overwhelmed by your suffering and death in order to accomplish the Father's plan of salvation. I am humbled by all you went through on the cross for my sake. Yet, I complain at the slightest inconvenience in following you. Deepen my commitment to you—at whatever cost. Amen.

22 I will proclaim your name to my brothers; in the midst of the assembly I will praise you. 23 You who fear the LORD, praise him; all you descendants of Jacob, glorify him, and stand in awe of him, all you descendants of Israel. 24 For he has not despised nor scorned the suffering of the afflicted; nor has he hidden his face from him; but when he cried to him for help, he heard. 25 From you comes my praise in the great assembly; I shall pay my vows before those who fear him. 26 The afflicted will eat and be satisfied; those who seek him will praise the LORD. May your heart live forever! (NASB)

"It will be well still to regard the words as a part of our Lord's soliloquy upon the cross, uttered in his mind during the last few moments before his death."

Motivation for worship. Spurgeon sees Jesus on the cross, who "exhorts the faithful to unite with him in thanksgiving." We are quite prone to dwell on our personal sorrows but "why are we so slow in declaring our deliverances?" What should give us reason for giving thanks? We praise the name of God revealed through Jesus in his character ("your name") and conduct on earth (v. 22). Thus, "one of the most excellent methods of showing our thankfulness for deliverances is to tell to our brethren what the Lord has done for us." The focus of our worship is on Jesus and the salvation he has accomplished on the cross for us. "The spiritually poor find a feast in Jesus, they feed upon him to the satisfaction of their hearts; they were famished until he gave himself for them" (v. 26). Spurgeon found the psalms to be an excellent aid for worship because they reflect the gospel—a wonderful reason to worship the Lord!

Prayer. Almighty God, teach me to worship you in the very difficult times, knowing that you are working out your purposes, even when I do not see what you are doing in my life or in the world. I want to depend on you, not because of my circumstances, but because you are the lover of my soul, the one who truly satisfies my heart. Amen.

February 9   Psalm 22:27–31

27 All the ends of the earth will remember and turn to the Lord, and all the families of the nations will worship before you. 28 For the kingdom is the Lord's and he rules over the nations. 29 All the prosperous of the earth will eat and worship, all those who go down to the dust will kneel before him, even he who cannot keep his soul alive. 30 A posterity will serve him; it will be told of the Lord to the coming generation. 31 They will come and will declare his righteousness to a people who will be born, that he has performed it. (NASB)

"He who by his own power reigns supreme in the domains of creation and providence, has set up a kingdom of grace, and by the conquering power of the cross, that kingdom will grow until all people shall own its sway."

God's kingdom. In this section, Spurgeon points to "the Messiah's missionary spirit." God's kingdom reigns on earth in various ways. First, it is true geographically (v. 27). "It is evidently his [Jesus'] grand consolation that Jehovah will be known throughout all places of his dominion . . . Out from the inner circle of the present church the blessing is to spread in growing power until the remotest parts of the earth shall be ashamed of their idols, mindful of the true God." Also, the kingdom is demographically broad. It includes all people who come to Christ, whether they are rich or poor (v. 20). Finally, the kingdom is generationally extensive. Generation after generation will follow Jesus Christ. "Posterity shall perpetuate the worship of the Most High . . . As one generation is called to rest, another will rise in its stead . . . he will reckon the ages by the succession of the saints" (v. 30). The growth of his kingdom encourages us when we see people oppose Jesus Christ.

Prayer. Eternal King, thank you for the reminder that suffering and death do not have the final say in this world. I thank you for the victorious power of Jesus, which has been witnessed for centuries. With confidence in your reign, help me to surrender to your rule so that your purposes may be accomplished in my life, for your honor. Amen.

1 The LORD is my shepherd; I have all that I need. 2 He lets me rest in green meadows; he leads me beside peaceful streams. 3 He renews my strength. He guides me along right paths, bringing honor to his name. 4 Even when I walk through the darkest valley, I will not be afraid, for you are close beside me. Your rod and your staff protect and comfort me. 5 You prepare a feast for me in the presence of my enemies. You honor me by anointing my head with oil. My cup overflows with blessings. 6 Surely your goodness and unfailing love will pursue me all the days of my life, and I will live in the house of the LORD forever. (NLT)

"We must by experience know the value of the blood-shedding, and see the sword awakened against the Shepherd, before we shall be able truly to know the sweetness of the good Shepherd's care."

Soul care. This psalm reminds us that throughout life there are dangers, opposition, and the reality of death (vv. 4–5). How can we not only survive, but see our inner life—our soul—thrive in this world? Knowing the shepherd heart of God is an encouragement to surrender to the One who desires to restore our soul (v. 3). "When the soul grows sorrowful he revives it; when it is sinful he sanctifies it; when it is weak he strengthens it." How does the Shepherd care for our soul? Verse 2 reflects the two aspects of the Christian life—"the contemplative and the active." Contemplation of Scripture is made possible by "the Lord who graciously enables us to perceive the preciousness of his truth, and to feed upon it." The Spirit then actively works in our soul "to cleanse, to refresh, to fertilize, to cherish." In response, we can lovingly obey the Shepherd and enjoy the daily blessings of God's goodness and mercy (vv. 3, 5–6).

Prayer. God my Shepherd, I confess that I can be overwhelmed and distressed by the busyness and challenges of daily living. Grant me a fresh vision of your great love for me. I want to let you nourish my soul through your word and your Spirit working in my heart. Amen.

1 The earth is the LORD's and the fullness thereof, the world and those who dwell therein, 2 for he has founded it upon the seas and established it upon the rivers. 3 Who shall ascend the hill of the LORD? And who shall stand in his holy place? 4 He who has clean hands and a pure heart, who does not lift up his soul to what is false and does not swear deceitfully. 5 He will receive blessing from the LORD and righteousness from the God of his salvation. 6 Such is the generation of those who seek him, who seek the face of the God of Jacob. *Selah* (ESV)

"Whose eye shall see the King in his beauty and dwell in his palace? In heaven he reigns most gloriously, who shall be permitted to enter into his royal presence?"

True worshippers. These verses provide us with three aspects for worship. One, the object of our worship is God the Creator (vv. 1–2). Two, since it is impossible for the "creature to reach the Creator" (v. 3), it is only by God's grace we can come into his presence. Three, we worship with God's people. What are the characteristics of true worshippers? They have clean hands (v. 4). Spurgeon writes, "Outward, practical holiness is a very precious mark of grace." But the outward must be a reflection of the inward. The pure heart (v. 4) reminds us of the "imperative need of purity within. There must be a work of grace in the core of the heart as well as in the palm of the hand, or our religion is a delusion." The integration of our inner and outer lives allows us to seek God's face in true worship (v. 6).

Prayer. Lord God, work in my heart. By your grace, enable me to worship you every day in spirit and truth. You are worthy and I want to exalt you with integrity in words, actions, and attitude. Amen.

February 12

Psalm 24:7–10

7 Lift up your heads, O gates! And be lifted up, O ancient doors, that the King of glory may come in. 8 Who is this King of glory? The LORD, strong and mighty, the LORD, mighty in battle! 9 Lift up your heads, O gates! And lift them up, O ancient doors, that the King of glory may come in. 10 Who is this King of glory? The LORD of hosts, he is the King of glory! *Selah* (ESV)

"All true glory is concentrated upon the true God, for all other glory is but a passing pageant, the painted pomp of an hour."

The glory of God. In these verses Spurgeon sees Jesus who has conquered his enemies (v. 8). Now victorious on the cross, Jesus reveals his majesty in heaven (v. 9). However, Jesus is perfect; what hope is there for any of us to be with God for eternity? We do not enter heaven based on our works but trust in the work of Christ. Fortunately, "you shall ride there too if you trust him . . . Faith in Jesus is the work of the Holy Spirit" who "will create in you a new heart and a right spirit." Thus, heaven is open to any follower of Jesus to enter. Through him we are able to experience God's glory for eternity.

Prayer. Lord, when I consider your glory I am enthralled by your majesty and intimidated by your holiness. I am so thankful for your grace, which makes it possible for me to enjoy you now and for all eternity. I am truly humbled knowing I can be in your presence forever. Amen.

February 13   Psalm 25:1–7

1 In you, LORD my God, I put my trust. 2 I trust in you; do not
let me be put to shame, nor let my enemies triumph over me. 3
No one who hopes in you will ever be put to shame, but shame
will come on those who are treacherous without cause. 4 Show
me your ways, LORD, teach me your paths. 5 Guide me in your
truth and teach me, for you are God my Savior, and my hope is in
you all day long. 6 Remember, LORD, your great mercy and love,
for they are from of old. 7 Do not remember the sins of my youth
and my rebellious ways; according to your love remember me,
for you, LORD, are good. (NIV)

> "[T]he bones of our youthful feastings at Satan's table will stick painfully
> in our throats when we are old men."

Looking back. In a time of trouble, David remembers when he failed to obey
God in his youth (vv. 1, 7). How often we wonder if our present struggles
and pain are due to past sins. This leaves us ashamed of both the past and the
present afflictions (v. 2). At such times, we may be tempted to fear God has
forgotten us (v. 6), which is "an unholy belief." David gives us two insights
to confront this fear. First, we live in light of God's lovingkindness, which is
based on his grace to us (vv. 6–7). "If the Lord will only do unto us in the
future as in the past, we shall be well content." Second, as we face the future,
we can ask God to continue teaching us his ways so we can obediently follow
him (vv. 4–5). Then we can trust God to deal with those who have brought
pain into our lives (vv. 2–3). Near the end of his life, Spurgeon looked back
at the revival in his early years of pastoral ministry in London as evidence
of God answering prayer. His congregation needed to be reminded of God's
faithfulness and we need to be reminded of the same from time to time.

Prayer. Gracious Father, help me to depend on the certainty of Christ's forgiveness for the guilt of my past—and present—sin. Free me from my shame
by your eternal love so I can follow you in your ways out of gratitude. Amen.

February 14   **Psalm 25:8–15**

8 Good and upright is the LORD; therefore he instructs sinners in his ways. 9 He guides the humble in what is right and teaches them his way. 10 All the ways of the LORD are loving and faithful toward those who keep the demands of his covenant. 11 For the sake of your name, LORD, forgive my iniquity, though it is great. 12 Who, then, are those who fear the LORD? He will instruct them in the ways they should choose. 13 They will spend their days in prosperity, and their descendants will inherit the land. 14 The LORD confides in those who fear him; he makes his covenant known to them. 15 My eyes are ever on the LORD, for only he will release my feet from the snare. (NIV)

"They know their need of guidance and are willing to submit their understandings to divine will, and therefore the Lord condescends to be their guide."

The Lord's leading. According to Spurgeon, this passage is mostly a meditation on God's attributes and acts, including leading his people. We often think of decision-making in very specific areas. However, Spurgeon takes us in a different direction. First, he states that our minds must be shaped by the word of God (vv. 8–10, 12). God "enlightens their mind to follow that which is just, and helps them to discern the way in which the Lord would have them to go." Second, Spurgeon states that our hearts must be aligned with God's heart. "Those whose hearts are right shall not err for want [lack] of heavenly direction." With humility individuals recognize their need to submit to God's direction (v. 9). When we do submit to the Lord, we can enjoy "confidential intimacy" with him (vv. 14–15).

Prayer. Thank you, Lord, for directing me in the past. Continue to shape my heart and inform my mind, that I may wisely and sensitively discern your leading in ways which are pleasing to you. Help me seek out times of quiet intimacy with you, where I will be in a better position to listen to your voice. Amen.

February 15   Psalm 25:16–22

16 Turn to me and be gracious to me, for I am lonely and afflicted.
17 Relieve the troubles of my heart and free me from my anguish.
18 Look on my affliction and my distress and take away all my
sins. 19 See how numerous are my enemies and how fiercely they
hate me! 20 Guard my life and rescue me; do not let me be put to
shame, for I take refuge in you. 21 May integrity and uprightness
protect me, because my hope, LORD, is in you. 22 Deliver Israel,
O God, from all their troubles! (NIV)

"Noble hearts can brook anything but shame."

Release from ridicule. Spurgeon highlights six descriptive words ("lonely,"
"afflicted," "troubles," "anguish," "affliction," "distress") in verses 16–18 as
reminders that we are not immune from life's trials. These external troubles
have a way of creating anguish in our hearts, which only makes matters even
worse (v. 17). "When trouble penetrates the heart it is trouble indeed." Will
we be able stand fast and hold up to all the problems we are facing? We may
also fear the ridicule of others who mock God (vv. 19–20). "This is the one
fear which like a ghost haunted the psalmist's mind. He trembled lest his faith
should become the subject of ridicule through the extremity of his affliction."
How can we hold firm to our faith? We wait on the integrity and uprightness
of God (v. 21) who will show us mercy in our afflictions (v. 16).

Prayer. Loving Father, I am grateful for your needed mercy amid all trials. I
am thankful for the reliability of your character and the word to sustain me
in these times. Come with your peace to my troubled heart. Amen.

1 Vindicate me, O Lord, for I have walked in my integrity, and I have trusted in the Lord without wavering. 2 Prove me, O Lord, and try me; test my heart and my mind 3 for your steadfast love is before my eyes, and I walk in your faithfulness. 4 I do not sit with men of falsehood, nor do I consort with hypocrites. 5 I hate the assembly of evildoers, and I will not sit with the wicked. 6 I wash my hands in innocence and go around your altar, O Lord, 7 proclaiming thanksgiving aloud, and telling all your wondrous deeds. 8 O Lord, I love the habitation of your house and the place where your glory dwells. (NASB)

"Our integrity is not absolute nor inherent, it is a work of grace in us, and is marred by human infirmity; we must, therefore, resort to the redeeming blood and the throne of mercy, confessing that though we are saints among men, we must still bow as sinners before God."

Cultivating integrity. By stating he is blameless, the psalmist is not suggesting he is perfect (v. 1). Instead, he is living with integrity among people who accuse him of wrongdoing. How did David cultivate integrity in his life? He lived with the awareness of God's character, which motivated him in the way he should live (vv. 1–3). "The goodness of the Lord to us should be before our eyes as a motive actuating our conduct . . . divine love when clearly seen, sanctifies the conversation." He hated evil (vv. 4–5). While we must interact with people who are opposed to God and his ways, we do not embrace the values of secular society. Finally, being in God's presence with those who worshipped him, motivated David to live for the Lord (vv. 6–8). In conclusion, for those who desire integrity, "[I]t is their deepest concern never to enter upon any course of action which would unfit them for the most sacred communion with God."

Prayer. Lord, living with integrity in this world is not easy. I confess my need for wisdom and dependence on your Spirit in order to do this. Help me to love people and hate evil in all its forms so that society will see your character reflected in the integrity of your people. Amen.

February 17   Psalm 26:9–12

9 Do not take away my soul along with sinners, my life with those who are bloodthirsty, 10 in whose hands are wicked schemes, whose right hands are full of bribes. 11 I lead a blameless life; deliver me and be merciful to me. 12 My feet stand on level ground; in the great congregation I will praise the Lord. (NIV)

"Worried and worn out by the injustice of men, the innocent spirit flies from its false accusers to the throne of Eternal Right."

God is judge. In these verses, David asks God not to put him "in the same basket with the best of sinners, much less with the worst of them" (v. 9). He rests in the knowledge that God is the judge (v. 1) who will separate those who reject him from those who love him. Their actions are the fruit of their evil hearts (v. 10). In contrast to them, David points to two qualities of his life. One, he leads a blameless life (v. 11). This is integrity which "is not absolute nor inherent, it is a work of grace in us, and is marred by human infirmity; we must, therefore, resort to the redeeming blood and to the throne of mercy, confessing that though we are saints among men, we must still bow as sinners before God." Two, David does not mock God but worships him (v. 12). He can do this because he is assured that God will one day judge all people fairly. Until that time, we stand on "the sure, covenant faithfulness, eternal promise and immutable oath of the Lord of Hosts . . . Established in Christ Jesus, by being vitally united to him, we have nothing left to occupy our thoughts but the praises of our God."

Prayer. Lord, despite what people might say about me, I am grateful that you are the judge who will make all things right one day. Although I want you to develop integrity in my life, I know my eternal destiny will not be judged by my actions. I rejoice that I stand righteous before you through the grace of Jesus who died for me. Amen.

February 18   Psalm 27:1–6

1 The LORD is my light and my salvation—so why should I be afraid? The LORD is my fortress, protecting me from danger, so why should I tremble? 2 When evil people come to devour me, when my enemies and foes attack me, they will stumble and fall. 3 Though a mighty army surrounds me, my heart will not be afraid. Even if I am attacked, I will remain confident. 4 The one thing I ask of the LORD—the thing I seek most—is to live in the house of the LORD all the days of my life, delighting in the LORD's perfections and meditating in his temple. 5 For he will conceal me there when troubles come; he will hide me in his sanctuary. He will place me out of reach on a high rock. 6 Then I will hold my head high above my enemies who surround me. At his sanctuary I will offer sacrifices with shouts of joy, singing and praising the LORD with music. (NLT)

"Let all our affection be bound up in one affection, and that affection set upon heavenly things."

Seeking God's presence. David had foes who sought to destroy him (v. 2). Nonetheless, he remains confident (v. 3). How could this be so in the face of incredible opposition? Rather than depending on his own resources, David found spiritual strength for such times. He knew the character of God, his light and strength in dark days (v. 1). Often we do not take the time to reflect on God and take matters into our own hands. David, on the other hand, has one overriding desire—to spend time in God's presence (v. 4). There, we spend time "learning more of the loving Father, more of the glorified Jesus, more of the mysterious Spirit, in order that we may the more lovingly admire, and the more reverently adore our gracious God." This will let us face troubles with confidence and worship him (vv. 5–6).

Prayer. Lord, I confess when troubles come I panic and take matters into my own hands. Recalibrate my heart's affections so that I reflect on your attributes. Enable me not only to face my present trials with greater confidence, but to give you all the praise you rightfully deserve. Amen.

7 Hear me as I pray, O LORD. Be merciful and answer me! 8 My heart has heard you say, "Come and talk with me." And my heart responds, "LORD, I am coming." 9 Do not turn your back on me. Do not reject your servant in anger. You have always been my helper. Don't leave me now; don't abandon me, O God of my salvation! 10 Even if my father and mother abandon me, the LORD will hold me close. 11 Teach me how to live, O LORD. Lead me along the right path, for my enemies are waiting for me. 12 Do not let me fall into their hands. For they accuse me of things I've never done; with every breath they threaten me with violence. 13 Yet I am confident I will see the LORD's goodness while I am here in the land of the living. 14 Wait patiently for the LORD. Be brave and courageous. Yes, wait patiently for the LORD. (NLT)

"[I]f we would have the Lord hear our voice, we must be careful to respond to his voice. The true heart should echo the will of God."

The true heart. Spurgeon observes that David's voice turns from singing in verse 6 to crying in verse 7. This shift in mood should not alarm us, as such changes are a part of the Christian life. This is the "pendulum of spirituality" which moves from praise to mourning and eventually back to thanksgiving. When we stop to consider the great challenges facing us, including family issues (v. 10), our minds can formulate many options to conquer our problems and fears. To counter this inclination requires more than sheer willpower. Desiring and seeking God's presence (vv. 4, 8) with God's word (v. 10) will soften and shape our hearts to respond appropriately to life's obstacles. "Would to God that we were more plastic to the divine hand, more sensitive to the touch of God's Spirit." Then we will pray with a "humble sense of personal ignorance, great teachableness of spirit, and cheerful obedience of heart," knowing that God will guide us. With honesty, we can then encourage others to wait on God in their circumstances (v. 14).

Prayer. Loving Father, I confess that my heart is too prone to wander from your will. How foolish this is! May your word and your Spirit mold my affections and mind, making me more sensitive to the touch of your Spirit. I wait on you to do your good work in every sphere of my inner and outer lives. Amen.

February 20   Psalm 28:1–5

1 Don't turn a deaf ear when I call you, God. If all I get from you is deafening silence, I'd be better off in the Black Hole. 2 I'm letting you know what I need, calling out for help and lifting my arms toward your inner sanctuary. 3–4 Don't shove me into the same jail cell with those crooks, with those who are full-time employees of evil. They talk a good line of "peace," then moonlight for the Devil. Pay them back for what they've done, for how bad they've been. Pay them back for their long hours in the Devil's workshop; then cap it with a huge bonus. 5 Because they have no idea how God works or what he is up to, God will smash them to smithereens and walk away from the ruins. (MSG)

"Not in this life, but certainly in the next, God will repay his enemies to their faces, and give them the wages of their sins."

Retributive justice. In this section, the psalmist describes the wicked. Spurgeon describes their speech as "soft words, oily with pretended love" (v. 3). We naturally want them to experience the fullness of God's justice (v. 4). While we may long to see this happen in this world, we painfully know that injustice continues to thrive. But "certainly in the next [life], God will repay his enemies to their faces, and give them the wages of their sins," not based on their "fawning words, but after the measure of their mischievous deeds" (vv. 4–5). This does not mean we become calloused to injustice but we should intensely long for the day when uprightness will prevail and Jesus judges all unjust actions.

Prayer. Lord, I confess I feel overwhelmed with evil both seemingly getting the upper hand in this world and your apparent lack of response. But I know you are the Judge who will one day deal with all forms of oppressive evil. In the meantime, help me to be concerned about social inequities by praying and acting in appropriate ways that honor you. Amen.

February 21   Psalm 28:6–9

6–7 Blessed be God—he heard me praying. He proved he's on my side; I've thrown my lot in with him. Now I'm jumping for joy, and shouting and singing my thanks to him. 8–9 God is all strength for his people, ample refuge for his chosen leader; save your people and bless your heritage. Care for them; carry them like a good shepherd. (MSG)

"God's mercy is not such an inconsiderable thing that we may safely venture to receive it without so much as thanks."

Responding to mercy. In these verses the psalmist praises God for hearing his prayer, which is rooted in trusting God (v. 7). Such trust depends on God and his power to work on our behalf. "Heart work is sure work; heart trust is never disappointed. Faith must come before help, but help will never be long behind-hand." The answer to his prayer is God's mercy giving him the help that he needed. When we receive this, we must acknowledge it with a response of heartfelt praise to him (vv. 6–7). So true are Spurgeon's words, "Real praise . . . rises, like a pure spring, from the deeps of experience . . . We should shun ingratitude, and live daily in the heavenly atmosphere of thankful love . . . When God blesses us, we should bless him with all our heart."

Prayer. Merciful God, I find myself not trusting and praising you enough. Deepen my trust in your character; enable me to praise you even in difficult circumstances. And make me more aware of the many subtle expressions of your love so that I may praise you more. Amen.

1 Ascribe to the Lord, sons of the mighty, ascribe to the Lord glory and strength. 2 Ascribe to the Lord the glory due his name; worship the Lord in holy attire. 3 The voice of the Lord is on the waters; the God of glory thunders, the Lord is over many waters. 4 The voice of the Lord is powerful, the voice of the Lord is majestic. 5 The voice of the Lord breaks the cedars; yes, the Lord breaks the cedars of Lebanon in pieces. 6 He makes Lebanon skip like a calf, and Sirion like a young wild ox. 7 The voice of the Lord divides flames of fire. 8 The voice of the Lord shakes the wilderness; the Lord shakes the wilderness of Kadesh. 9 The voice of the Lord makes the deer give birth and strips the forests bare; and in his temple everything says, "Glory!" 10 The Lord sat as King at the flood; yes, the Lord sits as King forever. 11 The Lord will give strength to his people; the Lord will bless his people with peace. (NASB)

"His voice, in nature or revelation, shakes both earth and heaven."

The voice of God. David uses the phrase "the voice of the Lord" seven times to refer to God's power over every sphere of nature (vv. 3–9). This voice has the same effect in people's lives through the spoken and written word of God. The gospel has power over people's "mountainous pride" for it "breaks hearts far stouter than the cedars." Thus, his voice through Scripture gives us strength to face the storms of life (v. 11).

Prayer. Lord, fill my heart and mind with awe at the power of your voice, not only in nature but also in Scripture. Increase my confidence that just as you can break and restore other people's lives you can transform mine. Help me to submit willingly to you as you speak through your word. Amen.

1 I will extol you, O Lᴏʀᴅ, for you have drawn me up and have not let my foes rejoice over me. 2 O Lᴏʀᴅ my God, I cried to you for help, and you have healed me. 3 O Lᴏʀᴅ, you have brought up my soul from Sheol; you restored me to life from among those who go down to the pit. 4 Sing praises to the Lᴏʀᴅ, O you his saints, and give thanks to his holy name. 5 For his anger is but for a moment, and his favor is for a lifetime. Weeping may tarry for the night, but joy comes with the morning. (ESV)

"Let your songs be grateful songs, in which the Lord's mercies shall live again in joyful remembrance."

Grace and gratitude. David confesses he experienced God's anger which may have brought him to the point of death. But God limited his anger out of mercy (vv. 3, 5). God's mercy is further revealed by healing David (v. 2). After much grief, he responds with gratitude to God. "David is quite sure, beyond a doubt, that God had done great things for him whereof he is exceedingly glad . . . he owned that nothing but grace had kept him from the lowest hell, and this made him doubly thankful." Spurgeon first experienced God's grace at the age of fifteen when he responded to a preacher's call to "look to Christ." Looking back on that event, Spurgeon said he could have shouted out, "I am forgiven! I am forgiven! A monument of grace! A sinner saved by blood!"* This is God's grace that saved us from the penalty of sin and then saves us from the power of sin on a daily basis. God receives all the glory for what he does!

Prayer. Father, thank you for your grace that brought me into a personal relationship with you and for your grace that continues to change my life. It's far too tempting to serve you out of sheer duty. But I don't want this approach! I want to live in obedience to you out of gratitude for all you have done for me. Amen.

---

* Morden, *C.H. Spurgeon*, 28–29.

February 24   Psalm 30:6–12

6 As for me, I said in my prosperity, "I shall never be moved." 7 By your favor, O LORD, you made my mountain stand strong; you hid your face; I was dismayed. 8 To you, O LORD, I cry, and to the LORD I plead for mercy: 9 "What profit is there in my death, if I go down to the pit? Will the dust praise you? Will it tell of your faithfulness? 10 Hear, O LORD, and be merciful to me! O LORD, be my helper!" 11 You have turned for me my mourning into dancing; you have loosed my sackcloth and clothed me with gladness, 12 that my glory may sing your praise and not be silent. O LORD my God, I will give thanks to you forever! (ESV)

"No temptation is as bad as tranquility."

Snare of tranquility. David had gone through a difficult time, but then his situation improved (vv. 1–5). Life would now be good and he could be more confident about his future (v. 6). "Prosperity had evidently turned the psalmist's head, or he would not have been so self-confident. He stood by grace, and yet forgot himself, and so met with a fall." In other words, he felt secure, believing it was due to God's favor toward him. Such thinking is precarious. "When God's children prosper one way, they are generally tried another, for few of us can bear unmingled prosperity . . . comfort breeds carnal security and self-confidence." With insight, Spurgeon says that this was a "time of peril . . . David, you said more than was wise to say, or even to think," since David did not know the future. "Instead of conceiving that we shall never be moved, we ought to remember that we shall very soon be moved altogether." God's silence (v. 7) reminded David of his continual need to depend on him (vv. 8–10) even when the good times return (vv. 11–12). At times, troubles are a blessing because God uses them to shake us out of our self-sufficiency and create greater dependence on him.

Prayer. Lord, I recognize my need for you throughout the day. I ask your forgiveness for my complacent attitude and for behaving as if I don't need you when life is tranquil. Change my spirit of self-sufficiency to a growing, wholehearted dependence on you—especially when life is going well. Amen.

February 25   Psalm 31:1–8

1 O Lord, I have come to you for protection; don't let me be disgraced. Save me, for you do what is right. 2 Turn your ear to listen to me; rescue me quickly. Be my rock of protection, a fortress where I will be safe. 3 You are my rock and my fortress. For the honor of your name, lead me out of this danger. 4 Pull me from the trap my enemies set for me, for I find protection in you alone. 5 I entrust my spirit into your hand. Rescue me, Lord, for you are a Faithful God. 6 I hate those who worship worthless idols. I trust in the Lord. 7 I will be glad and rejoice in your unfailing love, for you have seen my troubles, and you care about the anguish of my soul. 8 You have not handed me over to my enemies but have set me in a safe place. (NLT)

"The psalmist in dire affliction appeals to his God for help
with much confidence."

Confidence. The previous psalm reminds us of the danger of self-confidence. This psalm equally warns us that we should not blindly place our confidence in everyone (v. 4). David's enemies are cunning and crafty. His ultimate confidence is in the Lord (vv. 1, 6) marked by a prayer of submission to God who is absolutely trustworthy (v. 5). David's heart is in the right place because he does not trust in lifeless idols to deliver him (v. 6). As a result, rather than being trapped by evil, David enjoys his freedom (v. 8). "At all times we should commit and continue to commit our all to Jesus' sacred care, then . . . our soul shall dwell at ease and delight itself in quiet resting places." True freedom is not found in self-confidence but in the confident assurance of our relationship with Jesus Christ.

Prayer. Lord, when my heart is overwhelmed by life's adversities I am drawn to trust in useless idols. Forgive me for this. Shape my heart and mind to trust in you because you are totally reliable. Enable me, by your Spirit, to submit my whole being to your purposes. I want to live confidently in you! Amen.

9 Have mercy on me, LORD, for I am in distress. Tears blur my eyes. My body and soul are withering away. 10 I am dying from grief; my years are shortened by sadness. Sin has drained my strength; I am wasting away from within. 11 I am scorned by all my enemies and despised by my neighbors—even my friends are afraid to come near me. When they see me on the street, they run the other way. 12 I am ignored as if I were dead, as if I were a broken pot. 13 I have heard the many rumors about me, and I am surrounded by terror. My enemies conspire against me, plotting to take my life. 14 But I am trusting you, O LORD, saying, "You are my God!" 15 My future is in your hands. Rescue me from those who hunt me down relentlessly. 16 Let your favor shine on your servant. In your unfailing love, rescue me. 17 Don't let me be disgraced, O LORD, for I call out to you for help. Let the wicked be disgraced; let them lie silent in the grave. 18 Silence their lying lips—those proud and arrogant lips that accuse the godly. (NLT)

"It had become his daily occupation to mourn; he spent all his days in the dungeon of distress."

Handling grief. David experiences severe grief (v. 9) mostly caused by those who opposed him. His grief is even more painful when his friends turn away from him and want to end his life (vv. 11–13). Before God he sees beyond the afflictions to the guilt of "iniquity" in his life (v. 10 KJV). This external and internal misery affects his whole being (vv. 9, 10). How can one best respond to such angst? He doesn't lash out at those who have caused his grief. Rather, he turns to God, with whom he has a personal relationship ("my God," v. 14). He trusts the Lord during this period of time (v. 15), for his favor (v. 16), and to deal with his enemies (vv. 17–18). Ultimately, God brings healing to our soul so that we can once again experience his presence and goodness in our lives.

Prayer. Loving Savior, people bring great distress and overwhelming grief to my life, causing me to become angry and bitter toward them. This is not the way to live and especially before you! Hear my deep pain in order that my trust in you can be strengthened. Melt my heart to forgive and shine your love on my life. Amen.

February 27   Psalm 31:19-24

19 How abundant are the good things that you have stored up
for those who fear you, that you bestow in the sight of all, on
those who take refuge in you. 20 In the shelter of your presence
you hide them from all human intrigues; you keep them safe in
your dwelling from accusing tongues. 21 Praise be to the LORD,
for he showed me the wonders of his love when I was in a city
under siege. 22 In my alarm I said, "I am cut off from your sight!"
Yet you heard my cry for mercy when I called to you for help. 23
Love the LORD, all his faithful people! The LORD preserves those
who are true to him, but the proud he pays back in full. 24 Be
strong and take heart, all you who hope in the LORD. (NIV)

"[U]nbelief will have a corner in the heart of the firmest believer."

Dark suspicions. In this section, the psalmist praises God for his anticipated
mercy. How great is God's lovingkindness which should prompt us to praise
God (vv. 19, 21)! In this spirit, the psalmist encourages others to put their
hope in God (v. 24). We are naturally confused when David says, "I am cut
off from your sight" (v. 22). Why would he say this? In haste, David expressed
these words. He gave no real serious thought about the reality of God's mercy
extended to him. "Hasty words are for a moment on the tongue, but they
often lie for years on the conscience . . . unbelief will have a corner in the
heart of the firmest believer." In other words, when we panic, our words may
reveal the serious doubts we have. These need to be replaced with the truth
of God's word.

Prayer. Lord, I believe in you as you are revealed in the truth of your word.
However, in unguarded moments my words unexpectedly expose dark suspicions about your love for me. Continue to work in my life, that I may grow
in confidence in your character. Help dispel my unbelief! In the meantime,
I am thankful for your mercy, even when I have doubts about you. Amen.

1 Blessed is the one whose transgression is forgiven, whose sin is covered. 2 Blessed is the man against whom the LORD counts no iniquity, and in whose spirit there is no deceit. 3 For when I kept silent, my bones wasted away through my groaning all day long. 4 For day and night your hand was heavy upon me; my strength was dried up as by the heat of summer. *Selah* 5 I acknowledged my sin to you, and I did not cover my iniquity; I said, "I will confess my transgressions to the LORD," and you forgave the iniquity of my sin. *Selah* (ESV)

"The least thing we can do, if we would be pardoned, is to acknowledge our fault."

Confession. Not confessing our sin before God has negative effects on us, both spiritually and physically (vv. 3–4). When we come to grips with Jesus' forgiveness for the guilt of our sins, we can more readily confess our wrongdoing (v. 5), including the embarrassing ones we want to hide from God (v. 2). Now there is no further need for self-deception or hypocrisy in our hearts before God. As a consequence of our full confession of sin, we experience the blessing of his forgiveness in our lives (v. 1). Thus, confession "is beneficial to us to own it, for a full confession softens and humbles the heart. We must as far as possible unveil the secrets of the soul" for our spiritual well-being and growth. When the weeds of sin hiding in the dark places of our lives are exposed, God's love for us is not diminished. Instead, our intimacy with our Father grows.

Prayer. Lord, keep before me your forgiveness of my sins through your Son, Jesus. As my Father, you graciously invite me into your presence to confess how I have grieved you. I know you desire purity of heart. By your grace, create in my heart an openness to deal with those areas that I would rather hide from you. Amen!

February 29   Psalm 32:6–11

6 Therefore let everyone who is godly offer prayer to you at a time when you may be found; surely in the rush of great waters, they shall not reach him. 7 You are a hiding place for me; you preserve me from trouble; you surround me with shouts of deliverance. *Selah* 8 I will instruct you and teach you in the way you should go; I will counsel you with my eye upon you. 9 Be not like a horse or a mule, without understanding, which must be curbed with bit and bridle, or it will not stay near you. 10 Many are the sorrows of the wicked, but steadfast love surrounds the one who trusts in the LORD. 11 Be glad in the LORD, and rejoice, O righteous, and shout for joy, all you upright in heart! (ESV)

"He who is saved from sin has no need to fear anything else."

Confident living. When overwhelming troubles come our way, we are often prone to feel God is punishing us for our past or present sins. Once again, we often conclude God is against us. However, such thinking is corrected when we consider David's words. When difficult times arise, we can come running into God's presence (vv. 6–7). While we have faced many afflictions, we now find shelter in God, who stands with us in the most challenging seasons of life. Then we discover that we *want* to be directed by God rather than deliberately go our own way (vv. 8–9). "We are not pardoned that we may henceforth live after our own lusts, but that we may be educated in holiness and trained for perfection." Delighting in God brings us gladness (v. 11). Living with joy is a far better option than doubting his love for us.

Prayer. Lord, when life does not go well, how tempting it is to think you are punishing me. Thank you for allowing me not only to *know* that I am forgiven, but to *experience* the delights of forgiveness. I am thankful for the indescribable joy of forgiveness that lets me enjoy friendship with you. Amen.

March 1   Psalm 33:1–7

1 Sing for joy in the LORD, you righteous ones; praise is becoming to the upright. 2 Give thanks to the LORD with the lyre; sing praises to him with a harp of ten strings. 3 Sing to him a new song; play skillfully with a shout of joy. 4 For the word of the LORD is right, and all his work is done in faithfulness. 5 He loves righteousness and justice; the earth is full of the goodness of the LORD. 6 By the word of the LORD the heavens were made, and by the breath of his mouth all their lights. 7 He gathers the waters of the sea together as a heap; he puts the depths in storehouses. (NASB)

"That God is, and that he is such a God, ours for ever and ever, should wake within us an unceasing and overflowing joy."

Reasons for worship. Spurgeon outlines three excellent reasons why God's people should offer heartfelt praise to him. First, God's character is revealed by him speaking truthfully and acting rightly (vv. 4–5). In other words, his character, words, and actions are consistent. "His work is the outflow of his word, and it is true to it . . . There is no lie in God's word, and no sham in his works." He acts this way because he loves righteousness. Furthermore, God's majesty is evident in his creation, which was brought into existence by his word and breath (vv. 6–7). Spurgeon states that these are equivalent to the word (Col 1:16) and the Spirit (Gen 1:2). "Thus, the three persons of the Godhead unite in creating all things . . . A wise and merciful Word has arranged, and a living Spirit sustains all the creation of Jehovah." Finally, God's power over nature was not only demonstrated in the creation of the world, but in his dominion over nature (v. 7). No wonder we are called to exuberantly worship God with our whole being (vv. 1–3).

Prayer. Majestic God, I worship you this day for your perfect character is reflected in both what you say and what you do. When I consider this, forgive me for my lukewarm worship before you. I desire to give wholehearted exuberant praise that honors you. Amen.

8 Let the whole world fear the LORD, and let everyone stand in awe of him. 9 For when he spoke, the world began! It appeared at his command. 10 The LORD frustrates the plans of the nations and thwarts all their schemes. 11 But the LORD's plans stand firm forever; his intentions can never be shaken. (NLT)

"Men are bidden to fear before Jehovah because his purposes are accomplished in providence."

Fear of God. Spurgeon notes the psalmist now addresses those who do not submit to the Lord. Recognizing the immense power of God, their fear of him is involuntary and not true worship. In contrast, there is a fear that reverences God so that one stands in awe of him (v. 8). This fear causes people to disown their idols before turning to the one true living God. What would lead them to do this? They recognize the power of God in creation (v. 9) and they see that God is in charge of everything for he "overrules the evil, and brings good out of it. The cause of God is never in danger . . . he changes not his purpose, his decree is not frustrated, his designs are accomplished" (vv. 10–11). Therefore, people should revere God because he desires worship among the nations. Why would we not submit to God, who is in control of this world?

Prayer. Lord, may those who lack a personal relationship with you see not only your power over nature and your sovereignty over the nations, but also experience your great love for them. May they give up their idolatries in life and turn to you, the living God, with loving adoration and joy. Amen.

12 Blessed is the nation whose God is the LORD, the people he has chosen for his own inheritance. 13 The LORD looks from heaven; he sees all the sons of mankind; 14 from his dwelling place he looks out on all the inhabitants of the earth, 15 he who fashions the hearts of them all, he who understands all their works. 16 The king is not saved by a mighty army; a warrior is not rescued by great strength. 17 A horse is a false hope for victory; nor does it rescue anyone by its great strength. 18 Behold, the eye of the LORD is on those who fear him, on those who wait for his faithfulness, 19 to rescue their soul from death and to keep them alive in famine. 20 Our soul waits for the LORD; he is our help and our shield. 21 For our heart rejoices in him, because we trust in his holy name. 22 Let your favor, LORD, be upon us, just as we have waited for you. (NASB)

"We are selected to no mean estate, and for no ignoble purpose: we are made the peculiar domain and delight of the Lord our God."

Chosen by God. While we think God should bless us, Spurgeon reminds us that God is the one who takes the initiative (v. 12). "Election is at the bottom of it all. The divine choice rules the day; none take Jehovah to be their God till he takes them to be his people." What does God's choosing us mean for us? Living with the awareness of God knowing all things is reassuring (vv. 13–15). "It is one of our choicest privileges to be always under our Father's eye, to be never out of sight of our best Friend." We do not need to live fearfully for the Lord is always watching over us. When we feel powerless and weak, we have God's power to depend on (vv. 16–19). Therefore, we can patiently wait on God because we can trust him with our whole being (v. 20). We rejoice that he chooses us in his mercy (v. 21)!

Prayer. Thank you, Father, for choosing me to be your child. I am so undeserving but thankful for the blessings of your watchful care and for the strength you give me on a daily basis. In your great mercy and your love, continue to shape my mind and heart to worship you, to wait and to rely on you in all circumstances. Amen.

March 4   Psalm 34:1–10

1 I will bless the LORD at all times; his praise shall continually be in my mouth. 2 My soul will make its boast in the LORD; the humble will hear it and rejoice. 3 Exalt the LORD with me, and let's exalt his name together. 4 I sought the LORD and he answered me, and rescued me from all my fears. 5 They looked to him and were radiant, and their faces will never be ashamed. 6 This wretched man cried out, and the LORD heard him, and saved him out of all his troubles. 7 The angel of the LORD encamps around those who fear him, and rescues them. 8 Taste and see that the LORD is good; how blessed is the man who takes refuge in him! 9 Fear the LORD, you his saints; for to those who fear him there is no lack of anything. 10 The young lions do without and suffer hunger; but they who seek the LORD will not lack any good thing. (NASB)

"We may seek God even when we have sinned."

Imperfect prayers. Spurgeon describes this section as a hymn because the psalmist expresses his praise to God. However, the historical context of this psalm reveals David, who, rather than first turning to God in trust, takes matters into his own hands. Out of desperation and fear (v. 4) he feigns insanity (1 Sam 21:10–15). Despite David's foolish actions, God mercifully hears and answers his prayer (vv. 4, 6–7). Humbled by knowing God ultimately delivered him, David praises him for his great mercy (vv. 1–3) and exhorts the godly to join him in worship (vv. 3, 8–10). With knowledge we can speak about mercy; however, it is through our shortcomings we "can only know this reality and personally by experience."

Prayer. My heavenly Father, I confess that many times my prayers are not motivated by trust in you, but by reasons which do not honor you. I thank you for your extravagant, undeserved mercy, which both humbles and teaches me to trust you more. Amen.

March 5   Psalm 34:11–14

11 Come, my children, listen to me; I will teach you the fear of the LORD. 12 Whoever of you loves life and desires to see many good days, 13 keep your tongue from evil and your lips from telling lies. 14 Turn from evil and do good; seek peace and pursue it. (NIV)

"[H]e here aims by teaching the [youth] to undo the mischief which he had done aforetime."

Painful lessons. Spurgeon observes that David wants to provide us with insights if we are willing to listen and be taught (v. 11). Careful thought to his words is evident by this well-designed psalm which uses the Hebrew alphabet as an acrostic. What painful lessons did David learn and share with us? First, we must place the fear of the Lord above our fear of people (v. 11). Second, David instructs us that life is more than just surviving (v. 12). "Mere existence is not life; the art of living, truly, really, and joyfully living, it is not given to all men to know." Third, we must guard how we speak (v. 13). "Deceit must be very earnestly avoided by the man who desires happiness." And fourth, we must practice goodness (v. 14). In other words, we must continue being faithful by serving God and others. Yes, we can learn painful lessons and teach others to avoid the mistakes we have made by referring them to the wise counsel of God's word.

Prayer. Lord, when I do sin and fall short of your desires for me, remind me of the importance of learning from my past mistakes and teaching others with insights from my experiences. More importantly, I want to teach others to learn the wisdom of your word. Amen.

15 The eyes of the LORD watch over those who do right; his ears are open to their cries for help. 16 But the LORD turns his face against those who do evil; he will erase their memory from the earth. 17 The LORD hears his people when they call to him for help. He rescues them from all their troubles. 18 The LORD is close to the brokenhearted; he rescues those whose spirits are crushed. 19 The righteous person faces many troubles, but the LORD comes to the rescue each time. 20 For the LORD protects the bones of the righteous; not one of them is broken! 21 Calamity will surely destroy the wicked, and those who hate the righteous will be punished. 22 But the LORD will redeem those who serve him. No one who takes refuge in him will be condemned. (NLT)

"[W]e are again and again warned to expect tribulation while we are in this body."

God's loving protection. Using his personal situation with Abimelech, David uses these verses to teach. He begins by reminding the believer that our "afflictions come from all points of the compass" (v. 19). He addresses the issue of physical danger (v. 20). Spurgeon is well aware we are not immune from such harm because even godly people experience bodily injuries. Thus, one cannot use this verse to claim absolute physical protection. Instead, Spurgeon interprets verse 20 to mean that God's love will prevent us from experiencing spiritual death. When all life's trials are over, we will not experience fatal spiritual harm because we are preserved by the power of God. However, we may still experience broken hearts (v. 18). At such times, the Lord is our close friend who will comfort and console us. Whatever threats we may experience, God watches over the redeemed (v. 15). Spurgeon writes, "[T]hey are so dear to him that he cannot take his eyes off them; he watches each one of them as carefully and intently as if there were only that one creature in the universe."

Prayer. Almighty God, you are watching over me! Even if I go through life-threatening experiences, I know you are there to calm my questioning heart. Even when my heart is broken, I am thankful for your loving care that keeps me safe in your presence for the days to come. Amen.

1 Contend, LORD, with those who contend with me; fight against those who fight against me. 2 Take hold of buckler and shield and rise up as my help. 3 Draw also the spear and the battle-axe to meet those who pursue me; say to my soul, "I am your salvation." 4 Let those be ashamed and dishonored who seek my life; let those be turned back and humiliated who devise evil against me. 5 Let them be like chaff before the wind, with the angel of the LORD driving them on. 6 Let their way be dark and slippery, with the angel of the LORD pursuing them. 7 For they hid their net for me without cause; without cause they dug a pit for my soul. 8 Let destruction come upon him when he is unaware, and let the net which he hid catch him; let him fall into that very destruction. 9 So my soul shall rejoice in the LORD; it shall rejoice in his salvation. 10 All my bones will say, "LORD, who is like you, who rescues the afflicted from one who is too strong for him, and the afflicted and the poor from one who robs him?" (NASB)

> "The whole Psalm is the appeal to heaven of a bold heart and a clear conscience, irritated beyond measure by oppression and malice."

Complaining to God. Spurgeon notes how David mentions twice that his opponents are attacking him for no apparent reason (v. 7). Life is unfair! When we feel our complaints are valid, how should we respond to such malicious people? Rather than taking matters into his own hands, David takes his complaint to the Lord who will judge his opponents who are threatening him (v. 1). Spurgeon interprets David's opponents pleading to "litigate" against him. David gratefully concludes by recognizing that God will adjudicate these complaints (vv. 9–10). "David ascribes all the honour to the Judge of the right . . . he turns away from his adversaries to his God, and finds a deep unbroken joy in Jehovah, and in that joy his spirit revels."

Prayer. All-wise God, I confess and repent of my natural inclination to pay back those who have hurt me. Change my vindictive heart by seeing you as the One who will judge all wrongdoing. Then I will be filled with a greater degree of gratitude and able to praise you. Amen.

11 Malicious witnesses rise up; they ask me things that I do not know. 12 They repay me evil for good, to the bereavement of my soul. 13 But as for me, when they were sick, my clothing was sackcloth; I humbled my soul with fasting, but my prayer kept returning to me. 14 I went about as though it were my friend or brother; I bowed down in mourning, like one who mourns for a mother. 15 But at my stumbling they rejoiced and gathered themselves together; the afflicted people whom I did not know gathered together against me, they slandered me without ceasing. 16 Like godless jesters at a feast, they gnashed at me with their teeth. 17 Lord, how long will you look on? Rescue my soul from their ravages, my only life from the lions. 18 I will give you thanks in the great congregation; I will praise you among a mighty people. (NASB)

"He prays best who loves best."

Prayer for adversaries. In this section, David focuses on prayer (v. 13), which is the right response to the inequitable and false accusations against him (v. 11). Using Saul's unfair treatment of David as an illustration, Spurgeon gives us insight into verses 13–14. In the same way David did for Saul in his sickness, he mourned and humbly "prayed for his enemy, and made the sick man's case his own, pleading and confessing as if his own personal sin had brought on the evil" (v. 13). This humble attitude allowed David to use this prayer for his own heart as well. In essence he is saying, "I wished no worse to them than to myself." When David played on the harp and chased away the evil spirit from Saul (1 Sam 16:23), he treated Saul like a caring brother (v. 14). In addition, David grieved over Saul and his actions. His response to Saul challenges us to be more like Christ in our prayers for those who oppose us. With this perspective, we are better positioned to praise God with the right and proper attitude (v. 18).

Prayer. Lord, help me to pray for my adversaries with sadness and even grief for their actions. Enable me to love them with humility knowing, that I too am a sinner with a heart that needs to be changed by your grace. Amen.

19 Do not let those who are wrongfully my enemies rejoice over me; nor let those who hate me for no reason wink maliciously. 20 For they do not speak peace, but they devise deceitful words against those who are quiet in the land. 21 They opened their mouth wide against me; they said, "Aha, aha! Our eyes have seen it!" 22 You have seen it, LORD, do not keep silent; Lord, do not be far from me. 23 Stir yourself, and awake to my right and to my cause, my God and my Lord. 24 Judge me, LORD my God, according to your righteousness, and do not let them rejoice over me. 25 Do not let them say in their heart, "Aha, our desire!" Do not let them say, "We have swallowed him up!" 26 May those be ashamed and altogether humiliated who rejoice at my distress; may those who exalt themselves over me be clothed with shame and dishonor. 27 May those shout for joy and rejoice, who take delight in my vindication; and may they say continually, "The LORD be exalted, who delights in the prosperity of his servant." 28 And my tongue shall proclaim your righteousness and your praise all day long. (NASB)

"From morning till evening the grateful tongue would talk and sing, and glorify the Lord."

Holy rejoicing. In this section, David is well aware of his enemies who revel in the unjust and unreasonable challenges he faces (vv. 19, 24, 26). Their gloating at his expense reflects an awful self-congratulatory attitude. David leaves the situation with the Lord, who will rightly judge these people (vv. 23–24). This is the way God wants us to respond to those who oppose Jesus. Any rejoicing we do should not be out of personal satisfaction regarding our foes. Rather, we rejoice only for God's honor (v. 28) for he is the One who will vindicate us. This is holy rejoicing that pleases him. "O for such a resolve carried out by us all!"

Prayer. Lord, your word frequently challenges me to rejoice. Forgive me for being elated about those things that make my sinful heart glad. Change my heart and mind in order that I see life's injustices from your perspective. Teach me to wait on you so that I may truly delight in your will. Amen.

March 10   Psalm 36:1-4

1 Transgression speaks to the wicked deep in his heart; there is
no fear of God before his eyes. 2 For he flatters himself in his own
eyes that his iniquity cannot be found out and hated. 3 The words
of his mouth are trouble and deceit; he has ceased to act wisely
and do good. 4 He plots trouble while on his bed; he sets himself
in a way that is not good; he does not reject evil. (ESV)

"Rottenness smells sooner or later too strong to be concealed. There is a
time when the leprosy cannot be hidden."

The depth of sin. With these verses, David describes those who are rebellious and the depth of their evil. At the very root, they have no respect for
God (v. 1), who will judge them one day. They are practical atheists, for
though they believe in God they live as if there is no God. For this reason,
"Unholiness is clear evidence of ungodliness. Wickedness is the fruit of an
atheistic root." The evidence for their sinfulness is abundant. Such people
enjoy flattering themselves (v. 2). However, due to their wrongful actions,
they "are in the dark, for they cannot see what is so clearly within them and
around them that it stares them in the face." Also, sin affects one's speech (v.
3). "When the heart is so corrupt as to flatter itself, the tongue follows suit.
The open sepulcher of the throat reveals the fortress of the inner nature."
Lastly, sin affects behavior (v. 4) by which one schemes and "even rejoices in
it, and patronizes it. He never hates a wrong thing, because it is wrong, but he
meditates on it, defends it, and practices it." While sin includes our actions,
the extent of sin pervades every area of our lives, including attitudes and the
way we think of ourselves.

Prayer. Holy God, forgive my complacency toward sin when I only consider
my actions. When I see the depth of my rebellious nature affecting every area
of my life and injuring others, I realize how much your word and Spirit are
needed to transform my whole being to become more like Jesus. Amen.

March 11   Psalm 36:5-12

5 Your mercy, LORD, extends to the heavens, your faithfulness reaches to the skies. 6 Your righteousness is like the mountains of God; your judgments are like the great deep. LORD, you protect mankind and animals. 7 How precious is your mercy, God! And the sons of mankind take refuge in the shadow of your wings. 8 They drink their fill of the abundance of your house; and you allow them to drink from the river of your delights. 9 For the fountain of life is with you; in your light we see light. 10 Prolong your mercy to those who know you, and your righteousness to the upright of heart. 11 May the foot of pride not come upon me, and may the hand of the wicked not drive me away. 12 Those who do injustice have fallen there; they have been thrust down and cannot rise. (NASB)

"Divine mercy abides in its vastness of expanse, and matchless patience, all unaltered by the rebellions of man."

Attributes of God. The psalmist now shifts his thoughts from the wicked to the glory of God. In verses 5–9, we see God's glory revealed in his merciful love for us. His greatness is illustrated by the height and depth of creation which should captivate our attention (vv. 5–6a). "Towards his own servants especially, in the salvation of the Lord Jesus, he has displayed grace higher than the heaven of heavens, and wider than the universe." His love shelters and preserves us (vv. 6b–7) just as a hen protects her chicks. God also refreshes us providing all that we need (v. 8) and enlightens our minds to understand his word (v. 9). No wonder the Lord's love is priceless (v. 7)! We respond with a longing to continue experiencing his merciful love (v. 10). "This prayer is the heart of the believer asking precisely that which the heart of his God is prepared to grant." Since his glory is so great, it is not surprising that Spurgeon's primary purpose in preaching was to bring glory to Christ.*

Prayer. Lord, your love for me is so expansive! How can I ever tire of thinking and being awed by your divine love? Draw me away from sin and to your love. Lead me to obey and follow you. Amen.

* Dallimore, *Spurgeon*, 81–82; Morden, *C.H. Spurgeon*, 89.

March 12   Psalm 37:1-6

1 Do not fret because of those who are evil or be envious of those who do wrong; 2 for like the grass they will soon wither, like green plants they will soon die away. 3 Trust in the LORD and do good; dwell in the land and enjoy safe pasture. 4 Take delight in the LORD, and he will give you the desires of your heart. 5 Commit your way to the LORD; trust in him and he will do this: 6 he will make your righteous reward shine like the dawn, your vindication like the noonday sun. (NIV)

"The great riddle of the prosperity of the wicked and the affliction of the righteous . . . is here dealt with."

Four vital precepts. Spurgeon identifies eight precepts for life in this psalm. The first instructs us not to fret and fume about social injustices (v. 1). It takes grace to genuinely accept God's providence that he is right in all that he does. The second precept focuses on trust that obeys God and does what is good (v. 3). "Faith cures fretting . . . Doing good is a fine remedy for fretting. There is a joy in holy activity which drives away the rust of discontent." Since worrying is a heart issue, the third precept reminds us that we are to delight in pleasing God (v. 4) rather than envying the wicked. With this proper heart attitude, the fourth precept tells us to commit to God all of our worries and cares (vv. 5–6). "He does well to leave the whole matter to God; and so to all of us it is truest wisdom, having obediently trusted in God, to leave results in his hands, and expect a blessed issue."

Prayer. Lord, at times I fume at the wickedness flourishing in the world. Change my outlook and my anxious heart so that I may in delight in you and trust in your sovereign will. I personally and gladly submit to your will for my life. Amen.

7 Be still before the LORD and wait patiently for him; do not fret when people succeed in their ways, when they carry out their wicked schemes. 8 Refrain from anger and turn from wrath; do not fret—it leads only to evil. 9 For those who are evil will be destroyed, but those who hope in the LORD will inherit the land. 10 A little while, and the wicked will be no more; though you look for them, they will not be found. 11 But the meek will inherit the land and enjoy peace and prosperity. (NIV)

"If they find not abundance of gold, abundance of peace will serve their turn far better."

Rest from anger. We commonly experience anger in life and the instruction to stop being angry is not an easy one to practice (v. 8). How can we not be angry at the wickedness in the world and God's apparent inaction toward evil? The fifth precept states that we address our anger by not only waiting on God to act but by resting ("be still") in him (v. 7). The sixth precept reminds us God will deal with the wicked in his own time (vv. 9–10). These two precepts are interrelated. We cannot find true rest until we learn to wait patiently on God to accomplish his purposes. It is worth the wait! "In a story we wait until the end to clear up the plot; we ought not to prejudge the great drama of life, but stay till the closing scene" to see what God accomplishes. There is no benefit in worrying about evil around us because we will find that we only weary ourselves. Deal with our hearts by focusing on him now and wait for God to act in his good time. When we do this we will experience his blessings (v. 11).

Prayer. Righteous Father, my reaction to the flourishing of evil in society reminds me that this is a heart issue in my life. When I get angry, even at your ways, remind me to be silent and patient, knowing you will address all evil one day. Teach me to truly and humbly accept your ways in order that I can live with peace in my heart. Amen.

12 The wicked plot against the godly; they snarl at them in defiance. 13 But the Lord just laughs, for he sees their day of judgment coming. 14 The wicked draw their swords and string their bows to kill the poor and the oppressed, to slaughter those who do right. 15 But their swords will stab their own hearts, and their bows will be broken. (NLT)

"Why need we fret at the prosperity of the wicked when they are so industriously ruining themselves while they fancy they are injuring the saints?"

The reality of evil. It is foolhardy to think that resting and waiting on God to deal with evil is easy. Those who conspire against God's people plot and scheme to act out their evil (v. 12). They are like the serpent who was subtle and deceived Adam and Eve in the garden of Eden. The object of their animosity is often those who are defenseless (v. 14). However, the reality of evil has another side. The Lord laughs at those who love their wicked ways (v. 13). They boast about crushing the righteous, but he will defeat them. Besides, evil will turn on itself (v. 15). "Malice outwits itself. It drinks the poisoned cup which it mixed for another, and burns itself in the fire which it kindled for its neighbor." God's people do experience the reality of evil but the Lord will have the final say over the perpetrators.

Prayer. Jesus, I remember your statement that we will have troubles in this world because of its hatred of you. I recall how you faced people's animosity. You did not seek vengeance but allowed your Father to accomplish his purposes, which ultimately resulted in salvation for humanity. Thank you for your example and supernatural grace that enables me to live with peace. Amen.

16 Better is the little of the righteous than the abundance of many wicked. 17 For the arms of the wicked will be broken, but the Lord sustains the righteous. 18 The Lord knows the days of the blameless, and their inheritance will be forever. 19 They will not be ashamed in the time of evil, and in the days of famine they will have plenty. 20 But the wicked will perish; and the enemies of the Lord will be like the glory of the pastures, they vanish—like smoke they vanish away. 21 The wicked borrows and does not pay back, but the righteous is gracious and gives. 22 For those blessed by him will inherit the land, but those cursed by him will be eliminated. 23 The steps of a man are established by the Lord, and he delights in his way. 24 When he falls, he will not be hurled down, because the Lord is the One who holds his hand. 25 I have been young and now I am old, yet I have not seen the righteous forsaken or his descendants begging for bread. 26 All day long he is gracious and lends, and his descendants are a blessing. (NASB)

"Where grace does not keep from going down, it shall save
from keeping down."

God's faithfulness. In today's devotional the psalmist contrasts the godly and the ungodly. These two groups are differentiated in many ways: power and weakness (vv. 16-17); future destiny (vv. 18-20); character (vv. 21-22); and, blessings and curses (vv. 22-24). The purpose for showing these contrasts is found in verse 24. God is faithful to those he has chosen. "No saint shall fall finally or fatally . . . It is not that the saints are strong, or wise, or meritorious, that therefore they rise after every fall, but because God is their helper, and therefore none can prevail against them." Then David adds his observation (vv. 25-26), on which Spurgeon comments, "Never are the righteous forsaken; that is a rule without exception." This reality is not due to our efforts, but God's faithfulness to those who seek to follow him.

Prayer. Lord, I have heard previous generations bear testimony to your faithfulness and how you were faithful to them during financial distress, disease and sickness, and hostility. Through it all, they experienced your strength and love. Help me to remember your faithfulness so I can bear witness to the younger generations. Amen.

March 16   **Psalm 37:27–33**

27 Turn away from evil and do good; so shall you dwell forever. 28 For the LORD loves justice; he will not forsake his saints. They are preserved forever, but the children of the wicked shall be cut off. 29 The righteous shall inherit the land and dwell upon it forever. 30 The mouth of the righteous utters wisdom, and his tongue speaks justice. 31 The law of his God is in his heart; his steps do not slip. 32 The wicked watches for the righteous and seeks to put him to death. 33 The LORD will not abandon him to his power or let him be condemned when he is brought to trial. (ESV)

"No truce or parley is to be held with sin, we must turn away from it without hesitation, and set ourselves practically to work in the opposite direction."

Godly living. Capturing the essence of this psalm, the seventh precept (v. 27) instructs us to reject evil and do good. The verses following unpack the implications of this principle. We are to act justly as God does with all people (v. 28). Moreover, our concern for justice should not be motivated by media's social concerns but by speaking wisely (v. 30). A wise person is an advocate for honesty and fairness for all people. Finally, this person also loves uprightness because God's word is embedded in their heart (v. 31). "To love holiness, to have the motives and desires sanctified, to be in one's inmost nature obedient to the Lord—this is the surest method of making the whole run of our life efficient for its great ends." Godly living involves practicing God's word in society, thereby reflecting God's heart, which hates evil and loves good.

Prayer. Lord, I want to express your heart in this world by loving what is fair and advocating for justice with my words and actions. I do so not because of any contemporary agenda but because I want to reflect who you are in this dark world. Amen.

34 Wait for the LORD and keep his way, and he will exalt you to inherit the land; when the wicked are eliminated, you will see it. 35 I have seen a wicked, violent person spreading himself like a luxuriant tree in its native soil. 36 Then he passed away, and behold, he was no more; I searched for him, but he could not be found. 37 Observe the blameless person, and look at the upright; for the person of peace will have a future. 38 But wrongdoers will altogether be destroyed; the future of the wicked will be eliminated. 39 But the salvation of the righteous is from the LORD; he is their strength in time of trouble. 40 The LORD helps them and rescues them; he rescues them from the wicked and saves them, because they take refuge in him. (NASB)

> "This little word 'wait' is easy to say, but hard to carry out, yet faith must do it."

Waiting. The eighth and final precept challenges us to wait on the Lord (v. 34). Since this is not always easy to do it is fitting to ask why we should be so patient with God. The psalmist observes that people choose between two distinct outcomes in life. Those who oppose God will ultimately experience misery and pain (vv. 36, 38), whereas those who love Jesus will experience the blessing of God's peace (v. 37). "Peace without end comes in the end to the man of God. His way may be rough, but it leads home." In addition, God's salvation in its fullest sense will be ours (v. 39), both in the present and future. We ultimately inherit all that he has promised to us (v. 34). Thus, we can wait on the Lord. "Whoever truly believes in God will be no longer fretful against the apparent irregularities of this present life, but will rest assured that what is mysterious is nevertheless just, and what seems hard, is, beyond a doubt ordered by mercy." Yes, it is well worth waiting on God!

Prayer. My Lord, I confess that too often I fret and am impatient with you and others. I also admit it is hard to wait on you! Teach me how to wait on you, knowing you are working out your purposes in my life and in the world for your glory. Amen.

1 LORD, do not rebuke me in your wrath, and do not punish me in your burning anger. 2 For your arrows have sunk deep into me, and your hand has pressed down on me. 3 There is no healthy part in my flesh because of your indignation; there is no health in my bones because of my sin. 4 For my guilty deeds have gone over my head; like a heavy burden they weigh too much for me. 5 My wounds grow foul and fester because of my foolishness. 6 I am bent over and greatly bowed down; I go in mourning all day long. 7 For my sides are filled with burning, and there is no healthy part in my flesh. 8 I feel faint and badly crushed; I groan because of the agitation of my heart. 9 Lord, all my desire is before you; and my sighing is not hidden from you. (NASB)

"Soul sickness tells upon the entire frame; it weakens the body, and then bodily weakness reacts upon the mind."

Soul Sickness. While there are references to physical maladies in this section, the primary emphasis is on the sick soul. Spurgeon believes this psalm stands out because of its description of sin. "The fact is, it is a spiritual leprosy; it is an inward disease which is here described." David's sins weigh heavily on him, affecting his whole being (vv. 4–8). His sinful condition and guilt humble him before the Lord (vv. 1–3). What hope is there for any of us who recognize the pervasive and destructive impact sin has on our lives? Our only confidence is in God, to whom David turns (v. 9). When we are unable to express thoughts in words, it is God who "reads the longings of our heart . . . The good Physician understands the symptoms of our disease and sees the hidden evil which they reveal, hence our case is safe in his hands."

Prayer. All-powerful God, if I want to have a healthy heart, I need to confess my soul sickness to you. Through your word and Spirit, do your spiritual surgery on my sick heart and align it with your heart. I thank you that you are my great Physician who loves and heals me. Amen.

10 My heart pounds, my strength fails me; even the light has gone from my eyes. 11 My friends and companions avoid me because of my wounds; my neighbors stay far away. 12 Those who want to kill me set their traps, those who would harm me talk of my ruin; all day long they scheme and lie. 13 I am like the deaf, who cannot hear, like the mute, who cannot speak; 14 I have become like one who does not hear, whose mouth can offer no reply. 15 LORD, I wait for you; you will answer, Lord my God. (NIV)

"It is very hard when those who should be the first to come to the rescue, are the first to desert us."

Relational pain. This is the second of three sections expressing great sorrow before God. David's cruel friends have intentionally avoided him, causing deep pain in his heart (v. 11). Others have actively attacked him with lies and slander (v. 12). David guides us on how we should respond when we have been grievously hurt. First, we must intentionally guard ourselves from reacting and retaliating. David was silent (vv. 13–14). "A sacred indifference to the slanders of malevolence is true courage and wise policy. It is well to be as if we could not hear or see." Next, we turn to the Lord, who is our hope (v. 15). Spurgeon points out that we look to God because we believe in his intervention and in the power of prayer. By doing so, we entrust ourselves to God, who is "able to possess his soul . . . [and] we shall find the richest solace in waiting upon him . . . Rest then, O slandered one, and let not your soul be tossed to and fro with anxiety."

Prayer. Lord, I think of your Son, Jesus, who was deserted by his friends and maliciously slandered by his enemies. Amazingly, he did not retaliate, but silently honored you. Help me, Father, to reflect his life in my life when people abandon or attack me. Amen.

16 For I said, "Do not let them gloat or exalt themselves over me when my feet slip." 17 For I am about to fall, and my pain is ever with me. 18 I confess my iniquity; I am troubled by my sin. 19 Many have become my enemies without cause; those who hate me without reason are numerous. 20 Those who repay my good with evil lodge accusations against me, though I seek only to do what is good. 21 LORD, do not forsake me; do not be far from me, my God. 22 Come quickly to help me, my Lord and my Savior. (NIV)

"[W]e should often sit down, look back, retrace, and turn over in our meditation things that are past, lest at any time we should let any good thing sink into oblivion."

Retracing the past. In this section, David once again pours out his grief, reiterating some common themes that are important to remember in difficult times. He recalls his past trials and deliverances (vv. 16–17). The present afflictions we might encounter should not be surprising in light of our past experiences. He also reflects on the depravity of human nature. How can David be a man after God's heart when we know he deliberately sinned? Rather than denying this reality, he honestly confesses his sinfulness before God (v. 18). He reminds himself that he had enemies, not because he was evil but because he loved what was good (vv. 19–20). Finally, he remembers the graciousness of God, who he turns to in these three sections (vv. 9, 15–16, 21–22). He is gracious to us because our sin is forgiven through Jesus' redemption. Though we may be overwhelmed by our sin or people's rejection of us, Jesus is a friend who will never abandon us.

Prayer. Lord, in my moments of despair, it is valuable to reflect on the past, which often places the present in its proper perspective. But this is not enough! Your word and Spirit need to sink deep into my soul so that I may find rest in your gracious presence. You are my Savior and my friend! Amen.

1 I said, "I will keep watch over my ways so that I do not sin with my tongue; I will keep watch over my mouth as with a muzzle while the wicked are in my presence." 2 I was mute and silent, I refused to say even something good, and my pain was stirred up. 3 My heart was hot within me, while I was musing the fire burned; then I spoke with my tongue: 4 "LORD, let me know my end, and what is the extent of my days; let me know how transient I am. 5 Behold, you have made my days like hand widths, and my lifetime as nothing in your sight; certainly all mankind standing is a mere breath. *Selah* 6 Certainly every person walks around as a fleeting shadow; they certainly make an uproar for nothing; he amasses riches and does not know who will gather them. (NASB)

"[H]e rashly and petulantly desired to know the end of his wretched life, that he might begin to reckon the days till death should put a *finis* to his woe."

Deep despair. In these verses we hear David's despondence. He wrestles with God's mysterious providence and while "his heart was musing, it was fusing, for the subject was confusing." How do we respond at such times? One sensible approach is to remain silent (vv. 1–2). "If believers utter hard words of God in times of depression, the ungodly will take them up and use them as a justification for their sinful courses." Our silence guards us from wrongly speaking. However, to remain silent out of concern for speaking wrongly only aggravates the situation (v. 2). As one who personally knew depression, Spurgeon says, "Silence is an awful thing for a sufferer, it is the surest method to produce madness." This despondent silence stirs up our sinful nature and does not solve our despair. Spurgeon counsels us, "Mourner, tell your sorrow; do it first and most fully to God, but even to pour it out before some wise and godly friend is far from being wasted breath."

Prayer. Lord, like David I confess I experience dark days. I ask you to guard my tongue as well as my emotional life. Guide me to wise friends with whom I can share my sorrow in order to keep my heart right before you. Likewise, help me to be a trustworthy friend to others who are in deep despair. Amen.

7 And now, Lord, for what do I wait? My hope is in you. 8 Save me from all my wrongdoings; do not make me an object of reproach for the foolish. 9 I have become mute, I do not open my mouth, because it is you who have done it. 10 Remove your plague from me; because of the opposition of your hand I am perishing. 11 With rebukes you punish a person for wrongdoing; you consume like a moth what is precious to him; certainly all mankind is mere breath! *Selah* 12 Hear my prayer, LORD, and listen to my cry for help; do not be silent to my tears; for I am a stranger with you, one who lives abroad, like all my fathers. 13 Turn your eyes away from me, that I may become cheerful again before I depart and am no more. (NASB)

"Why should we dream of rest on earth when our fathers' sepulchers are before our eyes?"

A glimmer of hope. David's despair is further seen in these verses. Sensing God's discipline with him (vv. 10–11), he continues to weep, feeling like an alien in this world (v. 12). Nonetheless, there is a surprising degree of optimism. Though he feels like a stranger in this world, he dwells with God (v. 12). Spurgeon expressed the idea as follows: "I share the hospitality of God, like a stranger entertained by a generous host." In crying out to him, David expresses submission to God's grace, which enables him to be silent (v. 9). "It is his right to do as he wills, and he always wills to do that which is wisest and kindest." With hope and a submissive attitude, David pleads to God to remove the affliction from him (vv. 8, 10) before he dies (v. 13). Life is very difficult at times, but it is more bearable when we can submit ourselves to God.

Prayer. Father, forgive me when I wrongly think life should be easy. In fact, it can be intolerable. I am thankful that you understand what I am going through because your Son, Jesus experienced rejection and death, yet still submitted himself to you, the living hope. Amen.

1 I waited patiently for the LORD; he inclined to me and heard my cry. 2 He drew me up from the pit of destruction, out of the miry bog, and set my feet upon a rock, making my steps secure. 3 He put a new song in my mouth, a song of praise to our God. Many will see and fear, and put their trust in the LORD. 4 Blessed is the man who makes the LORD his trust, who does not turn to the proud, to those who go astray after a lie! 5 You have multiplied, O LORD my God, your wondrous deeds and your thoughts toward us; none can compare with you! I will proclaim and tell of them, yet they are more than can be told. (ESV)

"A simple, single-eyed confidence in God is the sure mark of blessedness."

Blessings of patience. Our impatient culture tempts us to take matters into our own hands, often creating a less-than-desired outcome. In this section, David and Jesus provide us with a better option. Jesus, who patiently waited on his Father's will to be accomplished, shows us the way to respond to the conflicts in our own lives (v. 1). When we learn the lesson of patience, we experience God's blessings (v. 4). The blessings are many: divine help (v. 2); a thankful heart (v. 3); a deeper trust in God (v. 4); and other innumerable wonders of God's grace (v. 5). Spurgeon states that these wonders pertain to the many aspects of our salvation, including our covenant relationship with God. "All the divine thoughts are good and gracious towards his elect. God's thoughts of love are very many, very wonderful, very practical!" When we are impatient we are often consumed with our own concerns. Patience allows us to wait on God and listen to his voice. Jesus is our example; by his life in us, we too can patiently wait on God to accomplish his purposes in our lives.

Prayer. Lord, forgive me for my impatience when I do not see you acting quickly enough in my difficult circumstances. Point me to your Son, Jesus, who saw your will being accomplished. Spirit of God, empower me to live patiently so I too can see your purposes being worked out in challenging situations. Amen.

March 24   Psalm 40:6–10

6 In sacrifice and offering you have not delighted, but you have given me an open ear. Burnt offering and sin offering you have not required. 7 Then I said, "Behold, I have come; in the scroll of the book it is written of me: 8 I delight to do your will, O my God; your law is within my heart." 9 I have told the glad news of deliverance in the great congregation; behold, I have not restrained my lips, as you know, O LORD. 10 I have not hidden your deliverance within my heart; I have spoken of your faithfulness and your salvation; I have not concealed your steadfast love and your faithfulness from the great congregation. (ESV)

"Here we enter upon one of the most wonderful passages in the whole of the Old Testament, a passage in which the incarnate Son of God is seen not through a glass darkly, but as it were face to face."

Dedication to God's will. Spurgeon applies these verses directly to Jesus, who knew and obeyed his Father's will. He did so because he had an obedient heart, which is far more important than "imposing performances of ritualistic worship" (v. 6). Rather than obeying out of sheer duty, Jesus delighted in the Father's will and work (v. 8). Even "from old eternity he had desired the work set before him . . . No outward, formal devotion was rendered by Christ; his heart was in his work." The application is clear for us. We should obey God not out of obligation, but with a grateful heart for all he has done for us. "Herein is the essence of obedience, namely, in the soul's cheerful devotion to God." To sum up, "Where there is no heart work, no pleasure, no delight in God's law, there can be no acceptance" to do God's will.

Prayer. Lord, I confess that I sometimes serve you out of obligation. Captivate me with your extravagant love and fill me with gratitude for all you have done, so that I may serve you with gladness and joy. Amen.

11 As for you, O LORD, you will not restrain your mercy from me;
your steadfast love and your faithfulness will ever preserve me!
12 For evils have encompassed me beyond number; my iniquities
have overtaken me, and I cannot see; they are more than the hairs
of my head; my heart fails me. 13 Be pleased, O LORD, to deliver
me! O LORD, make haste to help me! 14 Let those be put to shame
and disappointed altogether who seek to snatch away my life; let
those be turned back and brought to dishonor who delight in my
hurt! 15 Let those be appalled because of their shame who say to
me, "Aha, Aha!" 16 But may all who seek you rejoice and be glad
in you; may those who love your salvation say continually, "Great
is the LORD!" 17 As for me, I am poor and needy, but the LORD
takes thought for me. You are my help and my deliverer; do not
delay, O my God! (ESV)

"As the heart is warm with gladness let it incite the tongue to
perpetual praise."

Motive for prayer. In yesterday's reflections, we were reminded to obey the
Lord out of a glad and loving heart. With this renewed attitude, we can view
our difficulties from a different perspective. We do not selfishly pray, asking
God to rescue us from overwhelming circumstances. We confidently pray
that he will show us his lovingkindness in tough times (v. 11). Having experienced his love in the past, we know it will happen again. However, when
we pray for God's mercy it is not primarily for ourselves but for God to be
magnified (v. 16). When God does deliver us from painful circumstances, do
we give him the glory? Spurgeon rightfully challenges us, "[L]et us then, with
all our tongues proclaim the glory of God which is resplendent therein . . . Be
it ours to make God's glory the chief end of every breath and pulse." This is
our ultimate motive in prayer!

Prayer. Lord, I know I often pray for deliverance from my distressing circumstances. Lift my heart and mind beyond these situations so I can point
others to you and your great lovingkindness. I want to exalt you and give you
all the glory for what you have done in and through me! Amen.

March 26   Psalm 41:1–4

1 Blessed is one who considers the helpless; the LORD will save him on a day of trouble. 2 The LORD will protect him and keep him alive, and he will be called blessed upon the earth; and do not turn him over to the desire of his enemies. 3 The LORD will sustain him upon his sickbed; in his illness, you restore him to health. 4 As for me, I said, "LORD, be gracious to me; heal my soul, for I have sinned against you." (NASB)

> "The compassionate lover of the poor thought of others and therefore God will think of him."

God's mercy and sin. Verses 1–3 describe God's mercies promised to those who are afflicted and preface David's own plea for mercy in the rest of the psalm. Verse 1 is a benediction, a word of blessing to those who show mercy in the name of Christ. "The blessing is for those whose habit it is to love their neighbor as themselves, and who for Christ's sake feed the hungry and clothe the naked." Who are the poor? Whether in Spurgeon's day or ours, they are often the orphans, the widows, and the homeless. He knew they suffered physically and with a despondent spirit.* To those who are needy we are called to act with mercy in practical ways. To those who are compassionate, God will show his mercy in specific ways (vv. 1–3). Is this simply being rewarded by God for what we have done? No, for David has sinned and confesses it before the Lord (v. 4). The mercy God shows is based on his own character. "Even the fact that the confessing penitent had remembered the poor . . . but a direct appeal is made to mercy on the ground of great sin." This is God's immense mercy shown to each of us who have grieved God's heart.

Prayer. Lord, cultivate in me a compassionate heart for those who face so many kinds of need. I ask this because I not only desire your blessing on my life, but also want to reflect your merciful character by what I say and do. Make me more like Jesus, who showed enormous concern for the needy. Amen.

---

* Dallimore, *Spurgeon*, 128–29; Nettles, *Living by Revealed Truth*, 377–80.

5 My enemies speak evil against me, "When will he die, and his name perish?" 6 And when he comes to see me, he speaks empty words; his heart gathers wickedness to itself; when he goes outside, he tells it. 7 All who hate me whisper together against me; they plot my harm against me, saying, 8 "A wicked thing is poured out upon him, so that when he lies down, he will not get up again." 9 Even my close friend in whom I trusted, who ate my bread, has lifted up his heel against me. 10 But you, LORD, be gracious to me and raise me up, that I may repay them. 11 By this I know that you are pleased with me, because my enemy does not shout in triumph over me. 12 As for me, you uphold me in my integrity, and you place me in your presence forever. 13 Blessed be the LORD, the God of Israel, from everlasting to everlasting. Amen and Amen. (NASB)

"He had been a tender friend to the poor, and yet in the hour of his need the promised assistance was not forthcoming."

Delayed mercy. In addition to needing God's mercy because of his sin (v. 4), David desires it because of his circumstances. His enemies speak evil of David (vv. 5–8). They want him dead (v. 5) and spread false rumors that God's curse is on him (v. 8). The suffering is even greater because a friend has become his enemy (v. 9). When God's promised mercy is not immediately apparent and seemingly delayed, how should we respond? Rather than presuming God's mercy, we humbly ask him to be compassionate to us (v. 10a). Also, we need to look at God's supernatural power through Christ's resurrection that enables us to face and defeat the powers of evil (v. 10b). We rest in God who deeply loves us and gives us this assurance in our hearts (v. 11). Finally, we can depend on the Spirit's power, which enables us "to rise above the reach of slander by living in purity and righteousness. Our innocence and consistency are the result of divine upholding" (v. 12). We can depend on God's faithfulness even in such difficult experiences.

Prayer. Lord Jesus, I am thankful you empathize with my struggles and my need of your mercy. In your many afflictions on earth, you experienced your Father's faithful lovingkindness that was ultimately revealed by your resurrection. Thank you for your love and mercy, which give me hope in this life. Amen.

March 28   Psalm 42:1-5

1 As the deer pants for streams of water, so my soul pants for you, my God. 2 My soul thirsts for God, for the living God. When can I go and meet with God? 3 My tears have been my food day and night, while people say to me all day long, "Where is your God?" 4 These things I remember as I pour out my soul: how I used to go to the house of God under the protection of the Mighty One with shouts of joy and praise among the festive throng. 5 Why, my soul, are you downcast? Why so disturbed within me? Put your hope in God, for I will yet praise him, my Savior and my God. (NIV)

"[T]hirst is a perpetual appetite, and not to be forgotten, and even thus continual is the heart's longing after God."

Longing for God. Numerous factors may precipitate our desire for God's presence. The psalmist's opponents cruelly taunted him by suggesting that he had lost God's favor (v. 3). Dwelling on such things and being tempted to believe them is enough to discourage the strongest person who has experienced God's goodness. "Painful reflections were awakened by the memory of past joys" (v. 4). Then the "why" questions often surface in our minds (v. 5). For example, "Why am I experiencing deep melancholy and depression?" No wonder "the enjoyment of communion with God was an urgent need of his soul . . . his soul, his very self, his deepest life, was insatiable for a sense of the divine presence" (vv. 1–2). This thirst for God, in private and public worship, is both essential and an indication of our spiritual health. We are then able to recommit our hope in the Lord and praise him.

Prayer. Lord, rather than turning to cheap substitutes in painful times, increase my longing for you, the true, spiritual, living water. You have created our bodies to thirst in order that we may realize our need for water. Awaken my soul to thirst for you at all times because you alone are my hope! I want to be thirsty for you! Amen.

March 29   Psalm 42:6-11

6 My soul is downcast within me; therefore I will remember you from the land of the Jordan, the heights of Hermon—from Mount Mizar. 7 Deep calls to deep in the roar of your waterfalls; all your waves and breakers have swept over me. 8 By day the LORD directs his love, at night his song is with me—a prayer to the God of my life. 9 I say to God my Rock, "Why have you forgotten me? Why must I go about mourning, oppressed by the enemy?" 10 My bones suffer mortal agony as my foes taunt me, saying to me all day long, "Where is your God?" 11 Why, my soul, are you downcast? Why so disturbed within me? Put your hope in God, for I will yet praise him, my Savior and my God. (NIV)

"To know the reason for sorrow is in part to know how to escape it, or at least to endure it."

Questioning God. In this passage, the psalmist's dejection and despondency return like a hurricane drowning him in all his troubles (v. 7). He naturally raises the "why" question about God, who has apparently abandoned him (v. 9). It is natural to feel this way, especially when God's promises to us are not fulfilled. Fortunately, God graciously allows us to ask the hard questions so that we can discover the causes for our hardships. There is value in raising these questions before God. "Want [lack] of attentive consideration often makes adversity appear to be more mysterious and hopeless than it really is." Therefore, when the psalmist's opponents mock his God (v. 10), he realizes there is no basis for being so anxious or fearful. In response, he is drawn back to God's great love for him (v. 8). "The belief that we shall yet glorify the Lord for mercy given in extremity is a delightful stay to the soul. Affliction may put out our candle, but if it cannot silence our song we will soon light the candle again." With renewed confidence in God, the psalmist is able to praise him (v. 11).

Prayer. Thank you, Lord, that you allow me to ask tough questions when I wrestle with overwhelming situations in my life. Hear my doubts and searching questions as part of the process to see my faith in you strengthened. May this result in greater praise to you, with confidence of your great love for me. Amen.

1–2 Clear my name, God; stick up for me against these loveless, immoral people. Get me out of here, away from these lying degenerates. I counted on you, God. Why did you walk out on me? Why am I pacing the floor, wringing my hands over these outrageous people? 3–4 Give me your lantern and compass, give me a map, so I can find my way to the sacred mountain, to the place of your presence, to enter the place of worship, meet my exuberant God, sing my thanks with a harp, magnificent God, my God. 5 Why are you down in the dumps, dear soul? Why are you crying the blues? Fix my eyes on God—soon I'll be praising again. He puts a smile on my face. He's my God. (MSG)

"To have God in possession, and to know it by faith, is the heart's heaven—a fullness of bliss lies within."

Finding God. While Spurgeon recognizes this psalm is similar to the previous one, with its questions and dejected mood (vv. 2, 5), there is a positive and subtle shift. Now the psalmist rebukes himself for being so discouraged (v. 5). He asks God to reveal his light and truth in the present circumstance (v. 3). Today we can know the light of God's truth discovered in Jesus Christ. We also can possess the indwelling Holy Spirit, who enlightens our minds to God's truth. With these divine resources, we are able to enter and enjoy God's presence so that we may worship him with great delight (vv. 4–5). Thus, "the saints triumph in the manifestation of the love and fidelity of their God, which, like the golden sunbeam, lights up even the darkest surroundings with delightful splendor." Our hearts can be filled with joyful worship even in very difficult times.

Prayer. Father, when I think of the day you came into my life, I am filled with gratitude for knowing you through your Son, Jesus, and the Holy Spirit, who revealed who you are to me. I am amazed that I can experience your real presence and living truth in my life. I worship you for the joy of knowing you! Amen.

1 God, we have heard with our ears, our fathers have told us the work that you did in their days, in the days of old. 2 You with your own hand drove out the nations; then you planted them; you afflicted the peoples, then you let them go free. 3 For by their own sword they did not possess the land, and their own arm did not save them, but your right hand and your arm and the light of your presence, for you favored them. 4 You are my King, God; command victories for Jacob. 5 Through you we will push back our adversaries; through your name we will trample down those who rise up against us. 6 For I will not trust in my bow, nor will my sword save me. 7 But you have saved us from our adversaries, and you have put to shame those who hate us. 8 In God we have boasted all day long, and we will give thanks to your name forever. *Selah* (NASB)

> "There was nothing in the people themselves to secure them success, the Lord's favour alone did it."

Lessons from history. Spurgeon describes this section as rehearsing God's mighty acts of former days which strengthen our faith. What do we learn as we reflect on the past? We learn the importance of communicating stories of God's ongoing faithfulness (v. 1). Our parents' and grandparents' stories of former years make an indelible impression on young hearts and minds. We are reminded that it is God who is actively at work in history (vv. 1–3). "It is delightful to see the footprints of the Lord on the sea of changing events." We are reminded as well that past successes are ultimately due to God's goodness (v. 3). "[We] must not rest on anything in ourselves, but on the free and sovereign favour of the Lord of Hosts." In light of God's sovereignty and grace, we ought to reject sole self-reliance and learn to depend more on God (vv. 4–7). Lastly, we praise God for all he has done in the past (v. 8). "Praise should be perpetual. If there were no new acts of love, yet ought the Lord to be praised for what he has done for his people."

Prayer. Lord, when I fear the present and my trust in you wanes, remind me to look to the past, so that I can see your mighty acts in history. Use those to renew and strengthen my weak faith in you, and use me to tell others of your faithfulness experienced throughout my life. Amen.

April 1   Psalm 44:9-16

9 Yet you have rejected us and brought us to dishonor, and do not go out with our armies. 10 You cause us to turn back from the enemy; and those who hate us have taken spoils for themselves. 11 You turn us over to be eaten like sheep, and have scattered us among the nations. 12 You sell your people cheaply, and have not profited by their sale. 13 You make us an object of reproach to our neighbors, of scoffing and ridicule to those around us. 14 You make us a proverb among the nations, a laughingstock among the peoples. 15 All day long my dishonor is before me and I am covered with my humiliation, 16 because of the voice of one who taunts and reviles, because of the presence of the enemy and the avenger. (NASB)

"All this is ascribed to the Lord as being allowed by him, and even appointed by his decree. It is well to trace the hand of God in our sorrows, for it is surely there."

Complaints. In this section, we read about the psalmist's highs and lows in life. He complains to God, who abandoned his people and left them to be destroyed by their enemies (v. 11). One could assume that "Jehovah had grown weary of his people and put them away in abhorrence . . . loathing the sight of them" (v. 9). When one feels deserted by God it is true that "no calamity can equal the sorrow of being left of God, though it be but for a small moment." Even though we may *know* God's hand ("you" is mentioned six times) is behind the hardships, the *feeling* of rejection is still very painfully real. In one breath we may praise God, and in the next we may complain to him. Fortunately, God listens to our heartfelt complaints without rejecting us.

Prayer. Gracious Lord, I admit I am confused by the hardships that come my way. Thank you for not spurning me when I complain about your apparent lack of concern for me and others. I am thankful you allow me to express my heart to you even when I do not feel like praising you. Amen.

April 2   Psalm 44:17–26

17 All this has come upon us, but we have not forgotten you, and we have not dealt falsely with your covenant. 18 Our heart has not turned back, and our steps have not deviated from your way, 19 yet you have crushed us in a place of jackals and covered us with deep darkness. 20 If we had forgotten the name of our God or extended our hands to a strange god, 21 would God not find this out? For he knows the secrets of the heart. 22 But for your sake we are killed all day long; we are regarded as sheep to be slaughtered. 23 Wake yourself up, why do you sleep, Lord? Awake, do not reject us forever. 24 Why do you hide your face and forget our affliction and oppression? 25 For our souls have sunk down into the dust; our bodies cling to the earth. 26 Rise up, be our help, and redeem us because of your mercy. (NASB)

"Not petulantly, but piteously and enquiringly, we may question the Lord when his dealings are mysterious."

The hidden God. The psalmist has declared God has been actively involved with his people bringing many blessings to them (vv. 1–8). However, hardships have come their way, evoking complaints among them (vv. 9–16). Why do these painful times strike us? It puzzles us when we believe that our faithfulness to God exempts us from afflictions and suffering (vv. 17–18). Besides, he knows the secrets of our hearts and finds us innocent of wrongdoing (v. 21). Thus, we may conclude that our afflictions are based on other unknown causes. No clue or answer is given to the psalmist for the ultimate reason for the afflictions. In fact, it often appears God is sleeping and hiding from his people (vv. 23–24). In such situations, "it is hard, indeed, in the midst of persecution to see the reason why we are left to suffer so severely." As one who knew much sorrow, Spurgeon writes, "Heart sorrow is the very heart of sorrow." While we may not get an answer for our suffering, we can turn to God and plead for his mercy and love (v. 26). Ultimately, we depend not on the answers to our questions but on God's trustworthy and unchanging character.

Prayer. Father, I feel you are hiding from me because I do not see you acting on my behalf. But I remember that while Jesus suffered on the cross you were actively at work, bringing about my salvation. Help me to trust in your faithful love even when I think you have left me all alone. Amen.

1 My heart is stirred by a noble theme as I recite my verses for the king; my tongue is the pen of a skillful writer. 2 You are the most excellent of men and your lips have been anointed with grace, since God has blessed you forever. 3 Gird your sword on your side, you mighty one; clothe yourself with splendor and majesty. 4 In your majesty ride forth victoriously in the cause of truth, humility and justice; let your right hand achieve awesome deeds. 5 Let your sharp arrows pierce the hearts of the king's enemies; let the nations fall beneath your feet. 6 Your throne, O God, will last for ever and ever; a scepter of justice will be the scepter of your kingdom. 7 You love righteousness and hate wickedness; therefore God, your God, has set you above your companions by anointing you with the oil of joy. 8 All your robes are fragrant with myrrh and aloes and cassia; from palaces adorned with ivory the music of the strings makes you glad. 9 Daughters of kings are among your honored women; at your right hand is the royal bride in gold of Ophir. (NIV)

"This song has 'the King' for its only subject, and for the King's honour alone was it composed."

The beauty of Jesus. In this section, the psalmist pictures a wedding between the Messiah Jesus and the church. Spurgeon mentions that the word "excellent" (v. 2) is literally "beautiful, beautiful" in Hebrew. Thus, "Jesus is so emphatically lovely that words must be doubled, strained, yea, exhausted before he can be described." Jesus is the King (v. 1) who is beautiful in his grace (v. 2), his divine power and glory (v. 3), and his truth, humility, and righteousness (v. 4). He is the mighty and eternal King who reigns with justice (vv. 5–7). We need to allow these truths to soak into our whole being. No wonder Spurgeon said, "Let my name perish, but let Christ's name last forever! Jesus! Jesus! Jesus! Crown him Lord of all!"*

Prayer. Heavenly Father, I admit I do not often think about the beauty of Jesus. I fall down in humble adoration, with my whole being, to worship your Son, Jesus. Renew my vision of the matchless beauty of your Son so that I will want to worship and serve him for the rest of my life. Amen.

---

* Morden, *C.H. Spurgeon,* 169. Spurgeon uttered these words in a weakened physical condition at Exeter Hall in London.

April 4   Psalm 45:10–17

10 Hear, O daughter, and consider, and incline your ear: forget your people and your father's house, 11 and the king will desire our beauty. Since he is your lord, bow to him. 12 The people of Tyre will seek your favor with gifts, the richest of the people. 13 All glorious is the princess in her chamber, with robes interwoven with gold. 14 In many-colored robes she is led to the king, with her virgin companions following behind her. 15 With joy and gladness they are led along as they enter the palace of the king. 16 In place of your fathers shall be your sons; you will make them princes in all the earth. 17 I will cause your name to be remembered in all generations; therefore nations will praise you forever and ever. (ESV)

"This is no wedding song of earthly nuptials, but an Epithalamium [poem] for the heavenly Bridegroom and his elect spouse."

The beautiful church. This passage describes the mystic marriage of Jesus and the church composed of those who love him. We are called upon to give our allegiance to him for he is our bridegroom. How can we be faithful to the lover of our soul? We must give our wholehearted commitment to Jesus by being attentive to him (v. 10). We reject the allure of society "for a divided heart he cannot endure." "The church must forsake all others and cleave to Jesus only, or she will not please him nor enjoy the full manifestation of his love." We must also give serious consideration to the importance of developing godly character (v. 13). The beauty of the church is not superficial and external; it is internal and based on God's renewing work in our lives. We do well to remember that "the choicest of her charms are to be found in her heart, her secret character, her inward desires. Truth and wisdom in the hidden parts are what the Lord regards." Thankfully, we are clothed by the righteousness of Jesus Christ and have every reason to worship the Bridegroom!

Prayer. Lord, I confess that when I look at your church I see many faults and blemishes. Forgive me for my critical, even skeptical, spirit. Help me see your love for your church and to be faithful in loving you and your people, whom you died for. Amen.

April 5 Psalm 46:1–3

1 God is our refuge and strength, a very ready help in trouble. 2 Therefore we will not fear, though the earth shakes and the mountains slip into the heart of the sea; 3 though its waters roar and foam, though the mountains quake at its swelling pride. *Selah* (NASB)

"Great men who are like mountains may quake for fear in times of great calamity, but the man whose trust is in God need never be dismayed."

God over nature. In this the first of three sections divided by *selah*, the psalmist describes great natural calamities (vv. 2–3). But here is hope for us! "Let the worst come to the worst, the child of God should never give way to mistrust" because the focus is on God (v. 1). "He is their help, truly, effectually, constantly; he is present or near them, close at their side . . . he is more present than friend or relative can be." How appropriate that *selah* (a pause) is calling us to meditate on him. "We are in no hurry, but [the *selah*] can sit us down and wait while earth dissolves, and mountains rock, and oceans roar. Ours is not the headlong rashness which passes for courage, we can calmly confront the danger, and meditate upon terror." This is a far better approach than rushing to act out of fear and causing even greater calamities.

Prayer. Lord, I confess I am prone to act or speak too hastily when I see my world falling apart. Teach me to pause long enough to focus and meditate on you, my mighty fortress, to find true security in this chaotic world. Amen.

April 6   Psalm 46:4–7

4 There is a river whose streams make the city of God happy, the holy dwelling places of the Most High. 5 God is in the midst of her, she will not be moved; God will help her when morning dawns. 6 The nations made an uproar, the kingdoms tottered; he raised his voice, the earth quaked. 7 The LORD of armies is with us; the God of Jacob is our stronghold. *Selah* (NASB)

"[W]oe unto those who fight against him, for they shall fly like smoke before the wind when he gives the word to scatter them."

God over the nations. Now the psalmist turns the attention from nature to the general populace (v. 6). "The nations were in a furious uproar, they gathered against the city of the Lord like wolves ravenous for their prey." When we feel the wrath of nations against the Lord, we are often fearful of evil running rampant around the globe. Will the universal church be able to withstand the hatred of those opposed to Jesus Christ? The psalmist points us to the city of God (v. 4), which is the church, according to Spurgeon. God is with his people (v. 5) and his promised help is expressed in various ways. He provides a river (v. 4) so that "in seasons of trial all-sufficient grace will be given to enable us to endure unto the end." Not only do we have God's presence and grace for difficult times, but we possess his powerful word that speaks over his enemies (v. 6). "He gave forth a voice and stout hearts were dissolved, proud armies were annihilated, conquering powers were enfeebled." Thus, we can live with peace in our hearts, knowing the Lord is with us and his enemies will ultimately surrender to him.

Prayer. Sovereign God, once again I pause to remember you want me to be keenly aware of your powerful and reassuring presence, regardless of the tumult in today's world. May your people be a beacon of hope and an oasis of peace in the midst of the raging nations. Amen.

April 7   Psalm 46:8–11

8 Come, behold the works of the LORD, who has inflicted horrific events on the earth. 9 He makes wars to cease to the end of the earth; he breaks the bow and cuts the spear in two; he burns the chariots with fire. 10 "Stop striving and know that I am God; I will be exalted among the nations, I will be exalted on the earth." 11 The LORD of armies is with us; the God of Jacob is our stronghold. *Selah* (NASB)

"Either by terror or love God will subdue all hearts to himself."

God reigns. The psalmist invites the reader to ponder God's power in the world (vv. 8–9). "The destroyers he destroys, the desolaters he desolates." As Spurgeon points out, God's enemies are already robbed of their power to usurp his work and this will be fully realized when Christ returns to earth one day in the future. In the meantime, knowing God's power, we are to be still (v. 10). In other words, we are to patiently wait for the Lord to be exalted. "The whole round earth shall yet reflect the light of his majesty. All the more because of the sin, and obstinacy, and pride of man shall God be glorified when grace reigns unto eternal life in all corners of the world." In the meantime, we continually affirm God is with us (vv. 7, 11). When we do this, we can experience *selah* (v. 7), which is a hint to "lift up the heart. Rest in contemplation after praise. Still keep the soul in tune. It is easier to sing a hymn of praise than to continue in the spirit of praise, but let it be our aim to maintain the uprising devotion of our grateful hearts."

Prayer. Lord, calm my heart, not by the demonstrations of military might and political maneuvering, but by your presence and the knowledge you are the One who is sovereign in this world. Let my fretting mind experience a measure of stillness so that I can wait and rest in you. Amen.

1 Clap your hands, all peoples! Shout to God with loud songs of joy! 2 For the LORD, the Most High, is to be feared, a great king over all the earth. 3 He subdued peoples under us, and nations under our feet. 4 He chose our heritage for us, the pride of Jacob whom he loves. *Selah* 5 God has gone up with a shout, the LORD with the sound of a trumpet. 6 Sing praises to God, sing praises! Sing praises to our King, sing praises! 7 For God is the King of all the earth; sing praises with a psalm! 8 God reigns over the nations; God sits on his holy throne. 9 The princes of the peoples gather as the people of the God of Abraham. For the shields of the earth belong to God; he is highly exalted! (ESV)

"Sing a didactic Psalm. Sound doctrine praises God."

Spirituality of worship. After the previous psalm calls us to restfully wait on God to act, this psalm has a unified theme of worshipping him who has acted in history. Verse 7 urges us to sing a psalm—which means "understanding" in Hebrew. Thus, God should be praised "thoughtfully, intelligently, and with deep appreciation for the reason for the song." The psalmist provides sound theological reasons for such worship. The Lord is the Most High, who possesses great power, wisdom, and glory (v. 2). He will eventually reveal his ultimate victory over people and nations (v. 3) because he presently reigns over the nations (v. 8). "God holds a secret rule . . . and the rule now unrecognized shall be delighted in!" He will also give his people an inheritance (v. 4). In response, we clap our hands (v. 1) in enthusiastic worship to the Lord—"sing praises" is repeated five times (vv. 6–7). A proper spirituality of worship goes beyond the personal dimension to a global one (v. 9). "Not only the poor and the men of low estate are there, but nobles bow their willing necks to his sway . . . No people shall be unrepresented."

Prayer. Lord, I confess my worship is often more about the music than about you. It is far too commonplace to worship you half-heartedly as well. This is not what you desire! May I focus on who you are so that I, with the rest of God's people, can enthusiastically worship you with mind and heart. Amen.

April 9   Psalm 48:1–8

1 Great is the LORD, and greatly to be praised in the city of our God, his holy mountain. 2 Beautiful in elevation, the joy of the whole earth, is Mount Zion in the far north, the city of the great King. 3 In its palaces, God has made himself known as a stronghold. 4 For, behold, the kings arrived, they passed by together. 5 They saw it, then they were amazed; they were terrified, they fled in a hurry. 6 Panic seized them there, anguish, as that of a woman in childbirth. 7 With the east wind you smash the ships of Tarshish. 8 Just as we have heard, so have we seen in the city of the LORD of armies, in the city of our God; God will establish her forever. *Selah* (NASB)

> "In the church the Lord is to be extolled though all the nations rage against him."

The church. In these verses the psalmist is writing about Jerusalem as God's dwelling place. Since the Holy Spirit now indwells his people, Spurgeon makes several analogies to the universal church. One, since the church is how God reveals himself to society, worship is one tangible way to express who he is (v. 1). Two, in a world filled with despair, the church offers true joy and hope because God is our refuge amid confusion and chaos (vv. 2–3). Three, the spiritual nature of the church will evoke strong opposition (v. 4). Four, the church will be victorious over all of its adversaries (vv. 5–7). As Spurgeon expresses it, "They came like foam on the angry sea, like foam they melted away . . . The troublers were troubled. Their haste in coming was nothing to their hurry in going." Five, anticipated victory is not based on our strength, but rests in the nature of God, who is the Lord Almighty (v. 8). With this in mind, it is appropriate to pause (*selah*) to admire what God has done in the past and to face the future with confidence.

Prayer. Father, when I get discouraged about the church, with its shortcomings, remind me to focus on worshipping you, looking to you for hope, and anticipating your ultimate victory over all forms of injustice and wickedness. Thank you for your faithful love and power. Amen!

April 10   Psalm 48:9-14

9 We have thought over your goodness, God, in the midst of your temple. 10 As is your name, God, so is your praise to the ends of the earth; your right hand is full of righteousness. 11 Mount Zion shall be glad, the daughters of Judah shall rejoice because of your judgments. 12 Walk around Zion and encircle her; count her towers; 13 consider her ramparts; go through her palaces, so that you may tell of her to the next generation. 14 For such is God, our God forever and ever; he will lead us until death. (NASB)

"Holy men are thoughtful men; they do not suffer God's wonders to pass before their eyes and melt into forgetfulness."

Telling the church story. While one can see the blemishes and shortcomings of God's church throughout its history, the psalmist challenges us to embrace a different perspective. As his readers were invited to inspect Jerusalem, we are called on to do the same with the centuries-old church (v. 12). "We cannot too frequently or too deeply consider the origin, privileges, history, security, and glory of the church . . . this is worthy of the most patient consideration." When we do this, we see the strength of the church (v. 13). This strength does not come from our abilities, but from the security God promises his people. With this confidence in his church, we are called on to tell the next generation of God's faithfulness. For us, this is an "excellent reason for studious observation. We have received and we must transmit. We must be students that we may be teachers. The debt we owe to the past we must endeavor to repay by handing down the truth to the future." We are ultimately pointing to God, who has sustained the church and will continue to do so in the future. Thus, we do well to remember and retell all that God has done in the past.

Prayer. Lord, help me to see your church in a way that honors the faithfulness you have shown your people throughout the centuries. I want to see your name exalted when I tell the younger generation about the church here and around the world. Amen.

April 11   Psalm 49:1-4

1 Listen to this, all you people! Pay attention, everyone in the world! 2 High and low, rich and poor—listen! 3 For my words are wise, and my thoughts are filled with insight. 4 I listen carefully to many proverbs and solve riddles with inspiration from a harp. (NLT)

> "The writer was no mystic, delighting in deep and cloudy things, yet he was not afraid of the most profound topics."

Spiritual truth. In this preface to the rest of the psalm, Spurgeon gives us some insights to the nature of spiritual truth. First, spiritual truth is useful to all people (vv. 1–2). "The low will be encouraged, the high will be warned, the rich will be sobered, the poor consoled, there will be a useful lesson for each if they are willing to learn it." Second, this truth contains divine wisdom which is worthy of consideration and reflection in life (v. 3). Third, God's truth is not easily grasped (v. 4). In order to communicate effectively his word to others, we must follow the practice of the psalmist, who "would not leave the truth in obscurity, but he listened to its voice till he so well understood it as to be able to interpret and translate it into the common language of the multitude." We are thankful for godly men and women who teach the word and for the Holy Spirit who illumines the truth for our growth.

Prayer. Lord, I confess too often do I rush in the reading of your word, which is profound in its depth. When I consider the Scriptures contain divine wisdom, I realize I need to slow down and meditate on your spiritual truth. Give me the discipline to do this so I will be more effective in sharing your word. Amen.

April 12   Psalm 49:5-13

5 Why should I fear in days of adversity, when the injustice of those who betray me surrounds me, 6 those who trust in their wealth and boast in the abundance of their riches? 7 No one can by any means redeem another or give God a ransom for him—8 for the redemption of his soul is priceless, and he should cease imagining forever—9 that he might live on eternally, that he might not undergo decay. 10 For he sees that even wise people die; the foolish and the stupid alike perish and leave their wealth to others. 11 Their inner thought is that their houses are forever and their dwelling places to all generations; they have named their lands after their own names. 12 But man in his splendor will not endure; he is like the animals that perish. 13 This is the way of those who are foolish, and of those after them who approve their words. *Selah* (NASB)

"Eminence is evermore in imminence of peril. The hero of the hour lasts but for an hour."

Unfounded fear. Followers of Jesus are often oppressed and even persecuted by corrupt, powerful, and rich people. How should we respond? Should we be intimidated so that we yield like cowards? No! "Their enemies are too insignificant to be worthy of one thrill of fear" (v. 5). The psalmist gives us reasons not to fear our oppressors. He notes that the wealth of the powerful actually leaves them helpless in many life situations (vv. 6–9). All the wealth in the world cannot spare one from physical and spiritual death. Even the oppressor recognizes that people eventually die and leave their wealth behind (vv. 10–11). While the oppressors may have some short-term advantage over the righteous, the follower of Jesus need not fear them.

Prayer. Heavenly Father, help me to see life from your perspective so that I do not panic when others marginalize me because of my commitment to you. Those who appear powerful are truly limited in both their power and life itself. My fear is unfounded especially when my hope is placed in you. Amen.

April 13

Psalm 49:14-20

14 Like sheep they sink down to Sheol; death will be their shepherd; and the upright will rule over them in the morning, and their form shall be for Sheol to consume so that they have no lofty home. 15 But God will redeem my soul from the power of Sheol, for he will receive me. *Selah* 16 Do not be afraid when a person becomes rich, when the splendor of his house is increased; 17 for when he dies, he will take nothing with him; his wealth will not descend after him. 18 Though while he lives he congratulates himself—and though people praise you when you do well for yourself—19 he will go to the generation of his fathers; they will never see the light. 20 Mankind in its splendor, yet without understanding, is like the animals that perish. (NASB)

> "From the loftiest elevation of worldly honour to the uttermost depth of death is but a step."

Two destinies. Now the psalmist contrasts the future of those who reject God and those who follow him (v. 14). Those who trusted in their wealth rather than in God will be forever separated from him. "Death like a grim shepherd leads them on, and conducts them to the place of their eternal pasturage, where all is barrenness and misery." However, those who place their faith in God, through Jesus Christ, will enjoy the Lord forever. This is not based on earning our salvation but through God's redemption. "No redemption could one find in riches, but God has found it in the blood of his dear Son. Our Elder Brother has given to God a ransom, and we are the redeemed of the Lord." With these two different destinies in mind, the psalmist functions as a preacher who admonishes those who trust in earthly possessions rather than in Jesus Christ (vv. 16–20). "Comforting as the theme is to the righteous, it is full of warning to the worldly." Choose Jesus Christ, who is the only way to experience eternal life here and in the future.

Prayer. Lord, though I am very undeserving, I am thankful for your salvation through your Son, Jesus Christ. I pray that those who do not know you will see a shallowness in the wealth they trust and the things they pursue, while recognizing the richness of turning to you. May my life be used by your Spirit to draw them closer to you. Amen

April 14   Psalm 50:1–6

1 The Mighty One, God the LORD, speaks and summons the earth from the rising of the sun to its setting. 2 Out of Zion, the perfection of beauty, God shines forth. 3 Our God comes; he does not keep silence; before him is a devouring fire, around him a mighty tempest. 4 He calls to the heavens above and to the earth, that he may judge his people: 5 "Gather to me my faithful ones, who made a covenant with me by sacrifice!" 6 The heavens declare his righteousness, for God himself is judge! *Selah* (ESV)

"Observe how with trumpet voice and flaming ensign the infinite Jehovah summons the heavens and the earth to hearken to his word."

God's judgment. In this section, God summons people from around the world to hear what he has to say. In this case, he does not bring judgment on the nations but on his own people (vv. 4–5). "All are not saints who seem to be so—a severance must be made." According to Spurgeon, this judgment deals with God's discernment between those who have a genuine commitment to Christ and those who only profess to be followers of Jesus. With each person God will declare his verdict, revealing who has a genuine faith in him. This will not be based on an outward profession of faith but on the sacrificial death of Jesus Christ on the cross. Those who accept Jesus Christ as the Savior by faith are "objects of distinguishing grace while the formalists shall learn that outward sacrifices are all in vain." God is a righteous judge and we can be assured of the integrity of his verdict (v. 6).

Prayer. Lord, I am reminded I do not have to judge people's standing before you because you know their true relationship and status. Neither are you impressed by my acts of piety if my heart is cold toward you. I am humbled by your grace, which worked in my heart to confess you as my Savior. Amen.

7 Hear, O my people, and I will speak; O Israel, I will testify against you. I am God, your God. 8 Not for your sacrifices do I rebuke you; your burnt offerings are continually before me. 9 I will not accept a bull from your house or goats from your folds. 10 For every beast of the forest is mine, the cattle on a thousand hills. 11 I know all the birds of the hills, and all that moves in the field is mine. 12 If I were hungry, I would not tell you, for the world and its fullness are mine. 13 Do I eat the flesh of bulls or drink the blood of goats? 14 Offer to God a sacrifice of thanksgiving, and perform your vows to the Most High, 15 and call upon me in the day of trouble; I will deliver you, and you shall glorify me. (ESV)

"As helps to the soul, outward offerings were precious, but when people went not beyond them, even their hallowed things were profaned in the view of heaven."

External faith. This section "declares the futility of external worship when spiritual faith is absent and the mere outward ceremonial is rested in." While the people are not rebuked for the sacrifices which were prescribed by God in the Old Testament (v. 8), a more serious issue was at stake. They placed greater emphasis on the sacrifices than on the condition of their hearts before God. "What was greatest with them was least with God." When we do not love God and are not thankful to him, our outward religious expressions fall far short. What does God want? Verse 14 is instructive. Our actions should be expressions of gratitude and deep love for God. This includes prayer in times of trouble (v. 15). "For herein is faith manifested, herein is love proved, for in the hour of peril we fly to those we love." Thus, we are to be lovers of Jesus, who serve him out of genuine thanksgiving and go to him in genuine dependence. This is true spiritual worship.

Prayer. Lord, forgive me when I think my religious activities impress you, even though I do not truly love you. Remind me of your extravagant love so that my heart may be stirred to become a genuine lover of Jesus and to serve you out of gratitude for all you have done. Amen.

16 But to the wicked God says: "What right have you to recite my statutes or take my covenant on your lips? 17 For you hate discipline, and you cast my words behind you. 18 If you see a thief, you are pleased with him, and you keep company with adulterers. 19 You give your mouth free rein for evil, and your tongue frames deceit. 20 You sit and speak against your brother; you slander your own mother's son. 21 These things you have done, and I have been silent; you thought that I was one like yourself. But now I rebuke you and lay the charge before you. 22 Mark this, then, you who forget God, lest I tear you apart, and there be none to deliver! 23 The one who offers thanksgiving as his sacrifice glorifies me; to one who orders his way rightly I will show the salvation of God!" (ESV)

"Holy living is a choice evidence of salvation."

Phony faith. Now the psalmist moves from the "moral formalists," who do not have genuine hearts for God, to the "immoral pretenders," who are among God's people (v. 16). They actually hate God's word, casting it aside as worthless (v. 17). Without this moral base, their actions and speech are sinful, bringing harm to others (vv. 18–20). Spurgeon rephrases God's response, "you violate openly my moral law, and yet are great sticklers for my ceremonial commands!" To those who are hypocrites with a phony faith, God warns them not to forget he will deal harshly with them one day (v. 22). Such people need to allow God to change their hearts in order that they can genuinely worship him with gratitude (v. 23). Thus, the blessings of salvation are given not to those who are outwardly religious, with no change in their lives, but to those whose lives have been genuinely transformed by God's grace.

Prayer. Lord, I confess that I make great professions of loving you. At the same time, my actions and words violate your word and hurt those around me. I'm tired of a phony faith. Through your word and Spirit, renew my mind and change my heart so that my behavior, including worship, honors you. Amen.

April 17   Psalm 51:1–5*

1 Have mercy on me, O God, according to your unfailing love;
according to your great compassion blot out my transgressions.
2 Wash away all my iniquity and cleanse me from my sin. 3 For
I know my transgressions, and my sin is always before me. 4
Against you, you only, have I sinned and done what is evil in
your sight; so you are right in your verdict and justified when
you judge. 5 Surely I was sinful at birth, sinful from the time my
mother conceived me. (NIV)

"The fountain of my life is polluted as well as its streams."

The nature of sin. In these verses, David uses various words to describe the
nature of sin. There are the "transgressions" (vv. 1, 3) which reveal the many
ways we violate God's law. Sin is also viewed as "iniquity" (v. 2) which focuses
on the pollution of our entire human nature rather than one's actions (v. 5).
David is saying, "not only have I sinned this once, but I am in my very nature
a sinner . . . I naturally lean to forbidden things. Mine is a constitutional disease." In other words, we were born as sinful people. Finally, sin is described
as opposition to God, whereby we deliberately violate his laws before him
(v. 4). "To commit treason in the very court of the king and before his eye is
impudence indeed." How could David be a "man after God's own heart" (1
Sam 13:14)? Rather than denying his sin, "he is sick of sin as sin; his loudest
outcries are against the evil of his transgressions, and not against the painful
consequences of it." Given our sinfulness, what hope is there for David and
us? We can only depend on the mercy of God to forgive us (v. 1). "The sight
of mercy is good for eyes that are sore with penitential weeping."

Prayer. Lord, when I focus on the so-called big sins of David and others
I become smug and self-righteous, believing I am not as bad as they are.
Forgive me for minimizing the reality of sin in my own life. The confession
of my sinful nature and actions reminds me of how much I must depend on
your mercy to forgive me and to transform every area of my life. Amen.

---

* In reference to Psalm 51, Spurgeon wrote, "The Psalm is very human, its cries and
sobs are of one born of woman . . . Such a Psalm may be wept over, absorbed into the
soul, and exhaled again in devotion; but commented on—ah! Where is he who having
attempted it can do other than blush at his defeat?" (*Treasury of David*, 2:v)

6 Yet you desired faithfulness even in the womb; you taught me wisdom in that secret place. 7 Cleanse me with hyssop, and I will be clean; wash me, and I will be whiter than snow. 8 Let me hear joy and gladness; let the bones you have crushed rejoice. 9 Hide your face from my sins and blot out all my iniquity. (NIV)

"Pardon of sin must ever be an act of pure mercy, and therefore to that attribute, the awakened sinner flies."

Forgiveness. The pathway to a restored relationship with the Lord begins with the confession of sin (yesterday's reading), followed by asking God to cleanse and forgive us (v. 7). This request is based on Christ's sacrifice on the cross on our behalf. With this great provision to address our guilt, we can have confident assurance of God's forgiveness and mercy for us. What a relief to know there is nothing we can do to earn his forgiveness! When one grasps the wonder of forgiveness, pardon from God will give the individual "double joy—joy and gladness" (v. 8). This is David's "preposterous prayer" for he longs for joy to replace his crushed spirit. Such joy is only possible through forgiveness in Christ!

Prayer. Lord, my sin overwhelms me, but I am even more astounded that you should forgive me. Thank you for your mercy through your Son, Jesus Christ, who died on the cross, in my place, for the guilt and penalty of my sin. Reflecting on your boundless love for me, I am filled with wonder and joy far beyond anything society offers me. Amen.

10 Create in me a clean heart, O God. Renew a loyal spirit within me. 11 Do not banish me from your presence, and don't take your Holy Spirit from me. 12 Restore to me the joy of your salvation, and make me willing to obey you. (NLT)

"Salvation is a marvelous display of supreme power; the work *in* us as much as that *for* us is wholly of Omnipotence."

Spiritual renewal. The Christian life includes more than the confession and forgiveness of sin. Without any internal changes in our lives, attempts to sin less before God will be ineffective. Recognizing the futility of such an approach, David asks the Lord to make him a new person (v. 10). He has requested to be made clean (v. 7), which requires God to purify his heart (v. 10). Accepting this is divine work, David wants the core of his being to be renewed. This inner transformation occurs in two ways. One, we need to be exposed to God's truth (v. 6). Since the Lord desires inward purity, he searches every area of our inner life. When we allow God to do this, he will reveal to us those sinful areas that need to be changed in order to become more like Jesus. Two, we need the power of the Holy Spirit (v. 12). Like David, we need God's Spirit who "will not enslave but emancipate us; for holiness is liberty, and the Holy Spirit is a free Spirit." Then we can truly experience God's joy in our lives (v. 12). We seek both justification with a right standing before God and sanctification through the Holy Spirit to reflect Jesus Christ in our lives.

Prayer. Father, thank you for challenging me to grow and change as a person—regardless of my age. Renovate my life by your word and Holy Spirit so that I can become increasingly like Jesus Christ. Because you love me, do deep spiritual surgery in my life. Amen.

April 20   Psalm 51:13–19

13 Then I will teach wrongdoers your ways, and sinners will be converted to you. 14 Save me from the guilt of bloodshed, God, the God of my salvation; then my tongue will joyfully sing of your righteousness. 15 LORD, open my lips, so that my mouth may declare your praise. 16 For you do not delight in sacrifice, otherwise I would give it; you do not take pleasure in burnt offering. 17 The sacrifices of God are a broken spirit; a broken and a contrite heart, God, you will not despise. 18 By your favor do good to Zion; build the walls of Jerusalem. 19 Then you will delight in righteous sacrifices, in burnt offering and whole burnt offering; then bulls will be offered on your altar. (NASB)

> "[W]hen sin is pardoned our joyful gratitude is prepared for any sacrifice."

A life of gratitude. When we experience God's forgiveness and his renewing work in our lives, we can properly respond to him. Spurgeon points out the psalmist now resolves to express his gratefulness in various ways. First, he instructs others about God's ways (v. 14). From his painful experience he would teach others about the Lord's great mercy and love. "My fall shall be the restoration of others. You will bless my pathetic testimony to the recovery of many, who, like myself, have turned aside unto crooked ways." Second, the psalmist praises God, who acts rightly in his situation (vv. 14–15). Third, David lives paradoxically with both praise and a broken and contrite heart (v. 17). Being humbled by sin creates the proper heart attitude, which is pleasing to God. "A heart crushed is a fragrant heart . . . [God] despises what men esteem, and values that which they despise." Fourth, in addition to praying for himself, David prays for the well-being of God's people (vv. 18–19). Whatever negative consequences David's actions had on others, he asks God to correct the evil and ensure the security of his people.

Prayer. Lord, in response to your incredible mercy to me, I want to express my thankfulness by praising you, encouraging others by speaking of your mercy, and praying for the spiritual growth of others. I do so out of a broken and humbled heart, which is pleasing to you. Amen.

April 21   Psalm 52:1–5

1 Why do you boast of evil, O mighty man? The steadfast love of God endures all the day. 2 Your tongue plots destruction, like a sharp razor, you worker of deceit. 3 You love evil more than good, and lying more than speaking what is right. *Selah* 4 You love all words that devour, O deceitful tongue. 5 But God will break you down forever; he will snatch and tear you from your tent; he will uproot you from the land of the living. *Selah* (ESV)

> "God will turn the tables on malicious men, and mete to them a portion with their own measure."

Turned tables. Twice *selah* occurs in this brief section (vv. 3, 5), encouraging us to pause and reflect on what the psalmist is saying. In verses 1–3, we see the evil that is perpetuated by what a person loves. An individual, such as Doeg (1 Sam 22), delights in falsehoods and lying more than telling the truth. When we come to the first *selah* we might despair seeing the wicked, like Doeg, flourish and cause grief. "Let us pause and look at the proud blustering liar. Doeg is gone, but other dogs bark at the Lord's people." However, the second *selah* provides a reflective moment that refreshes our soul (vv. 4–5). "Pause again, and behold the divine justice proving itself more than a match for human sin." As for those who love evil and not God (v. 4), the latter will turn the tables on them. Their success is very brief because God will defeat them (v. 5). Rather than despairing, we do well to pause again and remember that human sin is no match for God's justice.

Prayer. Father, I see the tragic consequences all around me of people not loving you. Rather than being smug at the downfall of others, enlarge my heart to love you and others more. When I see evil flourishing, I will minimize my anxiety by focusing on you who reigns over this world. Amen.

April 22   Psalm 52:6-9

6 The righteous shall see and fear, and shall laugh at him, saying, 7 "See the man who would not make God his refuge, but trusted in the abundance of his riches and sought refuge in his own destruction!" 8 But I am like a green olive tree in the house of God. I trust in the steadfast love of God forever and ever. 9 I will thank you forever, because you have done it. I will wait for your name, for it is good, in the presence of the godly. (ESV)

"He was bearing fruit, and would continue to do so when all his proud enemies were withered like branches lopped from the tree."

Thriving in adversity. There are those who trust in their wealth and believe they can do whatever they want in society (v. 7). Such a person "found a fortress, but not in God; he gloried in his might, but not in the Almighty." In contrast to this very limited security, David shows us how to live even in very painful circumstances as he did with Doeg. Though the psalmist was pursued and oppressed by his enemies he was able to flourish like a thriving olive tree (v. 8). Spurgeon disagrees with those who interpret the "olive tree" to be in the pleasant setting of the tabernacle. Rather, David is in the barren desert where he experiences the presence of God ("the house of God"). Even in times of adversity, we can be in God's presence and thrive. One sign of this is the ability to praise God. David could essentially say, "While others boast in their riches I will boast in my God." Such dependence on God and praise in adversity is something only the Holy Spirit can do in our lives.

Prayer. Lord, I want to flourish in my life! However, when I look at society I am reminded of the foolishness of placing my hope in possessions and successes. Forgive me whenever I trust in anything but you. Woo me into your presence so that my soul may prosper, enabling me to give thanks to you—even in the tough times. Amen.

1 Only fools say in their hearts, "There is no God." They are corrupt, and their actions are evil; not one of them does good! 2
God looks down from heaven on the entire human race; he looks
to see if anyone is truly wise, if anyone seeks God. 3 But no, all
have turned away; all have become corrupt. No one does good,
not a single one! 4 Will those who do evil never learn? They eat
up my people like bread and wouldn't think of praying to God. 5
Terror will grip them, terror like they have never known before.
God will scatter the bones of your enemies. You will put them to
shame, for God has rejected them. 6 Who will come from Mount
Zion to rescue Israel? When God restores his people, Jacob will
shout with joy, and Israel will rejoice. (NLT)

"The Song of Man's Disease—the mortal, hereditary taint of sin."

The reality of sin. Though resembling Psalm 14, this psalm is "another edi-
tion by the same author, emphasized in certain parts, and re-written for
another purpose." Spurgeon explains the purpose of having two very similar
psalms in the psalter, "Holy Writ never repeats itself needlessly, there is good
cause for the second copy of this Psalm; let us read it with more profound
attention than before. If our age has advanced from fourteen to fifty-three,
we shall find the doctrine of this Psalm more evident than in our youth." To
illustrate, the psalmist uses strong language to show the reaction of those
who oppose God (v. 5). They panic at what God is doing to them. We do well
to heed our own sinfulness and turn back to the living God who forgives and
restores the repentant.

Prayer. Lord, while the world may be improving in some ways, our human
nature certainly is not. This is a reality check that I should never become
lackadaisical about my true human nature, even as I grow older. Keep me
humble, knowing I am forever dependent on your divine power to transform
my life. Amen.

April 24   Psalm 54

1 Save me, God, by your name, and vindicate me by your power.
2 Hear my prayer, God; listen to the words of my mouth. 3 For
strangers have risen against me and violent men have sought my
life; they have not set God before them. *Selah* 4 Behold, God is
my helper; the Lord is the sustainer of my soul. 5 He will pay
back the evil to my enemies; destroy them in your faithfulness. 6
Willingly I will sacrifice to you; I will praise your name, LORD, for
it is good. 7 For he has saved me from all trouble, and my eye has
looked with satisfaction upon my enemies. (NASB)

"The vigour of faith is the death of anxiety, and the birth of security."

A vigorous faith. David's plea focuses on complete strangers who are attacking him (vv. 1–3). In spite of this, he remarkably moves from passionate petition to praise. How is he able to do this? After his prayer, he pauses (*selah*).
When we feel the indignation of unfair treatment, pauses "as a rule, improve
our devotions . . . a little more holy meditation would make our words more
suitable and our emotions more fervent." In addition, David looks to God for
help (v. 4). Rather than paying attention to his opposition, David recognizes
that the Lord who champions his cause sustains him more than anyone else
can. This stirs him to praise God. David also knows that those who favor evil
will have evil come upon them (v. 5). "It is appointed, and so it must ever be,
that those who shoot upward the arrows of malice shall find them fall upon
themselves." In anticipation of God hearing his prayer, David promises he
will offer a sacrifice of praise to him (vv. 6–7). Thus, "if we are friendless as
this man of God, we may resort to prayer as he did, exercise the like faith, and
find ourselves, before long singing the same joyous hymn of praise."

Prayer. My Lord, when I am overwhelmed by unfair criticism, help me to
turn to you and patiently wait for you to accomplish your purposes. Then I
can humbly thank you for what I may learn without gloating over the fate of
those who oppose you. Amen.

April 25   Psalm 55:1-8

1 Listen to my prayer, God; and do not hide yourself from my pleading. 2 Give your attention to me and answer me; I am restless in my complaint and severely distracted, 3 because of the voice of the enemy, because of the pressure of the wicked; for they bring down trouble upon me and in anger they hold a grudge against me. 4 My heart is in anguish within me, and the terrors of death have fallen upon me. 5 Fear and trembling come upon me, and horror has overwhelmed me. 6 I said, "Oh, that I had wings like a dove! I would fly away and be at rest. 7 Behold, I would flee far away, I would spend my nights in the wilderness. *Selah* 8 I would hurry to my place of refuge from the stormy wind and heavy gale." (NASB)

"He gave himself up for lost. He felt that he was as good as dead. The inmost centre of his nature was moved with dismay."

Inner turmoil. When our outer world is falling apart we often find that our inner life, with its emotions and thoughts, is crumbling too. This is the case with David's outer circumstances (v. 3) and his inner world (vv. 4–5). He experienced agonizing inner turmoil and fear that made him shake. His thinking was adversely impacted, causing him to flee from his painful situation (vv. 6–8). "His love of peace made him sigh for an escape from the scene of strife." While we want to blame our circumstances, Spurgeon wisely points out that "in our ill estate we ever think the past to be better than the present." The desire to escape is natural, but we need to depend on God's grace if we are to endure our current troubles. By pouring our heart out to God, we can rest and trust in Jesus Christ.

Prayer. Heavenly Father, when I experience inner turmoil due to my circumstances, help me not to make wrong decisions, but to express all my feelings and thoughts to you. Lead my heart to trust in you in the midst of my chaos. Amen.

9 Confuse them, Lord, divide their tongues, for I have seen violence and strife in the city. 10 Day and night they go around her upon her walls, and evil and harm are in her midst. 11 Destruction is in her midst; oppression and deceit do not depart from her streets. 12 For it is not an enemy who taunts me, then I could endure it; nor is it one who hates me who has exalted himself against me, then I could hide myself from him. 13 But it is you, a man my equal, my companion and my confidant; 14 we who had sweet fellowship together, walked in the house of God among the commotion. 15 May death come deceitfully upon them; may they go down alive to Sheol, for evil is in their dwelling, in their midst. 16 As for me, I shall call upon God, and the LORD will save me. 17 Evening and morning and at noon, I will complain and moan, and he will hear my voice. 18 He will redeem my soul in peace from the battle which is against me, for they are many who are aggressive toward me. 19 God will hear and humiliate them—even the one who sits enthroned from ancient times—*Selah*—with whom there is no change, and who do not fear God. (NASB)

"[D]eep heart-thoughts should be attended with inarticulate but vehement utterances of grief."

Trusting intimacy. David laments the loss of a very close relationship (vv. 12-14). With such special friends, we can mutually share our most intimate thoughts and feelings. However, when we are betrayed in this kind of relationship, we experience deep hurt because "they are usually so well acquainted with our peculiar weaknesses that they know how to touch us where we are most sensitive, and to speak so as to do us most damage." While we may be tempted to withdraw to protect ourselves from the possibility of future hurt, David directs us to share our intimate thoughts and feelings with the Lord throughout the day (vv. 16-17). When we do this, God will not betray us, but will faithfully respond because he has pledged his love to us.

Prayer. Jesus, having experienced betrayal, I confess it is difficult to share my intimate thoughts and feelings. I am grateful that you understand, for you have been betrayed and yet you trusted your Father. I am thankful for you as a faithful friend—one who will never leave me. Amen.

20 My companion attacks his friends; he violates his covenant. 21 His talk is smooth as butter, yet war is in his heart; his words are more soothing than oil, yet they are drawn swords. 22 Cast your cares on the LORD and he will sustain you; he will never let the righteous be shaken. 23 But you, God, will bring down the wicked into the pit of decay; the bloodthirsty and deceitful will not live out half their days. But as for me, I trust in you. (NIV)

"The psalmist cannot forget the traitor's conduct, and returns again to consider it."

Continuing hurt. Even when we pour out our deepest pain to God in prayer, there is no guarantee that the anguish in our hearts and minds will evaporate. David's words in verses 20–21 remind us that it is often not what people *do* to us, but what they *say*, which often hurts us even more. In David's case, his so-called friend "buttered him with flattery and then battered him with malice." Thus, the reminder: "Beware of one who has too much honey on his tongue; a trap is to be suspected where the bait is so tempting. Soft, smooth, oily words are most plentiful where truth and sincerity are most scarce." How should we respond in such cases? We have to cast this burden on the Lord (v. 22). He gives us a measure of suffering that requires us to take this to God in prayer. We can confidently go to him, knowing he will sustain us with his divine resources. When we say, "This is in your hands," we can stand firm knowing he will strengthen us when we feel hurt and betrayed.

Prayer. Gracious Lord, I confess I pray about painful situations but then continue trying to deal with the hurt in my own ways. Teach me what it means to truly commit matters to you. I am thankful you are the Almighty One who is able to carry my burdens for me. Amen.

1 Be merciful to me, my God, for my enemies are in hot pursuit; all day long they press their attack. 2 My adversaries pursue me all day long; in their pride many are attacking me. 3 When I am afraid, I put my trust in you. 4 In God, whose word I praise—in God I trust and am not afraid. What can mere mortals do to me? 5 All day long they twist my words; all their schemes are for my ruin. 6 They conspire, they lurk, they watch my steps, hoping to take my life. (NIV)

"If I fear people, I have only to trust God, and I have the best antidote."

Fear and faith. Spurgeon notes the "deep spiritual knowledge" in Psalm 56, as it illustrates the dynamic relationship between fear and faith. The psalmist faces danger due to his enemies (vv. 1–2, 5–6). He wisely puts himself and the whole situation under the Lord's protection. He does this by placing his confidence in God and his word (vv. 3–4). He nevertheless admits he is still afraid (v. 3). We often assume trusting in God means denying our fears because we believe it is impossible for fear and faith to coexist. We do well to follow David's example by being willing to admit that we are not free from fear; it is a part of our human nature. Spurgeon writes, "[T]he condition of the psalmist's mind was complex—he feared but that fear did not fill the whole area of his mind." It is possible for fear and faith to comingle in our minds. The issue concerns the type of fear we have. "Unregenerate fear drives from God, gracious fear drives to him." With confidence in God and his word, our fear can drive us to a stronger trust in the Lord. With this kind of fear we can still praise God without feeling guilty for not having enough faith.

Prayer. Lord, often I hear I should not have fears, and so I deny them and chastise myself for what must be my feeble faith. Take my trepidations and use them to deepen my trust in you—even in times of great uncertainty. Amen.

7 Because of their wickedness do not let them escape; in your anger, God, bring the nations down. 8 Record my misery; list my tears on your scroll—are they not in your record? 9 Then my enemies will turn back when I call for help. By this I will know that God is for me. 10 In God, whose word I praise, in the LORD, whose word I praise—11 in God I trust and am not afraid. What can man do to me? 12 I am under vows to you, my God; I will present my thank offerings to you. 13 For you have delivered me from death and my feet from stumbling, that I may walk before God in the light of life. (NIV)

"What a God is this who hearkens to the cry of his children, and in a moment delivers them from the mightiest adversaries!"

Grief and faith. In the face of very difficult circumstances David experienced fear and much grief (v. 8). "His sorrows were so many that there would need a great wineskin to hold them all." But will God even notice his and our tears? Some theologians believe that God does not experience emotions and therefore he is not sensitive to our grief. However, this psalm paints a different picture. God is very aware of our pain for our tears are stored both in God's bottle and recorded in his scroll (v. 8). With both images, David is saying, "Look on my griefs as real things for these move the heart more than a mere account, however exact." In other words, God is touched by our grief and he responds when we, with our tears, call out to him (v. 9a). We do this with the confidence, knowing that God is for us (v. 9b). Moreover, we can trust his word, which gives us delight and enables us to enjoy God's presence even when we are grieving (vv. 10-13).

Prayer. Thank you Lord for hearing, receiving, and responding to my tears and grief. I recall your Son as the "man of sorrows" and you heard his cries. Fill my mourning heart with the gladness of your presence through your word and with the security of knowing your extravagant love. Amen.

April 30   Psalm 57:1–6

1 Have mercy on me, O God, have mercy! I look to you for protection. I will hide beneath the shadow of your wings until the danger passes by. 2 I cry out to God Most High, to God who will fulfill his purpose for me. 3 He will send help from heaven to rescue me, disgracing those who hound me. My God will send forth his unfailing love and faithfulness. 4 I am surrounded by fierce lions who greedily devour human prey—whose teeth pierce like spears and arrows, and whose tongues cut like swords. 5 Be exalted, O God, above the highest heavens! May your glory shine over all the earth. 6 My enemies have set a trap for me. I am weary from distress. They have dug a deep pit in my path, but they themselves have fallen into it. (NLT)

"Blessed be God, our calamities are matters of time, but our safety is a matter of eternity."

Responding to danger. Spurgeon describes this psalm as the first of four "Destroy not" psalms (58, 59, 75) containing a "distinct declaration of the destruction of the wicked and the preservation of the righteous." David likens his enemies to lions seeking to devour their prey (v. 4). They also use whatever means to trap David (v. 6). The psalmist reminds us that believers around the world are not immune from real dangers in life. However, too many times we complain about God not loving us or question why he allows us to face danger. David provides an alternative response: we can call out to God, who is merciful in his nature and actions (vv. 1, 3). Until he acts, we rest in the fact that we are secure under his divine power. With this confidence, we praise the Lord. More important than our deliverance should be the desire to see God's glory revealed in our circumstances (v. 5).

Prayer. Lord, I think of your people who live in very dangerous regions around the world. I pray that you would protect them for their sake, as well as for your name's sake, so that the nations will see your glorious power and mercy. May many people groups be drawn into your great love! Amen.

May 1   Psalm 57:7-11

7 My heart is confident in you, O God; my heart is confident.
No wonder I can sing your praises! 8 Wake up, my heart! Wake
up, O lyre and harp! I will wake the dawn with my song. 9 I will
thank you, Lord, among all the people. I will sing your praises
among the nations. 10 For your unfailing love is as high as the
heavens. Your faithfulness reaches to the clouds. 11 Be exalted,
O God, above the highest heavens. May your glory shine over all
the earth. (NLT)

"Believer, make a firm decree that your soul in all seasons shall
magnify the Lord."

A steady heart. In this section, the psalmist sings jubilantly before the Lord.
How could David be so joyful in such dire circumstances? The answer is
found in his repeated affirmation of steadfast faith in the Lord (v. 7). As Spurgeon comments, "One would have thought he would have said, 'my heart
is fluttered' but no, he is calm, firm, happy, resolute, established." With this
unwavering confidence in the Lord, David thrice calls upon his own heart
to awake and express adoration to God (v. 8). Similarly, we may still be in a
"cave" like David is, but we can focus on God's great love and mercy to steady
us in the storms of life. David gives thanks to God, for his goodness is greater
and more majestic than nature's beauty. For the second time in this psalm, we
shout out, with gusto, for God to be exalted (v. 11; see v. 5) in our individual
lives and around the world (v. 9).

Prayer. Almighty God, I ask you to give me a heart firmly fixed on your
greatness so that I will not be easily influenced by adversities and challenges.
When I wake up in the morning, I resolve to offer praise as my first act of the
day—and then throughout the day, for your glory. Amen.

May 2   Psalm 58:1-5

1 Justice—do you rulers know the meaning of the word? Do you judge the people fairly? 2 No! You plot injustice in your hearts. You spread violence throughout the land. 3 These wicked people are born sinners; even from birth they have lied and gone their own way. 4 They spit venom like deadly snakes; they are like cobras that refuse to listen, 5 ignoring the tunes of the snake charmers, no matter how skillfully they play. (NLT)

"Those very men who sat as judges . . . were in their own hearts perpetrating all manner of evil."

Evil leaders. Spurgeon points out it is wrong to assume that great leaders could not commit grievous errors. The one who experiences injustices "lays the axe at the root by requiring his judges to answer the question whether or not they were acting according to justice." Corrupt leadership is manifested not only by the actions taken but by taking no action. Seeing injustice and not speaking up is patently wrong (v. 1). These leaders "are asked to justify their silence. Silence gives consent. He who refrains from defending the right is himself an accomplice in the wrong." The fundamental issue is the human heart (v. 2). Deep in the hearts of corrupt people they rehearse the injustices they plan to practice. As Spurgeon puts it, "your hearts are in your wicked work, and your hands are therefore ready enough." Lest we point the finger at dishonest leaders in an attempt to exonerate ourselves, David reminds us we share the same human nature (v. 3). How can one's unethical ways be changed? Not by the arguments which seek to persuade a closed mind (v. 4) but by God, who works in our lives.

Prayer. Lord, your word instructs me to pray for those in positions of leadership. While I pray for their hearts to be moved from injustice to justice, continue to change my heart so I will desire to act in ways that are pleasing to you. Amen.

6 Break off their fangs, O God! Smash the jaws of these lions, O
LORD! 7 May they disappear like water into thirsty ground. Make
their weapons useless in their hands. 8 May they be like snails
that dissolve into slime, like a stillborn child who will never see
the sun. 9 God will sweep them away, both young and old, faster
than a pot heats over burning thorns. 10 The godly will rejoice
when they see injustice avenged. They will wash their feet in the
blood of the wicked. 11 Then at last everyone will say, "There
truly is a reward for those who live for God; surely there is a God
who judges justly here on earth." (NLT)

"All people shall be forced by the sight of the final judgment to see that
there is a God, and that he is the righteous ruler of the universe."

A just leader. In today's passage, David prays for God, who is just, to judge
corrupt leaders (vv. 6–8). Spurgeon paraphrases David's plea: "If they have
no capacity for good, at least deprive them of their ability for evil." God can
and will do this! "He will not suffer the malice of the wicked to triumph, he
will deal them such a blow as shall disable them from mischief." It may not
immediately happen but it will definitely occur in the future (v. 10). How
should the follower of Jesus view this eventual judgment? Commenting on
this verse, Spurgeon counsels us not to delight in revenge. Rather, we are to
submit to God's judgment and praise him for his justice.

Prayer. Lord, I must confess I am impatient to see you act in a world filled
with many forms of evil. Deepen my faith and expand my vision to trust in
your timing as a just God. My greatest reward will be people acknowledging
you as the one true living God. Amen.

May 4   Psalm 59:1-5

1-2 My God! Rescue me from my enemies, defend me from these
mutineers. Rescue me from their dirty tricks, save me from their
hit men. 3-4 Desperadoes have ganged up on me, they're hiding
in ambush for me. I did nothing to deserve this, God, crossed no
one, wronged no one. All the same, they're after me, determined
to get me. 4-5 Wake up and see for yourself! You're God, God-of-
Angel-Armies, Israel's God! Get on the job and take care of these
pagans, don't be soft on these hard cases. (MSG)

"[T]he bloodthirstiness of the foe is a fit reason for the interposition of
the righteous God, for the Lord abhors all those who delight in blood."

Persecution. The heading of this psalm provides us with the historical
context. King Saul was seeking to kill David (1 Sam 23:7-25). The psalmist
describes the nature of hatred toward him, giving us a glimpse into the persecution people currently experience around the globe. David had enemies,
such as Saul, who not only opposed him but sought to kill him (vv. 1-2). To
add to the pain, David asserts his innocence—their attacks are without cause,
motivated by sheer hatred (vv. 3-4). "To be thus gratuitously attacked is a
great grief. To a brave man the danger causes little distress of mind compared
with the injustice to which he is subjected." However, David's response is
instructive for today's persecuted people. He does not take matters into his
own hands but turns to God to take action. He cries out to a very personal
("my") God (vv. 1-2). The appeal for deliverance goes beyond himself to
cover others, for "the overthrow of oppression which was so needful for
himself must be equally desirable for multitudes of the godly placed in like
positions."

Prayer. Lord, I pray for your people who continually face persecution because
of their faith in Jesus Christ. I ask you to sustain them with your presence.
By looking to you, may they find strength and hope to live faithfully. Amen.

6 Each evening they come back, howling like dogs and prowling about the city. 7 There they are, bellowing with their mouths with swords in their lips—for "Who," they think, "will hear us?" 8 But you, O LORD, laugh at them; you hold all the nations in derision. 9 O my Strength, I will watch for you, for you, O God, are my fortress. 10 My God in his steadfast love will meet me; God will let me look in triumph on my enemies. 11 Kill them not, lest my people forget; make them totter by your power and bring them down, O Lord, our shield! 12 For the sin of their mouths, the words of their lips, let them be trapped in their pride. For the cursing and lies that they utter, 13 consume them in wrath; consume them till they are no more, that they may know that God rules over Jacob to the ends of the earth. *Selah* (ESV)

"It is a wise thing to find in the greatness of our difficulties a reason for casting ourselves upon the Lord."

The ways of God. When individuals seek to destroy God's people by one means or the other (vv. 6–7), the Lord responds in various ways. First, he laughs and scoffs at those who oppose him (v. 8). Second, he may delay his punishment for the benefit of his people (v. 11). Spurgeon explains that the hardships keep us spiritually alert, which is far better than living in a state of spiritual slumber. Third, God will allow the perpetrators of injustice to experience the consequences of their own proud actions (v. 12). Lastly, he will eventually destroy those who oppose him, thereby causing others to recognize his greatness. Spurgeon also draws attention to *selah* (v. 13) that serves not just to separate the sections in a psalm but to pause and reflect on what has been said. "Sit still awhile and consider the ways of God with man."

Prayer. Almighty Lord, I confess I struggle with your ways of dealing with evil in the world. You are infinitely wiser; let my heart be humbled and submissive to your ways. Amen.

14–15 They return when the sun goes down. They howl like coyotes, ringing the city. They scavenge for bones, and bite the hand that feeds them. 16–17 And me? I'm singing your prowess, shouting at dawn your largesse, for you've been a safe place for me, a good place to hide. Strong God, I'm watching you do it, I can always count on you—God, my dependable love. (MSG)

"The wicked howl, but I sing and will sing."

Howling and singing. Pausing to reflect on the ways God responds to evil enables us to praise and sing to him even in the face of oppression. Throughout the time David is pursued by Saul and his men, he does not forget the Lord's power and loving mercy that go before him (vv. 9–10). This same love sustains us in times of great turmoil and upheaval. With God as his focus, David rightly and wholeheartedly sings to the Lord regardless of circumstances (vv. 16–17). "Looking back upon a past all full of mercy, the saints will bless the Lord with their whole hearts, and triumph in him as the high place of their security." God is the one who acts; we cannot take the credit. David's safety is not due to his own power but to God's. Thus, all praise goes to him. "Sweet is the music of experience, but it is all for God . . . he [David] sees God in all, and all his own."

Prayer. Lord, I confess I can despair in times of great upheaval and turmoil. Turn my heart and mind toward you. Help me to find security and peace in your character and my relationship with you. By your grace, change my groaning into singing to you. You are the one who deserves all praise and worship. Amen.

May 7   Psalm 60:1–3

1–2 God! You walked off and left us, kicked our defenses to bits and stomped off angry. Come back. Oh please, come back! You shook earth to the foundations, ripped open huge crevasses. Heal the breaks! Everything's coming apart at the seams. 3 You made your people look doom in the face, then gave us cheap wine to drown our troubles. (MSG)

> "So far gone was Israel, that only God's interposition could preserve it from utter destruction."

The discipline of God. The heading of this psalm sheds light on a very difficult time in the history of the nation of Israel. Military defeats are discouraging; more so in this case, for the psalmist is aware that it is due to God's displeasure with his people. The psalmist buttresses this claim by stating God has rejected them (v. 1), bringing instability to the nation (v. 2). As a result, the people are confused like a drunken person (v. 3). What is behind God's strong measures? He is angry at his people (v. 1). However, even though God has rejected them, the psalmist affirms that they are still his treasured possession (v. 3). Though "[H]ardships had been heaped upon them . . . all had come by divine design and with a purpose." When we go through painful times, we must remember we are children of a heavenly Father who does not punish us but disciplines or corrects because he loves us very much (Heb 12:7–11).

Prayer. Father, when painful situations have come my way, I have sometimes wrongly assumed you are rejecting me. Instead, I want to remember your faithful love when I face hardships. Give me a heart to receive correction from you. Amen.

4 But you have raised a banner for those who fear you—a rallying point in the face of attack. 5 Now rescue your beloved people. Answer and save us by your power. 6 God has promised this by his holiness: "I will divide up Shechem with joy. I will measure out the valley of Succoth. 7 Gilead is mine, and Manasseh, too. Ephraim, my helmet, will produce my warriors, and Judah, my scepter, will produce my kings. 8 But Moab, my washbasin, will become my servant, and I will wipe my feet on Edom and shout in triumph over Philistia." 9 Who will bring me into the fortified city? Who will bring me victory over Edom? 10 Have you rejected us, O God? Will you no longer march with our armies? 11 Oh, please help us against our enemies, for all human help is useless. 12 With God's help we will do mighty things, for he will trample down our foes. (NLT)

"Strong to smite, he is also strong to save."

Spiritual victory. When we have been corrected by God's discipline, we are better positioned to experience spiritual victory in the same way David expected military victories over his enemies. The heading reminds us this psalm is for learning, and it offers illuminating insights for us. First, God loves us (v. 5), which is based on him choosing us by his grace. Second, we can act on God's promises just as David parceled the land to the tribes based on God's promises (vv. 6–7). Third, though we face the forces of spiritual darkness David reminds us that they serve God's purposes (v. 8). Thus, we should not be intimidated by Satan and his foes. Finally, God delivers us by granting victory (vv. 9–12). Though we depend on him, this does not mean we sit back and do nothing. "Divine working is not an argument for human inaction, but rather it is the best excitement for courageous effort." We move forward in expectation of spiritual victories because God is able to do far more than we could ever do in our own strength.

Prayer. Almighty God, I am so thankful for your supernatural power that you make available to me through your word and Spirit. I need and depend on you to conquer and defeat the evil one, who seeks to destroy me. Thank you for loving me and giving me strength for each day. Amen.

May 9

Psalm 61

1 Hear my cry, O God, listen to my prayer; 2 from the end of the earth I call to you when my heart is faint. Lead me to the rock that is higher than I, 3 for you have been my refuge, a strong tower against the enemy. 4 Let me dwell in your tent forever! Let me take refuge under the shelter of your wings! *Selah* 5 For you, O God, have heard my vows; you have given me the heritage of those who fear your name. 6 Prolong the life of the king; may his years endure to all generations! 7 May he be enthroned forever before God; appoint steadfast love and faithfulness to watch over him! 8 So will I ever sing praises to your name, as I perform my vows day after day. (ESV)

> "I will dwell with the Lord, enjoying his sacred hospitality, and sure protection."

True security. This psalm contains the expelled king's prayer of thanksgiving as he returns to his throne. Having been banished from the palace, David is in the desert, overwhelmed and crying out to God (vv. 1–2). He reflects on images of the Lord who is a rock, a strong tower, and a mother hen (vv. 2–4). These word pictures speak of God's omnipotence and care for us. The psalmist also refers to the tent, which is the tabernacle or dwelling place of God (v. 4). David is saying that "even now in my banishment my heart is there; and ever will I continue to worship you in spirit wherever my lot may be cast." Wherever we are located, we are at "home" when we are communing with God. His omnipresence continuously surrounds us—even in remote places. Since we are David's spiritual descendants through Christ, we can be assured we will live in God's presence forever (v. 7). Jesus is our true security now and for eternity.

Prayer. Loving Father, when society is in such chaos and turmoil, my heart can melt with fear. I need your presence to calm my heart so I can move on with strength. Thank you for your Holy Spirit who resides in me, giving me the great assurance of my eternal security in you. Amen.

1 Truly my soul finds rest in God; my salvation comes from him. 2 Truly he is my rock and my salvation; he is my fortress, I will never be shaken. 3 How long will you assault me? Would all of you throw me down—this leaning wall, this tottering fence? 4 Surely they intend to topple me from my lofty place; they take delight in lies. With their mouths they bless, but in their hearts they curse. (NIV)

"[T]rue faith is always in season, and is usually under trial."

Soul stillness. It is wonderful to experience a calm spirit in solitude, but it is quite a different matter when we are crushed by life's adversities. David was in this situation when ruthless enemies sought to topple him as the king (vv. 3–4). He instructs us on how we should respond in the heat of opposition. We are to call to mind the character of God, who is like a rock and fortress, offering us security and protection (v. 2). When we dwell on these attributes, we can experience rest in him (v. 1). Spurgeon comments, "The presence of God alone could awe his heart into quietude, submission, rest, and acquiescence . . . It is an eminent work of grace to bring down the will and subdue the affections to such a degree that the whole mind lies before the Lord . . . free from all inward and self-caused emotion, and also from all power to be moved by anything other than the divine will." To think seriously about the Lord's nature, we need to slow down enough. Spurgeon reminds us that the use of *selah* is an invitation to ponder the psalmist's situation (v. 4). "Here pause, and consider with astonishment the futile rancor of unholy men, and the perfect security of such as rest themselves upon the Lord."

Prayer. Lord, I confess that my faith can easily be thrown off-balance by the storms of life. I need to slow down and quiet my mind and heart to properly meditate on you. I can only do this when I recognize you are the only one who can truly help. Remind me that I can rely on your steadfast character during life's trials. Amen.

5 Yes, my soul, find rest in God; my hope comes from him. 6 Truly he is my rock and my salvation; he is my fortress, I will not be shaken. 7 My salvation and my honor depend on God; he is my mighty rock, my refuge. 8 Trust in him at all times, you people; pour out your hearts to him, for God is our refuge. (NIV)

"A living faith grows; experience develops the spiritual muscles of the saint."

The discipline of soul stillness. The word "rest" is used twice (vv. 1, 5), tying together these verses. Why does the psalmist repeat the theme of rest? "When we have already practiced a virtue, it is yet needful that we bind ourselves to a continuance of it. The soul is apt to be dragged away from its anchorage, or is readily tempted to add a second confidence to the one sole and sure ground of reliance." Since the practice of patiently waiting on God is not easy, it requires discipline on our part. As we learn to turn to him, we increasingly see how reliable he is (v. 6). We need not be rattled by life's challenges. David "will not stir an inch, nor be made to fear even in the smallest degree." Neither should we, as we develop the discipline of patiently waiting on God.

Prayer. Father, I confess I am too impatient for you to respond to my incessant pleas. I find myself demanding that you answer according to my schedule. Teach me to wait patiently on you by being reminded of your past faithfulness. I want to grow with confidence in you so that I will not be shaken by my circumstances. Amen.

9 Common people are as worthless as a puff of wind, and the powerful are not what they appear to be. If you weigh them on the scales, together they are lighter than a breath of air. 10 Don't make your living by extortion or put your hope in stealing. And if your wealth increases, don't make it the center of your life. 11 God has spoken plainly, and I have heard it many times: Power, O God, belongs to you; 12 unfailing love, O Lord, is yours. Surely you repay all people according to what they have done. (NLT)

"[O]ur faith should therefore patiently hope and quietly wait, for we shall surely see the salvation of God."

A rationale for soul stillness. David provides us with solid reasons why we can possess a calm heart in our relationship with Jesus. True soul-stillness is not attained by depending on people of high status or wealth (vv. 9–10). "As we must not rest in men, so neither must we repose in money. Gain and fame are only so much foam of the sea." In contrast, we can experience a calm spirit by paying careful attention to what God is saying to us (v. 11). Spurgeon advises that our "inner ears" must hear that God's power is more trustworthy than whatever society could offer. It is possible to experience spiritual rest by patiently waiting on God, who is both strong and mercifully loving (vv. 11–12). Here "we have power and mercy blended, and have a double reason for waiting only upon God. Humanity neither helps us nor rewards us; God will do both."

Prayer. Shepherd of my soul, on you alone I depend for a quiet and sill heart. Incline my ears to hear your word and my eyes to see your power at work through the most difficult situations. As I patiently wait for you, show your loving mercy so that I might see your deliverance. Amen.

1 O God, you are my God; I earnestly search for you. My soul thirsts for you; my whole body longs for you in this parched and weary land where there is no water. 2 I have seen you in your sanctuary and gazed upon your power and glory. 3 Your unfailing love is better than life itself; how I praise you! 4 I will praise you as long as I live, lifting up my hands to you in prayer. 5 You satisfy me more than the richest feast. I will praise you with songs of joy. (NLT)

"There was no desert in his heart, though there was a desert around him."

Our deepest desire. This "wilderness hymn" is inspired by David's flight from his son, Absalom. He knows he can experience God's presence in the desert, and with his whole being he longs for an encounter with the Lord (v. 1). It is encouraging to remember that fellowship with the Lord can occur in the most seemingly irreligious settings. This longing for God is based on a personal relationship ("my God" in v. 1). David recalls God's power and glory from his time in the temple, and now these "he desires to behold again in the place of his banishment" (v. 2). His desire for God is fueled by the recognition that God's love is greater than anything else life offers (v. 3). "Life is dear, but God's love is dearer. To dwell with God is better than life at its best." With such a singular desire, it is not surprising David is fully satisfied, leading him to praise God (vv. 4–5). Jesus Christ satisfies, transforming us from thirsty to contented people of God.

Prayer. Father, I recognize how important it is to desire fellowship with you. Increase my longing for you, the only one who truly satisfies. I am grateful that I can pursue your presence wherever I am and you will meet me there. Amen.

May 14   Psalm 63:6-8

6 I lie awake thinking of you, meditating on you through the
night. 7 Because you are my helper, I sing for joy in the shadow
of your wings. 8 I cling to you; your strong right hand holds me
securely. (NLT)

"Some revel in the night, but they are not a tithe so happy as those who
meditate in God."

Night reflections. At the end of a long day, it is not uncommon to dwell on
our shortcomings and failures. Our minds and hearts can also be filled with
worries stemming from today and in anticipation of tomorrow. But David
chooses to reflect on God when he lies awake during the night (v. 6). "If the
day's cares tempt us to forget God, it is well that night's quiet should lead us
to remember him." While we might repeat Bible verses to help us fall back
to sleep, David uses the night hours to ponder on God's past deliverances
(v. 7). "This is the grand use of memory, to furnish us with proofs of the
Lord's faithfulness, and lead us onward to a growing confidence in him." This
nocturnal ruminating evokes praise to God and his faithfulness to David
in the desert (v. 7). With this awareness, it is wise for us to stay glued to the
Lord (v. 8).

Prayer. My Lord, it is good to consider the ways I have seen you actively
working around me. Rather than musing on the troubles of the day, incline
my heart and mind to dwell on you and your faithfulness to me. I praise you,
even during the night, for your goodness to me. Amen.

9 But those plotting to destroy me will come to ruin. They will go down into the depths of the earth. 10 They will die by the sword and become the food of jackals. 11 But the king will rejoice in God. All who swear to tell the truth will praise him, while liars will be silenced. (NLT)

"As David earnestly sought for God, so there were men of another order who as eagerly sought after his blood."

Spiritual battle. David has reminded us that we should long for God's presence and reflect on his past faithfulness. This passage provides another reason for God to be so central in our lives. David was not in the desert for a spiritual retreat but because he was engaged in battle with men who sought to kill him (v. 9). Spurgeon points to an even greater danger we face. "The devil is a destroyer, and all his seed are greedy to do the same mischief." Neither David nor we are capable of defeating such powerful foes. What hope is there? If we take matters into our own hands, we will respond in ways that reflect our sinful nature. However, when Jesus is our central focus, we will turn to and depend on him. "O Lord, we seek you and your truth; deliver us from all malice and slander, and reveal to us thine own self, for Jesus sake." With unwavering allegiance to God, we will be able to praise God for what he overcomes on our behalf (v. 11).

Prayer. Most High God, you know I cannot face the enemy on my own. My futile attempts only remind me of my faulty thinking. Deliver me from my pride and teach me to depend on the power of your Spirit to confront the evil one. I humbly ask this in the name of Jesus, who conquered Satan on the cross. Amen.

1 Hear my voice, O God, in my complaint; preserve my life from dread of the enemy. 2 Hide me from the secret plots of the wicked, from the throng of evildoers, 3 who whet their tongues like swords, who aim bitter words like arrows, 4 shooting from ambush at the blameless, shooting at him suddenly and without fear. 5 They hold fast to their evil purpose; they talk of laying snares secretly, thinking, "Who can see them?" 6 They search out injustice, saying, "We have accomplished a diligent search." For the inward mind and heart of a man are deep. (ESV)

"He who deals with the serpent's seed has good need of the wisdom which is from above."

The ways of evil. Being in a spiritual battle, it is essential to be aware of how Satan tries to bring ruin to Jesus' followers. In this prayer, David describes his opponents' devious and cruel ways. They meet and encourage each another in their evil thinking and scheming (vv. 5–6). Spurgeon points out the irony that good people often discourage one another, but evildoers "know the benefit of cooperation and are not sparing of it . . . Diligently they consider, invent, devise, and seek for wicked plans to wreak their malice." As a result, they find manifold ways to do evil (v. 2). For example, they slander (v. 3), ambush, and attack innocent people (v. 4). All their plots reflect their wicked minds and hearts (v. 6). Considering the serpent's craftiness in the garden of Eden, this is a warning of "how dangerous is the believer's condition, and how readily may he be overcome if left to himself." We need Jesus to deliver us from the power of evil forces!

Prayer. Lord, once again your word reminds me of the daily spiritual battle I face. Awaken my mind so I am attentive to the schemes of the devil, who seeks to devour me. With this greater awareness, I recognize my desperate need for you. I call on you to give me victory. Amen.

May 17 Psalm 64:7–10

7 But God shoots his arrow at them; they are wounded suddenly. 8 They are brought to ruin, with their own tongues turned against them; all who see them will wag their heads. 9 Then all mankind fears; they tell what God has brought about and ponder what he has done. 10 Let the righteous one rejoice in the Lᴏʀᴅ and take refuge in him! Let all the upright in heart exult! (ESV)

"While strangers fear, the children are glad in view of their Father's power and justice."

The purposes of justice. In this section, the psalmist focuses not on his enemies but on his Almighty God. The Lord metes out justice against those who attack his people (vv. 7–8). "The Lord turns the tables on his adversaries, and defeats them at their own weapons." This is the case even with verbal attacks. "Their slander shall recoil. Their curses shall come home to roost. Their tongue shall cut their throats." Divine justice also inspires awe in people. Consequently, they take heed and change their ways (v. 9). God's uprightness causes his people to rejoice and deepens their trust in him (v. 10). We do not gloat over our enemies but glory in the Lord's power and justice.

Prayer. Lord, I despair when I see the rampant evil around the globe. Turn my fears into greater confidence in you, as I reflect on your justice now and in the future. While I want to see evil punished, give me a greater passion to see your Name exalted among all people. Amen.

1 There will be silence before you, and praise in Zion, God, and the vow will be fulfilled for you. 2 You who hear prayer, to you all mankind comes. 3 Wrongdoings prevail against me; as for our offenses, you forgive them. 4 Blessed is the one you choose and allow to approach you; he will dwell in your courtyards. We will be satisfied with the goodness of your house, your holy temple. (NASB)

"It [this psalm] is one of the most delightful hymns in any language."

Approaching God. David's personal relationship with God is seen in how he addresses God as "you" throughout this hymn of praise. Spurgeon writes that these verses show how we, too, can approach God in prayer despite our sinfulness (vv. 2-3a). We do so on the basis that God has forgiven our sins (v. 3b)! Our sins "would keep us away from God, but he sweeps them away before himself and us." Spurgeon reminds us that this forgiveness is only possible through Jesus Christ, "the Lamb that was slain." In addition, God has chosen and called us into a new relationship with him (v. 4). Thus, we can come to God in prayer, which is "the life of true religion; we come weeping in conversion, hoping in supplication, rejoicing in praise, and delighting in service." Spurgeon is correct to say this psalm is a song of grace!

Prayer. Father, I am awed and humbled by your grace, which enables me to come and enjoy being in your presence. I am undeserving apart from what you have done for me. Thank you for accepting and hearing my prayers each day. I am blessed by the goodness you show to me! Amen.

5 By awesome deeds you answer us in righteousness, God of our salvation, you who are the trust of all the ends of the earth and the farthest sea; 6 who establishes the mountains by his strength, who is encircled with might; 7 who stills the roaring of the seas, the roaring of their waves, and the turmoil of the nations. 8 They who dwell at the ends of the earth stand in awe of your signs; you make the sunrise and the sunset shout for joy. (NASB)

"God's memorial is that he hears prayer, and his glory is that he answers it in a manner fitted to inspire awe in the hearts of his people."

God's powerful response. In this section, God now replies to the prayers of his people (v. 5). Their enemies are defeated, reflecting God's justice or "severe righteousness." Their downfall is attributed to his great power, which is also revealed through nature (vv. 6–7). His "power everywhere meets you, sublimity, massive grandeur, and stupendous force are all around you; and God is there, the author and source of all." The impact of his power is three-fold. First, his power gives us hope or confidence (v. 5). Second, we do not fear God, but are awed by his mighty acts (v. 8a). Third, we praise him at the beginning and the end of the day for "he never ceases to make joy for those who find their joy in him" (v. 8b).

Prayer. Lord, your almighty power over nature makes me certain that nothing in this world can stop you from accomplishing your purposes. Fill my heart and mind with reverence as I come to you with my fears, knowing you respond in awesome ways. Amen.

9 You visit the earth and cause it to overflow; you greatly enrich it; the stream of God is full of water; you prepare their grain, for so you prepare the earth. 10 You water its furrows abundantly, you settle its ridges, you soften it with showers, you bless its growth. 11 You have crowned the year with your goodness, and your paths drip with fatness. 12 The pastures of the wilderness drip, and the hills encircle themselves with rejoicing. 13 The meadows are clothed with flocks and the valleys are covered with grain; they shout for joy, yes, they sing. (NASB)

"When the Lord goes on visitations of mercy, he has an abundance of necessary things for all his needy creatures."

A harvest song. The title Spurgeon gives this psalm captures the theme of this section. As we read yesterday, God's power not only brings down his enemies, but it also generously provides for all of his creation. He waters the earth so we have crops for nourishment (vv. 9–11). "He is represented here as going round the earth, as a gardener surveys his garden, and as giving water to every plant that requires it, and that not in small quantities, but until the earth is drenched and soaked with a rich supply of refreshment." God also provides vegetation for animals to graze on (v. 13a). In response, all creation responds with praise (v. 13b). His watchful care over nature to provide for our physical needs is a reminder of God's "common grace" extended to every person. Because we love God, we should love the world that he created and loves.

Prayer. Lord, I marvel at your wise plan of the life cycles in nature so that all you created can be sustained. This is a reminder for me to appreciate and care for your creation since you are the divine Gardener. I am thankful for everything your benevolent hand provides me with. Amen.

1 Shout for joy to God, all the earth! 2 Sing the glory of his name; make his praise glorious. 3 Say to God, "How awesome are your deeds! So great is your power that your enemies cringe before you. 4 All the earth bows down to you; they sing praise to you, they sing the praises of your name." (NIV)

"No meditation can be more joyous than that excited by the prospect of a world reconciled to its Creator."

Global worship. The call to worship God is extended beyond the covenant people to all the nations (v. 1). Worshipping the Lord includes giving honor to his name, nature, and deeds (v. 2). However, many around the world have not embraced Jesus Christ. What can influence them to turn to the living God? Evidence of God's judgment in the course of world events should cause people to "cringe" before him (v. 3). Spurgeon comments, though, that this is "a forced and false submission. Power brings a man to one's knee, but love alone wins the heart." When people respond to God's love, fear is replaced with joyful worship (v. 4). While global worship did not occur in the psalmist's day, "such a consummation was evidently expected by the writer of this psalm." Not every individual will accept Jesus as Savior, but there will be people from every corner of the world who will gladly acknowledge him as their personal Redeemer.

Prayer. Lord, may people around the world recognize your great power and turn to you because they accept your redeeming love for them. Thank you for the privilege of worshipping you with brothers and sisters around the globe. Amen.

5 Come and see the works of God, who is awesome in his deeds toward the sons of mankind. 6 He turned the sea into dry land; they passed through the river on foot; let's rejoice there, in him! 7 He rules by his might forever; his eyes keep watch on the nations; the rebellious shall not exalt themselves! *Selah* 8 Bless our God, you peoples, and sound his praise abroad, 9 who keeps us in life, and does not allow our feet to slip. 10 For you have put us to the test, God; you have refined us as silver is refined. 11 You brought us into the net; you laid an oppressive burden upon us. 12 You made men ride over our heads; we went through fire and through water. Yet you brought us out into a place of abundance. (NASB)

"Egypt was in his purposes *en route* to Canaan. The way to heaven is *via* tribulation."

Disciplined power. Here we see God's great deliverance of his people from Egypt by parting the Red Sea (vv. 5–7). When we see him intervening in the events of nations, we affirm, "He who did this can do anything, and must be God, the worthy object of adoration." However, our response may be quite different when we see God's people suffering through many afflictions (vv. 10–12a). Intriguingly, the psalmist calls us to praise God (v. 8) and gives some clues about how to do so when we might be questioning his might. God restrains his strength so that we can be refined and purified by the harsh realities of life (vv. 10–11). Even during these difficulties, God exercises his power to protect us (v. 9). "At any time, the preservation of life, and especially the soul's life, is a great reason for gratitude, but much more when we are called upon to undergo extreme trials." Ultimately, through perseverance by his grace, God delivers us after accomplishing his purposes (v. 12).

Prayer. Lord, I confess your supernatural power is questioned when it is not very evident. However, I acknowledge that your loving strength sustains me and accomplishes your purposes. I praise you for refining and preserving me. You have been faithful and will continue to be faithful in the future. Amen.

13 I will come into your house with burnt offerings; I will perform my vows to you, 14 that which my lips uttered and my mouth promised when I was in trouble. 15 I will offer to you burnt offerings of fattened animals, with the smoke of the sacrifice of rams; I will make an offering of bulls and goats. *Selah* (ESV)

"In these three verses we have gratitude in action, not content with words, but proving its own sincerity by deeds of obedient sacrifice."

Generous gratitude. God has sustained David and his people while they experienced trials which refined them (v. 10). Now, in these verses, the psalmist personally offers his response to God. "The child of God is so sensible of his own personal indebtedness to grace, that he feels he must utter a song of his own." David is indebted to God's faithfulness and expresses his deep gratitude through sacrifices ranging from the larger fat animals to the smaller goats (vv. 13, 15). "A perfect sacrifice, completing the circle of offerings, should show forth the intense love of his heart. We should magnify the Lord with great and little." Since God has been generous in his grace shown to us, we should reciprocate with generous gratitude. Outward expressions of gratitude do reflect our hearts' response to the grace and love God has shown to us.

Prayer. Father, you have lavishly expressed your love to me in diverse ways. I am filled with thankfulness for your grace. The best way I can express gratitude is to surrender my life as a living offering to you. I do so not to earn your good pleasure but to show my loving response to you. Amen.

16 Come and hear, all you who fear God, and I will tell what he has done for my soul. 17 I cried to him with my mouth, and high praise was on my tongue. 18 If I had cherished iniquity in my heart, the Lord would not have listened. 19 But truly God has listened; he has attended to the voice of my prayer. 20 Blessed be God, because he has not rejected my prayer or removed his steadfast love from me! (ESV)

"We must not be egotists, but we must be egotists when we bear witness for the Lord."

A personal testimony. Having committed to give thanks to God for his unfailing love (vv. 13–15), David now tells us why he is personally grateful. In his trials he cried out in praise to the Lord (v. 17), who showed his love by answering David's prayer (vv. 19–20)! Likewise, when God responds to our petitions, we are reminded to praise him. When we do this, we are also communicating to others how we have personally experienced God's love and goodness. We may wrongly believe this to be boasting and therefore choose to remain silent. "Let no mock modesty restrain the grateful believer from speaking of himself, or rather of God's dealings to himself, for it is justly due to God." By sharing how we have encountered his kindness, others may be instructed, consoled, inspired, or benefit in many other ways. Our personal testimony can have a real impact on people's lives. "Let each man speak for one's self, for a personal witness is the surest and most forcible" way of communicating God's way of loving us.

Prayer. Lord, I am very thankful for the many personal testimonies I have heard regarding your goodness to others. They have spurred me on in my daily walk with Christ. I often feel that there is nothing special for me to share which would benefit others, but your word encourages me to witness about your my personal experience of your unfailing love. I trust you with the impact of what I might tell others. Amen.

1 God be gracious to us and bless us, and cause his face to shine upon us—*Selah* 2 that your way may be known on the earth, your salvation among all nations. 3 May the peoples praise you, God; may all the peoples praise you. 4 May the nations be glad and sing for joy; for you will judge the peoples with fairness and guide the nations on the earth. *Selah* 5 May the peoples praise you, God; may all the peoples praise you. 6 The earth has yielded its produce; God, our God, blesses us. 7 God blesses us, so that all the ends of the earth may fear him. (NASB)

"When we bless God we do but little, for our blessings are but words, but when God blesses he enriches us indeed, for his blessings are gifts and deeds."

God's expanding blessings. Spurgeon reminds us that verse 1 is the benediction given by Aaron the high priest to the Israelites (Num 6:24–25). How wonderful to experience the blessing of the forgiveness of sin and God's smiling favor of his presence! However, it is selfish to enjoy his blessings only for ourselves, believing we have an exclusive claim to them (v. 2). "We are blessed for the sake of others as well as ourselves." Through our transforming encounter with Jesus Christ, others will learn of the salvation he offers (v. 1). This gives them the opportunity to turn to Jesus Christ and praise him (v. 3). In anticipation of the future, we should rejoice, knowing that people around the world will discover and accept Jesus Christ as the Savior. Blessings begin and conclude this psalm, reminding us "truly the Lord's blessing is manifold; he blesses and blesses and blesses again." Our response is to praise him!

Prayer. Father, I experience your favor in so many ways, and chief among them is the blessing of a personal relationship with you. It would be selfish of me not to tell my family members, neighbors and co-workers of your goodness. I pray that you will bless the people groups around the globe so that they will experience the blessing of knowing Jesus. Amen.

1 May God arise, may his enemies be scattered, and may those who hate him flee from his presence. 2 As smoke is driven away, so drive them away; as wax melts before a fire, so the wicked will perish before God. 3 But the righteous will be joyful; they will rejoice before God; yes, they will rejoice with gladness. 4 Sing to God, sing praises to his name; exalt him who rides through the deserts, whose name is the LORD, and be jubilant before him. 5 A father of the fatherless and a judge for the widows, is God in his holy dwelling. 6 God makes a home for the lonely; he leads out the prisoners into prosperity, only the rebellious live in parched lands. (NASB)

"To this day and forever, God is, and will be, the peculiar guardian of the defenseless."

The defenseless. The background of this psalm is related to the ark of the covenant which symbolized God's presence among his people. Moses asks God to scatter Israel's enemies while the ark is in transit to Mount Zion (vv. 1–2). His request is firmly rooted in God's past protection of his people when they were slaves in Egypt (v. 6). During their desert wanderings, "the people were like an orphan nation, but God was more than a father to them . . . there were many widows and fatherless ones in the camp" (v. 5). Though the Lord is in heaven, he is compassionate toward them. For this reason, they are called on to express exuberant worship to Jehovah, who cares for the weak and defenseless. As his children we are to reflect God's character by caring for society's weak and vulnerable, such as the homeless and orphans. Those who experience divine care and mercy (v. 6) can join the throngs of people already worshipping God (vv. 3–5).

Prayer. Lord, your word challenges me to be more concerned about those who are defenseless in society. Show me how to care for them as you have cared for the marginalized throughout the millennia. Guard me from a paternalistic attitude and remind me how you have cared for me as a needy person. Amen.

7 God, when you went forth before your people, when you marched through the desert, *Selah* 8 the earth quaked; the heavens also dropped rain at the presence of God; Sinai itself quaked at the presence of God, the God of Israel. 9 You made plentiful rain fall, God; you confirmed your inheritance when it was parched. 10 Your creatures settled in it; in your kindness you provided for the poor, God. 11 The Lord gives the command; the women who proclaim good news are a great army: 12 "Kings of armies flee, they flee, and she who remains at home will divide the spoils!" 13 When you lie down among the sheepfolds, you are like the wings of a dove covered with silver, and its pinions with glistening gold. 14 When the Almighty scattered the kings there, it was snowing in Zalmon. 15 The mountain of Bashan is a mountain of God; the mountain of Bashan is a mountain of many peaks. 16 Why do you look with envy, you mountains of many peaks, at the mountain God has desired as his dwelling? Indeed, the Lord will dwell there forever. 17 The chariots of God are myriads, thousands upon thousands; the Lord is among them as at Sinai, in holiness. 18 You have ascended on high, you have led captive your captives; you have received gifts among people, even among the rebellious as well, that the Lord God may dwell there. 19 Blessed be the Lord, who daily bears our burden, the God who is our salvation. *Selah* (NASB)

"[I]f others endeavor to oppress us, there is no cause for fear, for the Lord will come to the rescue of his people."

Our burden bearer. The congregation praises God, who bears his people's burdens (v. 19). The prior verses describe the various afflictions they experienced in the desert (vv. 7–10) and before powerful kings who sought to destroy them (vv. 11–14). During their trials, God sustained them by providing rain and food (vv. 9–10) and by defeating their enemies (v. 15). As a reminder that he uses the "weak things" of this world to show his power, God bypassed the high peaks of Bashan in favor of the much smaller Mount Zion (vv. 15–16). Likewise, while the Israelite army was smaller than those of the neighboring nations, Israel had at their disposal God's innumerable chariots (v. 17). Although we are weak and weighed down by our trials, Jesus is able to carry the heaviness of our burdens. "His yoke is easy, and his burden is light, therefore be the Savior's name for evermore."

Prayer. Lord, I confess that I often attempt to overcome problems on my own, but I am too weak and limited. Help me to entrust my burdens to you, the One who lovingly cares for me. Amen.

May 28   Psalm 68:20–23

20 God is to us a God of salvation; and to God the Lord belong ways of escape from death. 21 God certainly will shatter the heads of his enemies, the hairy head of one who goes about in his guilt. 22 The Lord said, "I will bring them back from Bashan. I will bring them back from the depths of the sea, 23 so that your foot may shatter them in blood, and the tongue of your dogs may have its portion from your enemies." (NASB)

"The Preserver is also the Destroyer."

Salvation and justice. Spurgeon notes that this brief section celebrates God's salvation for his people and his justice to those who oppose him. We should marvel at how God "has ways and means of rescuing his children from death; when they are at wit's end, and see no way of escape, he can find a door of deliverance for them" (v. 20). Today, our deliverance is found in Jesus Christ, who came to save people from the penalty (spiritual death) of their sin. On the other hand, the same God who preserves his people is also the destroyer of those who have resisted and rejected him (vv. 22–23). "Headstrong sinners will find that providence overcomes them despite their strong heads." We cannot soften the harsh reality of God's judgment described here. "Vengeance shall be awarded to the oppressed people, and that most complete and terrible."

Prayer. Lord, today your love has become greatly distorted by our society. Your word reminds me that you are a God who both loves and acts justly. While these attributes seem contradictory, I accept who you are by the witness of your word and the ways you have acted in history. Amen.

May 29   Psalm 68:24–31

24 They have seen your procession, God, the procession of my God, my King, into the sanctuary. 25 The singers went on, the musicians after them, in the midst of the young women beating tambourines. 26 Bless God in the congregations, even the LORD, you who are of the fountain of Israel. 27 Benjamin, the youngest, is there, ruling them, the leaders of Judah in their company, the leaders of Zebulun, the leaders of Naphtali. 28 Your God has commanded your strength; show yourself strong, God, you who acted in our behalf. 29 Because of your temple at Jerusalem kings will bring gifts to you. 30 Rebuke the animals in the reeds, the herd of bulls with the calves of the peoples, trampling the pieces of silver; he has scattered the peoples who delight in war. 31 Messengers will come from Egypt; Cush will quickly stretch out her hands to God. (NASB)

"The church of God, when truly spiritual, wins for her God the homage of the nations."

International homage. We have seen God's people carrying the ark (symbolizing his presence) to Zion and then worshipping him. One may conclude the ark's move was for the exclusive privilege of Israel's tribes. The psalmist corrects this faulty conclusion by looking to God's future conquests. The defeated nations brought gifts as an act of submission to the one true living God (vv. 29, 31). The nations' homage to him continued during the days of the early church and extends to our present time. "Great sinners shall yield themselves to the scepter of grace, and great men shall become good men, by coming to God." He is building a diverse international church, not through the sacrifices of animals, but through the sacrifice of Christ, who paid for our sins regardless of where we live on this planet.

Prayer. Lord, I think of the early church who made the kingdom of God known to their neighbors and the surrounding regions. Give me a global perspective of your church which will stir me to pray and support what you are doing internationally. I rejoice to see people of many ethnicities submitting to you and accepting your Son as Savior of the world. Amen.

32–34 Sing, O kings of the earth! Sing praises to the Lord! There he is: Sky-Rider, striding the ancient skies. Listen—he's calling in thunder, rumbling, rolling thunder. Call out "Bravo!" to God, the High God of Israel. His splendor and strength rise huge as thunderheads. 35 A terrible beauty, O God, streams from your sanctuary. It's Israel's strong God! He gives power and might to his people! O you, his people—bless God! (MSG)

"Our voices are fitly called to praise him whose voice spoke us into being, and gives us the effectual grace which secures our well-being."

Spiritual homage. Submission to powerful kings may be motivated by fear, which results in an unwilling compliance. In contrast, those who gladly submit to the Lord genuinely worship him among many nations around the world (v. 32). Why would they joyfully bow down to the King of the universe, whom they once opposed? God's great power was revealed through his voice speaking to people (vv. 33–34). "This gospel, which utters and reveals his word, is the power of God." Spurgeon writes that they gladly respond because they recognize that his greatness is for their good and his glory for their defense (v. 35). When there is a "yielding and trusting in him, let our hearts acknowledge his might. When we are reconciled to God, his omnipotence is an attribute of which we sing with delight." This willing submission of the heart is expressed in joyful worship with God's people.

Prayer. Lord, I am thankful you broke the monopoly of sin on the cross and in my life. When I think of those who do not know you, I do not want to pressure them into reluctant acceptance. Instead, may they gladly accept the gospel and joyfully submit to you. Amen.

May 31

Psalm 69:1–4

1 Save me, O God, for the floodwaters are up to my neck. 2 Deeper and deeper I sink into the mire; I can't find a foothold. I am in deep water, and the floods overwhelm me. 3 I am exhausted from crying for help; my throat is parched. My eyes are swollen with weeping, waiting for my God to help me. 4 Those who hate me without cause outnumber the hairs on my head. Many enemies try to destroy me with lies, demanding that I give back what I didn't steal. (NLT)

"Here our Lord pictures the close, clinging nature of his heart's woes."

Deep suffering. Spurgeon believes this psalm refers to Jesus Christ and his suffering. Like the prophet Jeremiah, Jesus was cast into a figurative dungeon of sorrows (vv. 1–2; Jer 38:6). We dare not limit our view of Jesus' suffering to the physical realm. "Sorrows, deep, abounding, deadly, had penetrated his inner nature . . . his sufferings were unlike all others in degree, the waters were such as soaked into the soul." That there was no justification for the hatred toward him worsened the suffering (v. 4). He was innocent but treated as guilty. When we go through similarly painful times, we are to follow the example of Jesus, who cried out to his Father and waited for an answer (v. 4). "There are times when we should pray till the throat is dry and watch till the eyes grow dim. Only then can we have fellowship with him in his sufferings." Jesus has great empathy for us when we endure suffering (Heb 4:15).

Prayer. Father, I feel all alone when I find myself in deep waters. Forgive me for those times when I think you do not care at all about what I am going through. When I pause to consider the depths of your suffering for my sin, I am grateful that you can empathize with my pain. Amen.

5 God, you know my foolishness, and my guilt is not hidden from you. 6 May those who wait for you not be ashamed because of me, Lord God of armies; may those who seek you not be dishonored because of me, God of Israel, 7 because for your sake I have endured disgrace; dishonor has covered my face. 8 I have become estranged from my brothers, and a stranger to my mother's sons. 9 For zeal for your house has consumed me, and the taunts of those who taunt you have fallen on me. 10 When I wept in my soul with fasting, it became my disgrace. 11 When I made sackcloth my clothing, I became a proverb to them. 12 Those who sit in the gate talk about me, and songs of mockery by those habitually drunk are about me. (NASB)

"Because he undertook to do the Father's will, and teach his truth, the people were angry."

Hated for uprightness. Verse 9 is quoted in the account of Jesus chasing people out of the temple (John 2:14–17). Their profits based on an abusive currency exchange prompted Jesus to act zealously. In this particular case, Spurgeon believes Jesus' actions stemmed from his great passion for God's glory and the reputation of his character. But why does ardor for God stir up people's hatred (vv. 9–12)? "Zeal for God is so little understood by men of the world, that it always draws down opposition, those who are inspired by it; they are sure to be accused of sinister motives, or of hypocrisy, or of being out of their senses." Spurgeon also makes the point that people had resolved to hate Jesus and everything he did further justified their decision to despise him. Jesus was innocent of their accusations but willingly suffered for the sake of his commitment to his Father (v. 7). He is our exemplar, reminding us that we are called to stand up for what is right and face the adverse consequences of our pledge to love him (1 Pet 3:14).

Prayer. Lord, I am committed to live uprightly to honor you. But, I admit I dislike people ridiculing and rejecting me because of my relationship to you. When I think of the pressure to conform to society's values, strengthen my resolve to obey you unreservedly. Amen.

13 But I keep praying to you, LORD, hoping this time you will show me favor. In your unfailing love, O God, answer my prayer with your sure salvation. 14 Rescue me from the mud; don't let me sink any deeper! Save me from those who hate me, and pull me from these deep waters. 15 Don't let the floods overwhelm me, or the deep waters swallow me, or the pit of death devour me. 16 Answer my prayers, O LORD, for your unfailing love is wonderful. Take care of me, for your mercy is so plentiful. 17 Don't hide from your servant; answer me quickly, for I am in deep trouble! 18 Come and redeem me; free me from my enemies. (NLT)

"[T]he nature of God is the great treasury of strong reasons which shall be to us most prevalent in supplication."

Our confidence in prayer. When he is overwhelmed by those who hate him (vv. 14–15), the psalmist pleads for God's deliverance. Our confidence that he should answer our prayers is not based on the severity of the opposition (v. 4) or the goodness of the cause (v. 9). Instead, our hope is rooted in the character of God, who is full of mercy and faithfulness (vv. 13, 16). It is very tempting to ask the Lord to bail us out from troubles without being concerned about our relationship with him. The essence of the psalmist's petition is a heart cry for God's presence (v. 17). "If ever a man needs the comforting presence of God it is when he or she is in distress; and, being in distress, it is a reason to be pleaded with a merciful God why he should not desert us."

Prayer. Lord, when I pray for your deliverance in dire situations, I appeal to you on my terms. Teach me to base my prayers on your unchanging and unfailing character. Your lovingkindness is a balm for my troubled soul and a witness to others of your great love for a troubled world. Amen.

June 3

Psalm 69:19–21

19 You know of my shame, scorn, and disgrace. You see all that my enemies are doing. 20 Their insults have broken my heart, and I am in despair. If only one person would show some pity; if only one would turn and comfort me. 21 But instead, they give me poison for food; they offer me sour wine for my thirst. (NLT)

"Here we have a sad recapitulation of sorrows, with more special reference to the persons concerned in their affliction."

A broken heart. Spurgeon applies these verses directly to Jesus' crucifixion on the cross, which gives insight to his intense agony. While we commonly focus on physical suffering (v. 21), we also see Jesus' emotional agony. Three descriptive words in verse 19 paint the hatred he encountered (v. 20). "Our Lord died of a broken heart, and reproach had done the deed. Intense mental suffering arises from slander . . . it sufficed to lacerate the heart till it broke." The pathos is reinforced because there was no one to comfort him after his disciples deserted him (v. 20). When we experience emotional anguish due to a loss or rejection, Jesus not only knows and feels our pain but shows us the appropriate response by turning to his loving Father in prayer (Matt 27:46).

Prayer. Lord, so many people have broken hearts, leaving them feeling incapacitated and unable to cope with life. Only you, in your tender mercy, can bring healing to their hearts as they cry out to you. Thank you for hearing their prayers and answering them in your right time and for your eternal purposes. Amen.

22 May the table set before them become a snare; may it become
retribution and a trap. 23 May their eyes be darkened so they
cannot see, and their backs be bent forever. 24 Pour out your
wrath on them; let your fierce anger overtake them. 25 May their
place be deserted; let there be no one to dwell in their tents. 26
For they persecute those you wound and talk about the pain of
those you hurt. 27 Charge them with crime upon crime; do not
let them share in your salvation. 28 May they be blotted out of the
book of life and not be listed with the righteous. (NIV)

"What can be too severe a penalty for those who reject the incarnate God,
and refuse to obey the commands of his mercy?"

Holy anger. When we read about Jesus' suffering on the cross, we often think
about him forgiving a criminal (Luke 23:42–43). The tone of this section
surprises us with such a sharp contrast. How do we explain the wide gulf
between forgiveness and the strong language here? Spurgeon suggests that
Jesus is predicting the eventual destruction of Jerusalem (Matt 23:38). Those
who despise God will face his wrath (vv. 23–24). "God's indignation is no
trifle; the anger of a holy, just, omnipotent, and infinite Being, is above all
things to be dreaded." His anger is also expressed by allowing people to reap
the consequences of their sins (v. 27). In some cases, human pride brings
justice upon their own actions. For example, they place their own names in
the Book of Life even though their names do not belong there (v. 28). "En-
rolled with honor, they shall be erased with shame." God's anger, based on his
character, determines his response to people's rejection of Christ's atonement
on the cross.

Prayer. Lord, when I see so many injustices in the world, anger wells up. The
desire is to take matters into my hands or to demand you act immediately.
Thank you for your word giving insight to your anger and justice that are
carried out in the present and future. Teach me to forgive and leave justice
to you. Amen.

29 But I am afflicted and in pain; let your salvation, O God, set me on high! 30 I will praise the name of God with a song; I will magnify him with thanksgiving. 31 This will please the LORD more than an ox or a bull with horns and hoofs. 32 When the humble see it they will be glad; you who seek God, let your hearts revive. 33 For the LORD hears the needy and does not despise his own people who are prisoners. 34 Let heaven and earth praise him, the seas and everything that moves in them. 35 For God will save Zion and build up the cities of Judah, and people shall dwell there and possess it; 36 the offspring of his servants shall inherit it, and those who love his name shall dwell in it. (ESV)

"In us, also, faith foresees the happy issue of all affliction, and makes us even now begin this music of gratitude."

Persevering faith. The intense tone of the previous verses has ended and now softens. In his pain, the psalmist could pray this way because of his faith in the Lord. With confidence that the Lord will hear him, he expresses praise (vv. 30–33). Spurgeon reminds us of the example of Jesus, who, in his sorrow, cried out to his Father and experienced his presence. "None can be brought lower than was the Nazarene, but see how highly he is exalted; descend into what depths we may, the prayer-hearing God can bring us up again." This is so encouraging for us. Thus, all creation is called on to praise God for his salvation (vv. 34–36). We persevere in faith, knowing "that through the atonement of the Christ of God, all the poor in spirit shall enjoy the mercies promised in the covenant of faith." We will go through deep waters (vv. 1–4). However, we can persevere by God's grace which makes it possible to praise him.

Prayer. Lord Almighty, at times I feel like giving up because the circumstances are so overwhelming. Knowing I cannot face these situations by myself I need to trust in you and live with your strength. I praise you, knowing you have seen my suffering and heard my cries to you. Amen.

June 6   Psalm 70

1 Make haste, O God, to deliver me! O Lord, make haste to help me! 2 Let them be put to shame and confusion who seek my life! Let them be turned back and brought to dishonour who delight in my hurt! 3 Let them turn back because of their shame who say, "Aha, Aha!" 4 May all who seek you rejoice and be glad in you! May those who love your salvation say evermore, "God is great!" 5 But I am poor and needy; hasten to me, O God! You are my help and my deliverer; O Lord, do not delay! (ESV)

"Make haste, for I'm in deep distress, my case is urgent; help me *now.*"

Urgent prayer. With some variations, this psalm is very similar to Psalm 40. The chief difference between them is the sense of urgency in today's psalm. David gets right to the point with a repeated plea for God's help (vv. 1, 5). His example is a good reminder for us. "It is not forbidden us, in hours of dire distress, to ask for speed on God's part in his coming to rescue us . . . It is most [appropriate] that we should day by day cry to God for deliverance and help." Also, verse 2 is more succinct than Psalm 40:14, a further reminder of the urgency of his prayer. Spurgeon points out that "a man in haste uses no more words than are actually necessary." The pressing need to come to God is based on the fact that we are poor and needy (v. 5). Paradoxically, "our poverty is our wealth, even as our weakness is our strength." Even though our prayers are urgent we have confidence in God, who is able to deliver us (v. 5). He is the Lord, who is faithful to his covenant with us.

Prayer. Lord, while I enjoy lengthy conversations with you, I am also thankful that I can cry out with short prayers to you throughout the day's overwhelming circumstances. I recognize how weak I am and how you are mighty and able to carry me through difficult times. Amen.

June 7   Psalm 71:1–8

1 In you, LORD, I have taken refuge; let me never be put to shame.
2 In your righteousness, rescue me and deliver me; turn your ear
to me and save me. 3 Be my rock of refuge, to which I can always
go; give the command to save me, for you are my rock and my
fortress. 4 Deliver me, my God, from the hand of the wicked,
from the grasp of those who are evil and cruel. 5 For you have
been my hope, Sovereign LORD, my confidence since my youth. 6
From birth I have relied on you; you brought me forth from my
mother's womb. I will ever praise you. 7 I have become a sign to
many; you are my strong refuge. 8 My mouth is filled with your
praise, declaring your splendor all day long. (NIV)

"We do well to reflect upon divine goodness to us in childhood, for it is
full of food for gratitude."

Reflecting on God's goodness. Once again David finds himself in a difficult
spot. He needs God's deliverance from people who ridiculed him (vv. 2, 4, 7).
He finds hope in God when he looks back over his life from the time of his
birth (vv. 5–6). The past is not problem-free for him, or for us. Nevertheless,
he sees clear evidence of God's faithfulness to him. Looking to the future,
"he felt persuaded that the God of his youth would not forsake him in his
old age." His confidence stems not from a blind faith but from a personal
relationship ("my" is used six times in verses 3–5) with a powerful and caring
God. In hard times, we do well to redirect our thoughts to past experiences of
God's faithfulness to us. When we do this, we are able to praise the Lord (v.
8). "He fills us with good; let us be also filled with gratitude."

Prayer. Heavenly Father, I join the many who have gone before me who bear
witness to your trustworthiness. When I begin to doubt and panic in my
circumstances, remind me of the countless times in the past you have shown
your unfailing love. Amen.

9 Do not cast me away at the time of my old age; do not abandon me when my strength fails. 10 For my enemies have spoken against me; and those who watch for my life have consulted together, 11 saying, "God has abandoned him; pursue and seize him, for there is no one to save him." 12 God, do not be far from me; my God, hurry to my aid! 13 May those who are enemies of my soul be put to shame and consumed; may they be covered with disgrace and dishonor, who seek to injure me. 14 But as for me, I will wait continually, and will praise you yet more and more. 15 My mouth shall tell of your righteousness and of your salvation all day long; for I do not know the art of writing. 16 I will come with the mighty deeds of the LORD God; I will make mention of your righteousness, yours alone. 17 God, you have taught me from my youth, and I still declare your wondrous deeds. 18 And even when I am old and gray, God, do not abandon me, until I declare your strength to this generation, your power to all who are to come. (NASB)

"Blessed are they who begin in youth to proclaim the name of the Lord, and cease not until their last hour brings their last word for their divine Master."

Aging well. David writes this psalm as an old man experiencing diminished strength (v. 9). His enemies are saying that God will forsake him (vv. 10–11) but he refutes them (vv. 12–13). "Old age robs us of personal beauty, and deprives us of strength for active service; but it does not lower us in the love and favor of God." David is not only thinking of *his* situation, but of *others* who belong to the younger generation (v. 18). He "longed to make them all acquainted with the power of God to support his people, that they also might be led to walk by faith . . . he would leave a record for unborn ages to read. He thought the Lord's power to be so worthy of praise, that he would make the ages ring with it till time should be no more." We age well when we find our confidence in God's presence and tell those younger than us to place their trust in the Lord.

Prayer. Gracious Father, despite a weakening body, help me not to become a grumbling old person. By your grace, may I find strength by rejoicing in your companionship and telling younger generations of your faithful love to followers of Jesus. Amen.

19 For your righteousness, God, reaches to the heavens, you who have done great things; God, who is like you? 20 You who have shown me many troubles and distresses will revive me again, and will bring me up again from the depths of the earth. 21 May you increase my greatness and turn to comfort me. 22 I will also praise you with a harp, and your truth, my God; I will sing praises to you with the lyre, Holy One of Israel. 23 My lips will shout for joy when I sing praises to you; and my soul, which you have redeemed. 24 My tongue also will tell of your righteousness all day long; for they are put to shame, for they are humiliated who seek my harm. (NASB)

"However low the Lord may permit us to sink, he will fix a limit to the descent, and in due time will bring us up again."

Old age, but revived. Like many of us, David has had more than his share of sorrow and afflictions throughout his lifetime. However, rather than becoming bitter, he lives with confidence that God will revive his spirit (v. 20). In essence, he is saying, "he has shown me many heavy and severe trials, and he will also show me many and precious mercies. He has almost killed me, he will speedily revive me." God will refresh us in his own ways. We are renewed by his Spirit in this life and by anticipating our resurrection to be with him forever (v. 20). In the meantime, with revived hearts we can praise God for his salvation and many other acts of love shown to us (vv. 23–24). "Soul-singing is the soul of singing."

Prayer. Loving Lord, even though my body is aging, continue to renew me by your living Spirit so that I can rejoice in you until I take my last breath. I look forward to that day when I will receive a new, resurrected, spiritual body, and be in your glorious presence. Amen.

1 Give the king your judgments, God, and your righteousness to the king's son. 2 May he judge your people with righteousness and your afflicted with justice. 3 May the mountains bring peace to the people, and the hills, in righteousness. 4 May he vindicate the afflicted of the people, save the children of the needy, and crush the oppressor. 5 May they fear you while the sun shines, And as long as the moon shines, throughout all generations. 6 May he come down like rain upon the mown grass, like showers that water the earth. 7 May the righteous flourish in his days, as well as an abundance of peace, until the moon is no more. (NASB)

"Our glorious King in Zion hath all judgment committed unto him. He rules in the name of God over all lands."

The reign of Jesus. This entire psalm comments on the reigns of David and his son Solomon. Spurgeon notes this song reflects more fully the future rule of Jesus, who is righteous (v. 1). All too often when tyrants rule, evil people thrive. Jesus will make impartial decisions concerning those who have been taken advantage of by those who oppressed them (vv. 2, 4). "True wisdom is manifest in all the decisions of Zion's King . . . [he] deals out evenhanded justice, to the delight of the poor and despised." As a result, people will flourish under Jesus' reign (vv. 3, 6–7). When uprightness rules, "[T]he best of men prosper most. A righteous king is the patron and producer of righteous subjects . . . The peace which Jesus brings is not superficial or short-lived; it is abundant in its depth and duration. Let all hearts and voices welcome the King of nations."

Prayer. Lord, when I see corrupt and oppressive governments around the world, my heart cries out for needed changes. The only true and lasting hope is through Jesus Christ, who desires to lovingly reign in people's lives. Grant me patience, knowing your kingship will be fully realized when you come with majesty and justice to exercise dominion over the world. Amen.

8 May he also rule from sea to sea, and from the Euphrates River to the ends of the earth. 9 May the nomads of the desert bow before him, and his enemies lick the dust. 10 May the kings of Tarshish and of the islands bring gifts; may the kings of Sheba and Seba offer tributes. 11 And may all kings bow down before him, all nations serve him. 12 For he will save the needy when he cries for help, the afflicted also, and him who has no helper. 13 He will have compassion on the poor and needy, and he will save the lives of the needy.14 He will rescue their life from oppression and violence, and their blood will be precious in his sight; (NASB)

"All other power shall be subordinate to his; no rival nor antagonist shall he know."

A universal and generous reign. Spurgeon summarizes Jesus' reign as universal (vv. 8–11) and generous (vv. 12–14). His cosmic rule will extend to every corner of the world and no nation will suffer under the dictatorship of Satan. This international kingdom will be manifest by powerful nations and leaders who give reverence to the Lord (v. 11). In the meantime, our great King is generous in his compassion toward the afflicted (vv. 12–13). He hears and responds to their cries. When people quote the proverb, "God helps those who help themselves," Spurgeon points out, "[I]t is yet more true that Jesus helps those who cannot help themselves, nor find help in others. All helpless ones are under the especial care of Zion's compassionate King." He even cares for those who are martyred for their faith in Jesus (v. 14). Although we do not currently see his total reign over every area of life, our King's generous compassion toward the needy is a sign he is ruling in our world.

Prayer. Sovereign God, help our churches to be generous in our compassion to warda hurting, needy world afflicted by pandemics and violence. As the world cries out, help us to be responsive as messengers of your hope and love. Amen.

15 So may he live, and may the gold of Sheba be given to him; and they are to pray for him continually; they are to bless him all day long. 16 May there be abundance of grain on the earth on top of the mountains; its fruit will wave like the cedars of Lebanon; and may those from the city flourish like the vegetation of the earth. 17 May his name endure forever; may his name produce descendants as long as the sun shines; and may people wish blessings on themselves by him; may all nations call him blessed. 18 Blessed be the LORD God, the God of Israel, who alone works wonders. 19 And blessed be his glorious name forever; and may the whole earth be filled with his glory. Amen and Amen. 20 The prayers of David the son of Jesse are ended. (NASB)

"He was slain, but is risen and ever lives."

An eternal reign. In this last section of the psalm, Spurgeon points to the eternal nature of Jesus Christ's reign (vv. 13, 17). How does this shape our response to him? We can pray for Jesus' cause to be accomplished through his people on earth, and we can praise him, for he is worthy of honor far above all other rulers (v. 15). "He himself shall be earth's greatest blessing; when men wish to bless others, they shall bless in his name." When we consider Jesus as our eternal King, our praise is filled with profound gratitude (vv. 18–19). "It is, and ever will be, the acme of our desires, and the climax of our prayers, to behold Jesus exalted King of kings, and Lord of lords . . . he is the blessed God, and his name shall be blessed; his name is glorious, and that glory shall fill the whole earth. For so bright a consummation our heart yearns daily, and we cry '*Amen and Amen.*'"

Prayer. Everlasting God, I ask you to be the Lord of my life as I look to the fullness of your eternal reign in this world. May I continue to pray for your purposes to be done on earth. I praise you for what you are doing and what you will continue to do for your glory. Amen.

1 Truly God is good to Israel, to those who are pure in heart. 2 But as for me, my feet had almost stumbled, my steps had nearly slipped. 3 For I was envious of the arrogant when I saw the prosperity of the wicked. (ESV)

"His eye was fixed too much on one thing; he saw their present, and forgot their future, saw their outward display, and overlooked their soul's discomfort."

The seed of an impure heart. The psalmist affirms that God is good to his people (v. 1). This truth is an anchor when the storms come blowing into our lives. However, the psalmist honestly admits his past struggle with the belief that God is always good to his people. He saw the prosperity of the wicked (v. 2), who should not thrive based on his own conviction in verse 1. Their success did not square with what he knew about God and he doubted the truth of his own convictions (v. 2). His heart influenced his uncertainties. He was envious of the proud and prosperous (v. 3). His questioning and desire to want what they had in life cautions us. "Errors of heart and head soon affect the conduct . . . How ought we to watch the inner being, since it has so forcible an effect upon the outward character." It is foolish to desire what evil people have, but it is more foolish not to desire what God wants from us—namely, a pure heart.

Prayer. Lord, I give excuses for my impure heart because my human nature craves what others have. I am also convicted about my doubts regarding the way you work in this world. Deepen my trust in you and your dealings with those who oppose you. Amen.

4 For they have no pangs until death; their bodies are fat and sleek. 5 They are not in trouble as others are; they are not stricken like the rest of mankind. 6 Therefore pride is their necklace; violence covers them as a garment. 7 Their eyes swell out through fatness; their hearts overflow with follies. 8 They scoff and speak with malice; loftily they threaten oppression. 9 They set their mouths against the heavens, and their tongue struts through the earth. (ESV)

"The prosperous wicked escape the killing toils which afflict the mass of mankind; their bread comes to them without care, their wine without stint."

Society's good life. The psalmist now reveals the cause of his envy. Simply put, the wicked have no troubles in life (v. 5). "While many saints are both poor and afflicted, the prosperous sinner is neither." They also have power to do what they want in life (v. 6). They "intend to have their own way, and achieve their own ends. They brag and bully, bluster and browbeat" to get what they want from others. Their actions allow them to get what they desire (v. 7). "Their wishes are gratified, and more; their very greediness is exceeded . . . The heart is beyond measure gluttonous." In light of this, they shockingly attempt to speak with authority on religious matters (v. 9). "Against God himself they aim their blasphemies. One would think, to hear them, that they were demi-gods themselves." Today's culture similarly craves possessions and power with an equal disdain for the Lord. When our envious hearts crave material goods and control, such objects become idols, displacing God as our primary object of adoration.

Prayer. Lord, my heart is so inclined to desire what my culture pursues. Now I see the further consequence of envy. Not only do I doubt your ways, but my pursuit of society's idols distracts and leads my heart away from you. Forgive me for following these illusions of the good life; lead my heart and mind back to you alone. Amen.

10 Therefore his people turn back to them, and find no fault in them. 11 And they say, "How can God know? Is there knowledge in the Most High?" 12 Behold, these are the wicked; always at ease, they increase in riches. 13 All in vain have I kept my heart clean and washed my hands in innocence. 14 For all the day long I have been stricken and rebuked every morning. (ESV)

"Such knots have we also sought to settle, and have sadly worn our fingers and broken our teeth."

A confused heart. The psalmist knows that God wants us to have a pure heart (v. 1). But we are often filled with envy for those who are successful and powerful (vv. 2–9). Now the psalmist declares that a godly disposition did not bring him the kind of life he expected from God (v. 13). He is still experiencing afflictions (v. 14). "Strange that saints should sigh and the sinners sing. Rest was given to the disturbers, and yet peace was denied to the peace makers." Now instead of saying possessions and power are vain pursuits, he laments his own piety. He concludes that "no advantage has come to him through his purity . . . it was a bitter thought that all this was useless, and left him in even a worse condition" than his enemies. What was his issue? The psalmist viewed upright living as a means to get from God what he wanted in life. His heart was not only envious, but self-centered and confused regarding the reason for a godly life.

Prayer. Lord, I confess that envy for worldly success is an affront to you. Neither can I have a clean heart and pursue this kind of success. Forgive me for such thinking and recalibrate my soul to passionately pursue you for true contentment. Amen.

15 If I had said, "I will speak thus," I would have betrayed the generation of your children. 16 But when I thought how to understand this, it seemed to me a wearisome task, 17 until I went into the sanctuary of God; then I discerned their end. 18 Truly you set them in slippery places; you make them fall to ruin. 19 How they are destroyed in a moment, swept away utterly by terrors! 20 Like a dream when one awakes, O Lord, when you rouse yourself, you despise them as phantoms. (ESV)

"Thus he shifted his point of view, and apparent disorder resolved itself into harmony."

The turning point. How do we handle the struggles with our envious desires that leave us feeling conflicted with God? To reveal our inner battles indiscriminately to others may leave them shocked and troubled in their own hearts (v. 15). For this reason, we benefit when we go to God. He gives us a very different outlook on those who have become prosperous by evil means (v. 17). "He had seen too little to be able to judge; a wider view changed his judgment; he saw with his mind's enlightened eye the future of the wicked, and his soul was in debate no longer as to the happiness of their condition." His new perspective on the wicked included realizing God was accomplishing his purposes with those who oppose him (vv. 18–20). The psalmist "sees that the divine had purposely placed these men in prosperous and eminent circumstances, not with the intent to bless them but the very reverse." Having God's perspective through his word is the turning point to liberate us from selfish desires which drive our hearts away from him.

Prayer. Lord, I come into your presence opening up to you my imperfect heart with all of its sinful desires. Thank you for your word, for your truth sheds new light on the way you work in today's world. It also convicts me not to pursue society's dreams, but to pursue you and your purposes for my life. Amen.

21 Then I realized that my heart was bitter, and I was all torn up inside. 22 I was so foolish and ignorant—I must have seemed like a senseless animal to you. 23 Yet I still belong to you; you hold my right hand. 24 You guide me with your counsel, leading me to a glorious destiny. (NLT)

"It is sin beloved and delighted in which separates us from the Lord, but when we bewail it heartily, the Lord will not withdraw from us."

Brokenness and grace. In today's passage, the psalmist condemns his own foolishness and admires God's grace. With a new glimpse of God's role in the world, the psalmist realizes he has become a bitter person. Now he is a broken man describing his emotional and mental anguish (vv. 21–22). "His pain had been intense . . . It was deep-seated sorrow, and one which penetrated his inmost being. His thinking had gone askew. Concerning the prosperous, he had envied them because he judged happiness by this mortal life, by outward appearances, and by fleshly enjoyments." He is wise enough to acknowledge that his thinking and desires were contrary to God's will. When we genuinely confess the reality of our sinful hearts, God graciously embraces and guides us in the way we should live (vv. 23–24). This is God's unconditional grace extended to us! "Our former mistakes are a blessing, when they drive us to this."

Prayer. Father, I admit that so often my thinking and desires are contrary to your ways. I am not only foolish, but I am also broken in the depths of my being. I am thankful you still love and receive me even when I confess my waywardness to you. Your grace is too profound for me to grasp, but you fill my heart with gratitude and a renewed longing to follow you. Amen.

June 18   Psalm 73:25-28

25 Whom have I in heaven but you? I desire you more than any-thing on earth. 26 My health may fail, and my spirit may grow weak, but God remains the strength of my heart; he is mine for-ever. 27 Those who desert him will perish, for you destroy those who abandon you. 28 But as for me, how good it is to be near God! I have made the Sovereign LORD my shelter, and I will tell everyone about the wonderful things you do. (NLT)

"He bade all things else go, that he might be filled with his God."

A renewed allegiance. Asaph concludes this psalm by renewing his commit-ment to God. Being in his presence Asaph knows the foolishness of envying the prosperous, whose hearts are far from God (v. 27). Thus, "he turns away from the glitter which fascinated him to the true gold which was his real trea-sure. He felt that his God was better to him than all the wealth, health, honor, and peace, which he had so much envied." What does it mean to renew our allegiance to the Lord? It involves guarding our hearts (v. 26). "His heart would be kept up by divine love, and filled eternally with divine glory . . . There is nothing desirable save God; let us, then, desire only him. All other things must pass away; let our hearts abide in him, who alone abides forever." A recommitment to the Lord includes a deeper trust in his sovereignty (v. 28). With greater confidence in him, Asaph has moved beyond his inner struggles (v. 15) to tell others the ways God works in the world.

Prayer. Lord, today I renew my commitment to you. I realize that there is nothing in society that truly satisfies the yearnings of the restless heart. I confidently turn to you and surrender my longings and hopes in adoration to you. With my love I trust your sovereign will to accomplish in my life what you know is best. Amen.

1 God, why have you rejected us forever? Why does your anger smoke against the sheep of your pasture? 2 Remember your congregation, which you purchased of old, which you have redeemed to be the tribe of your inheritance; and this Mount Zion, where you have dwelt. 3 Step toward the irreparable ruins; the enemy has damaged everything in the sanctuary. 4 Your adversaries have roared in the midst of your meeting place; they have set up their own signs as signs. 5 It seems like one bringing up his axe into a forest of trees. 6 And now they break down all its carved work with axes and hammers. 7 They have burned your sanctuary to the ground; they have defiled the dwelling place of your name. 8 They said in their heart, "Let's completely subdue them." They have burned all the meeting places of God in the land. 9 We do not see our signs; there is no longer any prophet, nor is there anyone among us who knows how long. 10 How long, God, will the enemy taunt you? Shall the enemy treat your name disrespectfully forever? 11 Why do you withdraw your hand, even your right hand? Extend it from your chest and destroy them! (NASB)

"Grief in its distraction asks strange questions and surmises impossible terrors."

Not rejected! This psalm deals with Israel's grief during the Babylonians' attack. Their enemies want to desecrate and destroy the temple (vv. 3–7) and every other place associated with the worship of God (v. 8). This national calamity, including exile, naturally raises questions: Why has he rejected us and for how long (vv. 1, 10–11)? In time, they would return from exile and then they would know God had not disowned them. When calamities strike us, we may feel God is rejecting us and find ourselves asking similar questions. In situations like this, it is important to remember God has not given up on us. "God is never weary of his people so as to abhor them, and even when his anger is turned against them, it is but for a small moment, and with a view to their eternal good." For Christ has purchased us through his redemption and we are his inheritance (v. 2).

Prayer. Father, I confess that I have felt abandoned by you when distressing circumstances have come my way. Your word teaches me not to evaluate my relationship based on my troubles. I will depend on your redemptive love that gives me the privilege of being your child forever. Amen.

12 Yet God is my King from long ago, who performs acts of salvation in the midst of the earth. 13 You divided the sea by your strength; you broke the heads of the sea monsters in the waters. 14 You crushed the heads of Leviathan; you gave him as food for the creatures of the wilderness. 15 You broke open springs and torrents; you dried up ever-flowing streams. 16 Yours is the day, yours also is the night; you have prepared the light and the sun. 17 You have established all the boundaries of the earth; you have created summer and winter. (NASB)

"Each past miracle of grace assures us that he who has begun to deliver will continue to redeem us from all evil."

God's great power. In the midst of our grief, we understandably ask questions like "Why?" and "How long?" We have a choice to make. We can either drown in our sorrows or we can intentionally redirect our thoughts to God. In this passage, the psalmist chooses to meditate on God's supernatural power. He recalls God's power revealed in opening up the Red Sea for the Israelites to cross and escape from the Egyptians (vv. 13–14). This same God stopped the Jordan River so his people could cross over into their promised land (v. 15). His power should not surprise us for he is the one who created nature (vv. 16–17). Years later, Jesus overthrew sin and death by dying on the cross. Jesus is "my king" (v. 12) and "if from eternity he has claimed us as his own, he will preserve us from the insulting foe." When we feel abandoned, we look to the cross and see Jesus' power to defeat evil. In the past, he was faithful to deliver his people and he continues to do so today.

Prayer. Almighty God, forgive me when I question your lack of power to rescue me in my distressing moments. When I consider Jesus' resurrection I know you can strengthen me in my struggles. May you receive the glory for what you accomplish in my present circumstances. Amen.

18 Remember this, LORD, that the enemy has taunted you, and a foolish people has treated your name disrespectfully. 19 Do not give the soul of your turtledove to the wild animal; do not forget the life of your afflicted forever. 20 Consider the covenant; for the dark places of the land are full of the places of violence. 21 May the oppressed person not return dishonored; may the afflicted and the needy praise your name. 22 Arise, God, and plead your own cause; remember how the foolish person taunts you all day long. 23 Do not forget the voice of your adversaries, the uproar of those who rise against you, which ascends continually. (NASB)

"It is not the way of the Lord to allow any of those who trust in him to be put to shame."

God responds. Today's meditation identifies two primary factors influencing God's power to act in times of national and personal calamities. One, God responds when he is continuously mocked and reviled by those who oppose him (vv. 18, 22). When this happens, "Jehovah is a jealous God, and will surely glorify his own name." He is committed to uphold his own honor and reputation through worship by those who have experienced his deliverance (v. 21). Two, through Jesus Christ, God has entered into a permanent covenant relationship with his people (v. 20). Out of love he will not break this eternal commitment and will show us compassion.

Prayer. Father, how can I ever question your love for me, when I know you have promised never to leave or forsake me? I rest not only in your love for me but also in your will to be revered and feared by all people. In the midst of tragedy, continue to remind me of your promised faithfulness to your people so that you may be exalted among the nations. Amen.

1 We praise you, God, we praise you, for your Name is near;
people tell of your wonderful deeds. 2 You say, "I choose the appointed time; it is I who judge with equity. 3 When the earth
and all its people quake, it is I who hold its pillars firm. 4 To the
arrogant I say, 'Boast no more,' and to the wicked, 'Do not lift up
your horns. 5 Do not lift your horns against heaven; do not speak
so defiantly.'" (NIV)

"How calm is he, how quiet are his words, yet how divine the rebuke."

A divine rebuke. From the past to the present, we are reminded that "tyrants
are in power, everything is unloosed, dissolution threatens all things" causing us to shudder (v. 3). While these power-mongers have great clout, intimi-
dating others, we need to know how God responds. Despite their apparent
power, he sets the appointed time to judge the wicked with justice (v. 3). He
puts these people in their place by commanding them not to boast in their
strength or "horns" (v. 4). He "rebukes the inane glories of the wicked, who
beyond measure exalt themselves in the day of their fancied power." In fact,
their arrogant boasting about their power brings a further reproof by God (v.
5). "For their abounding pride there is a double rebuke . . . Impudence before
God is madness. The outstretched neck of insolent pride is sure to provoke
his axe." God's divine reprimand is his way of humbling the proud in every
sector of society. They may flaunt their corrupted power and intimidate others for a while, but they will be firmly rebuked by a holy Judge.

Prayer. Lord, with evil running rampant throughout the world, I feel wickedness is getting the upper hand. Your response to evil reminds me of your
displeasure with all of its ugly forms. Enable me to walk in humility before
you; transform my life by your word and Spirit. Amen.

6 For no one on earth—from east or west, or even from the wilderness—should raise a defiant fist. 7 It is God alone who judges; he decides who will rise and who will fall. 8 For the LORD holds a cup in his hand that is full of foaming wine mixed with spices. He pours out the wine in judgment, and all the wicked must drink it, draining it to the dregs. 9 But as for me, I will always proclaim what God has done; I will sing praises to the God of Jacob. 10 For God says, "I will break the strength of the wicked, but I will increase the power of the godly." (NLT)

"Even now he is judging. His seat is not vacant; his authority is not abdicated; the Lord reigns evermore."

Divine justice. Despite all their corrupt power, arrogant people will be confronted by God one day. He exercises the sole ultimate authority to mete out divine justice (v. 6). As a result of his rightful role as judge, the nations around the world grow in dominance or fade away (v. 7). The intensity of his judgment cannot be minimized (v. 8). His wrath is analogous to a horrible drink forcibly swallowed by the wicked, illustrating the reality that "retribution is terrible, it is blood for blood, foaming vengeance for foaming malice" (v. 8). Jesus, the son of God, also broke the power of the proud and elevated those who recognized their need of him (v. 10). Reflecting Jesus' life requires us to love justice by living with uprightness and by depending on him to correct the injustices around us.

Prayer. Lord, I want you to bring immediate justice to those who are evil. Teach me to be patient, for you have your appointed time when you will judge equitably. Meanwhile, give me your mind to disdain the injustices in society, and the wisdom to respond in appropriate ways. Amen.

June 24   Psalm 76:1–6

1 God is known in Judah; his name is great in Israel. 2 His tabernacle is in Salem; his dwelling place also is in Zion. 3 There he broke the flaming arrows, the shield, the sword, and the weapons of war. *Selah* 4 You are resplendent, more majestic than the mountains of prey. 5 The stout-hearted were plundered, they sank into sleep; and none of the warriors could use his hands. 6 At your rebuke, God of Jacob, both rider and horse were cast into a dead sleep. (NASB)

"Without leaving his tranquil abode, he sent forth his word and snapped the arrows of his enemies before they could shoot them."

Our mighty warrior. In this first half of the psalm, Asaph points to God, who won the battles for his people. "The present Psalm is a most jubilant war song, a paean to the King of kings, the hymn of a theocratic nation in its divine power." His might is greater than the greatest military force against Israel (v. 3). His strength is not found in weapons but in his word of rebuke, which defeats his enemies (v. 6). God's power is not guided by his nature (v. 4). He is "glorious in holiness, and his terrible deeds are done in justice for the defense of the weak and the deliverance of the enslaved." He continues to fight on our behalf through our mighty warrior Jesus Christ, who defeated the strongest opponent, Satan, on the cross. Having defeated the devil, we can live victoriously and tell others confidently of God's greatness (v. 1).

Prayer. My King, I thank you that you have broken and shattered the powers of darkness through the death and resurrection of your Son, Jesus. By your indwelling Holy Spirit, I can experience victory over Satan and his demonic forces. Amen.

7 You, you indeed are to be feared, and who may stand in your presence, once you are angry? 8 You caused judgment to be heard from heaven; the earth feared and was still 9 when God arose to judgment, to save all the humble of the earth. *Selah* 10 For the wrath of mankind shall praise you; you will encircle yourself with a remnant of wrath. 11 Make vows to the LORD your God and fulfill them; all who are around him are to bring gifts to him who is to be feared. 12 He will cut off the spirit of princes; he is feared by the kings of the earth. (NASB)

"He who deserves to be praised, as our God does, should not have mere verbal homage, but substantial tribute."

Responding to God's victory. In this second half of the psalm, Asaph's comments now extend beyond Israel to the surrounding territories and rulers (vv. 11–12). How should they, and we, respond to battles clearly won by Almighty God? First, seeing his wrath, we should solemnly fear God (v. 7). Second, we should praise God's majestic nature, which his wrath reveals. The "most rampant evil is under the control of the Lord, and will in the end be overruled for his praise" (v. 10). Finally, we should live faithfully before the Lord for he has been faithful to us (vv. 11–12). "He keeps his promises, let not his people fail in theirs. He is their faithful God and deserves to have a faithful people." We do so with grateful praise and obedience to the Lord.

Prayer. Lord, in your sovereignty, you have used Jesus' suffering on the cross to make us recipients of your salvation. In turn, you receive praise around the globe for all you have done. Continue to work in people of all ages so that they will acknowledge your huge victory over Satan and come to know you personally. Amen.

1 I cry out to God; yes, I shout. Oh, that God would listen to me!
2 When I was in deep trouble, I searched for the Lord. All night
long I prayed, with hands lifted toward heaven, but my soul was
not comforted. 3 I think of God, and I moan, overwhelmed with
longing for his help. (NLT)

"This Psalm has much sadness in it, but we may be sure it will end well,
for it begins with prayer, and prayer never has an ill issue."

Despair before God. Asaph, a leader in David's Levitical choirs, is the writer
of this psalm. He begins on a note of despair, crying out to God. Even with
his weeping, seeking, and remembering God, he still could not find solace in
God (vv. 2–3). Spurgeon notes that God's attributes curiously have "a dark
side." Being confronted by his divine qualities, such as his perfect justice and
truth, can leave one feeling completely unworthy and unloved. As a result,
Asaph felt utterly crushed by life's burdens. Spurgeon, the great preacher,
shared these feelings. "Alas, my God, the writer of this exposition well knows
what thy servant Asaph meant, for his soul is familiar with the way of grief.
Deep glens and lonely caves of soul depressions, my spirit knows full well
your awful glooms." Committed followers of Jesus are not immune from the
depths of despair and depression. We must wisely and lovingly support those
who experience depression and other related suffering.

Prayer. Lord, depression has been stigmatized for too long, even among your
people. I am very thankful for those who are honest to admit their struggles
in this area. In your mercy, minister to them through individuals who can
understand and bring the care they desperately need. Please bring a degree
of peace to each troubled soul. Amen.

4 You kept my eyes from closing; I was too troubled to speak. 5 I thought about the former days, the years of long ago; 6 I remembered my songs in the night. My heart meditated and my spirit asked: 7 "Will the Lord reject forever? Will he never show his favor again? 8 Has his unfailing love vanished forever? Has his promise failed for all time? 9 Has God forgotten to be merciful? Has he in anger withheld his compassion?" (NIV)

"Thus with cord after cord unbelief is smitten and driven out of the soul: it raises questions and we will meet it with questions."

Sources of despair. When we go through a time of despondency we may find ourselves denying our pain in a number of injurious ways. Rather than escaping from our misery, the psalmist suggests a far better approach. We should take the time to search our inner life (v. 6).

> He did not cease from introspection, for he was resolved to find the bottoms of his sorrow, and trace it to its fountainhead. He made sure work of it by talking not with his mind only, but his inmost heart; it was heart work for him . . . He ransacked his experience, his memory, his intellect, his whole nature, his entire self, either to find comfort or to discover the reason why it was denied him.

What did he discover? Sleeplessness contributed to his despondency (v. 4). Spurgeon notes that when a dejected person loses sleep, the sadness only grows. In addition, some kinds of reminiscing can actually foster feelings of depression rather than joy (v. 5). It is a "sad calamity of a jaundiced mind to see nothing as it should be seen, but everything as through a veil of mist." Finally, the psalmist expressed a number of doubts in the form of questions (vv. 7–9). "Each one of the questions is a dart aimed at the very heart of despair." We then come to another *selah*, reminding us to ponder deeply the doubting questions and other causes of our despair.

Prayer. Lord, I am thankful that your word and your Spirit enable me to explore my inner life when I am feeling depressed. I am so glad that even when I cannot articulate the causes for my gloom, your Spirit prays for me with groans before you. Amen.

10 And I said, "This is my fate; the Most High has turned his hand against me." 11 But then I recall all you have done, O Lord; I remember your wonderful deeds of long ago. 12 They are constantly in my thoughts. I cannot stop thinking about your mighty works. 13 O God, your ways are holy. Is there any god as mighty as you? 14 You are the God of great wonders! You demonstrate your awesome power among the nations. 15 By your strong arm, you redeemed your people, the descendants of Jacob and Joseph. (NLT)

"Shall our trust be doubtful when his power is beyond all question? My soul see to it that these considerations banish thy mistrust."

Despair fades. Having wrestled with his questions, Asaph turns the corner in this section. "He has won the day, he talks reasonably now, and surveys the field with a cooler mind." Remembering God's goodness to himself and others, he accepts the grief which ultimately came from the sovereign hand of God (vv. 10–11). Now he does more than reminisce on the past; he meditates on God's works (v. 12). Meditation means to "lie down and ruminate" on God's revealed truth in Scripture. When we meditate on the word, we are reminded of God's great acts and his character (vv. 13–15). We move from despair to hope. "Herein is renewed reason for holy confidence. It would be a great wonder if we did not trust the wonder-working God." God's great acts of power and love bring us from a place of mistrust to a stronger and deeper trust in him.

Prayer. Lord, I am so thankful you are not silent, but have unmistakably revealed yourself in the course of world history. Since you have acted so powerfully in the past, I have confidence you are working out your purposes for my life in the present. You have turned my heart from despair to gladness. Amen.

June 29

Psalm 77:16–20

16 When the Red Sea saw you, O God, its waters looked and trembled! The sea quaked to its very depths. 17 The clouds poured down rain; the thunder rumbled in the sky. Your arrows of lightning flashed. 18 Your thunder roared from the whirlwind; the lightning lit up the world! The earth trembled and shook. 19 Your road led through the sea, your pathway through the mighty waters—a pathway no one knew was there! 20 You led your people along that road like a flock of sheep, with Moses and Aaron as their shepherds. (NLT)

"Therefore, with devout joy and full of consolation, we close this Psalm: the song of one who forgot how to speak and yet learned to sing far more sweetly than his fellows."

Renewed trust. This final section ends the psalm with a note of praise. The writer considers the events that enabled God's people to escape from the Egyptians. He could only conclude the Lord was displaying his might (vv. 16–19). Then the tone of the language changes. God's power is shown not for its own sake but to tenderly care for his people, who are like sheep. He is the shepherd who drives away the opposing threats by going ahead of his people (v. 20). The overall tenor of the entire psalm has also changed from despair to confidence. Spurgeon remarks, "The hymn now before us is for experienced saints only, but to them it will be of rare value as a transcript of their own inner conflict." With candor, the psalmist has provided us with wise insight: we can move on beyond darkness to joy, as we meditate on God's greatness revealed through history, including his victory over the forces of darkness and death.

Prayer. Lord, I am so thankful I do not need to be stuck in my own misery and pain. As I meditate on your power in the world, I see your love for your people, including me, throughout the ages. Thank you for defeating the strongest spiritual foe, Satan. Knowing this, I can live with confidence in you. Amen.

1 Listen, my people, to my instruction; incline your ears to the words of my mouth. 2 I will open my mouth in a parable; I will tell riddles of old, 3 which we have heard and known, and our fathers have told us. 4 We will not conceal them from their children, but we will tell the generation to come the praises of the LORD, and his power and his wondrous works that he has done. 5 For he established a testimony in Jacob, and appointed a law in Israel, which he commanded our fathers that they were to teach them to their children, 6 so that the generation to come would know, the children yet to be born, that they would arise and tell them to their children, 7 so that they would put their confidence in God and not forget the works of God, but comply with his commandments, 8 and not be like their fathers, a stubborn and rebellious generation, a generation that did not prepare its heart and whose spirit was not faithful to God. (NASB)

"[H]oliness towards God is the end we aim at, and not the filling of the head with speculative notions."

Heart obedience. Psalm 78 serves as a parable (v. 2) or an analogy between Israel and the church. This section (vv. 1–8) is a preface to the rest of the psalm. We should teach others the Bible (vv. 5–6), with its stories of God's gracious involvement in people's lives, both past and present (v. 4). The aim of this storytelling involves far more than imparting knowledge. People should be prompted to place their trust in the Lord and obey him (v. 7). However, history sadly reminds us that we disobey God because of the condition of the human heart (v. 8), which is "fickle as the winds, and changeful as the waves." The pages of sacred history continually remind us that obedience to God is possible only by a heart that is changed by the Holy Spirit.

Prayer. Lord, it is relatively easy to know and to teach your word, but it is much more difficult to obey it. I do not want my obedience to be based on duty or people's expectations. Continue transforming my heart and aligning my longing and my will with your word. Amen.

9 The sons of Ephraim were archers equipped with bows, yet they turned back on the day of battle. 10 They did not keep the covenant of God and refused to walk in his Law; 11 they forgot his deeds and his miracles that he had shown them. 12 He performed wonders before their fathers in the land of Egypt, in the field of Zoan. 13 He divided the sea and caused them to pass through, and he made the waters stand up like a heap. 14 Then he led them with the cloud by day and all the night with a light of fire. 15 He split the rocks in the wilderness and gave them plenty to drink like the ocean depths. 16 He brought forth streams from the rock and made waters run down like rivers. (NASB)

"Vows and promises were broken, idols were set up, and the living God was forsaken."

God's love spurned. The tribe of Ephraim is well prepared for battle but their faith and courage fail, forcing them to retreat (v. 9). The backdrop to this incident gives us insight. The Lord had entered into a covenant with Israel to protect his people, including during their days in the desert (vv. 12–16). However, they had violated their commitment to the agreement by deliberately refusing to obey God (v. 10). In their rebellion they forgot his incredible acts of loving care (v. 11). This was a heart issue. Spurgeon comments, "Grace cures bad memories; those who soon forget the merciful works of the Lord have need of teaching; they require to learn the divine art of holy memory." Our remembrance of all God has done for us fills us with awe and gratitude. We must be willing to repent of our own deliberate forgetfulness that leads us along the same path of disobedience travelled by those so long ago (v. 9).

Prayer. Almighty God, I am very thankful for the multitude of ways you have shown your love to me. When my heart has not been right, I have deliberately chosen to forget your love and have gone my own way. I ask for your forgiveness. Woo me with your love and strengthen my obedience. Amen.

17 Yet they still continued to sin against him, to rebel against the Most High in the desert. 18 And in their heart they put God to the test by asking for food that suited their taste. 19 Then they spoke against God; they said, "Can God prepare a table in the wilderness? 20 Behold, he struck the rock so that waters gushed out, and streams were overflowing; can he also provide bread? Will he prepare meat for his people?" 21 Therefore the LORD heard and was full of wrath; and a fire was kindled against Jacob, and anger also mounted against Israel, 22 because they did not believe in God and did not trust in his salvation. 23 Yet he commanded the clouds above and opened the doors of heaven; 24 he rained down manna upon them to eat, and gave them food from heaven. 25 Man ate the bread of angels; he sent them food in abundance. (NASB)

"They who will not be content will speak against providence even when it daily loads them with benefits."

The food test. Although God had been extremely generous toward his people by furnishing them with water in the desert (v. 20), they were not satisfied. They craved and demanded bread and meat (vv. 18, 20) and questioned whether God could meet their hankering for this food (v. 19). Their ultimatum tested God and his ability to cater to them (v. 18). "The sin began in their hearts, but it soon reached their tongues . . . To question the ability of one who is manifestly Almighty is to speak against him." How dare they question God who had already provided in the past! The root issue was unbelief or a lack of trust in him (v. 22). This is "the master sin, the crying sin . . . In the text it appears as if all Israel's other sins were as nothing compared with this." It is no wonder God is grieved and insulted when we question his power. When he does provide for us, he is not caving in to our demands, but is responding out of his undeserved lovingkindness (vv. 23–25).

Prayer. Lord, you have graciously provided in the past and I ask that you forgive me for questioning you and your power. Deepen my trust in you so that I may be content, knowing you will give me all that I need for life. Amen.

July 3   Psalm 78:26-31

26 He made the east wind blow in the sky and by his power he directed the south wind. 27 When he rained meat upon them like the dust, even winged fowl like the sand of the seas, 28 he let them fall in the midst of their camp, all around their dwellings. 29 So they ate and were well filled, and he satisfied their longing. 30 Yet before they had abandoned their longing, while their food was in their mouths, 31 the anger of God rose against them and killed some of their strongest ones, and subdued the choice men of Israel. (NASB)

"He showed them that when lust wins its desire it is disappointed, and by the way of satiety arrives at distaste."

The sin of greed. In response to the people's demand for bread and meat (v. 20), the Lord gave them an abundance of quails (v. 27; Num 11:31) they voraciously consumed (v. 29). Such ultimatums are often "a doubtful blessing, as easily acquired, and super-abounding riches generally are." Their greed had some negative consequences. They developed a revulsion for the food they had once craved (v. 30). "The food satiates, then it nauseates . . . they cried for it, they had it, and a curse with it." Also, God's anger at their greed led to the deaths of the strong and valiant (v. 31). The insatiable desire for more and more in today's consumerist society will leave us not only empty, but with an eventual distaste for our addictions. We will consume what we wrongly assume brings pleasure to us. "O my God, deny me my most urgent prayers sooner than answer them in displeasure. Better hunger and thirst after righteousness than to be well filled with sin's dainties."

Prayer. Lord, you have allowed me to see the danger of gratified desires. Forgive me for my selfish demands, leaving me soul-sick. Increase my hunger and thirst for you and your ways, for then I will be truly satisfied. Amen.

32 In spite of all this they still sinned and did not believe in his wonderful works. 33 So he brought their days to an end in futility, and their years to an end in sudden terror. 34 When he killed them, then they sought him, and they returned and searched diligently for God; 35 and they remembered that God was their rock, and the Most High God their Redeemer. 36 But they flattered him with their mouth and lied to him with their tongue. 37 For their heart was not steadfast toward him, nor were they faithful with his covenant. (NASB)

"There was no depth in their repentance; it was not heart work."

Shallow repentance. Crisis events, such as pandemics, often cause people to reconsider their relationship to God. This phenomenon is not unique to our day. When God's people suffered in the desert they eagerly turned to him (v. 34). They believed that their lives depended on God (v. 35). Such expressions of repentance appear satisfactory until we explore below the surface. The Israelites verbalized all the right statements to God, but their hearts were not fully committed to him (v. 37). "False on their knees, liars in their prayers. Mouth worship must be very detestable to God when dissociated from the heart." While the fear of death may evoke genuine contrition, in this case they expressed external remorse. This superficial repentance occurs when serious heart work is not thoroughly done and minds are not really set on the Lord. As a result, we can be "hot today for holiness, but cold towards it tomorrow." Genuine repentance extends beyond our words and tears; a changed heart is required.

Prayer. Father, I confess I have often come to you with half-hearted repentance while still clinging to what I love. Forgive me when I say all the right things and express sorrow but my heart has divided loyalties. Work in my heart so that I may genuinely turn from my wrongful ways and be more lovingly committed to you. Amen.

38 But he, being compassionate, forgave their wrongdoing and did not destroy them; and often he restrained his anger and did not stir up all his wrath. 39 So he remembered that they were only flesh, a wind that passes and does not return. 40 How often they rebelled against him in the wilderness and grieved him in the desert! 41 Again and again they tempted God, and pained the Holy One of Israel. (NASB)

"We see the fullness of God's compassion, but we never see all his wrath."

God's compassion. Yesterday's meditation focused on people's half-hearted repentance before God (vv. 36–37). Reflecting their shallow remorse, they constantly rebelled and tested him (v. 40). Before "they would believe in him they demanded signs, defying the Lord to do this and that, and acting as if he could be cajoled into being the minion of their lusts." Their actions deeply grieved him (v. 40), for they were biting the hand that fed them! Sandwiched between their questionable repentance and their outright rebellion, we surprisingly discover God restraining his anger by showing mercy and compassion (v. 38). "Not because of their pitiful and hypocritical pretensions to penitence, but because of his own real compassion for them he overlooked their provocations . . . he was slow, very slow, to anger." How could he respond this way? He knows how prone our fallen human nature is inclined to sin against him (v. 39). Although his wayward people were not faithful to their covenant with the Lord (v. 37), he kept loving them. As his people, we should not take for granted his grace but respond with gratitude for the lovingkindness he shows to us.

Prayer. My Lord, your extravagant love humbles me, especially when I realize how my thoughts, attitudes, words, and speech are not always pleasing to you. I do not want to take advantage of your grace. Your love fills me with gratitude so that I want to be increasingly aligned to you and your purposes. Amen.

42 They did not remember his power, the day when he redeemed them from the enemy, 43 when he performed his signs in Egypt and his marvels in the field of Zoan, 44 and turned their rivers to blood, and their streams, so that they could not drink. 45 He sent swarms of flies among them that devoured them, and frogs that destroyed them. 46 He also gave their crops to the grasshopper and the product of their labor to the locust. 47 He destroyed their vines with hailstones and their sycamore trees with frost. 48 He also turned their cattle over to the hailstones, and their herds to bolts of lightning. 49 He sent his burning anger upon them, fury and indignation and trouble, a band of destroying angels. 50 He leveled a path for his anger; he did not spare their souls from death, but turned their lives over to the plague, 51 and struck all the firstborn in Egypt, the first and best of their vigor in the tents of Ham. 52 But he led his own people out like sheep, and guided them in the wilderness like a flock; 53 he led them safely, so that they did not fear; but the sea engulfed their enemies. (NASB)

"He who forgets the natural returns of gratitude, may justly be charged with not remembering the obligation."

Forgetting God's power. In the desert, the people rebelled against God but he did not destroy them with his strength (v. 38). Experiencing his might through the plagues sent to the Egyptians should have humbled them (vv. 41–43). They saw him destroy their captors and preserve them (vv. 52–53). What a striking contrast they should never have forgotten, but they shockingly did (v. 42)! "Yet, it must have been difficult to forget it . . . it must have needed some more than usual effort to blot from the tablets of memory. It is probably meant that they practically, rather than actually, forgot." God could have struck them down in the desert, but instead he showed compassion (vv. 52–53). They should have responded with gratitude by loving and obeying God but they chose to forget his protective power. "The marvel is that the favored nation should live as if unmindful of it all, and yet such is human nature." We put aside our past experiences of God's powerful care at the risk of our own spiritual well-being.

Prayer. Lord, how could I fail to remember all the ways you have been so good? It should not happen, but history warns that I can forget. Fill me with gratitude so that I will not overlook all you have done. Amen.

54 So he brought them to his holy land, to this hill country which his right hand had gained. 55 He also drove out the nations from them and apportioned them as an inheritance by measurement, and had the tribes of Israel dwell in their tents. 56 Yet they tempted and rebelled against the Most High God and did not keep his testimonies, 57 but turned back and acted treacherously like their fathers; they turned aside like a treacherous bow. 58 For they provoked him with their high places and moved him to jealousy with their carved images. (NASB)

"Idols of any sort are highly abhorrent to God, and we must see to it that we keep ourselves from them through divine grace."

Pursuing other idols. The Lord was gracious to his people, leading them from the wilderness to the land he had promised to Abraham (vv. 54–55). We would expect to see them joyfully worshipping the Lord, who had been so faithful to them despite their past unfaithfulness, but they continued disobeying and testing God (v. 56). "They had left their nomadic habits, but not their tendencies to wander from God." Their actions were shocking in light of his faithfulness to them. Now they rebelled and forgot God, worshipping other tangible gods or idols (v. 58). God does not want us to love anything that would usurp his rightful claim to be our first love. He desires that we worship and love him with our whole being (Deut 6:5) because he is jealous for our love (v. 58). We must reject modern-day idolatry that places possessions or ambitions, status, and achievements above our love for Christ.

Prayer. Lord, what are the idols in my heart that control my actions? I confess I have pursued gods that have taken first place in my life. Deliver my heart and mind from being attached to them. I want to turn away from my distorted loves because I long to love you wholeheartedly! Amen.

July 8   Psalm 78:59–64

59 When God heard them, he was filled with wrath and he utterly rejected Israel; 60 so that he abandoned the dwelling place at Shiloh, the tent which he had pitched among people, 61 and he gave up his strength to captivity and his glory into the hand of the enemy. 62 He also turned his people over to the sword, and was filled with wrath at his inheritance. 63 Fire devoured his young men, and his virgins had no wedding songs. 64 His priests fell by the sword, and his widows could not weep. (NASB)

"He cast his idolatrous people from his favour, and left them to themselves, and their own devices."

Consequences. Having deliberately forgotten the power of God (vv. 42–53) and himself (vv. 54–58), they would now face the consequences of pursuing other gods. God was angry to the nth degree (v. 59) because idolatry led his people away from him. Also, God withdrew the Shekinah glory, or his presence (v. 60), symbolized by the capture of the ark by the Philistines. With his presence gone and his displeasure present, Shiloh was completely ruined. Finally, the Israelites lost their power because God's strength had been withdrawn (v. 61). As a result of their idolatry, they experienced defeat, death, and grief (vv. 62–64). The divine power that had protected them would now be used to discipline them. Rather than being delivered from their enemies, they would be punished by their adversaries. When we push God aside to pursue our idols, we quench the Holy Spirit (1 Thess 5:19). Rather than experiencing his enablement, we greatly diminish the awareness of God's strengthening presence in us.

Prayer. Lord, I confess that I have totally neglected you in my pursuit of other gods. By doing this, I have smothered the Holy Spirit's working in my life. This is not the way to live! Rather than facing more personal setbacks and grief, I come in repentance to you, the One who still loves me. Amen.

65 Then the Lord awoke as if from sleep, like a warrior overcome by wine. 66 He drove his adversaries backward; he put on them an everlasting disgrace. 67 He also rejected the tent of Joseph, and did not choose the tribe of Ephraim, 68 but chose the tribe of Judah, Mount Zion, which he loved. 69 And he built his sanctuary like the heights, like the earth which he has established forever. 70 He also chose his servant David and took him from the sheepfolds; 71 from the care of the ewes with nursing lambs he brought him to shepherd Jacob his people, and Israel his inheritance. 72 So he shepherded them according to the integrity of his heart, and guided them with his skillful hands. (NASB)

"It was an election of a sovereignly gracious kind, and it operated practically by making the chosen man a willing servant of the Lord."

God's gracious sovereignty. Israel had sadly disregarded their God and they experienced the tragic consequences. "This was the lowest depth; from this point things will take a gracious turn." God now takes action by defeating the Philistines, their enemies (vv. 65–66). He also addresses those who were steeped in religious idolatry (v. 67). In their place, God chooses another tribe, Judah, to become paramount in the nation. For example, God selects Mount Zion as the place where his temple will be built (vv. 68–69). Also, he appoints a new leader, David, who "was upright before God, and never swerved in heart from the obedient worship of Jehovah. Whatever faults he had, he was unfeignedly sincere in his allegiance to Israel's superior king" (vv. 70–72). From the tribe of Judah and David's lineage, Jesus our Savior would come. It may seem that the consequences of our disobedience disrupt and sideline God's plans. However, his ultimate sovereign purposes are not derailed, but rather are eventually fulfilled. This lengthy psalm provides us with hope in God's grace and sovereignty during times of disobedience.

Prayer. Heavenly Father, I am humbled by your hand of discipline that often brings sorrow. I am also humbled by your heart of grace that enables me to fulfill your sovereign purposes. Rather than chasing after idols, I want to be unwavering in my love and commitment to follow you. Amen.

1 O God, pagan nations have conquered your land, your special possession. They have defiled your holy temple and made Jerusalem a heap of ruins. 2 They have left the bodies of your servants as food for the birds of heaven. The flesh of your godly ones has become food for the wild animals. 3 Blood has flowed like water all around Jerusalem; no one is left to bury the dead. 4 We are mocked by our neighbors, an object of scorn and derision to those around us. 5 O LORD, how long will you be angry with us? Forever? How long will your jealousy burn like fire? 6 Pour out your wrath on the nations that refuse to acknowledge you—on kingdoms that do not call upon your name. 7 For they have devoured your people Israel, making the land a desolate wilderness. (NLT)

"Jerusalem, the beloved city, the joy of the nation, the abode of her God, was totally wrecked."

God's jealousy. The psalmist provides a descriptive glimpse into the destruction of Jerusalem and the impact on its citizens (vv. 1–4). When they plundered the city they desecrated God's holy temple (v. 1). They also killed and put to shame his people (vv. 2–3). After pillaging and defiling the city and its citizens, their cruel work was completed. The writer cries out to God, asking how long his jealous anger will persist toward his people (v. 5). "There was great cause for the Lord to be jealous, since idols had been set up, and Israel had gone aside from his worship." God's jealous love demands that his people not chase after other gods, but exclusively love him. On the other side of the coin, he is jealous for his covenant-people, and the psalmist rightfully asks when God is going to punish the aggressors who disdain him (v. 6). How can these cruelties continue against God's own people whom he has jealously loved for centuries (v. 7)? His jealousy moves him both to discipline us when we sin and to judge those who reject him.

Prayer. Lord, I confess I often do not consider that you are a jealous God. With fresh perspective I see why my sins grieve you so much. In light of today's meditation, I am so glad Jesus bore your anger on the cross. Yet, I accept your discipline flowing out of your jealous love for me. May I reciprocate by increasingly loving you! Amen.

8 Do not hold us guilty for the sins of our ancestors! Let your compassion quickly meet our needs, for we are on the brink of despair. 9 Help us, O God of our salvation! Help us for the glory of your name. Save us and forgive our sins for the honor of your name. 10 Why should pagan nations be allowed to scoff, asking, "Where is their God?" Show us your vengeance against the nations, for they have spilled the blood of your servants. 11 Listen to the moaning of the prisoners. Demonstrate your great power by saving those condemned to die. 12 O Lord, pay back our neighbors seven times for the scorn they have hurled at you. 13 Then we your people, the sheep of your pasture, will thank you forever and ever, praising your greatness from generation to generation. (NLT)

"From the direst calamities God's glory springs, and the dark days of his people become the prelude to unusual displays of the Lord's love and power."

God's glory. When we are in dire straits with our world falling apart, it is not uncommon to cry out to God to deliver us. Aware of his people's grievous sin, the psalmist calls to the Lord with a similar sentiment for national deliverance (v. 8). However, the writer goes beyond their problems to God's glorious name (v. 9). "This is masterly pleading. No argument has such force as this. God's majesty was tarnished in the eyes of the heathen by the defeat of his people, and the profanation of his temple; therefore, his distressed servants implore his aid, that his great name may no more be the scorn of blaspheming enemies." God's supremacy demands showing justice toward those who mock him (vv. 10, 12) and showing mercy to his afflicted people (v. 11). Then the Lord's name is exalted and for this reason we, as his people, praise him (v. 13). Our life's primary focus should not be on our deliverance, but to make known God's extraordinary mercy and justice.

Prayer. Father, I confess that many a time I am consumed with you bailing me out of my problems so life can be trouble-free and more enjoyable. You have reminded me that regardless of my circumstances, I should be ultimately concerned for your glory so that you will be exalted above all other names in the world. Amen.

1 Hear us, Shepherd of Israel, you who lead Joseph like a flock. You who sit enthroned between the cherubim, shine forth 2 before Ephraim, Benjamin and Manasseh. Awaken your might; come and save us. 3 Restore us, O God; make your face shine on us, that we may be saved. 4 How long, LORD God Almighty, will your anger smolder against the prayers of your people? 5 You have fed them with the bread of tears; you have made them drink tears by the bowlful. 6 You have made us an object of derision to our neighbors, and our enemies mock us. 7 Restore us, God Almighty; make your face shine on us, that we may be saved. (NIV)

"The best turn is not that of circumstances but of character."

The need for renewal. When difficulties fill us with despair, we are quick to cry out for God's help (v. 1). This was the case with the tribes of Israel and Judah facing military defeat and its consequences (vv. 2, 4–6). We often want God's deliverance, but nothing more (v. 2). However, in his mercy "God will reveal his grace, and only there can we hope to commune with him." It is in his presence we ask him to "restore us" (v. 3). On a personal level this request involves a spiritual renovation of character. This divine work begins at conversion and extends to those who have wandered away from the Lord. We can be confident this renewal project can be accomplished, for God is our shepherd who cares for his people (v. 1), our Almighty God (vv. 4, 7), and our faithful, covenant-keeping LORD (v. 19). Since he is the primary change agent, this restoration process brings his smiling favor upon us (vv. 3, 7, 19). It is in our times of need and brokenness that we are most aware of our dependence on Jesus our Shepherd to restore and change us by his Spirit.

Prayer. Lord Almighty, the brokenness and ashes of my life are not in vain. I want you to restore my walk with you with a greater sense of your presence. I know this means allowing you to renovate the damaged areas of my life. I place my confidence in you, my Shepherd, who indwells me through the Holy Spirit. Gracious Father, I desire your favor and smile on my life. Amen.

July 13   Psalm 80:8–11

8 You transplanted a vine from Egypt; you drove out the nations and planted it. 9 You cleared the ground for it, and it took root and filled the land. 10 The mountains were covered with its shade, the mighty cedars with its branches. 11 Its branches reached as far as the Sea, its shoots as far as the River. (NIV)

> "The Lord has planted us, we are growing downward, 'rooting roots,' and by his grace we are also advancing in manifest enlargement."

The life of renewal. Israel is described as a vine that was brought out of Egypt and planted in the land God had promised them (vv. 8–9). They could not take the credit for this. The thrice repeated "you" reminds us that Israel's new location became a reality because of God's singular action. For how else could a small and weak vine survive apart from God's care? Only the divine Gardener could make the nation grow and prosper (vv. 10–11). "This analogy might be applied to the experience of every believer in Jesus." It has always been God's intent to see his people mature so we can have a growing sphere of influence. He chose us so that we may bear fruit for his glory (John 15:16) and reveal his grace through us.

Prayer. Lord, you are like a horticulturalist who intimately watches over me and provides what is needed for my growth. Only you could produce the character of Jesus in my life. Continue to do your inward work in me so that my outward life will demonstrate the life-giving power of your Spirit! Amen.

July 14   Psalm 80:12–19

12 Why have you broken down its walls so that all who pass by
pick its grapes? 13 Boars from the forest ravage it, and insects
from the fields feed on it. 14 Return to us, God Almighty! Look
down from heaven and see! Watch over this vine, 15 the root
your right hand has planted, the son you have raised up for
yourself. 16 Your vine is cut down, it is burned with fire; at your
rebuke your people perish. 17 Let your hand rest on the man at
your right hand, the son of man you have raised up for yourself.
18 Then we will not turn away from you; revive us, and we will
call on your name. 19 Restore us, LORD God Almighty; make
your face shine on us, that we may be saved. (NIV)

"When he visits our souls anew we shall be revivified, and our praise shall
ascend unto the name of the Triune God."

The pathway to renewal. If we think we live a renewed life by our own effort,
we will sadly fall far short. Such moralistic attempts tragically fail because of
our own sinfulness. We then mercifully realize we, like a neglected house in
need of repair, must ask God to restore us (v. 14). He does this by elevating
his right-hand man, the Messiah, Jesus Christ (v. 17). He is the starting point
in our life with God, for he brings eternal life to us. We respond by calling him to do his good work in our lives so we may obey God (vv. 18–19).
Again, this desire to obey him requires more than sheer willpower. "It is in
Christ we abide faithful; because he lives we live also. There is no hope of
our perseverance apart from him . . . he is our life." We have confidence with
him renewing us because our God is the great I AM, who has made an eternal
covenant with his people (v. 19).

Prayer. Lord, thank you for restoring and renewing my life through your
Son, Jesus Christ. I am thankful for the abundant life he offers by dwelling
within me. I am thankful for your grace in allowing me to experience your
favor and blessing. Amen.

1 Sing for joy to God our strength; shout joyfully to the God of Jacob. 2 Raise a song, strike the tambourine, the sweet sounding lyre with the harp. 3 Blow the trumpet at the new moon, at the full moon, on our feast day. 4 For it is a statute for Israel, an ordinance of the God of Jacob. 5 He established it as a testimony in Joseph when he went throughout the land of Egypt. I heard a language I did not know. (NASB)

"For our part we delight in full bursts of praise . . . the heartiness of universal congregational song."

Public praise. The call for the congregation to worship the Lord provides some insights into corporate praise. The psalm's context centers on God's faithfulness to his people by delivering them out of slavery (v. 5a). As they are to testify to his deliverance, we are to praise God for our spiritual deliverance through Jesus Christ. He has a rightful claim to our worship. The Lord is both the cause and object of our praise because he strengthens and sustains his people (v. 1). Therefore, it is appropriate to set aside a particular time to celebrate God's salvation (v. 3). Spurgeon exhorts us, "let us feel the same exultation, and never speak of the Sabbath as though it could be other than 'a delight' and 'honorable.'" Setting aside a time to worship is not an option, but is mandated by God (v. 4). This divine requirement should lead to genuine praise (vv. 1, 2), not perfunctory worship! With our voices and instruments the expressions of worship flow from joyful hearts, for "Jehovah can only be adored with the heart, and that music is the best for his service which gives the heart most play."

Prayer. Father, sometimes my heart feels "down" when I consider tragic world events, such as acts of terrorism or a pandemic. However, Scripture reminds me to meet with your people to praise you for all you have done for us through Jesus Christ. As churches around the world praise you, the international celebration is a divine counterbalance to global tragedies. Amen.

6 "I relieved his shoulder of the burden, his hands were freed from the basket. 7 You called in trouble and I rescued you; I answered you in the hiding place of thunder; I put you to the test at the waters of Meribah. *Selah* 8 Hear, my people, and I will admonish you; Israel, if you would listen to me! 9 There shall be no strange god among you; nor shall you worship a foreign god. 10 I, the LORD, am your God, who brought you up from the land of Egypt; open your mouth wide and I will fill it." (NASB)

"The story of Israel is only our own history in another shape."

Recall the past. The psalmist twice recounts the deliverance of God's people from slavery (vv. 6, 10). Having heard their distressful cries to him, he shows his power *and* his compassionate heart. With such situations, we would expect them, and ourselves, to show gratitude with unreserved allegiance to the Lord. "Since God does not forsake us in our need, we ought never to forsake him at any time." The Lord tests our hearts to see how committed we are to him. Regrettably, the Israelites fail the test, having doubted and questioned God's love for them in the desert (v. 7). Our response is often similar. "God has heard us, delivered us, liberated us, and too often our unbelief makes the wretched return of mistrust, murmuring, and rebellion." Despite their past failure, God mercifully appeals to his people to turn away from idols and give their allegiance him (v. 9). He alone can supply all that they need in life (v. 11). "Because he had brought them out of Egypt he could do great things for them. He had proved his power and his good will; it remained only for his people to believe in him and ask large things of him." We are to remember the past and be committed to the Lord, who is faithful to us.

Prayer. Father, I tend to wander from you. I frequently forget you are testing my heart. When I consider the past, I realize I have failed the test. Forgive me! However, when I think about how faithful you have been to me, I renew my allegiance to you with gratitude! Amen.

July 17   Psalm 81:11–16

11 "But my people did not listen to my voice, and Israel did not obey me. 12 So I gave them over to the stubbornness of their heart, to walk by their own plans. 13 Oh that my people would listen to me, that Israel would walk in my ways! 14 I would quickly subdue their enemies and turn my hand against their adversaries. 15 Those who hate the LORD would pretend to obey him, and their time of punishment would be forever. 16 But I would feed you with the finest of the wheat, and with honey from the rock I would satisfy you." (NASB)

"The Lord can do great things for an obedient people."

The blessings of repentance. The psalmist laments that when our allegiance to God wanes we will choose a direction opposing God's will (v. 12). He grieves when this occurs (v. 13). "The condescending love of God expresses itself in painful regrets for Israel's sin and punishment . . . A God of mercy cannot see men heaping up sorrow for themselves through their sins without feeling his compassion excited toward them." He would have done much for his people if they had only followed him (vv. 14–15). They have paid the price for their wickedness. Fortunately, when we do turn back to the Lord, he graciously supplies us with more than we could ever expect (v. 16). Even though the psalmist is using hyperbole, he declares that God can do great things for us when we obey him. Let us allow God to use the hard times to soften our hard hearts and turn us back to him to experience his generous blessings!

Prayer. Lord, I confess that my soul is famished and I accept responsibility for my plight. When I see how much you want to bless me based on your unfathomable love, by your grace I turn aside from all empty things and allow you to satisfy my soul with your incredible riches. Amen.

1 God has taken his place in the divine council; in the midst of the gods he holds judgment: 2 "How long will you judge unjustly and show partiality to the wicked? *Selah* 3 Give justice to the weak and the fatherless; maintain the right of the afflicted and the destitute. 4 Rescue the weak and the needy; deliver them from the hand of the wicked." 5 They have neither knowledge nor understanding, they walk about in darkness; all the foundations of the earth are shaken. 6 I said, "You are gods, sons of the Most High, all of you; 7 nevertheless, like men you shall die, and fall like any prince." 8 Arise, O God, judge the earth; for you shall inherit all the nations! (ESV)

"We have here a clear proof that all Psalms and hymns need not be direct expressions of praise to God . . . he [Asaph] was praising God when he rebuked the sin which dishonoured him."

Unjust judges. There are various interpretations of who the "gods" in verse 1 are. Spurgeon views them as judges. "They are gods to other men, but he is GOD to them. He lends them his name, and this is their authority for acting as judges" in their offices. They are rebuked for their unjust and corrupt dealings, especially among the poor and the orphans (vv. 3–4). Unjust judges who have little regard for equitable ruling for all must keep in mind that they too will die like anyone else (v. 7). They must remember they are accountable to God, the one great judge, who will declare his verdict on all corrupt and unjust rulers (v. 8). "Come thou Judge of all mankind, put the bad judges to thy bar and end their corruption and baseness." This poignant psalm is a somber reminder: we are to love and embrace justice in our own lives and support others who are seeking justice for those who have very little voice in society.

Prayer. Lord, your word frequently addresses the sins of injustice and admonishes your people to love those who are oppressed in society. Stir my heart to pray for and support those who are addressing these injustices. Help me to act fairly toward all people, without prejudice. Amen.

July 19   **Psalm 83:1–8**

1 God, do not remain quiet; do not be silent and, God, do not be still. 2 For behold, your enemies make an uproar, and those who hate you have exalted themselves. 3 They make shrewd plans against your people, and conspire together against your treasured ones. 4 They have said, "Come, and let's wipe them out as a nation, so that the name of Israel will no longer be remembered." 5 For they have conspired together with one mind; they make a covenant against you: 6 the tents of Edom and the Ishmaelites, Moab and the Hagrites; 7 Gebal, Ammon, and Amalek, Philistia with the inhabitants of Tyre; 8 Assyria also has joined them; they have become a help to the children of Lot. *Selah* (NASB)

"At the Lord himself they aim through the sides of his saints."

Our enemies. Spurgeon gives the psalm's historical context based on 2 Chronicles 20. Jehoshaphat, king of Judah, and his people are facing their numerous enemies who have made an alliance to conquer Judah. Given the size of the confederate forces in comparison to Judah's troops, defeat appears certain. Just as their enemies were an undeniable fact, "how thoroughgoing are the foes of the church . . . men would be glad to cast the church out of the world because it rebukes them, and is thus a standing menace to their sinful peace." But here is another aspect of reality: our enemies are God's ("your") enemies (v. 2). Thus, we sense the urgency of the psalmist's prayer. With their hostile attitude toward the Lord, they form an alliance to make war against him (v. 5). People's opposition to the gospel is a reflection of their antipathy of God and his kingdom. Their animus, which we may personally experience, is directed at God, who is their true enemy.

Prayer. Lord, all too often I have viewed those who are antagonistic to the gospel as my adversaries. However, I too was an enemy of God until your grace changed my heart. Help me to love those who are resistant to the ways your Son, Jesus practiced and taught. Amen.

9 Deal with them as with Midian, as with Sisera and Jabin at the river of Kishon, 10 who were destroyed at En-dor, who became like dung for the ground. 11 Make their nobles like Oreb and Zeeb, and all their leaders like Zebah and Zalmunna, 12 who said, "Let's possess for ourselves the pastures of God." 13 My God, make them like the whirling dust, like chaff before the wind. 14 Like fire that burns the forest, and like a flame that sets the mountains on fire, 15 so pursue them with your heavy gale, and terrify them with your storm. (NASB)

"Faith delights to light upon precedents, and quote them before the Lord."

Confidence in God. When we view people who oppose the gospel not as our adversaries, but God's, this perspective reshapes our prayers. The spiritual conflict does not ultimately target us, but God himself. They are seeking to usurp everything that belongs to him (v. 12). Rather than angrily reacting in prayer when we have been insulted, we can intercede for them, knowing that they are attacking the Lord. Also, we have confidence in him because he has continually been faithful to us. As he had defeated the enemies in the past, he will do so again on behalf of his people (vv. 9–10). How amazing this is, when the odds were against Israel, whose adversaries far outnumbered them. Yet all their enemies were defeated! God revels in showing his strength through us who appear weak in society (2 Cor 4:7). It is appropriate for *selah* to be inserted before verse 9, where this prayer begins. Our prayers often lack a biblical perspective when we are in a panic. Spurgeon reminds us this hurry creates a lack of solid trust in God. We need the pause to reflect on God's character and his word, so that we can talk to him with confidence about those overwhelming circumstances.

Prayer. Almighty God, enable me to pray with confidence and love for those who oppose your ways. I pray this for your Name's sake, which is dishonored by those who resist you. By your grace enable me to love them as you do, for I am weak. Amen.

16–18 Knock the breath right out of them, so they're gasping for breath, gasping, "God." Bring them to the end of their rope, and leave them there dangling, helpless. Then they'll learn your name: "God," the one and only High God on earth. (MSG)

"Shame has often weaned men from their idols, and set them upon seeking the Lord."

Praying for God's enemies. We are disheartened and even angered when we hear accounts of God's people being persecuted for religious or ideological reasons. Our first impulse may be to see God punish the oppressors for their violent acts. The psalmist instructs us how we should intercede. We should pray that they will seek the Lord (v. 16) and come to know his majesty (v. 18). "The godless race of humanity disregards this, and yet at times the wonderful works of the Lord compel the most unwilling to adore his majesty." Spurgeon mentions that Israel's enemies' attitude shifted from disregard to fearing God after seeing his display of power against them (2 Chr 20:29). It should be our desire to see Jehovah honored among those who were his former enemies. They may gladly surrender out of reverence for God or by fearful necessity after seeing him vindicate his people and defeat his enemies (v. 17).

Prayer. Lord, do your mighty work among those who strongly oppose you. Change my heart so that I will pray for them to eventually and gladly acknowledge you. May they seek you, be drawn to your love, and gladly surrender to Jesus Christ. Accomplish your purposes so that you receive all the honor you rightfully deserve. Amen.

July 22   Psalm 84:1-4

1 How lovely is your dwelling place, O LORD of Heaven's Armies.
2 I long, yes, I faint with longing to enter the courts of the LORD.
With my whole being, body and soul, I will shout joyfully to the
living God. 3 Even the sparrow finds a home, and the swallow
builds her nest and raises her young at a place near your altar, O
LORD of Heaven's Armies, my King and my God! 4 What joy for
those who can live in your house, always singing your praises.
(NLT)

"It was God himself that he pined for, the only living and true God."

A holy longing. The psalmist addresses the desires of the human heart. At
first glance, one might assume the psalmist's greatest longing is to enjoy being in a religious place of worship such as the temple (vv. 1–2). While this is
understandable and good, our best aspiration should be for the Lord himself
(v. 2). "The desire was deep and insatiable—the very soul of the man was
yearning for his God." To emphasize his deep hunger for him, the writer
piles on three words to describe his "holy lovesickness" for God (v. 2). To
illustrate further, he observes the birds which make their home where God's
presence dwelled and longs for the same himself (v. 3). With this craving he
calls out to God. "The psalmist declared that he could not remain silent in his
desires, but began to cry out for God and his house; he wept, he sighed, he
pleaded for the privilege." The fruit of enjoying God's presence is expressed
by worship (v. 4). Our soul's joy is to personally know God and to enjoy
him forever. An interlude is appropriately placed here. "It is worthwhile to
pause and meditate upon the prospect of dwelling with God and praising
him throughout eternity."

Prayer. Lord, I confess it is far too easy to get caught up in religious settings
and activities. Reorient and shape my heart for you by creating a fiercer hunger for your presence. This will not only bring stronger satisfaction, but will
lead me into a greater love and joyful adoration for you. Amen.

5 What joy for those whose strength comes from the LORD, who have set their minds on a pilgrimage to Jerusalem. 6 When they walk through the Valley of Weeping, it will become a place of refreshing springs. The autumn rains will clothe it with blessings. 7 They will continue to grow stronger, and each of them will appear before God in Jerusalem. 8 O LORD God of Heaven's Armies, hear my prayer. Listen, O God of Jacob. (NLT)

"A company of pilgrims who had left their hearts at home would be no better than a caravan of carcasses, quite unfit to blend with living saints in adoring the living God."

The spiritual journey. At the age of five, Spurgeon read and fell in love with *The Pilgrim's Progress*, which he read more than a hundred times during his life.* Now the psalmist shifts from those who worship at the temple to those who make the journey to Jerusalem. This pilgrimage to worship God is a metaphor of the Christian life. God blesses us with his divine approval when we have a genuine heart for him on this spiritual pilgrimage (v. 5). It is necessary to have this hunger for God because the journey is often difficult, with many spiritually dry times. When these seasons in life occur, he is available to refresh us (v. 6). When we depend on God's resources, including the community of believers who walk with us, we gain spiritual strength (v. 7). However, the pilgrimage is more than the journey itself or the fellowship with others. The psalmist reminds us that the primary purpose is to encounter and experience God (v. 7). "This was the end of the pilgrims' march . . . to appear before God was the object of each devout Israelite . . . Unless we realize the presence of God we have done nothing; the mere gathering together is nothing worth." This desire should be our personal prayer to the Lord (v. 8).

Prayer. Lord, you know the powerful impact this passage has had on my life. As I journey through life with your people, keep me focused on you, and continue to refresh and sustain me with your spiritual resources. Amen.

---

* Nettles, *Living by Revealed Truth,* 22. This classic was one of Spurgeon's most valued books besides the Bible.

9 O God, look with favor upon the king, our shield! Show favor to the one you have anointed. 10 A single day in your courts is better than a thousand anywhere else! I would rather be a gatekeeper in the house of my God than live the good life in the homes of the wicked. 11 For the LORD God is our sun and our shield. He gives us grace and glory. The LORD will withhold no good thing from those who do what is right. 12 O LORD of Heaven's Armies, what joy for those who trust in you. (NLT)

"God has all good, there is no good apart from him."

The holy longing met. With this personal encounter of God in mind (v. 7), the psalmist unequivocally states the blessing of knowing God and being in his presence (v. 10). There is nothing like it! "To feel his love, to rejoice in the person of the anointed Saviour, to survey the promises and feel the power of the Holy Ghost in applying precious truth to the soul, is a joy which worldlings cannot understand but which true believers are ravished with. Even a glimpse at the love of God is better than ages spent in the pleasures of sense." When we personally know God, we benefit with his strength to live the Christian life (v. 11). "The Lord has both grace and glory in infinite abundance . . . Grace makes us walk uprightly and this secures every covenant blessing to us." For our part, we must genuinely place our trust in the Lord (v. 12). With a commitment to Jesus Christ, our long search for spiritual longing is satisfied.

Prayer. Lord, I confess that following you is not always easy. However, the joy of knowing you far surpasses life's challenges. I am grateful that you are with me every step of the way. I look forward to the day when I see you face to face. Amen.

1 Lᴏʀᴅ, you showed favor to your land; you restored the fortunes of Jacob. 2 You forgave the guilt of your people; you covered all their sin. *Selah* 3 You withdrew all your fury; you turned away from your burning anger. 4 Restore us, God of our salvation, and cause your indignation toward us to cease. 5 Will you be angry with us forever? Will you prolong your anger to all generations? 6 Will you not revive us again, so that your people may rejoice in you? 7 Show us your mercy, Lᴏʀᴅ, and grant us your salvation. (NASB)

"Because the God of Israel has been so rich in favor in bygone years, therefore he is entreated to reform and restore his backsliding nation."

Spiritual restoration. The psalmist prays for the spiritual revitalization of his people who have fallen away from the Lord. For hope, he looks to former times when God turned from anger to forgive based on his lovingkindness (vv. 1–3). The psalmist rhetorically asks if God will do it again (vv. 5–6). With this expectancy, spiritual renewal can occur when individuals return to God (v. 4). "This [is] the main business . . . It is not that God needs turning from his anger so much as we need turning from our sin; here is the hinge of the whole matter." Attempting to do this by sheer willpower is futile because we need God's grace to change our minds and hearts. He can revive us as he has revived others. Having experienced his unfailing love (v. 7), our lives are filled with joy (v. 6). "Those who were revived would rejoice not only in the new life but in the Lord who was the author of it. Joy in the Lord is the ripest fruit of grace, all revivals and renewals lead up to it."

Prayer. Father, my heart's tendency to wander away from you is no different than those of past generations. I give up my own futile attempts to resuscitate my spiritual life, and I surrender to you. Rejuvenate me by your Spirit so that I will follow you with joy. Amen.

8 I will hear what God the LORD will say; for he will speak peace to his people, to his godly ones; and may they not turn back to foolishness.9 Certainly his salvation is near to those who fear him, that glory may dwell in our land. 10 Graciousness and truth have met together; righteousness and peace have kissed each other. 11 Truth sprouts from the earth, and righteousness looks down from heaven. 12 Indeed, the LORD will give what is good, and our land will yield its produce. 13 Righteousness will go before him and will make his footsteps into a way. (NASB)

"[W]hen we are brought back to follow that which is good, the Lord abundantly enriches us with good things."

Evidence of spiritual restoration. After warning us not to wander from God (v. 8), the psalmist provides signs of spiritual restoration. Spiritually renewed people enjoy God's favor marked by his love, faithfulness, and peace shown to them (v. 10). Having experienced God's goodness, believers enjoy restored relationships marked by the same faithfulness or truthfulness with one another. A "hallowed harmony" exists between God in heaven and his people on earth (v. 11). His glory is not only seen in heaven but on earth whenever we honor him by our obedience (v. 9). Living with his favor allows us to experience the blessing of peace (v. 8) and good gifts which would be consistent with our spiritual well-being (v. 12). These blessings are possible only through Jesus Christ, who has reconciled us to our heavenly Father.

Prayer. Lord, you have accepted me as your child through Jesus. By your grace, now help me to be reconciled to those with whom broken relationships exist. I want to live rightly among them with the same love and mercy you have shown me. I long to experience your true peace and wholeness with you and them. Amen.

1 Incline your ear, LORD, and answer me; for I am afflicted and needy. 2 Protect my soul, for I am godly; you my God, save your servant who trusts in you. 3 Be gracious to me, LORD, for I call upon you all day long. 4 Make the soul of your servant joyful, for to you, LORD, I lift up my soul. 5 For you, Lord, are good, and ready to forgive, and abundant in mercy to all who call upon you. 6 Listen, LORD, to my prayer; and give your attention to the sound of my pleading! 7 On the day of my trouble I will call upon you, for you will answer me. (NASB)

"There can be no reason for praying if there be no expectation of the Lord's answering."

Persistent prayer. At times we plead incessantly with God to answer our requests. More important than the frequency of our prayers is the posture of our hearts before him. David is a good example because he is rightly positioned to call on the Lord. David unequivocally states his neediness, which reflects his humble dependence on God (v. 1). He also trusts God (v. 2), who is kind, forgiving, and full of lovingkindness (v. 5). With the correct heart attitude, he calls out to God throughout the day (v. 3). These prayers are not "vain repetitions" to impress others, which Jesus criticized (Matt 6:7 KJV). Instead, David's prayers are similar to a needy child's earnest repetition of the same simple phrases. Not fearing our Father will rebuke us, we can persistently cry out, expecting he will answer us (v. 7). "Our experience confirms us in the belief that Jehovah, the living God really does aid those who call upon him, and therefore we pray and mean to pray . . . because we really, indeed, and of a truth, find it to be a practical and effectual means of obtaining help from God in the hour of need."

Prayer. Lord, sometimes I feel like giving up on repeating my requests to you. You have reminded and encouraged me to be more persistent in my prayer life. I can do this by assuming the right heart posture, knowing you love your needy children. Amen.

July 28   Psalm 86:8–13

8 There is no one like you among the gods, Lord, nor are there
any works like yours. 9 All nations whom you have made will
come and worship before you, Lord, and they will glorify your
name. 10 For you are great, and you do wondrous deeds; you
alone are God. 11 Teach me your way, LORD; I will walk in your
truth; unite my heart to fear your name. 12 I will give thanks to
you, Lord my God, with all my heart, and I will glorify your name
forever. 13 For your graciousness toward me is great, and you
have saved my soul from the depths of Sheol. (NASB)

"To fear God is both the beginning, the growth, and the maturity of wisdom, therefore should we be undividedly given up to it, heart, and soul."

Singleheartedness. Our heart's posture is influenced by God's nature.
Among all the deities, none are powerful like the Almighty God (v. 8). Since
he is the only God worthy of worship (vv. 9, 12), our heart's affections are
exclusively centered on him. "When my heart is one, I will give you all of it.
Praise should never be rendered with less than all our heart, and soul, and
strength, or it will be both unreal and unacceptable." Worship is not a stand-
alone in the Christian life but a starting point. With the right heart attitude,
we long for him to teach us from his word (v. 11a). We learn in order to live
singleheartedly for God (v. 11b). However, such a life does not come easily.
Our sinful nature, competing for our hearts, seeks to control and leave us
inwardly conflicted. "A man of divided heart is weak, the man of one object
is *the* man." Spiritual strength comes from our heart allegiance to Jesus.

Prayer. Lord, I find myself straying from you and your purposes for my life.
By my own effort, I cannot be completely devoted to you. Flood my mind
with your greatness so that I may unreservedly give you my devotion. It is on
this basis I want to worship and obey you. Amen.

July 29   Psalm 86:14–17

14 God, arrogant men have risen up against me, and a gang of violent men have sought my life, and they have not set you before them. 15 But you, Lord, are a compassionate and gracious God, slow to anger and abundant in mercy and truth. 16 Turn to me, and be gracious to me; grant your strength to your servant, and save the son of your maidservant. 17 Show me a sign of good, that those who hate me may see it and be ashamed, because you, LORD, have helped me and comforted me. (NASB)

"A truly glorious doxology, in which there is not one redundant word."

Singleheartedness applied. Now David reveals the specific issue which prompted his prayer. He faced death at the hands of those who hated him (v. 14). When we feel secure, we can quickly make bold declarations of our sole commitment to love Jesus Christ. It is quite another matter when troubles confront us. However, in the midst of his enemies, David affirmed God's character. It is this singlehearted devotion to the Lord which allows David to worship him (v. 15). On this basis, David asks for God's mercy and strength (v. 16). In addition to depending on his character, David also humbly mentions that he is a servant before the Lord (v. 16). His status reflects how secure he is in God's love for him. With the right heart, focused only on the Lord, David can trust him for help and comfort (v. 17). David's total devotion to God in the midst of adversity encourages us to imitate him.

Prayer. Father, I readily declare my commitment to you when life is good. But my allegiance to you has wavered when adversities have come my way. Continually remind me of your great love so my devotion to you will be firm and strong in the days to come. I am thankful to be your child and servant. Amen.

1 On the holy mount stands the city he founded; 2 the LORD loves the gates of Zion more than all the dwelling places of Jacob. 3 Glorious things of you are spoken, O city of God. *Selah* 4 Among those who know me I mention Rahab and Babylon; behold, Philistia and Tyre, with Cush—"This one was born there," they say. 5 And of Zion it shall be said, "This one and that one were born in her"; for the Most High himself will establish her. 6 The LORD records as he registers the peoples, "This one was born there." *Selah* 7 Singers and dancers alike say, "All my springs are in you." (ESV)

"[T]he queen of all the cities of the universe; the true 'eternal city,' the metropolitan, the mother of us all."

The city of God. The psalmist paints a glorious description of those who will be with God in the future New Jerusalem (vv. 2–3). In this city, the populace consists of gentile believers from nations which once opposed the gospel (v. 4). There is also an emphasis on individuals (v. 5). While there is a diversity of people, they equally share the same registry because of their birth in Zion (v. 6). The names of those who experience the new birth in Christ are written in the "book of life" (Rev 20:15). Jesus is in their midst as the fountain or "the eternal source of all our supplies, and looking to him we shall never flag or fail" (v. 7). What a glimpse of the future church, with its diverse peoples focused on their loving God!

Prayer. Everlasting Lord, with all the good things in this life, I get so caught up in the here and now. I confess that I easily forget about spending eternity with you and everyone you have redeemed. Increase my longing for my true home so that my priorities are changed until the day I see you. Amen.

July 31   **Psalm 88:1–9**

1 LORD, you are the God who saves me; day and night I cry out to you. 2 May my prayer come before you; turn your ear to my cry. 3 I am overwhelmed with troubles and my life draws near to death. 4 I am counted among those who go down to the pit; I am like one without strength. 5 I am set apart with the dead, like the slain who lie in the grave, whom you remember no more, who are cut off from your care. 6 You have put me in the lowest pit, in the darkest depths. 7 Your wrath lies heavily on me; you have overwhelmed me with all your waves. 8 You have taken from me my closest friends and have made me repulsive to them. I am confined and cannot escape; 9 my eyes are dim with grief. I call to you, LORD, every day; I spread out my hands to you. (NIV)

"Assuredly, if ever there was a song of sorrow and a Psalm of sadness, this is one."

A description of darkness. The writer has suffered physically and nearly died (vv. 3–4). Concerning his afflictions he is saying, "I am satiated and nauseated with them . . . Trouble in the soul is the soul of trouble." To add to his misery, he feels God has abandoned him (v. 5). "To feel utterly forsaken of the Lord and cast away as though hopelessly corrupt is the very climax of heart desolation." Not surprisingly he feels God is angry with him (v. 7). Perhaps due to an infectious disease or moral defilement, even his closest friends have abandoned him (v. 8). "Yet it is a piercing pain which arises from the desertion of dear associates; it is a wound which festers and refuses to be healed . . . he was a prisoner in his room." The deep darkness envelopes him with grief and weeping (v. 9). When we feel we are all alone with our suffering, Scripture is replete with other believers who have experienced the "dark night of the soul."

Prayer. Father, as I reflect on my personal pain, I take comfort in knowing that others have also gone through times of profound darkness. The assurance that my dark days are not unique delivers me from unnecessary guilt and self-pity. Thank you, Lord, that you understand me. Amen.

August 1   Psalm 88:10–18

10 Do you show your wonders to the dead? Do their spirits rise up and praise you? 11 Is your love declared in the grave, your faithfulness in Destruction? 12 Are your wonders known in the place of darkness, or your righteous deeds in the land of oblivion? 13 But I cry to you for help, LORD; in the morning my prayer comes before you. 14 Why, LORD, do you reject me and hide your face from me? 15 From my youth I have suffered and been close to death; I have borne your terrors and am in despair. 16 Your wrath has swept over me; your terrors have destroyed me. 17 All day long they surround me like a flood; they have completely engulfed me. 18 You have taken from me friend and neighbor—darkness is my closest friend. (NIV)

"I am familiar only with sadness, all else has vanished. I am a child crying alone in the dark."

Embracing the darkness. Using darkness as a metaphor for painful afflictions, we will face dark times. Rather than becoming bitter, we do well to acknowledge God's sovereignty. Knowing he is in control and has his purposes allows us to embrace the darkest hours. The psalmist, Heman, reminds us it is permissible to ask God the hard questions in these situations (vv. 11–12, 14). "We may put these questions to the Lord, nay, we ought to do so. It is not undue familiarity, but holy boldness." Heman teaches us to cry out to God about these perplexing questions (v. 13). When caught up in the immediate situation, we risk distorting or losing perspective of God's love (v. 11) and Jesus' suffering on the cross for our sake (vv. 11, 15). Spurgeon mentions that Heman has had an opportunity to reflect before writing about his bleak experience. Time often gives us a fresh perspective when we cannot see in the darkness of the night. It is also helpful to see suffering from the perspective of the cross. "Since the Savior became the acquaintance of grief, sorrow has become honorable in believers' eyes." We do not suffer alone; Jesus knows what our suffering is like.

Prayer. Merciful God, it is very hard to embrace the dark times. Thank you for hearing my cries and questions. Grant me a fresh perspective by remembering your love and giving myself time to reflect. Thank you for giving me the cross to remind me that the darkest days can also be redemptive for your purposes. Thank you that you are with me during such times. Amen.

August 2   **Psalm 89:1–4**

1 I will sing of the graciousness of the LORD forever; to all generations I will make your faithfulness known with my mouth. 2 For I have said, "Graciousness will be built up forever; in the heavens you will establish your faithfulness." 3 "I have made a covenant with my chosen; I have sworn to my servant David, 4 I will establish your descendants forever and build up your throne to all generations." *Selah* (NASB)

"Because God is, and ever will be, faithful, we have a theme for song which will not be out of date for future generations."

God's eternal faithfulness. In the midst of a national disaster, the psalmist is pleading for God's deliverance based on his faithfulness to his people. The Lord's commitment to be faithful was established in the covenant made between himself and David (2 Sam 7:12–16). The writer will expand on the covenant later (vv. 19–37), but in this section he wants to dwell on God's faithfulness. He is faithful because of his nature. "It is *Jehovah* who deigns to deal out to us our daily benefits, and he is the all-sufficient and immutable God" whose faithful love we experience. In light of his faithfulness, we respond in praise to God (v. 1). "Whatever we may observe abroad or experience in our own persons, we ought still to praise God for his mercies, since they most certainly remain the same, whether we can perceive them or not." This is particularly true in hard times. "In times of trouble it is the divine faithfulness which the soul hangs upon" for God's people are prone to forget or doubt his faithfulness. For this reason, it is important to remember that God's faithfulness is forever (vv. 1, 2, 4). With this truth it is very appropriate to pause (*selah*) and reflect.

Prayer. Lord, I know I have not always been faithful to you. This causes me to marvel at your faithfulness to me, especially in very difficult times when it is tempting to doubt you. Thank you for your faithful love. Amen.

August 3   Psalm 89:5-14

5 The heavens will praise your wonders, LORD; your faithfulness also in the assembly of the holy ones. 6 For who in the skies is comparable to the LORD? Who among the sons of the mighty is like the LORD, 7 a God greatly feared in the council of the holy ones, and awesome above all those who are around him? 8 Lord God of armies, who is like you, mighty LORD? Your faithfulness also surrounds you. 9 You rule the surging of the sea; when its waves rise, you calm them. 10 You yourself crushed Rahab like one who is slain; you scattered your enemies with your mighty arm. 11 The heavens are yours, the earth also is yours; the world and all it contains, you have established them. 12 The north and the south, you have created them; Tabor and Hermon shout for joy at your name. 13 You have a strong arm; your hand is mighty, your right hand is exalted. 14 Righteousness and justice are the foundation of your throne; mercy and truth go before you. (NASB)

"Before we argue our case before the Lord, it is most becoming to acknowledge that we know him to be supremely great and good."

Moral power. Should we complain before God? Before the psalmist laments, he offers praise for God's attributes. Spurgeon advises that we are wise to follow this pattern. By dwelling on God, we can experience greater peace in the midst of our troubles. In his particular situation, the psalmist first focuses on God's power (vv. 5-13). There is no one who can rival God (vv. 6-8) whose power enables him to rule over everything. He has power over nature (v. 9) and the nations (v. 10), for he created everything (v. 12). God has not relinquished the throne or surrendered it to Satan. His great power does not abuse his people because he leads with justice and wisdom (vv. 13-14). "God as a sovereign is never unjust or unwise. He is too holy to be unrighteous, too wise to be mistaken." Our complaints to him are mitigated when we meditate on his character.

Prayer. Almighty Lord, I find myself complaining to you far too much. Teach me to focus first on you and your relationship to the world. I am thankful that I do not have to fear your power. Instead, your power gives me hope you are in control of my life and the nations. Amen.

15 Blessed are the people who know the joyful sound! LORD, they walk in the light of your face. 16 In your name they rejoice all the day, and by your righteousness they are exalted. 17 For you are the glory of their strength, and by your favor our horn is exalted. 18 For our shield belongs to the LORD, and our king to the Holy One of Israel. (NASB)

"Who among his saints will not rejoice in the God of election? Are they not indeed a people greatly blessed who can call this God their God for ever and ever?"

Praise expected. When we consider God's greatness (vv. 5–14), we are called on to praise him at all times (vv. 15–16). When we think of God's faithful commitment to us, we "need no other reason for rejoicing . . . If God were unjust, or if he regarded us as being without righteousness, we must be filled with misery, but as neither of these things is so, we are exalted indeed, and would extol the name of the Lord." We also praise the Lord because he is holy and protects us (v. 18). Both qualities are related to his faithfulness. Since God is holy, he will not break his promises or act unjustly with us. He is committed to be our ultimate shield and protector against the evil forces. We can praise him at all times because of his abiding relationship with us.

Prayer. Lord, I confess my praise to you is often conditioned by my circumstances. However, when I think of your unconditional love commitment to me, I am overwhelmed. This motivates me to express deep gratitude to you for what you have done and are doing in my life. Amen.

August 5   Psalm 89:19-29

19 Once you spoke in vision to your godly ones, and said, "I have given help to one who is mighty; I have exalted one chosen from the people. 20 I have found my servant David; with my holy oil I have anointed him, 21 with whom my hand will be established; my arm also will strengthen him. 22 The enemy will not deceive him, nor will the son of wickedness afflict him. 23 But I will crush his adversaries before him, and strike those who hate him. 24 My faithfulness and my favor will be with him, and in my name his horn will be exalted. 25 I will also place his hand on the sea, and his right hand on the rivers. 26 He will call to me, 'you are my Father, my God, and the rock of my salvation.' 27 I will also make him my firstborn, the highest of the kings of the earth. 28 I will maintain my favor for him forever, and my covenant shall be confirmed to him. 29 So I will establish his descendants forever, and his throne as the days of heaven." (NASB)

"David was God's elect, elect out of the people, as one of themselves, and elect to the highest position of the state."

God chooses. The psalmist discusses the covenant God made with David (2 Sam 7:8–16). He chooses and anoints David as the king of Israel (vv. 19–20). His military victories are a reflection of God's faithful love which exalted David (v. 24). In time, David's lineage fell away from God, threatening the very existence of the nation and his descendants. It was only God's grace which preserved David's lineage until Jesus, the son of Mary, came (v. 28). Through him, David's lineage would be established forever (v. 29). Now God's covenant with us continues through the death of Jesus Christ. Through the cross, "David's seed lives on in the person of the Lord Jesus, and the seed of Jesus in the persons of believers." Jesus is, and always will be, the King of kings and Lord of lords (v. 27).

Prayer. Sovereign God, I am astounded that you should choose me to be one of your children. Like David, I am so imperfect. However, when I see how you used him, I am humbled that you can also use my life to accomplish your purposes. I am thankful for your commitment to stand by me. Amen.

August 6   Psalm 89:30–37

30 "If his sons abandon my Law and do not walk in my judgments, 31 if they violate my statutes and do not keep my commandments, 32 then I will punish their wrongdoing with the rod, and their guilt with afflictions. 33 But I will not withhold my favor from him, nor deal falsely in my faithfulness. 34 I will not violate my covenant, nor will I alter the utterance of my lips. 35 Once I have sworn by my holiness; I will not lie to David. 36 His descendants shall endure forever, and his throne as the sun before me. 37 It shall be established forever like the moon, and a witness in the sky is faithful." *Selah* (NASB)

"Mercy may seem to depart from the Lord's chosen, but it shall never altogether do so."

Faithfulness clarified. Having heard God's declaration of his faithfulness to his people, this would eventually trigger questions which deserved to be answered now. One question centered on disobedience (vv. 30–31). When one fears God's rejection because of disobedience, the concern of losing one's salvation surfaces. When one experiences hardships, questions about God punishing and rejecting a believer are raised (v. 32). God responds by adamantly declaring his unfailing love to his people (vv. 33–34)! This covenant relationship rests on God's holy character (v. 35). "He does as good as say that if he ceases to be true to his covenant he will have forfeited his holy character." His promise to us is absolute and he would be lying if he is not faithful to us. When we do go through painful situations, God is not using a "penal sword" to destroy us, but rather, a "gospel rod" to discipline us due to his committed love to us.

Prayer. Lord, I am thankful for your word that allows me to understand more and more of your faithfulness to me. This guards my mind and heart from the unnecessary fear of you rejecting me. When I go through trying times, forgive me for thinking you are punishing me. I now see your discipline as an expression of your faithful love to me. Amen.

August 7   Psalm 89:38-45

38 But you have rejected and refused, you have been full of wrath against your anointed. 39 You have repudiated the covenant of your servant; you have profaned his crown in the dust. 40 You have broken down all his walls; you have brought his strongholds to ruin. 41 All who pass along the way plunder him; he has become a disgrace to his neighbors. 42 You have exalted the right hand of his adversaries; you have made all his enemies rejoice. 43 You also turn back the edge of his sword, and have not made him stand in battle. 44 You have put an end to his splendour and cast his throne to the ground. 45 You have shortened the days of his youth; you have covered him with shame. *Selah* (NASB)

"Is this according to the covenant? Can this be as the Lord has promised?"

Faithfulness questioned. Biblical truths may comfort us when life is great. But, how do we respond to these truths when the good times evaporate and are replaced by the storms of adversity? The psalmist now discusses God's people who have experienced his anger. They assume God has rejected them because their king has been put to shame (vv. 38–39, 44–45). In addition, their enemies have devastated their nation (vv. 40–43). However, this painful situation is eclipsed by God apparently breaking his commitment to be faithful to his own people (v. 39). Moreover, destruction at the national level appears to be in conflict with God's promised commitment to his people. Here is what we need to keep in mind. "God's actions may appear to us to be the reverse of his promises, and then our best course is to come before him in prayer and put the matter before him" to get his perspective on the matter. When we meditate on the word and talk to the Lord, we are reminded that nothing shall separate us from God's great love for us (Rom 8:38–39).

Prayer. Father, in the face of difficulties it is very tempting to doubt your unreserved love for me and even believe you are punishing me. When I question your faithfulness to me, lead me deeper into your truth, which assures me of your constant fatherly love. Amen.

August 8   Psalm 89:46–52

46 How long, LORD? Will you hide yourself forever? Will your wrath burn like fire? 47 Remember what my lifespan is; for what futility you have created all the sons of mankind! 48 What man can live and not see death? Can he save his soul from the power of Sheol? *Selah* 49 Where are your former acts of favor, Lord, which you swore to David in your faithfulness? 50 Remember, Lord, the taunt against your servants; how I carry in my heart the taunts of all the many peoples, 51 with which your enemies have taunted, LORD, with which they have taunted the footsteps of your anointed. 52 Blessed be the LORD forever! Amen and Amen. (NASB)

"If the kingdom of heaven should fail, everything is a failure. Creation is a blot, providence an error, and our own existence a bell, if the faithfulness of God can fail and his covenant of grace can be dissolved."

Faithfulness realized. In this section, the writer pleads with the Lord regarding the calamities that have befallen his people. Though the scene is dark, all is not gloomy. Spurgeon applies these verses not primarily to Jesus' suffering but to the universal church. After Israel's long exile in captivity and God's subsequent silence, he reveals himself through Jesus Christ, who came from the lineage of David. He conquered death and now reigns as the eternal King. Through him, God's covenant is reestablished and he continues to be faithful to his people today. Even though the church has experienced, and will continue to experience, hardships, our reigning King will never reject his people. This psalm begins and ends with affirmations of God's faithfulness to us (vv. 1, 52), reminding us not to despair when trials come our way.

Prayer. Lord, I thank you for the covenant relationship with Jesus, the Son of David, who is both my Savior and my King. My faith in you is deepened by reflecting on your unconditional, loving faithfulness to me. Amen.

August 9   Psalm 90:1–6

1 Lord, you have been our dwelling place in all generations. 2 Before the mountains were brought forth, or ever you had formed the earth and the world, from everlasting to everlasting you are God. 3 You return man to dust and say, "Return, O children of man!" 4 For a thousand years in your sight are but as yesterday when it is past, or as a watch in the night. 5 You sweep them away as with a flood; they are like a dream, like grass that is renewed in the morning: 6 in the morning it flourishes and is renewed; in the evening it fades and withers. (ESV)

"Moses sings of the frailty of man, and the shortness of life, contrasting therewith the eternity of God."

Eternality and mortality. Frequently used at funeral services, this well-known passage reminds us of our mortality. Moses, the author of this the oldest psalm, mentions why we are finite. We are frail people, made from dust, and will return to dust (v. 3). Life is fleeting (v. 4) like a blink of the eye. Moreover, life is unpredictable, like a surging flood which we have no control over (v. 5). Lush vegetation that dies within a day is analogous to our lives that come to an end (vv. 5–6). With this realistic portrait of life, we are given a snapshot of God's eternality (vv. 1–2). What does his life offer us? Since God is preexistent, all life is derived from him (v. 2). "The eternal existence of God is here mentioned to set forth, by contrast, the brevity of human life." God is also our dwelling place (v. 1). By abiding or making our home in Jesus Christ, we find eternal life (John 15:4).

Prayer. Lord, when I consider the devastating toll of disasters around the world, I see the reality of how unpredictable and brief life is! I am so thankful that I have found my eternal home and life in Jesus. Amen.

7 For we have been consumed by your anger, and we have been terrified by your wrath. 8 You have placed our guilty deeds before you, our hidden sins in the light of your presence. 9 For all our days have dwindled away in your fury; we have finished our years like a sigh. 10 As for the days of our life, they contain seventy years, or if due to strength, eighty years, yet their pride is only trouble and tragedy; for it quickly passes, and we disappear. 11 Who understands the power of your anger and your fury, according to the fear that is due you? 12 So teach us to number our days, that we may present to you a heart of wisdom. 13 Do return, LORD; how long will it be? And be sorry for your servants. 14 Satisfy us in the morning with your graciousness, that we may sing for joy and rejoice all our days. 15 Make us glad according to the days you have afflicted us, and the years we have seen evil. 16 Let your work appear to your servants and your majesty to their children. 17 May the kindness of the Lord our God be upon us; and confirm for us the work of our hands; yes, confirm the work of our hands. (NASB)

"We come and go, but the Lord's work abides."

Anger and grace. Due to sin, God's people experienced his anger and death in the wilderness (v. 7). Given the brevity of life (v. 10) it is wise to rethink our existence on earth (v. 12). "People are led by reflections upon the brevity of time to give their earnest attention to eternal things . . . A short life should be wisely spent." Living wisely includes moving from independence to dependence on God. This new posture allows us to experience his unfailing love (vv. 13–14) and joy (v. 15). We are inspired when we see God at work around us (v. 16). This delight stands in stark contrast to coming to life's finish line with a groan (v. 9). We also enjoy God's love when we see that our own work has a lasting impact (v. 17). This is a much better way to live than a life that fades away with no results (v. 10). "Since the Lord abides forever the same, we trust our work in his hands, and feel that since it is far more his work than ours he will secure it immortality." Living by God's grace is the best way to live!

Prayer. Lord, a life apart from you will short-circuit your blessings for my life. I want to live wisely by using my days for your eternal purposes. Flood my heart with joy as I observe signs of your grace at work around, in, and through me. Amen.

1 Those who live in the shelter of the Most High will find rest in the shadow of the Almighty. 2 This I declare about the LORD: he alone is my refuge, my place of safety; he is my God, and I trust him. 3 For he will rescue you from every trap and protect you from deadly disease. 4 He will cover you with his feathers. He will shelter you with his wings. His faithful promises are your armor and protection. (NLT)

"To take up a general truth and make it our own by personal faith is the highest wisdom."

My protector. Spurgeon believes this psalm is one of the most cheerful in the psalter because of the writer's strong faith. He focuses on God's protection. In this case, it is not displayed by his great power. Rather, his protection is experienced when we rest in God (v. 1). This involves communion or fellowship with him. It is an intimate relationship with God, indicated by the use of "my" three times (v. 2). For this reason we can trust in God, who is like a protective mother hen (v. 4). "Even as a hen covers her chickens so does the Lord protect the souls which dwell in him; let us cower down beneath him for comfort and for safety. Hawks in the sky and snares in the field are equally harmless when we nestle so near the Lord." God protects us with his tender love.

Prayer. Almighty God, your word informs me that you are strong and powerful. However, events such as global terrorism and pandemics make me feel very unsafe. Help me to live wisely by trusting in your protection. I know that I can live with joy because of your promise to take care of me. Amen.

5 Do not be afraid of the terrors of the night, nor the arrow that flies in the day. 6 Do not dread the disease that stalks in darkness, nor the disaster that strikes at midday. 7 Though a thousand fall at your side, though ten thousand are dying around you, these evils will not touch you. 8 Just open your eyes, and see how the wicked are punished. 9 If you make the LORD your refuge, if you make the Most High your shelter, 10 no evil will conquer you; no plague will come near your home. 11 For he will order his angels to protect you wherever you go. 12 They will hold you up with their hands so you won't even hurt your foot on a stone. 13 You will trample upon lions and cobras; you will crush fierce lions and serpents under your feet! (NLT)

"Ill to him is no ill, but only good in a mysterious form."

God's protection. Spurgeon refers to a German physician who believed this psalm was "the best preservative in times of cholera, and in truth it is a heavenly medicine against plague and pest." During a thirty-year span, this epidemic killed 40,000 residents of London. In 1854, when he had been living in London for one year, Spurgeon wrote that many people in his congregation had suffered and died from cholera. Consequently, "almost every day I was called to visit the grave" and he himself became exhausted emotionally and physically. One day he came across verses 9–10, which greatly encouraged him. In our era, we have experienced the ravages of the COVID-19 pandemic. This psalm tells us that those who know the Lord are secure from disaster and harm (vv. 9–10). How can we say God protects us from illnesses and other dangers? Spurgeon acknowledges that every believer will die, but goes on to say, "No evil in the strict sense of the word can happen to him, for everything is overruled for good." In addition to our security in the Lord, God's angels aid us when needed, as seen in Jesus' life (vv. 11–12; Matt 4:6). Besides, premature death brings the reward of heaven to us sooner than expected. Rather than promising immunity from dangers, God provides security and resources through our relationship with him.

Prayer. Lord, I know many of your children live in fear of disasters and disease. Like those of many years ago who found hope in your word during similar situations, help us find rest in you, our God who offers true security and peace. Amen.

14 The LORD says, "I will rescue those who love me. I will protect those who trust in my name. 15 When they call on me, I will answer; I will be with them in trouble. I will rescue and honor them. 16 I will reward them with a long life and give them my salvation." (NLT)

"God first gives us conquering grace, and then rewards us for it."

The grace of protection. Spurgeon notes that God does not protect us because we deserve it; he does so based on our status as his elect or chosen children. Our love for him (v. 14) is the key indicator of God's grace. As his children, we honor the Father by calling out to him in prayer (v. 15). God's grace that saved us also allows us to be secure in him during times of need. God and his angels may directly intervene when we are in harm's way. Although he does not always step in and remove us from danger, he protects us with his "special divine presence in times of severe trial. God is always near in sympathy and in power to help his tried ones." In the midst of peril, we can still experience his presence filling us with peace and joy because of our relationship with our Father. Therefore, if our lives are in jeopardy, we can experience not only his power but his presence. Being secure in God and our relationship with him throughout the years brings great satisfaction to us (v. 16).

Prayer. Lord, I know there are believers around the world who have died for their faith while others are spared. It is reassuring that above all physical dangers is the reality of being secure in a relationship with you through union with Jesus Christ. Amen.

August 14   Psalm 92:1-4

1 It is good to give thanks to the LORD, to sing praises to the Most High. 2 It is good to proclaim your unfailing love in the morning, your faithfulness in the evening, 3 accompanied by a ten-stringed instrument, a harp, and the melody of a lyre. 4 You thrill me, LORD, with all you have done for me! I sing for joy because of what you have done. (NLT)

"Devout praise is always good, it is never out of season, never superfluous, but it is especially suitable to the Sabbath."

Sabbath praise. This psalm was intended to be sung on the Sabbath, the day of rest. "The subject is the praise of God; praise is Sabbatic work, the joyful occupation of resting hearts. Since a true Sabbath can only be found in God, it is wise to meditate on him on the Sabbath day." In fact, it is beneficial to meditate and give thanks to God (v. 1). "It is good ethically, for it is the Lord's right; it is good emotionally, for it is pleasant to the heart." Rather than limiting praise to a few hours on a certain day, mornings and evenings are appropriate times to worship God (v. 2). Specifically, the mornings are a suitable time to focus on God's immeasurable love for us. In the evening we can praise him for his faithfulness. "Evening is the time for retrospect, memory is busy with the experiences of the day; hence the appropriate theme for song is the divine *faithfulness.*" While the psalmist focused his worship on God's completed creation (v. 4) we can gladly praise him for his complete salvation.

Prayer. Lord, I confess that I complain too much throughout the day. This is not pleasing to you or me. I want to cultivate a more thankful heart. As I begin and end each day, would you make me more conscious of your countless acts of love and faithfulness? I long to be filled with gratitude instead of constantly grumbling. Amen.

August 15   Psalm 92:5-8

5 O Lord, what great works you do! And how deep are your
thoughts. 6 Only a simpleton would not know, and only a fool
would not understand this: 7 though the wicked sprout like
weeds and evildoers flourish, they will be destroyed forever. 8
But you, O Lord, will be exalted forever. (NLT)

"Humanity is superficial, God is inscrutable; humanity is shallow, God is deep."

Thoughtful Sabbath praise. The psalmist paints a stark contrast of responses to the works of God. On one hand, there are those who are blind to
God's plans and works (v. 6). The person may be a philosopher but does not
acknowledge the wisdom of a divine Creator who made the "ten thousand
matchless creations around him which wear, even upon their surface, the
evidences of profound design." The lack of acknowledgment is not an issue of
the intellect, but a spiritual one. When one does not believe in God, it is impossible to understand spiritual truth. On the other hand, when our spiritual
"eyes" are opened, we recognize the majesty of God's works and thoughts (v.
6). "The Lord's plans are as marvelous as his acts; his designs are as profound
as his doings are vast. Creation is immeasurable, and the wisdom displayed
in it unsearchable . . . Redemption is grand beyond conception, and the
thoughts of love which planned it are infinite." Being mindful of all God's
great works, we exalt him above everything else (v. 8).

Prayer. Lord, thank you for revealing your involvement in the creation of
this world. As I consider the universe or the intricate design of the human
body, I recognize your majesty and wisdom. I give you praise for your creation. Thank you for making me a new creation in Christ. May my life bring
you honor in praise and the way I live for you. Amen.

9 For surely your enemies, LORD, surely your enemies will perish; all evildoers will be scattered. 10 You have exalted my horn like that of a wild ox; fine oils have been poured on me. 11 My eyes have seen the defeat of my adversaries; my ears have heard the rout of my wicked foes. 12 The righteous will flourish like a palm tree, they will grow like a cedar of Lebanon; 13 planted in the house of the LORD, they will flourish in the courts of our God. 14 They will still bear fruit in old age, they will stay fresh and green, 15 proclaiming, "The LORD is upright; he is my Rock, and there is no wickedness in him." (NIV)

"If a man abide in Christ he brings forth much fruit . . . those who dwell in habitual fellowship with God shall become men of full growth, rich in grace, happy in experience, mighty in influence, honoured and honourable."

Sabbath renewal. Sabbath rest provides the opportunity for God to strengthen ("my horn") and refresh us in the midst of life's challenges (vv. 10–11). This renewal occurs when we choose to invest time in his presence (v. 13). A habitual, intimate friendship with Jesus enables us to be like a tree flourishing in adverse conditions (vv. 12, 13). We are able to thrive because we can draw from God the needed resources. Even in old age, we need to keep doing this if we want to continue being fruitful (v. 14). While the strength of the elderly may recede, "aged believers possess a ripe experience" which will encourage others. Besides, God receives the praise for renewing and refreshing us regardless of circumstances (v. 15). "Happy they who can sing this Sabbath Psalm, enjoying the rest which breathes through every verse of it," which God gives us to us when we recognize our daily dependence on him.

Prayer. Lord, I confess that as I get older it is tempting to coast and plateau in my spiritual life. Would you continue to renew me as a vibrant witness of your grace in my life? I want to continue being fruitful for your purposes even as my physical strength diminishes. Amen.

August 17   Psalm 93

1 The LORD reigns; he is robed in majesty; the LORD is robed; he has put on strength as his belt. Yes, the world is established; it shall never be moved. 2 Your throne is established from of old; you are from everlasting. 3 The floods have lifted up, O LORD, the floods have lifted up their voice; the floods lift up their roaring. 4 Mightier than the thunders of many waters, mightier than the waves of the sea, the LORD on high is mighty! 5 Your decrees are very trustworthy; holiness befits your house, O LORD, forevermore. (ESV)

"Whatever turmoil and rebellion there may be beneath the clouds, the eternal King sits above all in supreme serenity; and everywhere he is really Master, let his foes rage as they may."

The Lord reigns. When we see the world in chaos with wars and disease, it is tempting to question if God has lost control. However, despite the angry raging of people and nations (v. 3), God still reigns as the eternal King who exercises dominion and sovereignty over the nations (vv. 1–2). For this reason, Spurgeon comments, "It is the Psalm of Omnipotent Sovereignty: Jehovah, despite all opposition, reigns supreme." His rule reveals both his power and holy character (v. 5). This is most encouraging when we panic in the midst of current political, economic, and military upheavals. His righteous reign also deserves our willing submission and heartfelt devotion. Our "due esteem for the great King will lead us to adopt a behavior becoming his royal presence. Divine sovereignty both confirms the promises as sure testimonies, and enforces the precepts as seemly and becoming in the presence of so great a Lord."

Prayer. Eternal God, I am thankful you reign and are still in control of this world. While your kingly power encourages me, draw me closer to your holy character so that I may willingly submit to you and gladly obey your word. I want you, my King, to reign over my life. Amen.

1 LORD, God of vengeance, God of vengeance, shine forth! 2 Rise up, Judge of the earth, pay back retribution to the proud. 3 How long, LORD, shall the wicked—how long shall the wicked triumph? 4 They pour out words, they speak arrogantly; all who do injustice boast. 5 They crush your people, LORD, and afflict your inheritance. 6 They kill the widow and the stranger and murder the orphans. 7 They have said, "The LORD does not see, nor does the God of Jacob perceive." 8 Pay attention, you stupid ones among the people; and when will you understand, foolish ones? 9 He who planted the ear, does he not hear? Or he who formed the eye, does he not see? 10 He who disciplines the nations, will he not rebuke, he who teaches mankind knowledge? 11 The LORD knows human thoughts, that they are mere breath. (NASB)

"The toleration of injustice is here attributed to the Lord's being hidden."

Tolerated oppression. The psalmist queries how long God will tolerate those who oppress others. He pleads for God to deal with this cruelty (vv. 1–3). Their tyranny is manifested in different ways. Their language is full of boasting while they threaten and insult others (v. 4). They also hate God's people (v. 5), "grinding them with oppression, crushing them with contempt." Lastly, rather than showing kindness to the vulnerable, they pervert justice (v. 6). Their oppressive behavior stems from their character. Thinking themselves wise, they are actually fools (v. 8). They may be knowledgeable but they lack wisdom. Spurgeon reminds us of the proverb, "No fool like a learned fool." Their character also reveals their dismissive attitude toward God. They did not think God noticed their oppression (v. 7) but now they are called to notice God's verdict about them (v. 8). They are futile in the sense that their thoughts and actions are vain (v. 11). "How foolish are those who think that God does not know their actions, when the truth is that their vain thoughts are all perceived by him! How absurd to make nothing of God when in fact we ourselves are as nothing in his sight."

Prayer. Holy God, I am upset by the ways cruel people harass the vulnerable in society. Break into their lives by softening their hardened hearts. May they turn to Jesus, who died for those who hated him. Give me a heart to love even those who despise you. Amen.

August 19   Psalm 94:12–15

12 Blessed is the man whom you discipline, LORD, and whom you teach from your Law, 13 so that you may grant him relief from the days of adversity, until a pit is dug for the wicked. 14 For the LORD will not abandon his people, nor will he abandon his inheritance. 15 For judgment will again be righteous, and all the upright in heart will follow it. (NASB)

> "The psalmist's mind is growing quiet . . . for his faith perceives that with the most afflicted believer all is well."

Hope for the oppressed. The psalmist turns his attention to God's people who are oppressed by those who hate them and God. He offers various reasons we can have hope in times of affliction. We are blessed because we experience God's discipline and training through his word (v. 12)! We should not equate punishment with discipline because each believer "is precious in God's sight, or the Lord would not take the trouble to correct him, and right happy will the results of his correction be." When we learn to be submissive to God's lessons for us in trials we can also gladly surrender to his plans. We find relief for our souls when we learn to trust God's designs in the most adverse circumstances (v. 13). This is finding true rest in God. In adversities, the Lord never rejects or withdraws from us for we are his chosen people (v. 14). "He may cast them down, but he never can cast them off." Even though we face antagonism, righteousness will be restored one day when Jesus Christ returns (v. 15). We can patiently and victoriously live through trials and oppression, knowing God is working out his sovereign purposes in our lives and in the world.

Prayer. Merciful Lord, I think of the many followers of Jesus around the world who are oppressed for their faith in you. Their lives, with unflagging confidence in the midst of opposition and persecution, are inspiring examples of how to live for you. Grant me humility to learn from them. Amen.

16 Who will stand up for me against evildoers? Who will take his stand for me against those who do injustice? 17 If the LORD had not been my help, my soul would soon have dwelt in the land of silence. 18 If I should say, "my foot has slipped," your faithfulness, LORD, will support me. 19 When my anxious thoughts multiply within me, your comfort delights my soul. 20 Can a throne of destruction be allied with you, one which devises mischief by decree? 21 They band themselves together against the life of the righteous and condemn the innocent to death. 22 But the LORD has been my refuge, and my God the rock of my refuge. 23 He has brought back their injustice upon them, and he will destroy them in their evil; the LORD our God will destroy them. (NASB)

"Never is the soul safer or more at rest than when, all other helpers failing, she leans upon the Lord alone."

Our true champion. Surrounded by people who attack us for our faith in God, it may seem nobody will advocate for us (v. 16). In his own day, Spurgeon wondered who the real defenders of the faith were. Though there appeared to be none, he asserted, "Our grand consolation is that the God of Knox and Luther is yet with us, and in due time will call out his chosen champions." God is our biggest supporter who offers his unfailing love (v. 18). As a pastor who promoted many causes, Spurgeon knew this reality. "Ten thousand times has this verse been true in relation to some of us, and especially to the writer of this comment." God offers comfort when we are filled with serious doubts (v. 19). When we are totally confused, Jesus offers us rest and a calm spirit. When we feel too weak to face our challenges, we can confidently come to him because he is reliably strong (v. 22). This same quality applies to the future when he comes to judge the oppressors (v. 23). Jesus is our true champion who stands by us at all times!

Prayer. Lord, it is tiresome promoting various initiatives. I am so glad you are my champion who loves me when I fail or when others criticize me. When I am drained and weak, I am thankful I can come to you for strength and encouragement. Thank you for being my faithful supporter. Amen.

August 21   Psalm 95:1–5

1–2 Come, let's shout praises to GOD, raise the roof for the Rock who saved us! Let's march into his presence singing praises, lifting the rafters with our hymns! 3–5 And why? Because GOD is the best, High King over all the gods. In one hand he holds deep caves and caverns, in the other hand grasps the high mountains. He made Ocean—he owns it! His hands sculpted Earth! (MSG)

"Other nations sing unto their gods, let us sing unto Jehovah. We love him, we admire him, we reverence him, let us express our feelings with the choicest sounds, using our noblest faculty for its noblest end."

Joyful worship. The psalmist invites us to worship God, for he is the creator of the world (vv. 4–5). The vastness of his creation with its ocean depths and mountains reminds us of God's dominion over this world. For this reason, he is above all other gods (v. 3) and is worthy of our praise (vv. 1–2). "God is our abiding, immutable, and mighty rock . . . therefore it becomes us to praise him with heart and with voice from day to day; and especially should we delight to do this when we assemble as his people for public worship." While we are to come before God with reverence, this does not preclude offering him exuberant thanksgiving. Spurgeon acknowledges it is difficult to combine reverence and enthusiastic praise. It is easy to forget that "joy is as much a characteristic of true worship as solemnity itself."

Prayer. Lord, I confess my worship is often motivated by my feelings and the quality of the worship music. But you are so great, so mighty, so creative, and so worthy of my joyful adoration. May my exuberant praise be combined with holy reverence for you! I offer you my heartfelt praise today. Amen.

6–7 So come, let us worship: bow before him, on your knees before GOD, who made us! Oh yes, he's our God, and we're the people he pastures, the flock he feeds. Drop everything and listen, listen as he speaks: (MSG)

"The adoration is to be humble."

Reverential worship. Congregations worship with different styles. For example, some church traditions practice bowing and kneeling before God (v. 6). Does our posture really matter? In Spurgeon's opinion, posture is not the most important but can indicate one's attitude before the Lord. "We are to worship in such a style that the bowing down shall indicate that we count ourselves to be as nothing in the presence of the all-glorious Lord." With a humble attitude, what should be the primary motivation to worship him? Jesus, our Great Shepherd, cares for us who are dependent on him for life now and forever (v. 7). "He is ours, and our God; ours, therefore will we love him; our God, therefore will we worship him . . . As he belongs to us, so do we belong to him."

Prayer. Majestic Lord, I know there are many expressions of worship among the global church. Grant me the humility to appreciate these different styles that can lead me into a stronger love for you. Whatever means of praise I use, may they reflect my genuine heart's desire to exalt you. Amen.

August 23   Psalm 95:7-11

7-11 "Don't turn a deaf ear as in the Bitter Uprising, as on the day of the Wilderness Test, when your ancestors turned and put me to the test. For forty years they watched me at work among them, as over and over they tried my patience. And I was provoked—oh, was I provoked! 'Can't they keep their minds on God for five minutes? Do they simply refuse to walk down my road?' Exasperated, I exploded, 'They'll never get where they're headed, never be able to sit down and rest.'" (MSG)

"Let us in reading this Psalm examine ourselves, and lay these things to heart."

The heart of worship. The psalmist has already called us to worship God the Creator who rules, and the Shepherd who guides. We are to praise him from the depths of our being for his great acts of faithful love. However, there is the danger of hardening our hearts whereby we test God's patience (vv. 8–9). Spurgeon notes we do this when we are unwilling to submit to God's will. "We tempt [test] him to alter his plans to suit our imperfect views of how the universe should be governed." Consequently, we demand miracles, divine intervention and other evidence of his presence. However, testing God clearly violates the very nature of worship, which is an expression of our confidence in God. When we test him we do not trust him. In this situation, our hearts need to be changed. Why is the heart so important? "The heart is the main spring of a man, and if it be not in order, the entire nature is thrown out of gear." For this reason, we must search for the cause of unbelief that has hardened our hearts. When we discover the cause, our hearts soften and we cease our relentless demands on God. We begin to experience true rest in God's ways (Heb 4:10). "Ours is the true Sabbatic rest, it is ours to rest from our own works as God did his." Then we can truly worship the Lord with thanksgiving and psalms of praise (v. 1).

Prayer. Lord, you have led me deeper into the essence of worship, trusting you rather than childishly demanding from you. Worship addresses the condition of my heart. Soften my heart so that I gladly trust and submit to your inscrutable ways. Then I can truly worship you each day. Amen.

August 24   Psalm 96:1–9

1 Sing a new song to the LORD! Let the whole earth sing to the LORD! 2 Sing to the LORD; praise his name. Each day proclaim the good news that he saves. 3 Publish his glorious deeds among the nations. Tell everyone about the amazing things he does. 4 Great is the LORD! He is most worthy of praise! He is to be feared above all gods. 5 The gods of other nations are mere idols, but the LORD made the heavens! 6 Honor and majesty surround him; strength and beauty fill his sanctuary. 7 O nations of the world, recognize the LORD; recognize that the LORD is glorious and strong. 8 Give to the LORD the glory he deserves! Bring your offering and come into his courts. 9 Worship the LORD in all his holy splendor. Let all the earth tremble before him. (NLT)

"All the earth Jehovah made, and all the earth must sing to him."

Worship the supreme God. The psalmist exhorts his readers to worship God (vv. 1–2) for very good reasons. He has saved his people (v. 2). While this may refer to the ways he has delivered his people from their enemies, Spurgeon applies the passage to our time. "The gospel is the clearest revelation of himself, salvation outshines creation and providence; therefore let our praises overflow in that direction." The gospel is so wonderful that all nations need to hear of God's salvation (v. 3). "His salvation is his glory, the word of the gospel glorifies him; and this should be published far and wide, till the remotest nations of the earth have known it." God is not only the Savior, but the Creator who is supreme over any other gods (vv. 4–5). "The idol gods have no existence, but our God is the author of all existences; they are mere earthly vanities, while he is not only heavenly, but made the heavens. This is mentioned as an argument for Jehovah's universal praise." Three times we are told to worship God because of his nature (vv. 6–7). He is worthy of worship by people groups around the globe because there is no one like him in holiness and splendor (vv. 8–9).

Prayer. Lord, it is wonderful to see people from many nations come to know Jesus as Savior. Let his redemptive love and the truth of your word increasingly draw people of all ethnic groups to come to know you. Use my life to communicate and demonstrate the good news in Jesus Christ. Amen.

August 25   Psalm 96:10–13

10 Tell all the nations, "The LORD reigns!" The world stands firm and cannot be shaken. He will judge all peoples fairly. 11 Let the heavens be glad, and the earth rejoice! Let the sea and everything in it shout his praise! 12 Let the fields and their crops burst out with joy! Let the trees of the forest sing for joy 13 before the LORD, for he is coming! He is coming to judge the earth. He will judge the world with justice, and the nations with his truth. (NLT)

"This is the gladdest news which can be carried to them—the Lord Jehovah, in the person of his Son has assumed the throne."

Worship the King. The psalmist praises God, who reigns as King over the world. His equitable rule (v. 10) is shaped by his commitment to do what is right and faithful to the truth (vv. 10, 13). Therefore no nation will receive special favor from, nor suffer, prejudice. In fact, all creation is glad and worships this kind of King (vv. 11–12)! Even the created angels, who have seen formerly wicked people turn to God, worship their Creator. Spurgeon comments that nature rejoices with God's reign as well. No longer does nature suffer the effects of the curse of sin (Rom 8:20–22) and people's greedy exploitation of the land. God will judge the perpetrators of sin. In light of this, we praise him because his kingdom extends to every sphere of life. Regardless of the overwhelming circumstances we may be facing, Spurgeon is reminding us that "already we are in his presence."

Prayer. In a world filled with violence, one shudders at what is happening. It is good news to know you have not lost control and are reigning over this world. I look forward to that day when your reign will be fully realized. Until then, I will worship you, the Almighty King, who is with me wherever I go. Amen.

August 26   Psalm 97:1–5

1 The LORD reigns, let the earth be glad; let the distant shores rejoice. 2 Clouds and thick darkness surround him; righteousness and justice are the foundation of his throne. 3 Fire goes before him and consumes his foes on every side. 4 His lightning lights up the world; the earth sees and trembles. 5 The mountains melt like wax before the LORD, before the Lord of all the earth. (NIV)

"So was it at Sinai, so must it be: the very Being of God is power, consuming all opposition; omnipotence is a devouring flame."

Holy fire. Spurgeon notes the imagery in this section points to Mount Sinai, where God met Moses (Exod 19). This event describes God's nature, which has also been revealed throughout history and in our own lives. The imagery of a powerful fire (v. 3) symbolizes the advent of Jesus and the Holy Spirit. "Even now where the gospel is preached in faith, and in the power of the Spirit, it burns its own way, irresistibly destroying falsehood, superstition, unbelief, sin, indifference, and hardness of heart." The lightning (v. 4) portrays the gospel of Jesus Christ, which came "with such a blaze of truth and grace as was never seen or even imagined before." Throughout the centuries, "the Word flashed from one end of the heavens to the other, no part of the civilized globe was left unilluminated." On a personal level, with Jesus' presence in our lives, he is able to "to consume our lusts and melt our souls to obedience." Also, when the dark clouds of doubt inevitably come our way, Jesus lights up our lives and our hearts are softened in his warm presence.

Prayer. Lord, may your word and Spirit ignite a spiritual fire throughout the world, so that people will irresistibly come to know Jesus as Savior. May your holy fire purify my life and warm my heart with your presence. Like the early church, may those who do not know you see evidence of your fire in my life and be drawn to you. Amen.

August 27   Psalm 97:6–9

6 The heavens proclaim his righteousness, and all peoples see his glory. 7 All who worship images are put to shame, those who boast in idols—worship him, all you gods! 8 Zion hears and rejoices and the villages of Judah are glad because of your judgments, LORD. 9 For you, LORD, are the Most High over all the earth; you are exalted far above all gods. (NIV)

"A man who worships an image is but the image of a man, his senses must have left him. He who boasts of an idol makes an idle boast."

Homage to the exalted One. The forces of nature (vv. 2, 4) clearly demonstrate God's righteousness and glory (v. 6). Observing his majesty should prompt three groups to give homage to God. The first represents the idols (v. 7) and those who worship them. This group should instead worship God, because he is exceedingly superior to the false gods (v. 9). The second grouping includes the angels, who should give reverence to God (v. 7). "If the false gods are thus bidden to worship the coming Lord, how much more shall they adore him who are godlike creatures in heaven, even angelic beings." The third and final group represents God's people, who render joyful homage to him because they love to see him exalted (v. 8). As a consequence, the follower of Jesus "is glad when he see false systems broken up and idol gods broken down" so that God receives the rightful honor.

Prayer. Lord, forgive me when I see others worshipping their idols but fail to see the idols that I worship. Wean my heart from attachments that draw my heart's devotion away from you. I want to give you homage, for nothing else compares to you, exalted one. Amen.

10 Let those who love the LORD hate evil, for he guards the lives of his faithful ones and delivers them from the hand of the wicked. 11 Light shines on the righteous and joy on the upright in heart. 12 Rejoice in the LORD, you who are righteous, and praise his holy name. (NIV)

"If all others fail to praise the Lord, the godly must not. To them God is peculiarly revealed, by them he should be specially adored."

Until then. The psalmist provides two responses for those who follow the Lord. The first response is to hate evil (v. 10). "We cannot love God without hating that which he hates." Godly living requires us to confront evil in our lives and in society. This posture is not easy because it will stir up some people to threaten our lives. Though God guards our lives, he does not guarantee protection from death. In fact, we may lose our lives (v. 10). However, we need not fear the possibility of death. "He [God] may leave the bodies of his persecuted saints in the hand of the wicked, but not their souls, these are very dear to him, and he preserves them safe in his bosom." The second response encourages us to rejoice in God even in the midst of spiritual battle (vv. 11–12). Wherever the gospel shines or is "sown" (v. 11 KJV) around the globe, it brings joy to people. "The full harvest of delight is not yet ours, but it is sown for us; it is springing, it will appear in fullness." We continue praising God while he is doing his work in people's lives.

Prayer. Lord, even though I continually face a spiritual battle in this world, I want to praise you at all times. I know you are defeating the powers of darkness through the word being planted in people's lives. Amen.

August 29   Psalm 98:1-3

1 Sing to the LORD a new song, for he has done marvelous things; his right hand and his holy arm have worked salvation for him. 2 The LORD has made his salvation known and revealed his righteousness to the nations. 3 He has remembered his love and his faithfulness to Israel; all the ends of the earth have seen the salvation of our God. (NIV)

"[T]he present Psalm is a kind of CORONATION HYMN, officially proclaiming the conquering Messiah as Monarch over the nations."

Jesus the reigning King. Spurgeon describes Psalm 98 as one of several "royal" songs exalting God as the reigning king. While the previous psalms (96 and 97) focus on the Lord's coming kingdom, this psalm focuses on the king who does *now* reign over the world. As with the rest of the psalter, Spurgeon also sees Jesus as the full revelation of this psalm. He did wonderful things during his ministry on earth (v. 1). "Jesus, our King, has lived a marvelous life, died a marvelous death, risen by a marvelous resurrection, and ascended marvelously into heaven." These events occurred because Jesus was victorious on the cross, paying for our sin and conquering death. He has made salvation available for everyone throughout the world (vv. 2–3). With the Holy Spirit's coming, Jesus continues to reign through his followers, who demonstrate God's power through signs and miracles.

Prayer. I thank you Lord that you are reigning on your throne. Reign in my life! As one of your followers, I want to join with others to make you known. May they notice the great things you have done in the past and continue to do today! Amen.

4 Shout for joy to the LORD, all the earth, burst into jubilant song with music; 5 make music to the LORD with the harp, with the harp and the sound of singing, 6 with trumpets and the blast of the ram's horn—shout for joy before the LORD, the King. 7 Let the sea resound, and everything in it, the world, and all who live in it. 8 Let the rivers clap their hands, let the mountains sing together for joy; 9 let them sing before the LORD, for he comes to judge the earth. He will judge the world in righteousness and the peoples with equity. (NIV)

"Loud let our hearts ring out the honors of our conquering Savior . . . The rule of Christ is the joy of nature."

Praise to the King. All creation is called to praise Jesus, the reigning king (vv. 6, 9). As his people, we can use all means, such as instruments, to praise him with exuberance. Reference to the harp (v. 5) suggests that we may elegantly express adoration to God. However, Spurgeon was wary of the use of musical instruments to adulate God. They can become a substitute for a proper heart attitude and the focus of worship, rather than God himself. "There is no fear of our being too hearty in magnifying the God of our salvation, only we must take care that the song comes from the heart, otherwise the music is nothing but a noise in his ears, whether it is caused by human throats, or organ pipes, or far-resounding trumpets." With the universal acknowledgment of Jesus' reign, his entire creation praises him (vv. 7–9).

Prayer. Eternal King, I confess I can pay more attention to the worship teams rather than rightly focusing on you. This is a reminder that I need to keep a check on my heart attitude before I come to praise you. I want you to be reigning in my life during the week when I worship you with your people. Then my adoration of you will truly come from my heart. Amen.

1 The LORD is king! Let the nations tremble! He sits on his throne between the cherubim. Let the whole earth quake! 2 The LORD sits in majesty in Jerusalem, exalted above all the nations. 3 Let them praise your great and awesome name. Your name is holy! 4 Mighty King, lover of justice, you have established fairness. You have acted with justice and righteousness throughout Israel. 5 Exalt the LORD our God! Bow low before his feet, for he is holy! (NLT)

"This [psalm] may be called THE SANCTUS or, the HOLY, HOLY, HOLY Psalm (a hymn in the 1549 *Book of Common Prayer*)."

A holy King. The exuberant praise of Psalm 98 is expressed to the king who not only rules but is also holy. His throne is surrounded by flaming angels (v. 1). They worship him because he is holy (vv. 3, 5, 9). "In him is no flaw or fault, excess or deficiency, error or iniquity. He is wholly excellent, and is therefore, holy. In his words, thoughts, actions, and revelations, as well as in himself, he is perfection itself." He expresses his holy nature by establishing justice (v. 4) and demolishing every form of injustice in society. At the same time, this holy God is our Lord (v. 5). It is possible to have a relationship with him through Jesus Christ, who made it possible to stand before a holy God. In sheer gratitude, we have the privilege of praising him (vv. 3, 5). We do so with humility, prostrating our hearts before our holy God.

Prayer. Father, I kneel in humble reverence and adoration before you. I know it is impossible to make myself holy before you. I am thankful for Jesus, who gave me a right standing before you. Now I ask you to transform my life to become more like him. Amen.

September 1   Psalm 99:6–9

6 Moses and Aaron were among his priests; Samuel also called on his name. They cried to the LORD for help, and he answered them. 7 He spoke to Israel from the pillar of cloud, and they followed the laws and decrees he gave them. 8 O LORD our God, you answered them. You were a forgiving God to them, but you punished them when they went wrong. 9 Exalt the LORD our God, and worship at his holy mountain in Jerusalem, for the LORD our God is holy! (NLT)

"Reader, are you a believer? Then your sin is forgiven you."

A holy and forgiving King. Worshipping and praying to God, our holy King, is a privilege. The psalmist mentions three men (Moses, Aaron, Samuel) who prayed to God and he answered them (v. 6). It is very encouraging to know that the Lord does hear his children's prayers! Though these men faithfully obeyed God (v. 7), they did seem brash to come before a perfect God on behalf of a sinful nation. Nevertheless, God forgave the people for their sin (v. 8). God is holy and yet he still forgives. "So to forgive sin as at the same time to express abhorrence of it, is the peculiar glory of God, and is best seen in the atonement of our Lord Jesus." God answers our prayers for others, which is only possible by God's forgiveness through Jesus Christ, who paid for the guilt of our sin. We praise the holy and forgiving Lord (mentioned four times in this passage), who is faithfully committed to his people.

Prayer. Father, aware of my sinfulness, I am glad for your forgiveness. Even though you forgive, it is still humbling to know that that I can approach you in prayer. I am thankful for your Son, Jesus Christ, who has made it possible for me to come into your presence. Amen.

September 2   Psalm 100

1 Make a joyful noise to the Lord, all the earth! 2 Serve the Lord with gladness! Come into his presence with singing! 3 Know that the Lord, he is God! It is he who made us, and we are his; we are his people, and the sheep of his pasture. 4 Enter his gates with thanksgiving, and his courts with praise! Give thanks to him; bless his name! 5 For the Lord is good; his steadfast love endures forever, and his faithfulness to all generations. (ESV)

"Nothing can be more sublime this side of heaven than the singing of this noble Psalm by a vast congregation."

Thanksgiving. Spurgeon notes, "This is the only Psalm bearing this precise inscription [a psalm of thanksgiving]." The writer invites us to express thanks to God for two primary reasons. First, knowing God deserves thanksgiving (v. 3). While our praise may include an emotional component, worship also involves an informed response. "Our worship must be intelligent. We ought to know whom we worship and why . . . Only those who practically recognize his Godhead are at all likely to offer acceptable praise." Second, our relationship to God prompts us to give thanks (v. 4). Since he created us, we should give honor to our Creator. He also shepherds us by guiding, caring, and nurturing through the word. He is a good shepherd because he faithfully loves us (v. 5). He is worthy of praise! It is no wonder this psalm of thanksgiving has been "a great favorite with the people of God ever since it was written."

Prayer. Lord, I confess that my praise is conditioned by my emotional state. I want to offer my thanksgiving because of the greatness of your nature and for all you have done in my life. You are my Shepherd, who has faithfully cared for me throughout the years. I give you all the praise due to you. Amen.

1 I will sing of your love and justice, LORD. I will praise you with songs. 2 I will be careful to live a blameless life—when will you come to help me? I will lead a life of integrity in my own home. 3 I will refuse to look at anything vile and vulgar. I hate all who deal crookedly; I will have nothing to do with them. 4 I will reject perverse ideas and stay away from every evil. 5 I will not tolerate people who slander their neighbors. I will not endure conceit and pride. 6 I will search for faithful people to be my companions. Only those who are above reproach will be allowed to serve me. 7 I will not allow deceivers to serve in my house, and liars will not stay in my presence. 8 My daily task will be to ferret out the wicked and free the city of the LORD from their grip. (NLT)

"David's resolve was excellent, but his practice did not fully tally with it . . . he who does not even resolve to do well is likely to do very ill."

Resolutions of integrity. David makes commitments resolving to establish a particular lifestyle to reflect his love for God. In this "Psalm of pious resolutions" he wants to live with integrity (v. 2). Positively stated, integrity includes, among many other characteristics, emulating important qualities such as love and justice (v. 1). Negatively stated, living with integrity requires despising every form of corruption, including an evil heart (v. 4), slander (v. 5), and enjoying the company of dishonest people (v. 7). Integrity also requires us to repel forms of injustice (v. 8). Living with integrity is a challenge, but we can experience a measure of success. "We are no more perfect than David, nay, we fall far short of him in many ways." This is a solemn reminder that we need the Lord's forgiveness and his Spirit's enablement to obey and love Jesus.

Prayer. Lord, I am tired of making resolutions, knowing that I will fail to keep them. Yet, I am challenged and encouraged to make specific determinations for my spiritual growth. I want to walk with integrity before you and others. Amen.

September 4   Psalm 102:1-11

1 LORD, hear my prayer! Listen to my plea! 2 Don't turn away from me in my time of distress. Bend down to listen, and answer me quickly when I call to you. 3 For my days disappear like smoke, and my bones burn like red-hot coals. 4 My heart is sick, withered like grass, and I have lost my appetite. 5 Because of my groaning, I am reduced to skin and bones. 6 I am like an owl in the desert, like a little owl in a far-off wilderness. 7 I lie awake, lonely as a solitary bird on the roof. 8 My enemies taunt me day after day. They mock and curse me. 9 I eat ashes for food. My tears run down into my drink 10 because of your anger and wrath. For you have picked me up and thrown me out. 11 My life passes as swiftly as the evening shadows. I am withering away like grass. (NLT)

"[W]e have frequently met with individuals so disordered by sorrow . . . and we must confess that we have passed through the same condition ourselves."

Heartbreak. In this section, "the moaning monopolizes every verse, the lamentation is unceasing, sorrow rules the hour." Various factors contribute to the psalmist's anguish. He feels God has turned away and is hiding from him (vv. 1–2). Consequently, he feels God is angry at him and his people (v. 10). He knows God is listening to him, but his emotions cloud what he knows to be true. Also, his angry adversaries mock him (v. 8). As a result, David experiences symptoms such as fever (v. 3), a loss of appetite (v. 4), and "all-saturating, all-embittering sadness" (v. 9). He is left with the distinct impression that life has no meaning (v. 11). "There are times when through depression of spirit a man feels as if all life were gone from him, and existence had become merely a breathing death." When we go through grief, we often conclude our depressed outlook is unique. Although each person's circumstances are unique, many others have also experienced intense heartbreak and a profound sense of hopelessness.

Prayer. Father, I am thankful that you understand the pain people go through in their lives. You understand because your own Son, Jesus, experienced the hiddenness of your face and the ridicule of others. Come alongside those who are depressed and comfort them with a sense of your gentle presence. Amen.

September 5   Psalm 102:12–17

12 But you, O Lord, will sit on your throne forever. Your fame will endure to every generation. 13 You will arise and have mercy on Jerusalem—and now is the time to pity her, now is the time you promised to help. 14 For your people love every stone in her walls and cherish even the dust in her streets. 15 Then the nations will tremble before the Lord. The kings of the earth will tremble before his glory. 16 For the Lord will rebuild Jerusalem. He will appear in his glory. 17 He will listen to the prayers of the destitute. He will not reject their pleas. (NLT)

"The sovereignty of God in all things is an unfailing ground for consolation; he rules and reigns whatever happens, and therefore all is well."

Disconsolation and consolation. The psalmist has been dejected. His nation has been devastated by its enemies, leaving the country in ruins (v. 14). The citizens have either been exiled to another country or remain destitute in their own impoverished nation (v. 17). "Only the poorest of the people were left to sigh and cry among the ruins of the beloved city" of Jerusalem. It is no wonder that the psalmist is feeling disconsolate! In this state, he turns his attention to God, who is securely reigning on his throne (v. 12). Knowing this, he is consoled. The Lord, who appeared to be inattentive to his people's plight, will rise and show mercy to them (v. 13). Jerusalem will be rebuilt because God will be involved in its restoration (v. 16). God does mercifully hear and respond to the cries of the poor (v. 17). He is "the true source of all consolation," making it possible to have an abrupt turnaround in our outlook on life. We can have hope whether in our personal life, marriage, family, or church.

Prayer. Gracious God, at times I am disheartened about any number of areas in my sphere of influence. Some situations seem so hopeless and beyond repair. Your word has reminded me to turn my attention to your sovereignty and love for your people. You are attentive to my cries and I look forward to what you will do in these situations to bring honor to your name. Amen.

September 6   Psalm 102:18–22

18 Let this be recorded for future generations, so that a people not yet born will praise the LORD. 19 Tell them the LORD looked down from his heavenly sanctuary. He looked down to earth from heaven 20 to hear the groans of the prisoners, to release those condemned to die. 21 And so the LORD's fame will be celebrated in Zion, his praises in Jerusalem, 22 when multitudes gather together and kingdoms come to worship the LORD. (NLT)

"[T]he rebuilding of Jerusalem would be a fact in history for which the Lord would be praised from age to age."

The future generations. We are encouraged when we see God answer our prayers regarding desperate life situations (v. 17). While this has an inspiring impact on us, the psalmist is also thinking about future generations (v. 18). When they eventually read about God's mercy being shown in the past through the rebuilding of Jerusalem they will be encouraged. With this big-picture perspective, "we ought to have an eye to posterity, and especially should we endeavor to perpetuate the memory of God's love to his church and to his poor people, so that young people as they grow up may know that the Lord God of their fathers is good and full of compassion." It is easy to get caught up in the present. With a short-term perspective, we often fail to consider the future impact of our actions and decisions. When we adopt a long-term view, we will want to see countless future generations praising God for his loving faithfulness (vv. 21–22).

Prayer. Lord, forgive me when I get caught up with myself and my struggles. I have failed to consider how my reactions will influence the next generation. I pray that your faithfulness to me over the years will be a clear testimony to my family and friends. I want them to be inspired to follow you because they have heard of your goodness being revealed to previous generations. Amen.

23 He broke my strength in midlife, cutting short my days. 24 But I cried to him, "O my God, who lives forever, don't take my life while I am so young! 25 Long ago you laid the foundation of the earth and made the heavens with your hands. 26 They will perish, but you remain forever; they will wear out like old clothing. You will change them like a garment and discard them. 27 But you are always the same; you will live forever. 28 The children of your people will live in security. Their children's children will thrive in your presence." (NLT)

"[T]he psalmist remembered that when Israel was vanquished, her capital destroyed, and her temple levelled with the ground, her God remained the same self-existent, all-sufficient being, and would restore his people, even as he will restore the heavens and the earth, bestowing at the same time a new glory never known before."

The eternal, unchanging God. In this section, the psalmist is once again filled with sorrow realizing he may pass away before he sees the restoration of Jerusalem's glory (v. 22). Sadness is multiplied when one's life is cut short (v. 23) without the opportunity to see the completion of God's work (v. 24). It is possible Spurgeon may have had himself in mind when he penned these words, "Perhaps this may be our lot, and it will materially help us to be content with it." The exposition of this psalm and the others contained within volume 4 of *The Treasury of David* was completed in 1874. With more volumes to write, during his times of illness Spurgeon wondered if he would complete this major project. After thirteen years, he did accomplish his task well before his death at the early age of fifty-seven. In contrast to our frail and finite lives, God is eternal (vv. 25–26) and unchanging (vv. 27–28). When the psalmist saw the destruction of Jerusalem, his confidence depended on the Lord, who would intervene and restore his people once again (v. 28). Our desire for future generations to see God's work rests on the same basis with those generations prior to us.

Prayer. Everlasting God, I want to see you do great things during my lifetime. However, I accept the sober reality that my life is very short in comparison to your eternal timetable. Take my uncompleted work and do what you may for the sake of the next generation and for your glory. Amen.

September 8   Psalm 103:1–5

1 Bless the LORD, my soul, and all that is within me, bless his holy name. 2 Bless the LORD, my soul, and do not forget any of his benefits; 3 who pardons all your guilt, who heals all your diseases; 4 who redeems your life from the pit, who crowns you with favor and compassion; 5 who satisfies your years with good things, so that your youth is renewed like the eagle. (NASB)

"He selects a few of the choicest pearls from the casket [trunk] of divine love, threads them on the string of memory, and hangs them about the neck of gratitude."

The benefits of grace. David provides a litany of God's blessings as just cause for praising God. First, God forgives or pardons our sin (v. 3a), which is the foundation for all the other blessings we can enjoy. Spurgeon notes that this pardon is present, continual, and comprehensive. Second, God can heal our physical and spiritual disease because he is able to remove the effects of sin within us (v. 3b). Third, he removes us from the sphere of spiritual death (v. 4). He reverses the curse of spiritual death and crowns us with his compassion (v. 4). "Thus is the endless chain of grace complete. Sin is forgiven, its power subdued, and its penalty averted, then we are honoured, supplied, and our very nature renovated." These expressions of God's grace satisfy and renew us (v. 5). When we experience his love, we respond with thanksgiving (vv. 1–2). "Soul-satisfaction loudly calls for soul-praise, and when the mouth is filled with good it is bound to speak good of him who filled it." For us to do any less would be ungrateful on our part. Considering God's grace to Spurgeon throughout his lifetime, it is fitting that this psalm was his last reading and exposition before he passed away two weeks later.*

Prayer. Father, you have given me so many blessings. I am awed by your unconditional love for me. I cannot pay you back other than to live with gratitude for all you have done. What a satisfying and renewing way to live for you! Amen.

---

* Nettles, *Living by Revealed Truth*, 652.

September 9   Psalm 103:6–12

6 The LORD performs righteous deeds and judgments for all who are oppressed. 7 He made known his ways to Moses, his deeds to the sons of Israel. 8 The LORD is compassionate and gracious, slow to anger and abounding in mercy. 9 He will not always contend with us, nor will he keep his anger forever. 10 He has not dealt with us according to our sins, nor rewarded us according to our guilty deeds. 11 For as high as the heavens are above the earth, so great is his mercy toward those who fear him. 12 As far as the east is from the west, so far has he removed our wrongdoings from us. (NASB)

"Rich in it [mercy], quick in it, overflowing with it; and so had he need to be or we should soon be consumed."

Compassionate mercy. As his children, we often take God's mercy for granted. However, his deliverance of the children of Israel in Moses' day (v. 7) reminds us not to do this. Spurgeon rightfully places verse 8 within the context of Exodus 34:6, where God declares he will show mercy to people who sin against him. He has done this with us when he curtailed his anger (v. 9) through Christ's death. With his wrath satisfied on the cross, God does not punish those he has forgiven (vv. 10, 12). For this to occur, "he lingers long, with loving pauses, tarrying by the way to give space for repentance and opportunity for accepting mercy." When we express our desire to turn away from our former way of life, he shows his compassionate mercy (v. 11) by forgiving us. "Boundless in extent towards his chosen is the mercy of the Lord . . . [his] mercy from above covers all his chosen, enriches them, embraces them, and stands forever as their dwelling place." Spurgeon reminds us to give thanks for what we did not receive (his punishment) as well as what we did receive (his salvation).

Prayer. Lord, I am overwhelmed by the mercy you have shown with the offer of eternal salvation. Having known you for many years, I tend to take your mercy for granted. Forgive me for this. I also ask that I might show your compassionate mercy to others who have offended or hurt me. To do so, make my heart tender by helping me see them the way you do. Amen.

September 10   Psalm 103:13-18

13 Just as a father has compassion on his children, so the Lord has compassion on those who fear him. 14 For he himself knows our form; he is mindful that we are nothing but dust. 15 As for man, his days are like grass; like a flower of the field, so he flourishes. 16 When the wind has passed over it, it is no more, and its place no longer knows about it. 17 But the mercy of the Lord is from everlasting to everlasting for those who fear him, and his justice to the children's children, 18 to those who keep his covenant and remember his precepts, so as to do them. (NASB)

"Blessed be his holy name for this gentleness towards his frail creatures."

The Father's compassion. Some fathers are aloof or harsh toward their children. In contrast, God's nature is full of loving kindness (v. 13). "He is at this moment compassionating us, for the word is in the present tense; his pity never fails to flow, and we never cease to need it." As our heavenly Father, he expresses tenderheartedness to his adopted children, who respond with love and obedience (v. 13). His continual mercy to us is assured due to the eternal covenant relationship between God and those who believe and obey him (v. 18). He is also lovingly attentive to the needs of our frail humanity—regardless of our age or health (v. 14). While we are prone to compassion-fatigue, God's compassion remains eternally for those who are a part of his family (v. 17)! Spurgeon sees the irony in this. "How wonderful that his mercy should link our frailty with his eternity, and make us everlasting too!"

Prayer. Father, I thank you for being so compassionate to me with my weaknesses. I confess that I get weary of the relentless requests to show compassion to the homeless near me and the valid needs around the world. By your Spirit, enable me to have an enlarged, compassionate heart, that I may continue showing mercy to those struggling with their issues. This is my prayer because I want to reflect your character to these people. Amen.

19 The LORD has established his throne in the heavens, and his sovereignty rules over all. 20 Bless the LORD, you his angels, mighty in strength, who perform his word, obeying the voice of his word! 21 Bless the LORD, all you his angels, you who serve him, doing his will. 22 Bless the LORD, all you works of his, in all places of his dominion; bless the LORD, my soul! (NASB)

"[H]e gathers up all his energies for one final outburst of adoration, in which he would have all unite, since all are subjects of the Great King."

Adoring the merciful King. As his children, we can anticipate God's eternal kindness because he has firmly established his throne and reign (v. 19). "This matchless sovereignty is the pledge of our security, the pillar upon which our confidence may safely lean." While Spurgeon wrote during Queen Victoria's growing empire, we cannot forget that it is God who continually rules over the whole universe (v. 19). "He is the only universal monarchy, he is the blessed and only Potentate, King of kings, and Lord of lords." In light of this universal reign, all of his creation is called on to praise the Lord (vv. 20–22). Within these verses, threefold praise is expected from the angels (v. 20), his servants (v. 21), and his created work on earth (v. 22). This is an expanding praise to God for "each one of the three blessings is an enlargement upon that which went before. This [v. 22] is the most comprehensive of all, for what can be a wider call than to all in all places?" But each one must praise and sing, "Praise the Lord, my soul" (v. 22) in anticipation of God's further mercy.

Prayer. Lord, you are my King and I join the rest of creation in praising you. I am awed by your incredible kindness and mercy shown to me, yet I grumble, questioning your kindness to me. I ask for your forgiveness. Reign in my life so that I may show mercy to others as you have shown me mercy. Amen.

September 12   Psalm 104:1–6*

1 Bless the Lord, my soul! Lord my God, you are very great; you are clothed with splendor and majesty, 2 covering yourself with light as with a cloak, stretching out heaven like a tent curtain. 3 He lays the beams of his upper chambers in the waters; he makes the clouds his chariot; he walks on the wings of the wind; 4 he makes the winds his messengers, flaming fire his ministers. 5 He established the earth upon its foundations, so that it will not totter forever and ever. 6 You covered it with the deep sea as with a garment; the waters were standing above the mountains. (NASB)

"The Psalm gives an interpretation to the many voices of nature, and sings sweetly both of creation and providence."

Days one and two. Spurgeon notes this psalm was written poetically to describe each day of the creation account in Genesis. However, the real focus is the greatness and majesty of God, who created everything (v. 1). Therefore, it is not surprising that God is praised throughout this entire psalm. This is the only fair conclusion one can arrive at. "He must be blind indeed who does not see that nature is the work of a king." With this statement, perhaps Spurgeon is referring to Charles Darwin's evolutionary theory which was fairly recent in his day. In contrast to Darwin's theory, it is God who creates light (v. 2), which points to his personal glory. Poetic imagery using the king's chambers and chariots describe the skies, clouds, winds, and angels (vv. 3–4). The creation of earth covered with water concludes the second day of creation. As we reverently ponder these creative acts, we are filled with adoration for God our Creator.

Prayer. Majestic God, some deny your role in creation, while others worship creation but not you. Both perspectives fail to honor you who created the world. I marvel at your creation on earth and in the universe because they are awesome reflectors of your power, wisdom, and glory. Amen.

---

* Spurgeon wrote, "The grand *Cosmos* of Psalm CIV [104] was not to be dismissed in a few days; even now, after laying our best efforts at its feet, we feel dissatisfied with the poor result. However, we have done our best, and have grappled honestly with all hard places" (*Treasury of David*, 4:v–vi).

September 13   Psalm 104:7-18

7 They fled from your rebuke, at the sound of your thunder they hurried away. 8 The mountains rose; the valleys sank down to the place which you established for them. 9 You set a boundary so that they will not pass over, so that they will not return to cover the earth. 10 He sends forth springs in the valleys; they flow between the mountains; 11 they give drink to every animal of the field; the wild donkeys quench their thirst. 12 The birds of the sky dwell beside them; they lift up their voices from among the branches. 13 He waters the mountains from his upper chambers; the earth is satisfied with the fruit of his works. 14 He causes the grass to grow for the cattle, and vegetation for the labor of mankind, so that they may produce food from the earth, 15 and wine, which makes a human heart cheerful, so that he makes his face gleam with oil, and food, which sustains a human heart. 16 The trees of the LORD drink their fill, the cedars of Lebanon which he planted, 17 where the birds build their nests, and the stork, whose home is the juniper trees. 18 The high mountains are for the wild goats; the cliffs are a refuge for the rock hyrax. (NASB)

"[H]e describes the separation of the waters . . . the formation of the rain, brooks, and rivers and the uprising of green herbs . . . of the third day."

Day three. Spurgeon describes with awe the emergence of land, water, and vegetation, which provides him with important insights. God cares for us because he does the same for all of his creation (vv. 11, 13–14). This same attentiveness which extends even to wild animals is a reminder of the high value he places on each of his creatures. "Must everything exist for man or else be wasted? What but our pride and selfishness could have suggested such a notion?" In addition to God's care, we see his power at work, including in the plants (v. 14). This truth implies that without God working in the situation our efforts are in vain. We should also be attentive to the signs of his ongoing activity as we go through our day. A further insight reveals a God who wisely designed everything for a purpose. The trees are created so that the birds have a place for their nests (v. 17). When we walk through a forest, we hear the birds singing, which is a testimony of God's creativity. Lastly, nature provides illustrations for our spiritual lives. Like the birds which fly and have nests (v. 12), we should sing as "we flit through time into eternity," knowing God is our dwelling place.

Prayer. Lord, I thank you for botanists and zoologists who give us great insight into the splendor of your creative work. Continue to give me a new and deeper appreciation for your wise design and caring provision in nature. Your creation fills me with awe of your majesty. Amen.

September 14   Psalm 104:19–23

19 He made the moon to mark the seasons, and the sun knows when to go down. 20 You bring darkness, it becomes night, and all the beasts of the forest prowl. 21 The lions roar for their prey and seek their food from God. 22 The sun rises, and they steal away; they return and lie down in their dens. 23 Then people go out to their work, to their labor until evening. (NASB)

"For all this man should praise the Lord of the sun and moon, who has made these great lights to be our chronometers, and thus keeps our world in order, and suffers no confusion to distract us."

Day four. We have a glimpse of God's purposes in the creation of the moon and sun. The moon's waning and waxing arrange the months, weeks, and days for worship (v. 19). Thus, the movement of the moon is not based on an "inanimate impersonal law, but as the appointment of our God." God has also created a rhythm in life (vv. 20–23). Night is a benefit to us, because without darkness it would be much more difficult to sleep. While we slumber, nocturnal animals commence their day by hunting (v. 22). Then, when the sun rises, they return to sleep while we start our day (v. 23). This daily rhythm is a powerful dynamic at work in creation. For example, who can domesticate a roaming lion? "The sun suffices to do it. He is the true lion-tamer." Once again, we note that nature provides illustrations for our spiritual benefit. When the lions roar, they are appealing to their Creator for food (v. 21). When we groan with unexpressed words in prayer, "the Spirit translates the voice of a lion" and finds we are seeking spiritual food from our Creator.

Prayer. Lord, I take the daily and monthly patterns of nature so much for granted. When I consider the exactness of the movements of the earth and moon, I am thankful they govern the rhythms in my life. I am amazed how your arrangement of the sun and moon perfectly fit the ways you have designed nature. Amen.

September 15   Psalm 104:24-30

24 LORD, how many are your works! In wisdom you have made them all; the earth is full of your possessions. 25 There is the sea, great and broad, in which are swarms without number, animals both small and great. 26 The ships move along there, and Leviathan, which you have formed to have fun in it. 27 They all wait for you to give them their food in due season. 28 You give to them, they gather it up; you open your hand, they are satisfied with good. 29 You hide your face, they are terrified; you take away their breath, they perish and return to their dust. 30 You send forth your Spirit, they are created; and you renew the face of the ground. (NASB)

"It is ours to study his works, for they are great."

Days five and six. God created the waters and vegetation, the moon and stars for his creatures' survival. This passage provides us with further insights into our creative God. He loves the rich variety of living species, from the smallest forms of life to the largest animals (vv. 24–25). Diversity originates with him! These creatures are wisely made, with each one situated in its proper place within the ecosystem. God also liberally provides for all his creatures (vv. 27–29). Although they must gather their food, it is God who ultimately supplies what they need. In addition, God sustains life (v. 30). Without him, all life would end. Since the words "breath" and "Spirit" (vv. 29–30) are interchangeable Hebrew words, "we see the Divine Spirit going forth to create life in nature even as we see him in the realms of grace." God's wise and loving care for his creatures gives us the assurance he will do the same for us who bear his image.

Prayer. Lord, I cannot take for granted the countless ways you sustain me throughout the day. Each breath is a gift from you for which I am deeply thankful. I also thank you for your creativity in providing so much variety in the world. You have given me a new appreciation for those who exercise their creative talents for the well-being of society. What a gift they are! Amen.

September 16   Psalm 104:31–35

31 May the glory of the LORD endure forever; may the LORD rejoice in his works; 32 he looks at the earth, and it trembles; he touches the mountains, and they smoke. 33 I will sing to the LORD as long as I live; I will sing praise to my God while I have my being. 34 May my praise be pleasing to him; as for me, I shall rejoice in the LORD. 35 May sinners be removed from the earth and may the wicked be no more. Bless the LORD, my soul. Praise the LORD! (NASB)

"We may regard the closing verses . . . as a Sabbath meditation, hymn, and prayer."

Day seven. With his creation completed, God rejoices with all that he has made (v. 31). It is only appropriate that we praise him for his creation (v. 33). "The birds sang God's praises before men were created, but redeemed men will sing his glories when the birds are no more." However, our praise to God is tempered by sin's curse, which has left its ugly mark on creation. We can still praise God because nature is stunningly beautiful, belying the negative effect of sin on creation. There will come a day when all evil is vanquished and God will "more fully [rejoice] when the earth is renovated." At that time, he will also deal with sinful humanity (v. 35). Until then, our responsibility is to pray for people to turn from their sinful ways and to the Lord. Through the restoration of nature and the redemption of individuals, God's glory will be seen and will endure. For our part, we are wisely called on to meditate on God himself and his creative work (v. 34).

Prayer. Lord Almighty, it has been good to pause and meditate on your creation through this psalm. Your word has enlarged my mind and heart because I have gained a greater appreciation for your created world. More importantly, it has given me more reason to praise you as my Creator and Savior. Amen.

September 17   Psalm 105:1-7

1 Give thanks to the LORD, call upon his name; make his deeds known among the peoples. 2 Sing to him, sing praises to him; tell of all his wonders. 3 Boast in his holy name; may the heart of those who seek the LORD be joyful. 4 Seek the LORD and his strength; seek his face continually. 5 Remember his wonders which he has done, his marvels and the judgments spoken by his mouth, 6 you descendants of Abraham, his servant, you sons of Jacob, his chosen ones! 7 He is the LORD our God; his judgments are in all the earth. (NASB)

"[S]urely the believer in the living God has before him the most amazing series of wonders ever heard of or imagined, his themes are inexhaustible and they are such as should hold men spellbound."

The value of remembering. Most of this psalm is found in 1 Chronicles 16, which is David's praise for the arrival of the ark of the covenant in Jerusalem. With this backdrop, the psalmist exhorts the people to be mindful of everything God has done for them throughout many years. His wonderful actions (v. 2) include wonders, miracles, and judgments on his enemies (v. 5). Spurgeon suggests that beyond sentimental reminiscing, it is important to remember what God has done for a spiritual reason. "If we would keep these [actions] in remembrance our faith would be stronger, our gratitude warmer, and our devotion more fervent, and our love more intense." Remembering God's activity kindles our spiritual growth. Our worship is enriched with gratitude for the many ways God shows his commitment to us (vv. 1–2). Our conversations are more about God's great activities (v. 2). Reflecting on his past faithfulness, we are stirred to seek God (mentioned three times in verses 3–4). "First we seek *him*, then his *strength*, and then his *face*." This active reflection leads us to place a higher priority on pursuing God for himself rather than for our own benefit. We can confidently come to him because of our relationship with him. He is our Father, who has chosen us to be his spiritual children (vv. 6–7).

Prayer. Lord, when I look back on my life, my mind is filled with so many ways you have shown your faithfulness. Gratitude and praise flood my soul. Your devotedness spurs me to long for a deeper relationship with you. I want to be faithfully committed to you because of my love for you. Amen.

September 18   Psalm 105:8–15

8 He has remembered his covenant forever, the word which he commanded to a thousand generations, 9 the covenant which he made with Abraham, and his oath to Isaac. 10 Then he confirmed it to Jacob as a statute, to Israel as an everlasting covenant, 11 saying, "To you I will give the land of Canaan as the portion of your inheritance," 12 when they were only a few people in number, very few, and strangers in it. 13 And they wandered from nation to nation, from one kingdom to another people, 14 he allowed no one to oppress them, and he rebuked kings for their sakes, saying, 15 "Do not touch my anointed ones, and do not harm my prophets." (NASB)

"[W]e are like sheep in the midst of wolves, but the wolves cannot hurt us, for our shepherd is near."

A promise with security. Global events, such as pandemics, serve as a reminder that very little is secure in this life. In contrast, God entered into a covenant as an unconditional promise to give Abraham and his descendants a homeland (vv. 8–9, 11). God pledged to protect and preserve his people wherever they would go (vv. 14–15). They would be secure apart from God because they were too few in number. Their situation reminds us of our dependence on God (v. 12). Through Jesus Christ, a new covenant is established (1 Cor 11:25) between God and his people. He makes an unconditional promise of an eternal inheritance for those whom he has chosen (Heb 9:15). Until we inherit heaven, divine protection gives us security. "Even so at this present time the remnant according to the election of grace cannot be destroyed, nay, nor so much as touched, without the divine consent. Against the church of Christ the gates of hell cannot prevail." We do well to remember God will be faithful because he promised to be with us (v. 8).

Prayer. Lord, at times life feels brutal and I wonder how I can survive in this world. Thank you that you have chosen me as your child and you are with me protecting me with your presence and strength. This is all I need to be secure in you. Amen.

September 19   Psalm 105:16–24

16 And he called for a famine upon the land; he broke the whole staff of bread. 17 He sent a man before them, Joseph, who was sold as a slave. 18 They forced his feet into shackles, he was put in irons; 19 until the time that his word came to pass, the word of the LORD refined him. 20 The king sent and released him, the ruler of peoples, and set him free. 21 He made him lord of his house, and ruler over all his possessions, 22 to imprison his high officials at will, that he might teach his elders wisdom. 23 Israel also came into Egypt; so Jacob lived in the land of Ham. 24 And he made his people very fruitful, and made them stronger than their enemies. (NASB)

"Thus was he in the best conceivable position for preserving alive the house of Israel with whom the covenant was made."

Timely provisions. God not only faithfully protects but also provides for us. During a famine, Joseph was sold by his brothers and ended up in Egypt (vv. 16–17). In time, Pharaoh gave Joseph the responsibility to oversee the country's grain supply (v. 21). Over a period of seven years, Joseph stored an adequate amount to last during the famine. Joseph wisely distributed the grain so that there was enough for the Egyptians and for his family who came from Canaan (vv. 22–23). As time went on, Joseph and his family grew in number and prospered (v. 24). God uses the most unlikely ways to supply the needs of his people. Spurgeon needed ongoing financial support for his orphanages. When some people withheld funds, God raised new supporters who contributed the required funds.* It is helpful for us to remember the ways God has faithfully met past needs, so that we can be encouraged when facing new challenges.

Prayer. Lord, in this journey of life, there are twists and turns which feel like significant setbacks. It is encouraging when I hear stories of your miracle-like, unexpected ways of meeting people's needs. Help me not to panic, but to trust in your sovereign purposes. As I learn to do this, I will patiently wait on you to provide what I need at just the right time. Amen.

* Dallimore, *Spurgeon*, 224.

September 20   Psalm 105:25-38

25 He turned their heart to hate his people, to deal cunningly with his servants. 26 He sent his servant Moses, and Aaron, whom he had chosen. 27 They performed his wondrous acts among them, and miracles in the land of Ham. 28 He sent darkness and made it dark; and they did not rebel against his words. 29 He turned their waters into blood, and caused their fish to die. 30 Their land swarmed with frogs even in the chambers of their kings. 31 He spoke, and a swarm of flies and gnats invaded all their territory. 32 He gave them hail for rain, and flaming fire in their land. 33 He also struck their vines and their fig trees, and smashed the trees of their territory. 34 He spoke, and locusts came, and creeping locusts, beyond number, 35 and they ate all the vegetation in their land, and ate the fruit of their ground. 36 He also fatally struck all the firstborn in their land, the first fruits of all their vigor. 37 Then he brought the Israelites out with silver and gold, and among his tribes there was not one who stumbled. 38 Egypt was glad when they departed, for the dread of them had fallen upon the Egyptians. (NASB)

"O give thanks unto Jehovah; call upon his name, make known his deeds among the people."

Signs of goodness. The psalmist continues to praise God for the many miracles performed while the Israelites were in Egypt. The Lord turned the Egyptians' hearts against the foreigners whom they had long enslaved (v. 25). God aroused the oppressors' hatred to accomplish his purpose to deliver the Israelites from the country. Furthermore, through Moses and Aaron, God demonstrated the power of his word (vv. 31, 34) by performing miraculous signs (vv. 26-27). Finally, God miraculously delivered his people from slavery. They left Egypt generously blessed with riches and good health (v. 37). Considering the harsh treatment they received, their physical well-being was a miracle. In contrast to the Egyptians, who experienced death in every household, Spurgeon notes, "Poverty and oppression had not enfeebled them." It is no wonder the Egyptians gladly paid them to leave (vv. 37-38).

Prayer. Lord, when I feel overwhelmed by the forces of darkness, you graciously show your love to me. Sometimes, your expressions of love are obvious. Other times, your love seems so mysterious. Let me trust in you and allow your powerful word to speak to me. Amen.

39 He spread out a cloud as a covering, and fire to illumine by night. 40 They asked, and he brought quail, and satisfied them with the bread of heaven. 41 He opened the rock and water flowed out; it ran in the dry places like a river. 42 For he remembered his holy word with his servant Abraham; 43 and he led out his people with joy, his chosen ones with a joyful shout. 44 He also gave them the lands of the nations, so that they might take possession of the fruit of the peoples' labor, 45 and that they might keep his statutes and comply with his laws; praise the LORD! (NASB)

"From the most unlikely sources the all-sufficient God can supply his people's needs."

Unlikely provisions. We often assume God will respond in predictable ways to our needs. However, he loves to surprise us. Having left Egypt, a large number of Israelites now faced the challenge to survive with a lack of water in the heat. The Lord lovingly cared for them in ways they could not imagine (vv. 39–41). These unexpected gifts were further indicators of God's past promised agreement with his people (v. 42). "Here is the secret reason for all this grace . . . he remembered his people because he remembered his covenant." Consequently, they not only survived; they thrived (v. 42). "They were *his* people, *his* chosen, and hence in them he rejoiced, and upon them he showered his favors that they might rejoice in him as their God, and their portion." Based on his faithfulness to the covenant relationship, God brought them to the land he promised them. "[T]his Psalm selects the happier theme and dwells only upon covenant love and faithfulness." They arrived in this new land so that they would obey him (vv. 44–45). Would they? Their poor response to God made his provision for them even more surprising.

Prayer. Father, in times of great need I recognize my dependence on you. I am thankful that I experience your grace through your presence. I am also delighted when I experience your faithful care in the most unexpected ways. Even though I am thrilled in these situations, forgive me for my failure to express thanks for your love packages sent my way. Amen.

September 22   Psalm 106:1–5

1 Praise the LORD! Oh give thanks to the LORD, for he is good; for his mercy is everlasting. 2 Who can speak of the mighty deeds of the LORD, or can proclaim all his praise? 3 How blessed are those who maintain justice, who practice righteousness at all times! 4 Remember me, LORD, in your favor toward your people. Visit me with your salvation, 5 so that I may see the prosperity of your chosen ones, that I may rejoice in the joy of your nation, that I may boast with your inheritance. (NASB)

"Israel's history is here written with the view of showing human sin, even as the preceding Psalm was composed to magnify divine goodness."

Sin and grace. In light of God's great love for his people (Ps 105), one would expect them to respond with gratitude and obedience. If they did, God would bless their nation (v. 3). However, they disobeyed him. "Hence the story which follows is in sad contrast to the happiness" God desired for his people. It is natural to ask why this psalm begins and concludes with shouts of "Praise the Lord" (vv. 1, 48). The answer is in God's exceptional patience with those he has chosen to have a personal relationship with (vv. 4–5). He shows them his grace and love even when they sin. His mercy certainly does not condone disobedience because he wants us to obey (v. 3) and praise (v. 1) him. Then God blesses us (v. 3). "Holiness is happiness. The way of right is the way of peace." We unfortunately miss out on these blessings when we choose to go our own way.

Prayer. Lord, how can I experience so much of your goodness and then disobey you? My lack of gratitude saddens me and grieves you. Apart from your persistent patience, it is amazing that you still love me! I am profoundly thankful for your faithful commitment. Turn my heart toward you so that I may experience your blessings. I want my life to be a witness of your incredible grace! Amen.

September 23   Psalm 106:6-12

6 We have sinned like our fathers, we have gone astray, we have behaved wickedly. 7 Our fathers in Egypt did not understand your wonders; they did not remember your abundant kindnesses, but rebelled by the sea, at the Red Sea. 8 Nevertheless he saved them for the sake of his name, so that he might make his power known. 9 So he rebuked the Red Sea and it dried up, and he led them through the mighty waters, as through the wilderness. 10 So he saved them from the hand of one who hated them, and redeemed them from the hand of the enemy. 11 The waters covered their adversaries; not one of them was left. 12 Then they believed his words; they sang his praise. (NASB)

"Sins of omission, commission, and rebellion we ought to acknowledge under distinct heads, that we may show a due sense of the number and heinousness of our offences."

The confession of sin. The nation's escape from their Egyptian captors highlights God's miraculous deliverance (vv. 8–11). However, they did not grasp and believe in God's power revealed in Egypt. Neither did they remember God's faithfulness repeatedly shown to them (v. 7). "The sin of the understanding leads on to the sin of the memory. What is not understood will soon be forgotten." They rebelled against the Lord "by doubting his power to deliver and questioning his faithfulness to his promise" (v. 7). No excuses could be given. For the distant past, a present national confession is made using three different terms (v. 6). Those in the desert eventually did believe when they looked back and saw all their captors had died (v. 12). But their response was "not to their credit but to their shame." Their belief rested on the miracle of the widespread death and not on God, who had acted on behalf of his people. They praised God (v. 12), but it was short-lived, as we will discover in the next meditation.

Prayer. Lord, it's too easy to excuse my sin altogether by denying, minimizing, or blaming. Or, when I focus on my sinful actions, I ignore my thoughts, attitudes, and emotions. I confess my sin by what I have done and also in the ways I have failed to love others. I confess my sin includes my lack of trust in you. Deepen my dependence on you. Help me to learn more of your nature and rely less on the tangible expressions of your faithfulness to me. Amen.

13 They quickly forgot his works; they did not wait for his plan,
14 but became lustfully greedy in the wilderness, and put God to
the test in the desert. 15 So he gave them their request, but sent
a wasting disease among them. 16 When they became envious
of Moses in the camp, and of Aaron, the holy one of the LORD,
17 the earth opened and swallowed up Dathan, and engulfed the
company of Abiram. 18 And a fire blazed up in their company;
the flame consumed the wicked. (NASB)

"[W]e are long in learning to wait for the Lord, and upon the Lord. With
him [the Lord] is counsel and strength, but we are vain enough to look for
these to ourselves, and therefore we grievously err."

Lust and envy. Changing our circumstances does not fundamentally change
our nature. Although the Israelites crossed the Red Sea, also known as the
"sea of weeds," Spurgeon notes that "far worse weeds grew in their hearts."
Ungrateful to God, they chose what they wanted to do (v. 13). Rather than
trusting in God's wise ways, they foolishly "would have him change the plans
of his wisdom, supply their sensual appetites, and work miracles to meet
their wicked unbelief" (v. 14). This passion to have their way paradoxically
left them bitterly disappointed and spiritually lean (v. 15). In addition to
lust, they envied and rebelled against their leaders, Moses and Aaron (v. 16).
Instead of thanking God, they selfishly complained about Moses' choice of
Aaron as the high priest who would intercede for them. "It is the mark of bad
men that they are envious of the good, and spiteful against their best benefac-
tors." If we want to have our hearts transformed, God's word and Spirit can
gradually uproot the "weeds" of lust and envy which are deeply planted there.

Prayer. Lord, forgive me when I think my way is the best approach to life
rather than depending on your power. This faulty thinking leaves me spiritually famished, while I continue to feed on the sins of lust and envy. I confess
my lack of trust in you. Give me a hunger for your ways so that I can be richly
satisfied and transformed by you. Amen.

September 25   Psalm 106:19-23

19 They made a calf in Horeb, and worshiped a cast metal image. 20 So they exchanged their glory for the image of an ox that eats grass. 21 They forgot God their Savior, who had done great things in Egypt, 22 wonders in the land of Ham, and awesome things by the Red Sea. 23 Therefore he said that he would destroy them, if Moses, his chosen one, had not stood in the gap before him, to turn away his wrath from destroying them. (NASB)

"[I]dols are worthy of no respect, scorn is never more legitimately used than when it is poured upon all attempts to set forth the Invisible God."

Idolatry. This passage explains the reason idolatry is a sin and an affront to God. Idolatry violates the second commandment (not to have any other gods) which was given to Moses on Mount Horeb. With irony, the Israelites made an idol at "the very place where they had solemnly pledged themselves to obey the Lord" (v. 19). Rather than worshipping the one true living God, they now revered a metal calf (v. 20). What a poor exchange! God, who had delivered them, was now pushed out of their minds and hearts (vv. 21–22). They did not only forget his commands, but they had "forgotten the nature and character of Jehovah or they could never have likened him to a grass eating animal." Had it not been for Moses' intercession for his people, God's anger at their idolatry would have resulted in their death (v. 23). Revering other gods is insidious because it distorts the heart's affections for anything other than God. Adulation of our human idols is pernicious, stopping us from loving the Lord and obeying his word. Why would we exchange the living God for anything else?

Prayer. Lord, I think I am above worshipping metal calves. When I look into my heart, however, I see my propensity to adore and pursue the good things in life rather than passionately following you. Given all you have done for me, increase my heart's affection and worship for you. Amen.

September 26   Psalm 106:24–31

24 Then they rejected the pleasant land; they did not believe his word, 25 but grumbled in their tents; they did not listen to the voice of the LORD. 26 Therefore he swore to them that he would have them fall in the wilderness, 27 and that he would bring down their descendants among the nations, and scatter them in the lands. 28 They also followed Baal-peor, and ate sacrifices offered to the dead. 29 So they provoked him to anger with their deeds, and a plague broke out among them. 30 Then Phinehas stood up and intervened, and so the plague was brought to a halt. 31 And it was credited to him as righteousness, to all generations forever. (NASB)

"If we do not believe the Lord's word, we shall think lightly of his promised gifts."

The sin of unbelief. With all the troubles they were experiencing in the desert, the people began to despise the land God promised them (v. 24). They now preferred Egypt over Canaan. Here was the fundamental problem: they did not believe God's promise of a new homeland. "This is the root sin." They doubted God and very soon began grumbling among themselves (v. 25). "Murmuring is a great sin and not a mere weakness; it contains within itself unbelief, pride, rebellion, and a whole host of sins." Instead of entering the land promised to them, God pledged that he would strike them down in the desert where they would die (vv. 26–27). Even divine judgment did not change their hearts! They chose to worship a false god and eat sacrifices to the idols (v. 28). To show his anger, God brought a plague upon them (v. 29). Only his mercy, through intercession, spared the people from further destruction (v. 30). A refusal to trust in God has profound effects in our hearts and with our relationships with God and those around us.

Prayer. Lord, your word reminds me that people will not usually move from unbelief to faith in you with warnings of your judgment on their sin. Only your Spirit can effectively give them regenerated hearts that can trust and follow you. Amen.

September 27   Psalm 106:32–39

32 They also provoked him to wrath at the waters of Meribah, so that it went badly for Moses on their account. 33 Because they were rebellious against his Spirit, he spoke rashly with his lips. 34 They did not destroy the peoples, as the Lord had commanded them, 35 but they got involved with the nations and learned their practices, 36 and served their idols, which became a snare to them. 37 They even sacrificed their sons and their daughters to the demons, 38 and shed innocent blood, the blood of their sons and their daughters whom they sacrificed to the idols of Canaan; and the land was defiled with the blood. 39 So they became unclean in their practices, and were unfaithful in their deeds. (NASB)

"Dalliance with sin is fatal to spiritual liberty."

Spiritual complacency. If we adopt a lackadaisical attitude regarding our spiritual life, we will experience tragic consequences. The Israelites knew this reality all too well. Without Moses in their newly settled land of Canaan (vv. 32–33), they continued to disobey God. Rather than destroying the surrounding nations as God had commanded (v. 34), they adopted their customs (v. 35). "They found evil company, and delighted in it. Those whom they should have destroyed they made their friends." Their conformity to the Canaanite culture included worshipping their idols, which became a snare to them (v. 36). Now enslaved by sin, they sacrificed their own children to these false gods (vv. 37–38). How ironic! "People will sooner wear the iron yoke of Satan than carry the pleasant burden of the Lord." As a result of their sins, they prostituted themselves (v. 39). They loved what was prohibited, while failing to love God and his word. They had broken "the marriage bond between them and the Lord, and fell into spiritual adultery . . . This was provocation of the severest sort." Conformity to values and practices contrary to Scripture ensnare us and lead us further from God.

Prayer. Lord, when I make compromises by deliberately disobeying your word, I fool myself into thinking my decisions are innocuous. However, I confess that I hurt myself, those around me, and, most importantly, you. By your Spirit, free me from the grip of sin's influence. Grant me the courage to be faithful to your word in a culture that increasingly opposes it. Amen.

40 Therefore the anger of the LORD was kindled against his people, and he loathed his inheritance. 41 So he handed them over to the nations, and those who hated them ruled over them. 42 Their enemies also oppressed them, and they were subdued under their power. 43 Many times he would rescue them; they, however, were rebellious in their plan, and they sank down into their guilt. 44 Nevertheless he looked at their distress when he heard their cry; 45 and he remembered his covenant for their sake, and relented according to the greatness of his mercy. 46 He also made them objects of compassion in the presence of all their captors. 47 Save us, LORD our God, and gather us from the nations, to give thanks to your holy name and glory in your praise. 48 Blessed be the LORD, the God of Israel, from everlasting to everlasting. And all the people shall say, "Amen." Praise the LORD! (NASB)

"[H]e had a father's heart, and a sight of their sorrows touched his soul, the sound of their cries overcame his heart, and he looked upon them with compassion."

The Father's heart. God's love for us is manifested in diverse ways. When we choose to disobey the Lord, he disciplines us (v. 42) to bring us back into a proper relationship with him. "God can make our enemies to be rods in his hands to flog us back to our best Friend." We often do not appreciate what he is doing in our lives, and subsequently, we may turn away from him (v. 43). Surprisingly, he continues to love us even when we are willfully disobedient children. When he hears our cries (v. 44), "his love burns on forever like the light of his own immortality." In our distress, he does not to turn his back on us because of his covenant with us (v. 45). This permanent commitment made to us is "the sure foundation of mercy . . . the fundamental basis of love which is never moved." Despite our many failings, he faithfully and unconditionally loves us. Filled with gratitude, we praise the Lord (vv. 47–48). Adoring the Savior is far better than grieving him.

Prayer. Heavenly Father, knowing that I have failed you countless times, I feel so undeserving to receive your grace. I am overwhelmed by your continued love for me. My greatest praise to you is to lovingly obey you. Amen.

September 29   Psalm 107:1–9

1 Give thanks to the Lord, for he is good, for his mercy is everlasting. 2 The redeemed of the Lord shall say so, those whom he has redeemed from the hand of the enemy 3 and gathered from the lands, from the east and from the west, from the north and from the south. 4 They wandered in the wilderness in a desert region; they did not find a way to an inhabited city. 5 They were hungry and thirsty; their souls felt weak within them. 6 Then they cried out to the Lord in their trouble; he saved them from their distresses. 7 He also had them walk on a straight way, to go to an inhabited city. 8 They shall give thanks to the Lord for his mercy, and for his wonders to the sons of mankind! 9 For he has satisfied the thirsty soul, and he has filled the hungry soul with what is good. (NASB)

"The Lord sets us longing and then completely satisfies us."

Wandering to longing satisfied. After returning (v. 3) from exile, the psalmist glances back to describe Israel's initial entry into the promised land many years before. Their wandering in the wilderness while hungry and thirsty, with no hope of supplies, had been daunting (v. 4). "The loneliness of a desert has a most depressing influence upon the man who is lost in the boundless waste." In their impoverished state, they cried to the Lord, who delivered them by leading them to the city (vv. 6–7). After reflecting on this account in the desert, the psalmist states a life principle: when we allow God to direct our lives, he will truly satisfy our deepest longings (v. 9). "That longing leads us into solitude, separation, thirst, faintness, and self-despair, and all these conduct us to prayer, faith, divine guidance, satisfying of the soul's thirst, and rest." When we are filled with good things (v. 9), the psalmist is not referring to material possessions but a quality of life found only in God. Today, Jesus is the way for people to enjoy a truly satisfied life that includes praising God for his goodness (v. 8).

Prayer. Lord, people are wandering around in life, attempting to fill their soul's longings with cheap substitutes. I pray that they will find Jesus, the true living bread and water, who will richly satisfy them. Spare me from looking anywhere else so that I may continually feast on you and your goodness. Amen.

September 30   Psalm 107:10–16

10 There were those who lived in darkness and in the shadow of death, prisoners in misery and chains, 11 because they had rebelled against the words of God and rejected the plan of the Most High. 12 Therefore he humbled their heart with labor; they stumbled and there was no one to help. 13 Then they cried out to the Lord in their trouble; he saved them from their distresses. 14 He brought them out of darkness and the shadow of death and broke their bands apart. 15 They shall give thanks to the Lord for his mercy, and for his wonders to the sons of mankind! 16 For he has shattered gates of bronze and cut off bars of iron. (NASB)

> "So also he frees men from care and trouble, and especially from the misery and slavery of sin."

From bondage to freedom. Lest we discount the grip sin can have on our lives, the psalmist confronts us with the harsh reality of sin's enslaving power. With poetic language, his people sat in a dark gloomy place, imprisoned with no physical escape (v. 16). In their cells, they were bound and chained with afflictions (v. 10). These "poor captives cannot stir because of their bonds, cannot rise to hope because of their grief, and have no power because of their despair." They could not blame their circumstances for their plight. There was only one reason—they rebelled against God's word (v. 11). "Those who will not be bound by God's law will, ere long, be bound by the fetters of judgment." As a result of their disobedience, they collapsed, and no one could lift them up (v. 12). Fortunately, their sorrow was not in vain. "When a soul finds all its efforts at self-salvation prove abortive . . . then the Lord is at work . . . preparing the afflicted one to receive his mercy." When they cried to the Lord, he responded by breaking down the powers of darkness and brought spiritual freedom (vv. 14, 16). Jesus Christ has broken the potency of spiritual bondage and delivers people so that they can experience true freedom.

Prayer. Father, I confess that sometimes sin is appealing. However, I only need to look around me to realize that its attractiveness is an illusion meant to trap and enslave me. Thank you for delivering me from the prison of sin through the power of the Holy Spirit and your word. Experiencing true freedom through you is better than enjoying the allure of sin. Amen.

October 1   Psalm 107:17–22

17 Fools, because of their rebellious way, and because of their guilty deeds, were afflicted. 18 Their souls loathed all kinds of food, and they came close to the gates of death. 19 Then they cried out to the LORD in their trouble; he saved them from their distresses. 20 He sent his word and healed them, and saved them from their destruction. 21 They shall give thanks to the LORD for his mercy, and for his wonders to the sons of mankind! 22 They shall also offer sacrifices of thanksgiving, and tell of his works with joyful singing. (NASB)

"Sin-sick souls should remember the power of the Word."

From diseased to healing. Some who suffer physically do so because they have wrongly mistreated their own bodies. Unhealthy decisions affect us in the spiritual realm as well (vv. 17–18). People make foolish choices when they sense their spiritual guilt before God. They may initially refuse divine treatment, the gospel, for their troubled souls and then they deteriorate further in their spiritual condition. In desperation, they may eventually turn to the Lord for help (v. 19). In his mercy, God brings spiritual healing through his word (v. 20). "Then is the soul driven to cry in the bitterness of its grief unto the Lord, and Christ, the eternal Word, comes with healing power in the direct extremity, saving to the uttermost." The most appropriate response is to praise God, the great physician who heals us (vv. 21–22).

Prayer. Gracious Father, I thank you for your continual healing power from the disease of sin in my life. Use your word and Spirit to expose the hidden and deep pockets of emotional wounds and hurts. I am grateful that you can restore me to become more like Jesus in my relationships with others. Amen.

October 2   Psalm 107:23–32

23 Those who go down to the sea in ships, who do business on great waters; 24 they have seen the works of the LORD, and his wonders in the deep. 25 For he spoke and raised a stormy wind, which lifted the waves of the sea. 26 They rose up to the heavens, they went down to the depths; their soul melted away in their misery. 27 They reeled and staggered like a drunken person, and were at their wits' end. 28 Then they cried out to the LORD in their trouble, and he brought them out of their distresses. 29 He caused the storm to be still, so that the waves of the sea were hushed. 30 Then they were glad because they were quiet, so he guided them to their desired harbor. 31 They shall give thanks to the LORD for his mercy, and for his wonders to the sons of mankind! 32 They shall also exalt him in the congregation of the people, and praise him at the seat of the elders. (NASB)

"Here the spiritual mariner's log agrees with that of the sailor on the sea."

From soul-storms to peace. Spurgeon draws from the imagery in this passage, of sailors in their battered boat on a tumultuous sea, to draw spiritual parallels for our life's storms. We can find ourselves "in troubled waters, tossed to and fro with a thousand afflictions. Doubts, fears, terrors, anxieties lift their heads like so many angry waves, when once the Lord allows the storm-winds to beat upon us." Spurgeon says of his own life, "Some of us have weathered many such an internal hurricane." The thought of being in control is shattered when we cannot figure out how to manage life (v. 27). In desperation, we cry out to God for his help (vv. 27–28). To teach us that we should not attempt to be in charge of our lives, God "sends some of his saints to the sea of soul-trouble, and there they see as others do not, the wonders of divine grace . . . they need God above all others, and they find him." As a consequence, he mercifully transforms our troubled and fearful minds so that we can experience his peace (vv. 29–30). No wonder the Lord should be praised for his mercy and grace shown to us in the adversities of life (vv. 31–32)!

Prayer. Lord, forgive me when I believe am in charge of my own life. Such thinking is foolhardy because it means denying your rightful role as the Lord of my life. Transform my faulty thinking and incline my heart to spare me from needless desperation. Thank you for granting me your supernatural peace in the midst of troubles. Amen.

October 3   Psalm 107:33-43

33 He turns rivers into a wilderness, and springs of water into a thirsty ground; 34 and a fruitful land into a salt waste, because of the wickedness of those who dwell in it. 35 He turns a wilderness into a pool of water, and a dry land into springs of water; 36 and he has the hungry live there, so that they may establish an inhabited city, 37 and sow fields and plant vineyards, and gather a fruitful harvest. 38 He also blesses them and they multiply greatly, and he does not let their cattle decrease. 39 When they become few and lowly because of oppression, misery, and sorrow, 40 he pours contempt upon noblemen and makes them wander in a pathless wasteland. 41 But he sets the needy securely on high, away from affliction, and makes his families like a flock. 42 The upright see it and are glad; but all injustice shuts its mouth. 43 Who is wise? He is to pay attention to these things, and consider the mercy of the LORD. (NASB)

"Those who notice providence shall never be long without a providence to notice."

Providential lovingkindness. This psalm describes people's calamities and the Lord who rescued them. Their deliverance is an indication of his merciful care (v. 41). We are wise to acknowledge this, not as good luck, but as God's providential hand (v. 43). Shortly after his conversion, Spurgeon began recognizing signs of God's providence and continued to do so throughout his life. He remarks on God's providence, "It is wise to observe what the Lord doth . . . we must observe wisely, otherwise we may soon confuse ourselves and others with hasty reflections upon the dealings of the Lord. . . In a thousand ways the lovingkindness of the Lord is shown, and if we will but prudently watch, we shall come to a better understanding of it." In fact, we can become "proficient scholars in this art" which will encourage us to praise God for his goodness.

Prayer. Lord, in my times of need I have experienced your love through very clear divine intervention. Improve my spiritual eyesight so that I can discern your hand in the day's activities. I ask this, not so much to bail me out of my troubles, but that I might notice your love and praise you for it. Amen.

October 4   Psalm 108:1–5

1 My heart is steadfast, O God! I will sing and make melody with all my being! 2 Awake, O harp and lyre! I will awake the dawn! 3 I will give thanks to you, O Lord, among the peoples; I will sing praises to you among the nations. 4 For your steadfast love is great above the heavens; your faithfulness reaches to the clouds. 5 Be exalted, O God, above the heavens! Let your glory be over all the earth! (ESV)

"He would march to battle praising Jehovah."

A resolute heart. Spurgeon observes the similarity between this psalm and the latter section of Psalm 57. However, the arrangement of verses leads to a slightly different focus in each psalm. Psalm 57 moves from prayer to praise; whereas Psalm 108 moves in the reverse order. In the latter case, we praise God in order to strengthen our faith in prayer before him. David is resolute in his commitment to sing to the Lord (v. 1). He is determined to do this even when he travels to the surrounding nations (v. 3). His thanksgiving has an impact on others. "He would carry his religion with him wherever he pushed his conquests, and the vanquished should not hear the praises of David, but the glories of the Lord of Hosts." As we live in the various sectors of society, our passion should be to see God exalted and receive glory (v. 5). This will occur as individuals learn more about Jesus Christ and the gospel. When we are known as thankful people, some will be drawn to find out the source of our joy and they will have the opportunity to join the groundswell of praise to Jesus!

Prayer. Lord, knowing how faithful you have been to me in the past, I am committed to praising and worshipping you even before the day's battles begin. May people around me see Jesus in my actions and attitudes so that they may come to know you as their Savior. Amen.

October 5   Psalm 108:6–13

6 That your beloved ones may be delivered, give salvation by your right hand and answer me! 7 God has promised in his holiness: "With exultation I will divide up Shechem and portion out the Valley of Succoth. 8 Gilead is mine; Manasseh is mine; Ephraim is my helmet, Judah my scepter. 9 Moab is my washbasin; upon Edom I cast my shoe; over Philistia I shout in triumph." 10 Who will bring me to the fortified city? Who will lead me to Edom? 11 Have you not rejected us, O God? You do not go out, O God, with our armies. 12 Oh grant us help against the foe, for vain is the salvation of man! 13 With God we shall do valiantly; it is he who will tread down our foes. (ESV)

"Now prayer follows upon praise, and derives strength of faith and holy boldness therefrom."

Prayer of holy confidence. With a heart resolutely committed to God, the psalmist now moves from praise to prayer. With "holy boldness" he asks God to give him victory against his enemies (vv. 6–9). His courage is rooted in God's covenant and guaranteed promise to David (1 Chr 17:10). In light of this, he goes into battle, knowing God is with him. His confidence will be tested by various challenges. Doubts may surface over the ability to conquer impregnable fortified cities (v. 10) or the existence of God's presence with his people (v. 11). Occasions such as this take "grand faith which can trust the Lord even when he seems to have cast us off. Some can barely trust him when he pampers them." We must ultimately trust in God's power to do what no one else can accomplish (vv. 12–13). While we may publicly experience victory, in the final analysis, God provides the resources for us.

Prayer. Almighty God, it is true that my confidence in prayer increases when I praise you for your character. I face great challenges, but I know your power is far greater than anything I face. Guard me from taking credit for successes when I know that you should receive all the glory and praise. Amen.

October 6   Psalm 109:1–5

1 God of my praise, do not be silent! 2 For they have opened a wicked and deceitful mouth against me; they have spoken against me with a lying tongue. 3 They have also surrounded me with words of hatred, and have fought against me without cause. 4 In return for my love they act as my accusers; but I am in prayer. 5 So they have repaid me evil for good, and hatred for my love. (NASB)

"He did nothing else but pray. He became prayer as they became malice."

A response to slander. It is difficult to receive criticism but much more so when it is unfair. David extended his friendship to a hostile group (vv. 4–5). In response, they retaliated with verbal attacks (vv. 2–3). Like David, Spurgeon was slandered by individuals who opposed his ministry and his commitment to God's word.[*] He comments on the impact of the accusations on David, and perhaps, on himself: "The misery caused to a good man by slanderous reports no heart can imagine but that which is wounded by them; in all Satan's armoury there are no worse weapons than deceitful tongues." In response to these verbal attacks, David prays (v. 4). "This was his answer to his enemies . . . True bravery alone can teach a man to leave his traducers unanswered, and carry the case unto the Lord." God enables us not to retaliate but graciously respond. When we do, it is a testimony of God working in our lives. We emulate the life of Jesus, who loved and prayed for those who viciously attacked him.

Prayer. Loving Father, when I am heartlessly criticized, I am deeply hurt. I need to confess my pain and the need to forgive those who have badmouthed me. I desperately need your grace to love them. I ask you for your Spirit's help so that I can become more like Jesus. Amen.

---

[*] Dallimore, *Spurgeon*, 66–68, 211–13. He was mocked by the press and accused by his fellow pastors within the same denomination. He chose not to respond to these verbal attacks.

October 7   Psalm 109:6-15

6 Appoint a wicked person over him, and may an accuser stand
at his right hand. 7 When he is judged, may he come out guilty,
and may his prayer become sin. 8 May his days be few; may another take his office. 9 May his children be fatherless, and his wife
a widow. 10 May his children wander about and beg; and may
they seek sustenance far from their ruined homes. 11 May the
creditor seize everything that he has, and may strangers plunder
the product of his labor. 12 May there be none to extend kindness
to him, nor any to be gracious to his fatherless children. 13 May
his descendants be eliminated; may their name be wiped out in a
following generation. 14 May the guilt of his fathers be remembered before the LORD, and do not let the sin of his mother be
wiped out. 15 May they be before the LORD continually, so that
he may eliminate their memory from the earth. (NASB)

"But what are we to make of such strong language? Truly this is one of the
hard places of Scripture."

Righteous indignation. David's language and the tone of this passage
shocks us. How could he write numerous love songs in the psalter and now
want to see families afflicted with economic ruin and death (vv. 9–11)?

> The gentlest hearts burn with indignation when they hear of bar-
> barities to women and children, of crafty plots for ruining the
> innocent, of cruel oppression of helpless orphans, and gratuitous
> ingratitude to the good and gentle . . . We wish well to all man-
> kind, and for that very reason we sometimes blaze with indigna-
> tion against the inhuman wretches

who trample on our fellow citizens. In other words, this passage rouses us
from our complacent attitudes when social injustices are perpetuated. We
should also take stock of our own attitude toward sin. We can have a namby-
pamby view toward evil, which would be just reason to confess this sin to
God. Like David and the prophets, we are to cry out for justice in society
where there is racism, mistreatment of the poor, genocide of ethnic minori-
ties, and oppression of the powerless. This is a way to be an advocate for our
fellow human beings.

Prayer. Lord, I know one day you will bring complete justice to this world, but this does not remove me from my active concern for social justice. Show me how I can reflect your grief and love for those who are afflicted by the evil deeds of others. Amen.

16 Because he did not remember to show mercy, but persecuted
the afflicted and needy person, and the despondent in heart, to
put them to death. 17 He also loved cursing, so it came to him;
and he did not delight in blessing, so it was far from him. 18 But
he clothed himself with cursing as with his garment, and it entered his body like water, and like oil into his bones. 19 May it be
to him as a garment with which he covers himself, and as a belt
which he constantly wears around himself. 20 May this be the
reward of my accusers from the LORD, and of those who speak
evil against my soul. (NASB)

"Retaliation, not for private revenge, but as a measure of public justice, is
demanded by the psalmist, and deserved by the crime."

Social sins. In this passage, David asks God to act equitably toward those
who have committed social injustices. Sin recoils upon the perpetuators of
evil. To those who did not show compassion to the poor and brokenhearted,
no mercy should be shown (v. 16). Those who cursed the oppressed will be
cursed (vv. 17, 19). "It is but common justice that he should receive a return
for his malice, and receive it in kind, too." David's prayer is not motivated
by revenge; instead, he seeks public justice for the sake of society. For this
reason, "even Christian love would not wish to see the sentence mitigated."
This prayer also reflects the law of blessings and cursings (Deut 28). If an
individual violates God's laws, including the mistreatment of foreigners
(28:43-44), the garment of cursing will wrap itself around the offender (v.
19). In other words, the psalmist's prayer reflects the will and holy nature
of God, who is most offended by evil. At the same time, the gospel invites
people to repent and turn to the Lord; thus we "would all pray for the conversion of our worst enemy."

Prayer. Lord, the grave social injustices that inflict suffering on innumerable others makes me angry. Guard my heart from a spirit of meanness and
revenge. I pray that the unjust may experience the consequences of their actions, so that their hearts will be changed and they will genuinely turn to
Jesus. Amen.

October 9   Psalm 109:21–29

21 But you, God, the LORD, deal kindly with me for the sake of your name; because your mercy is good, rescue me; 22 for I am afflicted and needy, and my heart is wounded within me. 23 I am passing like a shadow when it lengthens; I am shaken off like the locust. 24 My knees are weak from fasting, and my flesh has grown lean, without fatness. 25 I also have become a disgrace to them; when they see me, they shake their head. 26 Help me, LORD my God; save me according to your mercy. 27 And may they know that this is your hand; you, LORD, have done it. 28 They will curse, but you bless; when they arise, they will be ashamed, but your servant will be glad. 29 May my accusers be clothed with dishonor, and may they cover themselves with their own shame as with a robe. (NASB)

> "The Lord has always a tender regard to brokenhearted ones, and such the psalmist had become."

A prayer of the brokenhearted. David's enemies have left him physically emaciated and emotionally wounded, a mere shadow of his former self (vv. 22–24). Events at the end of Spurgeon's life left him feeling weary and ill. The bitter treatment he had received from his fellow ministers left him deeply injured.* He wrote, "Slander and malice are apt to produce nervous disorders and to lead on to pining diseases." Pivotal to his outlook, David responds by turning to the Lord (v. 21). "Weak knees are strong with God, and failing flesh has great power in healing." Recognizing his own weakness and the fury of his foes, David appeals to the honor of God's name and his mercy (v. 21). Spurgeon notes that there are two aspects of divine mercy. One, God brings justice upon the evildoers (vv. 26–27). Two, the Lord blesses those who are heartbroken (v. 28a). We rejoice (v. 28b), but not for selfish reasons. "It ought to be our greatest joy that the Lord is honored in our experience."

Prayer. Merciful Father, many times I have experienced physical and emotional afflictions due to the attacks of others. Turning to you in desperate prayer, I have also experienced your gentle and healing mercy, which has restored me and, more importantly, honored your name. Amen.

---

* Dallimore, *Spurgeon*, 224.

October 10   Psalm 109:30–31

30 With my mouth I will give thanks abundantly to the LORD; and I will praise him in the midst of many. 31 For he stands at the right hand of the needy, to save him from those who judge his soul. (NASB)

"Never let us despair, yea, never let us cease to praise."

The brokenhearted rejoices. David has been grievously hurt by others and now he "praises, praises greatly, praises aloud . . . and praises with a right joyous spirit" (v. 30). He does not focus his praise on himself but on God (v. 31). "God will not be absent when his people are on their trial; he will hold a brief for them and stand in court as their advocate, prepared to plead on their behalf." What a contrast to the wicked, who have Satan as their advocate on their right hand (v. 6). It does not matter because God the King rejects their sentence of condemnation on David and others (v. 31). Those who are guilty will receive that same sentence. We do well not to retaliate when others unfairly criticize us. Since Jesus Christ stands with us as our advocate (1 John 2:1–2), we can go through unfair criticisms and accusations knowing he does not condemn us.

Prayer. Father, thank you for giving us men and women who stood faithful in their commitment to you and your word. They knew you as their defender when they were mistreated. Help me to follow in their footsteps by not caving in to stinging, unfounded accusations, and instead by turning to you. I praise you for backing me, not because I am perfect, but because your Son is my advocate. Amen.

1 The LORD says to my Lord: "Sit at my right hand, until I make your enemies your footstool." 2 The LORD sends forth from Zion your mighty scepter. Rule in the midst of your enemies! 3 Your people will offer themselves freely on the day of your power, in holy garments; from the womb of the morning, the dew of your youth will be yours. 4 The LORD has sworn and will not change his mind, "you are a priest forever after the order of Melchizedek." 5 The Lord is at your right hand; he will shatter kings on the day of his wrath. 6 He will execute judgment among the nations, filling them with corpses; he will shatter chiefs over the wide earth. 7 He will drink from the brook by the way; therefore he will lift up his head. (ESV)

> "As he is a Priest-King, so are his people all priests and kings, and the beauties of holiness are their priestly dress, their garments for glory and for beauty; of these priests unto God there shall be an unbroken succession."

The Priest-King. In the previous psalm, David cried to God, asking for mercy for himself and justice upon the wicked. In this psalm, David looks to the distant future and sees God revealing his mercy and justice. Jehovah God is speaking to "my Lord" (v. 1). This is a reference to Jesus Christ (Matt 22:41–45), whom Spurgeon calls the "Priest-King." Sitting at the Father's right hand, he reigns as king over the world by bringing judgment on those who have scorned him and his righteousness (vv. 1, 5–7). Jesus reigns also by extending his "scepter" or the good news of salvation to people who once opposed him (v. 2). The gospel's power draws many people to Jesus (v. 3). We have the privilege of communicating the gospel to others in order that they may come to know and enjoy life with him. We are secure knowing that in addition to being our king, Jesus is our priest (v. 4) who atoned for our sins by his death.

Prayer. Lord, I see your church is not always strong and the gospel is so readily resisted and rejected. Yet, my heart is encouraged when I see the big picture of your messianic reign in people's lives around the globe. I am truly thankful you are the Priest-King. Amen.

1 Praise the LORD! I will thank the LORD with all my heart as I meet with his godly people. 2 How amazing are the deeds of the LORD! All who delight in him should ponder them. 3 Everything he does reveals his glory and majesty. His righteousness never fails. 4 He causes us to remember his wonderful works. How gracious and merciful is our LORD! 5 He gives food to those who fear him; he always remembers his covenant. 6 He has shown his great power to his people by giving them the lands of other nations. 7 All he does is just and good, and all his commandments are trustworthy. 8 They are forever true, to be obeyed faithfully and with integrity. 9 He has paid a full ransom for his people. He has guaranteed his covenant with them forever. What a holy, awe-inspiring name he has! 10 Fear of the LORD is the foundation of true wisdom. All who obey his commandments will grow in wisdom. Praise him forever! (NLT)

"In design, in size, in number, in excellence, all the works of the Lord are great. Even in the little things of God are great."

God's glory in acts. This psalm declares God's glory through his many acts. His creative work reveals his wisdom requiring us to study what he has done (v. 2). His most important work revolves around his salvation and righteousness (v. 3) through Jesus Christ. Through him, we see his grace and compassion (vv. 4–5). With our new relationship, God acts faithfully according to his covenant with us (v. 5). He also demonstrates his power (v. 6) through the miraculous work of the Holy Spirit. Finally, God's actions are marked by integrity (vv. 7–8). We ponder on his various deeds so that we may know him better. In turn, this knowledge should evoke different responses from us (v. 10). As Spurgeon points out, "Holy reverence of God leads us to praise him, and this is the point which the Psalm drives at, for it is a wise act on the part of the creature towards his Creator . . . Practical godliness is the best of wisdom."

Prayer. Lord, I know it is important to develop a sound biblical understanding of your nature and work in our world. I also need to translate a sound theology of you into action. Enable me by your Spirit to respond with praise and obedience to you. Knowing who you are and living for you is a wise way to live! Amen.

1 Praise the LORD! Blessed is the man who fears the LORD, who greatly delights in his commandments! 2 His offspring will be mighty in the land; the generation of the upright will be blessed. 3 Wealth and riches are in his house, and his righteousness endures forever. 4 Light dawns in the darkness for the upright; he is gracious, merciful, and righteous. 5 It is well with the man who deals generously and lends; who conducts his affairs with justice. 6 For the righteous will never be moved; he will be remembered forever. 7 He is not afraid of bad news; his heart is firm, trusting in the LORD. 8 His heart is steady; he will not be afraid, until he looks in triumph on his adversaries. 9 He has distributed freely; he has given to the poor; his righteousness endures forever; his horn is exalted in honor. 10 The wicked man sees it and is angry; he gnashes his teeth and melts away; the desire of the wicked will perish! (ESV)

"We are at best but humble copies of the great original; still we are copies, and because we are so, we praise the Lord who hath created us anew in Christ Jesus."

God's glory in his people. The one who reveres God delights in obeying in his word (v. 1). When we obey him, we find ourselves becoming more upright individuals (v. 2). This does not happen by self-effort. Rather, we can stand firm against the winds of wickedness because uprightness "springs from the same root as the righteousness of God, and is, indeed, the reflection of it" (vv. 3–4, 9). With him actively working in our lives, we become more compassionate toward the poor (vv. 5, 9). Our concern for others reflects the way God responded to us in our spiritual poverty. Jesus came to indwell us in order to change our inner and outer lives. Besides making us better people, this spiritual transformation makes us more like Jesus so that we reflect God's glory or character (2 Cor 3:18).

Prayer. Lord, when I consider your glory, reflecting it in my life seems impossible. But I am thankful for your Holy Spirit indwelling and changing my life to become more like Jesus. Continue to do your supernatural work to transform my thoughts and emotions, as well as my speech and behavior. I want to reflect your glorious character to those around me. Amen.

October 14   Psalm 113

1 Praise the LORD! Yes, give praise, O servants of the LORD. Praise the name of the LORD! 2 Blessed be the name of the LORD now and forever. 3 Everywhere—from east to west—praise the name of the LORD. 4 For the LORD is high above the nations; his glory is higher than the heavens. 5 Who can be compared with the LORD our God, who is enthroned on high? 6 He stoops to look down on heaven and on earth. 7 He lifts the poor from the dust and the needy from the garbage dump. 8 He sets them among princes, even the princes of his own people! 9 He gives the childless woman a family, making her a happy mother. Praise the LORD! (NLT)

"How great a stoop from the height of his throne to a dunghill!"

Our God who stoops. National leaders who are obsessed with the trappings of power are seldom concerned about those considered least important in society. The psalmist paints a very different picture of God. His power and glory are above everything else that exists (vv. 4–5). "None can be compared to him for an instant . . . his throne, his whole character, his person, his being, everything about him is lofty, and infinitely majestic, so that none can be likened unto him." To emphasize his exalted position, the psalmist uses the imagery of a person bending down to observe everything (v. 6). Unlike many powerful leaders, God watches his creatures in order that he may act on behalf of the poor and needy (vv. 7–9). He picks them up and elevates them to a position higher than those who are viewed as great in society. Spurgeon writes that throughout history individuals such as John Bunyan and Mary, the mother of Jesus, experienced God's "gracious stoop of love." Jesus came down to earth so that he could lift us, with the stench of our spiritual filth, out of the dunghill of sin. We have the privilege of being with his family forever (v. 9).

Prayer. Father, I am grateful you showed your love by humbling and sending your Son, Jesus, to earth. Thank you for reaching out, rescuing and cleaning me of my sin. Create within me the same mindset of reaching out to those in need around me so they may come to know your love. Amen.

1 When Israel went out from Egypt, the house of Jacob from a people of strange language, 2 Judah became his sanctuary, Israel his dominion. 3 The sea looked and fled; Jordan turned back. 4 The mountains skipped like rams, the hills like lambs. 5 What ails you, O sea, that you flee? O Jordan, that you turn back? 6 O mountains, that you skip like rams? O hills, like lambs? 7 Tremble, O earth, at the presence of the Lord, at the presence of the God of Jacob, 8 who turns the rock into a pool of water, the flint into a spring of water. (ESV)

"Let the believer feel that God is near, and he will serve the Lord with fear and rejoice with trembling."

Trembling in God's presence. In his comments on Psalm 113, Spurgeon pointed out that this is the commencement of the Hallel psalms. These songs were read during the Passover feast to celebrate the Jews' deliverance from Egypt. According to Spurgeon, "no human mind has ever been able to equal, much less excel, the grandeur of this Psalm." The historical account provides rich parallels for us. When God led the people out of Egypt, all nature worshipped his majesty (vv. 3–8). If creation responds in this manner to his presence (v. 6), Spurgeon reminds us that in Jesus Christ "God has come nearer to us than ever he did to Sinai, or to Jordan, for he has assumed our nature." His incarnation should prompt us to serve him with reverence and love. Also, just as God brought the Israelites out from slavery, Jesus has given us victory because we are no longer slaves to the power of death and hell. Therefore, the Hallel psalms become our songs celebrating God's deliverance and provision for us throughout our spiritual journey.

Prayer. Lord, your presence and power are evident through nature and the demonic forces of this world. I thank you for coming into my life to deliver me from the clutches of Satan and enabling me to experience victory and freedom through Jesus. I bow in your presence to worship you, and I rise to continue my journey with you. Amen.

October 16   Psalm 115:1–8

1 Not to us, LORD, not to us, but to your name give glory, because of your mercy, because of your truth. 2 Why should the nations say, "Where, then, is their God?" 3 But our God is in the heavens; he does whatever he pleases. 4 Their idols are silver and gold, the work of human hands. 5 They have mouths, but they cannot speak; they have eyes, but they cannot see; 6 they have ears, but they cannot hear; they have noses, but they cannot smell; 7 they have hands, but they cannot feel; they have feet, but they cannot walk; they cannot make a sound with their throat. 8 Those who make them will become like them, everyone who trusts in them. (NASB)

"[T]he heathen were presuming upon the absence of miracles, were altogether denying the miracles of former ages."

The silent God. Spurgeon reminds us that this psalm was sung at the Passover celebrating God's past deliverance. Many centuries later, when God is not performing miracles, outsiders mock him for his apparent silence (v. 2). This incenses the psalmist, who aims his sarcasm at their gods. This section gives us some insights into how we should respond to such people. First, in trying to explain God's silence, we should not accept others' grossly distorted views of him. The idols or gods of the past (vv. 4–7) and the present do not bear any resemblance to Almighty God. He is silent because he lives and does as he pleases, unlike any other gods (v. 3). Second, we recognize that those who mock the living God are spiritually dead (v. 8). Their "god is fashioned like themselves [and] they will by degrees fashion themselves like their god." Their attitude to God reflects who they are and what they have become. Third, we should ask God to reveal his glory at the right time. We ask this not for our sake but for his sake (v. 1).

Prayer. Lord, I can be intimidated by those around me who jeer at you. Give me the grace to firmly and politely challenge their views of "God." I do so not to win arguments but to see you receive all the glory that you alone deserve. Amen.

October 17   Psalm 115:9-18

9 Israel, trust in the Lord; he is their help and their shield. 10 House of Aaron, trust in the Lord; he is their help and their shield. 11 You who fear the Lord, trust in the Lord; he is their help and their shield. 12 The Lord has been mindful of us; he will bless us. He will bless the house of Israel; he will bless the house of Aaron. 13 He will bless those who fear the Lord, the small together with the great. 14 May the Lord increase you, you and your children. 15 May you be blessed of the Lord, Maker of heaven and earth. 16 The heavens are the heavens of the Lord, but the earth he has given to the sons of mankind. 17 The dead do not praise the Lord, nor do any who go down into silence; 18 but as for us, we will bless the Lord from this time and forever. Praise the Lord! (NASB)

"The Lord has many blessings, each one worthy to be remembered, he blesses and blesses and blesses again."

Expect God to act. The Lord is not silent forever with his people. Three times the psalmist tells us God is our help and shield (vv. 9–11). He will defend them when they face their many opponents. Also, we are told five times that God will bless or show his favor to his people (vv. 12–15). "It is his nature to bless, it is his prerogative to bless, it is his glory to bless, it is his delight to bless; he has promised to bless, and therefore be sure of this, that he will bless and bless and bless without ever ceasing." God's blessings, fortunately, depend not on our social status but on our attitude of reverence for him (v. 13). We reveal this outlook by trusting the Lord (mentioned three times in verses 9–11). Why this emphatic exhortation to God's people? Their adversaries' continuous mocking could rattle their dependence on the Lord. However, as they persisted in trusting him, they would eventually experience his favor. They would discover they had good reason to bless the Lord (v. 18). Even though God seems silent, we can still praise him for what he has done in the past and will do in the future.

Prayer. Lord, I am impatient and want you to act now! Forgive me for my lack of trust in you. As I reflect on your past faithfulness, deepen my confidence in you. I ask this, for I want your favor and approval on my life, so that you receive all the praise and glory for what you will do. Amen.

October 18   Psalm 116:1-8

1 I love the LORD, because he hears my voice and my pleas. 2 Because he has inclined his ear to me, therefore I will call upon him as long as I live. 3 The snares of death encompassed me and the terrors of Sheol came upon me; I found distress and sorrow. 4 Then I called upon the name of the LORD: "Please, LORD, save my life!" 5 Gracious is the LORD, and righteous; yes, our God is compassionate. 6 The LORD watches over the simple; I was brought low, and he saved me. 7 Return to your rest, my soul, for the LORD has dealt generously with you. 8 For you have rescued my soul from death, my eyes from tears, and my feet from stumbling. (NASB)

"David's reason for his love [for God] was the love of God in hearing his prayers."

Resolved to pray. This psalm continues the Hallel prayer, with its focus on deliverance. The psalmist had faced death (vv. 3, 8) and cried out to God, who heard his petition and rescued him (v. 1). God did more than answer his request. Notice how the Lord responded (v. 2). God is pictured as "a tender physician or loving friend leaning over a sick man whose voice is faint and scarcely audible, so as to catch every accent and whisper." When we feel weak and overwhelmed by our circumstances, the Lord compassionately responds to us (vv. 5-6). Having experienced divine kindness, the psalmist reciprocates by declaring his love for God (v. 1). With this heightened awareness of God's love, the psalmist can enjoy genuine rest in him (v. 7). The commitment to pray is rooted in our relationship with God, who profoundly loves us at all times.

Prayer. Father, when I come to you with my needs, you are the one who lovingly answers. In response to your incredible love, I want to deepen my prayer life. Rather than approaching you with a list of my needs, I want my prayer life to be motivated out of love for you. How can I not when you love me so much? Amen.

October 19   Psalm 116:9–11

9 I shall walk before the LORD In the land of the living. 10 I believed when I said, "I am greatly afflicted." 11 I said in my alarm,
"All people are liars." (NASB)

"This is the psalmist's second resolution, to live as in the sight of God."

Resolved to godliness. Our love for God (v. 1) is measured by our obedience
to him (v. 9). We cultivate this obedience when we are consciously walking
before the Lord. Wherever we go, we are aware that he is with us and watching us. This proper perspective of God's omnipresence and omniscience
should prompt us to a holy lifestyle. This includes the manner of our conversation with God and others. The psalmist spoke to the Lord with honesty
because he trusted him (v. 10). All too often, there is a glaring gap between
how we converse with God and how we talk with others. In this case, the
psalmist hastily accused others (v. 11). "He believed, and therefore he rightly
prayed to God; he disbelieved, and therefore he wrongly accused mankind."
His accusations could not be justified and he confesses it to the Lord (and
to us). Acknowledgment of wrongdoing is an important aspect of godliness.

Prayer. Lord, I realize my resolve to lead a godly life fails miserably without
your strength. By your Spirit, do your work in me so that my inner life will
be integrated with my outer life. I want my conversation with others to be
marked by integrity. Amen.

October 20 Psalm 116:12-19

12 What shall I repay to the LORD for all his benefits to me? 13 I will lift up the cup of salvation, and call upon the name of the LORD. 14 I will pay my vows to the LORD; may it be in the presence of all his people! 15 Precious in the sight of the LORD is the death of his godly ones. 16 O LORD, I surely am your slave, I am your slave, the son of your female slave, you have unfastened my restraints. 17 I will offer you a sacrifice of thanksgiving, and call upon the name of the LORD. 18 I will pay my vows to the LORD, May it be in the presence of all his people, 19 in the courtyards of the LORD's house, in the midst of you, Jerusalem! Praise the LORD! (NASB)

"I will bring that which is more suitable, namely, the thanksgiving of my heart. My inmost soul shall adore thee in gratitude."

Resolved to live gratefully. Having seen God's great mercy, the psalmist asks the question (v. 12) on behalf of us: "How can I repay the Lord for all his goodness to me?" Having been close to death (vv. 15, 16b), it is only appropriate to express thanks and love to God for his mercy (v. 17). He desires both our praise and our commitment. Freed from the bonds of death, he now binds himself to the Lord (v. 16a). For us, Jesus is our Master and we are his servants. In gratitude for God's overwhelming mercy, we invite others to join in with praise to him (v. 19). "God's praise is not to be confined to a closet . . . but in the thick of the throng, and in the very center of assemblies, we should lift up heart and voice unto the Lord, and invite others to join with us in adorning him." Spurgeon reminds us that we began our spiritual pilgrimage with "hallelujah" (Ps 113:1) and we continue our journey living with gratitude, shouting hallelujah to our Master Jesus, who walks with us.

Prayer. Lord, there is no bondage greater than the power of sin. Neither is there any greater freedom than submitting to and serving you, my Master. Forgive me for complaining when life is tough. Teach me to live gratefully by recalling all the ways you show your tender love to me. Amen.

October 21   Psalm 117

1 Praise the LORD, all you nations; extol him, all you peoples. 2 For great is his love toward us, and the faithfulness of the LORD endures forever. Praise the LORD. (NIV)

> "This Psalm, which is very little in its letter, is exceedingly large in its spirit."

International deliverance. This, the fourth Hallel psalm, is the shortest psalm in the psalter. The writer looks beyond his people's deliverance from Egypt to the potential deliverance for all nations. God's love is extended beyond the Jewish people and to the rest of humanity (v. 2). Some believe these two verses suggest that every individual will spend eternity with God. However, the psalmist uses the name "LORD" to highlight God's faithfulness, which was expressed by establishing a covenant with Abraham (Gen 12:3). Through this patriarch "all nations of the earth [will] be blessed, and [God] will eternally keep every single promise of that covenant to all those who put their trust in him." God reveals his mercy by providing spiritual deliverance from the guilt of sin to anyone who believes in Jesus Christ (Titus 3:4–7). With people from nations and people groups around the world coming to know Christ, a global wave of praise to God erupts (v. 1). What a motivation to tell others of God's great love so that they can join this global song of hallelujah!

Prayer. Lord, it often seems I am preoccupied with my own little world. Broaden my vision as I ponder your love for every nation and ethnic group. When I worship you every Sunday, I am joining brothers and sisters from every corner of the world in an international festival of praise. Grant me wisdom as to how I can be involved in making the gospel known throughout the world. Amen.

October 22   Psalm 118:1-9

1 Oh give thanks to the LORD, for he is good; for his steadfast love endures forever! 2 Let Israel say, "His steadfast love endures forever." 3 Let the house of Aaron say, "His steadfast love endures forever." 4 Let those who fear the LORD say, "His steadfast love endures forever." 5 Out of my distress I called on the LORD; the LORD answered me and set me free. 6 The LORD is on my side; I will not fear. What can man do to me? 7 The LORD is on my side as my helper; I shall look in triumph on those who hate me. 8 It is better to take refuge in the LORD than to trust in man. 9 It is better to take refuge in the LORD than to trust in princes. (ESV)

"The fourfold testimonials to the everlasting mercy of God which are now before us speak like four evangelists."

His enduring love. In this last Hallel psalm, the writer focuses on God's love as revealed to four groups of people, including himself (vv. 2–7). In times of distress, God answered his prayer, prompting him to declare that God is on his side (v. 6). "The psalmist naturally rejoiced in the divine help; all men turned against him, but God was his defender and advocate, accomplishing the divine purposes of his grace." The takeaway is clear: it is better to rely on the Lord than any other person (vv. 8–9). Spurgeon outlines five succinct reasons to support this claim. First, we are wiser to place confidence in God, who is able to help us more than anyone else. Second, we make a better moral decision when we place our hope in God. Creatures naturally put their trust in their Creator, who deserves such trust. Third, we are safer with God's security than the limited security people offer us. Fourth, when we depend on God, we are positively affected. Trusting in people can make us totally dependent on them and miserable. In contrast, "confidence in God elevates, produces a sacred quiet of spirit, and sanctifies the soul." Fifth, while people will let us down, we can count on God, who can do far more than we could ever imagine.

Prayer. Lord, you know my confidence in you fades in the heat of discouraging situations. Forgive me for trusting in anything other than you, which ultimately leads to disappointment. I have every reason to rely on you. I am thankful that you care for me with your enduring love. Amen.

10 All nations surrounded me; in the name of the LORD I cut
them off! 11 They surrounded me, surrounded me on every side;
in the name of the LORD I cut them off! 12 They surrounded me
like bees; they went out like a fire among thorns; in the name of
the LORD I cut them off! 13 I was pushed hard, so that I was falling, but the LORD helped me. 14 The LORD is my strength and my
song; he has become my salvation. 15 Glad songs of salvation are
in the tents of the righteous: "The right hand of the LORD does
valiantly, 16 the right hand of the LORD exalts, the right hand of
the LORD does valiantly!" 17 I shall not die, but I shall live, and
recount the deeds of the LORD. 18 The LORD has disciplined me
severely, but he has not given me over to death. (ESV)

"The gardener prunes his best roses with most care."

His chastening love. When trials come, we tend to doubt God's love. We
wrongly believe that we should be immune from serious afflictions. This
thinking is contrary to the way God loves us. The psalmist had been surrounded by his enemies who were determined to kill him (vv. 10–13). He
believed God was chastening him because God spared him from death (v.
18). To those going through similar afflictions, Spurgeon would say, "[T]heir
pains are for their instruction, not for their destruction . . . for if he [God]
intended our final rejection he would not take the pains to place us under
his fatherly discipline." Drawing from his knowledge of flowers and shrubs,*
Spurgeon knew the value of God pruning our lives. "Chastisement is sent to
keep successful saints humble, to make them tender toward others, and to
enable them to bear the high honours which their heavenly Father puts upon
them." Even in grief we can "gather sweet flowers from the garden in which
the Lord has planted [bitter plants]."

Prayer. Father, I confess I need your loving discipline in my life. Though it
may hurt, give me grace to accept your pruning in those areas of my life that
need to be changed. I really do want to become more like Jesus so that others
may detect his fragrance in my life. Amen.

---

* Nettles, *Living by Revealed Truth*, 160, 169; Dallimore, *Spurgeon*, 186; Bacon,
Spurgeon, 145.

October 24   Psalm 118:19–29

19 Open to me the gates of righteousness, that I may enter through them and give thanks to the LORD. 20 This is the gate of the LORD; the righteous shall enter through it. 21 I thank you that you have answered me and have become my salvation. 22 The stone that the builders rejected has become the cornerstone. 23 This is the LORD's doing; it is marvelous in our eyes. 24 This is the day that the LORD has made; let us rejoice and be glad in it. 25 Save us, we pray, O LORD! O LORD, we pray, give us success! 26 Blessed is he who comes in the name of the LORD! We bless you from the house of the LORD. 27 The LORD is God, and he has made his light to shine upon us. Bind the festal sacrifice with cords, up to the horns of the altar! 28 You are my God, and I will give thanks to you; you are my God; I will extol you. 29 Oh give thanks to the LORD, for he is good; for his steadfast love endures forever! (ESV)

"In raising [Jesus] from the dead the Lord God exalted him to be the head of his church, the very pinnacle of her glory and beauty."

His victorious love. At one level, this passage is about the psalmist, David, entering the gates of Jerusalem, where he is enthroned as king. On another level, this passage finds it fullest meaning in Jesus Christ. The apostle Peter described Jesus as the stone that was rejected (v. 22; 1 Pet 2:4). As a result of the resurrection, he is now known as the "living stone." He is the only entrance to God for those who want to move into a relationship with him (vv. 19–20). We collectively praise the Lord with shouts of "Hosanna" because he has saved us from sin and death (vv. 19–20) and will return one day to deliver us from this world (v. 25). Yes, his love endures from the past to the future. He is worthy of our praise (v. 29). Hallelujah!

Prayer. Almighty God, thank you for the victory on the cross over sin and death. I am thankful that I can be a part of your universal church through faith in Jesus. I praise you as the King who rules in the lives of people around the world. One day your reign will be fully manifest, and every nation and power will acknowledge you as the victorious and eternal king. You are worthy of praise. Amen.

1 Blessed are those whose ways are blameless, who walk according to the law of the LORD. 2 Blessed are those who keep his statutes and seek him with all their heart—3 they do no wrong but follow his ways. 4 You have laid down precepts that are to be fully obeyed. 5 Oh, that my ways were steadfast in obeying your decrees! 6 Then I would not be put to shame when I consider all your commands. 7 I will praise you with an upright heart as I learn your righteous laws. 8 I will obey your decrees; do not utterly forsake me. (NIV)

"The one theme [of the Psalm] is the word of the Lord."

His word blesses. This section centers on those who experience God's blessing by obeying the word and living blamelessly (v. 1). They are not perfect, but they are steadily progressing in their daily walk with God. They sincerely seek after him (v. 2). "Seeking after God signifies a desire to commune with him more closely, to follow after him more fully, to enter into more perfect union with his mind and will, to promote his glory, and to realize completely all he is to holy hearts." They pursue the Lord with their whole being (v. 2). Anything competing with our loyalty to him must not be allowed to create a rift. While a divided heart is never whole, a broken heart may be. Spurgeon comments on this paradox, "[N]o heart is so whole in its seeking after God as a heart which is broken, whereof every fragment sighs and cries after the great Father's face." Broken people may wholeheartedly pursue God because they ardently love him and want to obey his word. He fills them with an enjoyment of him expressed with praise (v. 7). True happiness is found in a godly life.

Prayer. Father, I want to continue growing in my relationship with you. Through your word and Spirit, shape my heart to seek you consistently. I want to be motivated by a growing love for you, but this requires the hard work of examining my heart for anything that challenges my loyalty to you. May I delight in you by obeying and praising you! Amen.

---

* Spurgeon described this psalm as "vast" like the oceans. He admitted, "I confess I hesitated to launch upon it." Expounding on this psalm was "no mean feat of patient authorship and research" (*Treasury of David*, 5:v).

October 26　　　　Psalm 119:9-16

9 How can a young person stay on the path of purity? By living according to your word. 10 I seek you with all my heart; do not let me stray from your commands. 11 I have hidden your word in my heart that I might not sin against you. 12 Praise be to you, Lord; teach me your decrees. 13 With my lips I recount all the laws that come from your mouth. 14 I rejoice in following your statutes as one rejoices in great riches. 15 I meditate on your precepts and consider your ways. 16 I delight in your decrees; I will not neglect your word. (NIV)

"There is no hiding from sin unless we hide the truth in our souls."

His word is a treasure. The psalmist asks how we may grow in our spiritual life without succumbing to sin (v. 9a). His answer to his own question involves obedience to the word, which we must know (v. 9b). This knowledge includes the study of Scripture, but extends to the pursuit of God himself (v. 10a). We study the biblical text with our minds and hide the word in our hearts (v. 11). This exercise goes beyond Scripture memory. Spurgeon believes we joyfully store God's word in our affections like a treasure kept in a safety deposit box. When we do this, the heart is kept by the word because it is stored in our heart. This respect for God's word allows us to properly meditate on it (v. 15). As one frequently returns to fawn over new treasure, "so does the devout believer by frequent meditation turn over the priceless wealth he has discovered in the book of the Lord." With our affections set on God and his word we have an aversion to wander from him (v. 10 b). We would rather rejoice in the word (v. 14), and this indicates it is cleansing our lives.

Prayer. Lord, I confess the Bible has become so commonplace in my life and I have failed to treasure it. Spare me from the temptation to view Scripture only as a biblical text. Increase my appetite for studying and meditating on your word so I may pursue you. I want your truth to seep into the recesses of my heart and transform me from the inside out. This is the best way to live a pure life before you. Amen.

October 27   Psalm 119:17–24

17 Be good to your servant while I live, that I may obey your word. 18 Open my eyes that I may see wonderful things in your law. 19 I am a stranger on earth; do not hide your commands from me. 20 My soul is consumed with longing for your laws at all times. 21 You rebuke the arrogant, who are accursed, those who stray from your commands. 22 Remove from me their scorn and contempt, for I keep your statutes. 23 Though rulers sit together and slander me, your servant will meditate on your decrees. 24 Your statutes are my delight; they are my counselors. (NIV)

"It was *their* delight to slander and *his* delight to meditate."

His word is applicable. Spurgeon astutely notices the interconnection and the progression of the various stanzas of this psalm. The psalmist has already stated his resolve to meditate on the word (v. 15). Now he discusses the value of this meditation. He feels he is a foreigner in this world (v. 19) because arrogant people contemptuously slander him (vv. 21–23a). Now he has to apply what he has learned and promised to do. By knowing and meditating on Scripture he is reminded that God will deal with the proud (v. 21). Instead of responding to their accusations, he can remain silent and continue meditating on, and delighting in, God's word (vv. 23–24). He will allow God to deal with the arrogant while he obeys the Lord (v. 17). "Those who feed upon the word grow strong and peaceful, and are by God's grace hidden from the strife of tongues." Meditation on Scripture is a preventative measure to guard us from a response contrary to God's written revelation.

Prayer. Lord, I cannot separate my spiritual rhythms, such as meditation, from the demands and pressures of the day. Enable me to delight in your word so that it shapes my attitudes and responses to today's challenges. May my meditation on you guard me from wrong reactions because I want to obey you. Amen.

October 28   Psalm 119:25–32

25 I am laid low in the dust; preserve my life according to your word. 26 I gave an account of my ways and you answered me; teach me your decrees. 27 Cause me to understand the way of your precepts that I may meditate on your wonderful deeds. 28 My soul is weary with sorrow; strengthen me according to your word. 29 Keep me from deceitful ways; be gracious to me and teach me your law. 30 I have chosen the way of faithfulness; I have set my heart on your laws. 31 I hold fast to your statutes, LORD; do not let me be put to shame. 32 I run in the path of your commands, for you have broadened my understanding. (NIV)

"In these verses we shall see the influence of the divine word upon a heart which laments its downward tendencies."

His word revives. How can we go from groveling in our misery (v. 25) to energetically running in life (v. 32)? Soul work is required on our part. Spurgeon mentions how frequently the psalmist gives an account of his "inner soul life." In his particular case, he experienced genuine sorrow (v. 28). "Heaviness of heart is a killing thing, and when it abounds it threatens to turn life into a long death," resulting in an atrophied soul. At such times, we plead with God for help to survive (v. 25). The tone of this section reflects a cry not only for physical well-being but an emotional and spiritual revival. God, who breathed life into Adam, revitalizes us by his word (v. 25) and Spirit. We can pray using Scripture to strengthen us when we are weakened by life's crushing blows (v. 28). "Let us always resort to prayer in our desponding times, for it is the surest and shortest way out of the depths. In that prayer let us plead nothing but the Word of God." By God's grace, we can rise from the dust to run with a revived heart (v. 32).

Prayer. Father, I have discovered my soul can be suffocated by toxic attitudes and emotions. My heart can be hardened by destructive behavioral patterns and unhealthy relationships. Breathe new life into me so that I may once again find joy in being with you and obeying your word. Amen.

October 29   Psalm 119:33–40

33 Teach me, LORD, the way of your decrees, that I may follow it to the end. 34 Give me understanding, so that I may keep your law and obey it with all my heart. 35 Direct me in the path of your commands, for there I find delight. 36 Turn my heart toward your statutes and not toward selfish gain. 37 Turn my eyes away from worthless things; preserve my life according to your word. 38 Fulfill your promise to your servant, so that you may be feared. 39 Take away the disgrace I dread, for your laws are good. 40 How I long for your precepts! In your righteousness preserve my life. (NIV)

> "[T]he holy man would not only learn the *statutes*, but the *way* of them, the daily use of them."

His word provides a pathway. Living for Jesus Christ can be very challenging when society offers so many competing voices and options. Like the psalmist, we need practical direction to follow Jesus in a secular society. Thankfully, God's word provides a pathway for godly living (v. 35). We need the Lord to teach us his word in order that we may obey it for the duration of our life (v. 33). Since living in today's world is complicated, we also need spiritual discernment (v. 34) to know how to respond to specific situations. We may feel prepared for our life journey but the heart is one critical area that needs to be addressed (vv. 36–37). If we are honest, we will admit that our hearts are often shaped by fears (v. 39) or self-interest (v. 36) and can lead us to pursue "worthless things" (v. 37). Since "the leaning of the heart is the way in which life will lean," the "only way to cure a wrong leaning is to have the soul bent in the opposite direction." We need God's grace to redirect us to the right path in life.

Prayer. Lord, there are so many competing voices in society offering appealing options on how to enjoy life. From observation and personal experience, I know that those options lead to a dead end. Thank you for showing me the best path. Shape my heart to delight in following you. Grant me your wisdom and strength to persevere. Amen.

October 30   Psalm 119:41–48

41 May your unfailing love come to me, LORD, your salvation, according to your promise; 42 then I can answer anyone who taunts me, for I trust in your word. 43 Never take your word of truth from my mouth, for I have put my hope in your laws. 44 I will always obey your law, for ever and ever. 45 I will walk about in freedom, for I have sought out your precepts. 46 I will speak of your statutes before kings and will not be put to shame, 47 for I delight in your commands because I love them. 48 I reach out for your commands, which I love, that I may meditate on your decrees. (NIV)

"This is a part of his liberty; he is free from fear of the greatest, proudest, and most tyrannical of men."

His word emboldens. It is not uncommon to hold back in communicating the gospel with others. We can be intimidated by those who are skeptical or critical of the gospel (v. 42). Or, we feel personally ashamed when we consider other people's social status (v. 46). Despite these challenges, the psalmist states it is quite possible for us to experience freedom among those who differ from us (v. 45). If we want to know this freedom, we cannot be ashamed of God's word (v. 46). "The great hindrance to our speaking upon holy topics in all companies is shame, but the psalmist will 'not be ashamed'; there is nothing to be ashamed of, and there is no excuse for being ashamed." An unapologetic attitude is reinforced by a fervent love for God's word ("love" is twice mentioned in verses 47–48). With this mindset, we will have the courage to answer people's objections to the Christian faith (v. 42). For ourselves, we discover Scripture has applicable promises for daily living (v. 41). No wonder we can delight in the Scriptures (v. 47)!

Prayer. Lord, I confess I have been ashamed and intimidated to share the gospel with others. Create in my heart a greater love for your word, which emboldens and frees me to communicate truth to those who desperately need your salvation. Amen.

October 31   Psalm 119:49–56

49 Remember your word to your servant, for you have given me hope. 50 My comfort in my suffering is this: your promise preserves my life. 51 The arrogant mock me unmercifully, but I do not turn from your law. 52 I remember, LORD, your ancient laws, and I find comfort in them. 53 Indignation grips me because of the wicked, who have forsaken your law. 54 Your decrees are the theme of my song wherever I lodge. 55 In the night, LORD, I remember your name, that I may keep your law. 56 This has been my practice: I obey your precepts. (NIV)

"Some have comfort and no affliction, others have affliction and no comfort; but saints have comfort in their affliction."

His word comforts. Like us, the psalmist experienced trials, including being mocked by others (v. 51) and being left gripped by indignation (v. 53). In such times, the word can bring comfort to our troubled hearts (vv. 50, 52), but not with pious platitudes. Rather, comfort is derived by the choice to "remember," which is mentioned three times (vv. 49, 52, 55). For his part, the psalmist remembers God's laws (v. 52) which are true and just. Facing mockery (v. 51), the psalmist "finds comfort in the fact that there is a Judge of all the earth" who will make all things right in due time. He also takes the time to remember and reflect on God's character and past faithfulness to him. This backward glance encourages him to obey God's laws (v. 55). He is confident that God will remember him in his troubles (v. 49). "[T]hat word 'remember' . . . is used in Scripture in the tenderest sense, and suits the sorrowing and depressed." God does not forget us when we are experiencing difficult and painful times. This fills us with hope (v. 49).

Prayer. Father, I recall Jesus' words, "Do not let your hearts be troubled." Thank you for your promises which comfort, and for being the God who does not forget. You tenderly care for me when I am navigating deep waters. Yes, I trust in you and your word. Amen.

November 1   Psalm 119:57-64

57 You are my portion, LORD; I have promised to obey your words. 58 I have sought your face with all my heart; be gracious to me according to your promise. 59 I have considered my ways and have turned my steps to your statutes. 60 I will hasten and not delay to obey your commands. 61 Though the wicked bind me with ropes, I will not forget your law. 62 At midnight I rise to give you thanks for your righteous laws. 63 I am a friend to all who fear you, to all who follow your precepts. 64 The earth is filled with your love, LORD; teach me your decrees. (NIV)

"God has revealed as the word reveals . . . God is his portion, and yet he begs for a look at his face."

His word is an encounter. The psalmist believes that Scripture's primary purpose centers on developing a personal relationship with the living God. In comparison to all the world's riches, the Lord is his greatest possession (v. 57a). The psalmist backs up his desire for him with a resolute commitment to obey the word (v. 57b). We are reminded of Jesus' words, "If you love me, keep my commands" (John 14:15). Obedience is the practical side of our relationship with Jesus Christ. In addition to this, the psalmist expresses the desire to be in God's presence at any time (vv. 58a, 62). During his intimate time with the Father, the writer considers the way he is living (v. 59). "Consideration is the commencement of conversion: first, we think and then we turn . . . Action without thought is folly, and thought without action is sloth: to think carefully and then to act promptly is a happy combination." When he becomes very aware of his need to turn away from sin, he commits himself to turn to the word and obey it (vv. 59-60). This transformative relationship with God is reflected by those whom he befriends. He wisely spends time with those who also love and obey the Lord (v. 63).

Prayer. Lord, what a treasure it is to know you and to be in your presence. This is an opportunity for transformative encounters to reveal areas in my life that need to be aligned with your word. Forgive me for the rushed times which short-circuit this process. There are pockets of my life where I need to change and obey you. Give me wisdom to carve out adequate space for you to speak into them. Amen.

November 2   Psalm 119:65–72

65 Do good to your servant according to your word, LORD. 66 Teach me knowledge and good judgment, for I trust your commands. 67 Before I was afflicted I went astray, but now I obey your word. 68 You are good, and what you do is good; teach me your decrees. 69 Though the arrogant have smeared me with lies, I keep your precepts with all my heart. 70 Their hearts are callous and unfeeling, but I delight in your law. 71 It was good for me to be afflicted so that I might learn your decrees. 72 The law from your mouth is more precious to me than thousands of pieces of silver and gold. (NIV)

"Good judgment is the form of goodness which the godly man most needs and most desires, and it is one which the Lord is most ready to bestow."

His word provides discernment. The psalmist describes a time when people smeared him with their lies (v. 69). When this happens to us, we might hastily conclude that God does not love us. Due to the psalmist's lack "of knowledge he had misjudged the chastening hand of the heavenly Father, and therefore he now asks to be better instructed." In view of his unfair assessment of God, the psalmist now prays for discernment to better understand God's purpose for this affliction (v. 66a). With new insight, he recognizes he went astray when life was going well prior to his hardship (v. 67). "Why is it that a little ease works in us so much disease?" Spiritual insight enables him to see that God's discipline was for his good (v. 71). Now, rather than going astray, he obeys the word (v. 67). Having gone through a hard situation, he knows by experience that God's truth is much better than anything this world offers (v. 72). God is good to us (vv. 65, 68), but when we go through trials we need divine perception to affirm he is good at all times.

Prayer. Father, forgive me when I question your goodness in difficult circumstances. At such times, I need a proper perspective to see that such moments and situations are for my good. While I cannot fully understand your ways, enable me to perceive from your word how I can respond well by obeying you. Amen.

November 3   Psalm 119:73-80

73 Your hands made me and formed me; give me understanding to learn your commands. 74 May those who fear you rejoice when they see me, for I have put my hope in your word. 75 I know, LORD, that your laws are righteous, and that in faithfulness you have afflicted me. 76 May your unfailing love be my comfort, according to your promise to your servant. 77 Let your compassion come to me that I may live, for your law is my delight. 78 May the arrogant be put to shame for wronging me without cause; but I will meditate on your precepts. 79 May those who fear you turn to me, those who understand your statutes. 80 May I wholeheartedly follow your decrees, that I may not be put to shame. (NIV)

"We care neither for devout dunces nor for intellectual icebergs."

The word supplies divine understanding. God's word transcends our natural ability to grasp it. Since we are finite creatures made by our Creator, we are unable to understand his eternal truth (v. 73a). The good news is that he created us with a spiritual capacity to fathom the depths of Scripture. In his creation of humanity, he fashioned us with both a body to do his will and a soul to learn his divine will (v. 73b). With a reverential awe of God and a desire to know him, we have a primary motivation for understanding his word (v. 79). With the aid of the Holy Spirit, who gives insight to the word, we must "think much" on it so that we are able to apply the truth to our circumstances. When we do this, we protect ourselves from taking wrongful actions (vv. 77-78). In the psalmist's case, he "would study the law of God and not the law of retaliation." Spurgeon notes that some believers are all heart and no head, or vice versa. When we possess both a devoted heart and a teachable mind, we can fully obey God's word (v. 80).

Prayer. Lord, I am thankful you created humanity with the capacity to receive spiritual truth from you. Guard my heart from a piety without knowledge, and intellectual pursuits without a passion for you. Open my mind to understand your truth. Enlarge my heart to embrace it. Strengthen my resolve to obey your word. Amen.

November 4   Psalm 119:81–88

81 My soul faints with longing for your salvation, but I have put my hope in your word. 82 My eyes fail, looking for your promise; I say, "When will you comfort me?" 83 Though I am like a wineskin in the smoke, I do not forget your decrees. 84 How long must your servant wait? When will you punish my persecutors? 85 The arrogant dig pits to trap me, contrary to your law. 86 All your commands are trustworthy; help me, for I am being persecuted without cause. 87 They almost wiped me from the earth, but I have not forsaken your precepts. 88 In your unfailing love preserve my life, that I may obey the statutes of your mouth. (NIV)

"Hope sustains when desire exhausts."

His word offers hope. God's people, including Spurgeon, are not spared from devastating experiences. In this section, we see "the psalmist *in extremis*. His enemies have brought him to the lowest condition of anguish and depression" (vv. 82–87). Nevertheless, together with the psalmist, we can have unwavering confidence in the word because it is God who speaks into our lives (v. 81). The Lord cannot break his promise to us because his words are trustworthy (v. 86). This gives us solid assurance in the midst of confusing situations. With hope rooted in God's character and his word, one could wrongly conclude that prayer is not necessary. But hope does not preclude prayer (v. 82). In fact, Spurgeon suggests that confident trust in the Lord increases our persistence in prayer and sustains us while we wait for answered prayer.

Prayer. Lord, when life's storms come along and my faith wavers, I am glad I am rooted in you. You are trustworthy and your word is reliable. I am thankful I can place my confidence in you. This is not wishful thinking, but a steadfast faith that is based on your character. Amen.

November 5   Psalm 119:89-96

89 Your word, LORD, is eternal; it stands firm in the heavens. 90 Your faithfulness continues through all generations; you established the earth, and it endures. 91 Your laws endure to this day, for all things serve you. 92 If your law had not been my delight, I would have perished in my affliction. 93 I will never forget your precepts, for by them you have preserved my life. 94 Save me, for I am yours; I have sought out your precepts. 95 The wicked are waiting to destroy me, but I will ponder your statutes. 96 To all perfection I see a limit, but your commands are boundless. (NIV)

"The power and glory of heaven have confirmed each sentence which the mouth of the Lord has spoken."

His word is eternal. The psalmist uses various words and insights from the created order to emphasize the eternal nature of God's truth (v. 89). "There is an analogy between the word of God and the works of God . . . both of them are constant, fixed, and unchangeable. God's Word which established the world is the same as that which he has embodied in the Scriptures." Just as the ordered movements of the planets, seasons, and oceans continue to exist for millennia, his eternal word endures or stands the test of time (v. 91). Both creation and his word serve God's purposes. As God holds together his creation (Col 1:17), his word sustains us in our trials (v. 92). God, who breathed life into his created world, provides the "life-giving energy" through the word for our lives (v. 93). The universe's vast expanse illustrates that God's truth has no limits (v. 96). His word "touches every act, word and thought . . . it judges the motives, desires, and emotions of the soul."

Prayer. Everlasting Lord, you know how society's attitude toward your word has changed over the years. Even though it is ridiculed as being outdated with respect to today's issues, I am thankful that your written revelation with its eternal truths speaks into personal and social issues. Your word endures because it reflects the breadth of your wisdom and faithfulness. Amen.

November 6 Psalm 119:97–104

97 Oh, how I love your law! I meditate on it all day long. 98 Your commands are always with me and make me wiser than my enemies. 99 I have more insight than all my teachers, for I meditate on your statutes. 100 I have more understanding than the elders, for I obey your precepts. 101 I have kept my feet from every evil path so that I might obey your word. 102 I have not departed from your laws, for you yourself have taught me. 103 How sweet are your words to my taste, sweeter than honey to my mouth! 104 I gain understanding from your precepts; therefore I hate every wrong path. (NIV)

"A holy life is the highest wisdom and the surest defense."

His word provides wisdom. The psalmist offers us a better alternative to today's countless philosophies—biblical wisdom. Spurgeon defines it as "knowledge put to practical use." The main source for this is God's word (v. 98), which is qualitatively superior to other teachers or philosophers (v. 99). Through Scripture, we gain the spiritual acuity to see our way through difficult situations, enabling us to make right responses and choices (vv. 98, 104). This provides guardrails to protect us in the pursuit of a godly life (vv. 101–2). We do not quickly amass wisdom; we gather it slowly by meditating on and delighting in God's word (vv. 97, 99, 103). Having ruminated on his truth, we can prudently obey the Lord (v. 100). Therefore, "we may count ourselves happy to have such a wise, prudent, and beneficial law to be the rule of our lives. We are wise if we obey and we grow wise by obeying" (v. 104).

Prayer. Lord, I confess that I have not always lived wisely and the consequences have been painful. Use my meditation on your word to make me wiser and let me honor you in my decisions and responses. Amen.

November 7   Psalm 119:105-12

105 Your word is a lamp for my feet, a light on my path. 106 I have taken an oath and confirmed it, that I will follow your righteous laws. 107 I have suffered much; preserve my life, LORD, according to your word. 108 Accept, LORD, the willing praise of my mouth, and teach me your laws. 109 Though I constantly take my life in my hands, I will not forget your law. 110 The wicked have set a snare for me, but I have not strayed from your precepts. 111 Your statutes are my heritage forever; they are the joy of my heart. 112 My heart is set on keeping your decrees to the very end. (NIV)

"One of the most practical benefits of Holy Writ is guidance in the acts of daily life."

His word reveals a pathway. The psalmist's adversaries placed figurative hidden traps along the darkened road to kill him (vv. 109–10). "We are walkers through the city of the world and we are often called to go out into its darkness . . . This is a true picture of our path through this dark world; we should not know the way or how to walk in it, if the Scripture . . . did not reveal it." God's truth illumines our path, guiding us on how to live in this darkened world (v. 105). To follow his truth, a firm resolve is required (v. 106) in order to avoid being tempted by other voices in society. This unyielding decision is not based merely on sheer willpower, but with a joyful attitude toward God's word (v. 111) and a genuine desire to obey the truth (v. 112). "To this end create in us a clean heart, and daily renew a right spirit within us, for only so shall we incline in the right direction."

Prayer. Lord, there many luminaries who advise us to follow their road to success and happiness. But I do not want to be ensnared by their so-called enlightened approaches to life. Illumine my mind and heart with your word so I more clearly see your way through this dark and treacherous world. I humbly ask you for your Spirit to strengthen my resolve, soften my heart, and quicken my feet to follow you. Amen.

November 8   Psalm 119:113-20

113 I hate double-minded people, but I love your law. 114 You are
my refuge and my shield; I have put my hope in your word. 115
Away from me, you evildoers, that I may keep the commands of
my God! 116 Sustain me, my God, according to your promise,
and I will live; do not let my hopes be dashed. 117 Uphold me,
and I will be delivered; I will always have regard for your decrees.
118 You reject all who stray from your decrees, for their delusions
come to nothing. 119 All the wicked of the earth you discard like
dross; therefore I love your statutes. 120 My flesh trembles in fear
of you; I stand in awe of your laws. (NIV)

"When we love the law it becomes a law of love, and we cling to it with
our whole heart."

His word demands commitment. The psalmist speaks of those who are
double-minded (v. 113). They waver in their minds but they have a firm de-
termination to mislead others (v. 118). God is not pleased with such people
(vv. 118-19) and he calls us to have a steadfast commitment to him and his
word. This commitment starts with an awe for God himself, which fosters a
love for his word (vv. 113, 119-20). When our hearts are rightly positioned
before God, we hate all forms of evil, including deceitfulness (v. 113a). "In
proportion to his love to the law was his hate for men's inventions." We should
not minimize these two strong emotions because they "are as important as
the acts of life, for they are the fountain and spring from which the actions
proceed." We will want to obey God's word (v. 115). With this attitude, God
gives us the grace to sustain us with our commitment (v. 116).

Prayer. Lord, today so many are constantly thrashing around, trying to figure out how to survive in life. They pursue every novel approach they think
will help them to live better. I would rather follow you, but I cannot do this
on my own. I want to revere you and wholeheartedly commit myself to obey
your word. Amen.

November 9   Psalm 119:121-28

121 I have done what is righteous and just; do not leave me to my oppressors. 122 Ensure your servant's well-being; do not let the arrogant oppress me. 123 My eyes fail, looking for your salvation, looking for your righteous promise. 124 Deal with your servant according to your love and teach me your decrees. 125 I am your servant; give me discernment that I may understand your statutes. 126 It is time for you to act, LORD; your law is being broken. 127 Because I love your commands more than gold, more than pure gold, 128 and because I consider all your precepts right, I hate every wrong path. (NIV)

"Because the ungodly found fault with the precepts of God, therefore David was all the more sure of their being right."

His word provides absolutes. In light of society's general conviction that there are no absolutes, the psalmist's contrary belief certainly seems outdated to many. His conviction that there are absolutes is not based on personal opinion but on the very nature of God and his word. Facing perpetual wickedness by those who take God lightly, he longs for the Lord to deliver him (v. 123). He acts according to God's moral standard of what is right and wrong (v. 126). God's certain response has a practical implication for us. If we love God, then we also love his word, with its ethical standards (v. 127). We should equally despise that which is contrary to his moral will (v. 128). "Love to truth begat hatred of falsehood . . . he was a good lover or a good hater, but he was never a waverer . . . he had not a good word for any practice which would not bear the light of truth." For the psalmist, his own moral character guided him to act consistently within this framework (v. 121). Regardless of society's stance on morals, God's word does not vacillate on its benchmark for ethical living.

Prayer. Lord, society is confused about what is right and wrong in every area of life. I am so thankful your word provides a clear compass by which I should live. Your moral standard provides a social ethic that encourages personal well-being and flourishing relationships. Grant me the courage to hold to, and live out, your standards in this messy world. Amen.

November 10   Psalm 119:129-36

129 Your statutes are wonderful; therefore I obey them. 130 The unfolding of your words gives light; it gives understanding to the simple. 131 I open my mouth and pant, longing for your commands. 132 Turn to me and have mercy on me, as you always do to those who love your name. 133 Direct my footsteps according to your word; let no sin rule over me. 134 Redeem me from human oppression, that I may obey your precepts. 135 Make your face shine on your servant and teach me your decrees. 136 Streams of tears flow from my eyes, for your law is not obeyed. (NIV)

"David was always practical, and the more he wondered the more he obeyed."

His word is wonderful. The psalmist declares that God's word is wonderful (v. 129) and Spurgeon suggests a few reasons. Scripture is inerrant and effective in teaching, encouraging, and strengthening our walk with the Lord. His word is also remarkable because its supernatural truth can illuminate our finite understanding (v. 130). His divine light dispels the spiritual darkness of our minds with spiritual understanding (1 Cor 2:14–16). With a renewed heart and mind, personal changes occur. We have a hunger to learn more about God's truth (v. 131). God shows his favor by teaching us his will (v. 135). With this spiritual appetite for his truth, we desire to obey the word because we do not want sin to dominate our lives or others' (vv. 133, 136). We view God's divine truth with awe, knowing it inwardly and outwardly transforms our lives.

Prayer. Father, forgive me when I view your word with anything less than wonder and awe. Create in me an increased hunger for your word so its truths may seep into my heart and mind, transforming my attitudes toward, and conduct with, others. Amen.

137 You are righteous, LORD, and your laws are right. 138 The statutes you have laid down are righteous; they are fully trustworthy. 139 My zeal wears me out, for my enemies ignore your words. 140 Your promises have been thoroughly tested, and your servant loves them. 141 Though I am lowly and despised, I do not forget your precepts. 142 Your righteousness is everlasting and your law is true. 143 Trouble and distress have come upon me, but your commands give me delight. 144 Your statutes are always righteous; give me understanding that I may live. (NIV)

"Here he extols God's Word, or recorded judgments, as being right, even as their Author is righteous."

His word is righteous. The psalmist declares God to be righteous and his word is in accord with this (v. 137). His promises have been thoroughly tested over time (v. 140) and found to be pure and true (v. 142). "It is pure in its sense, pure in its language, pure in its spirit, pure in its influence. As God is love, so his law is the truth, the very essence of truth, truth applied to ethics, truth in action." We can trust his unchanging and reliable word (v. 138). We can also allow the pure truth of his word to test our heart's spiritual condition (v. 140). For the psalmist, loving God's promises "is a proof that he himself was pure in heart, for only those who are pure love God's Word because of its purity." When we are troubled, we can be encouraged by the promises and assurances in Scripture (v. 143).

Prayer. Lord, I am so thankful that your word is so trustworthy when so much in today's world is unreliable. The reliability of your word fills me with gratitude. Incline my heart to regularly delight in the truth of Scripture so that I might obey you. Amen.

November 12   Psalm 119:145-53

145 I call with all my heart; answer me, LORD, and I will obey your decrees. 146 I call out to you; save me and I will keep your statutes. 147 I rise before dawn and cry for help; I have put my hope in your word. 148 My eyes stay open through the watches of the night that I may meditate on your promises. 149 Hear my voice in accordance with your love; preserve my life, LORD, according to your laws. 150 Those who devise wicked schemes are near, but they are far from your law. 151 Yet you are near, LORD, and all your commands are true. 152 Long ago I learned from your statutes that you established them to last forever. 153 Look on my suffering and deliver me, for I have not forgotten your law. (NIV)

"He who has been with God in the closet will find God with him in the furnace."

His word shapes prayer. Throughout the centuries, God's people have used the psalter to orientate their prayer life. The psalmist prays when he faces his adversaries (v. 150). Three times he calls or cries out to God (vv. 145-47). "Heart cries are the essence of prayer . . . his whole soul pleaded with God, his entire affections, his united desires all went out towards the living God." However, without Scripture, our prayers may be misguided by our selfishness. The psalmist's prayer emerges after pondering on the word (v. 148). Throughout this psalm, he uses eight different words to describe the many aspects of God's word. This variety of terms suggests how Scripture can inform and influence the patterns of our prayer life. With this hope in the word, he prays to God throughout the day (vv. 147-48). When there is a pressing need, such as nearby enemies, he knows God is also close (v. 151). Having meditated on God's truth, and being assured of his presence and protection, he asks God's help to obey what he knows is true (vv. 151, 153).

Prayer. Lord, teach me to pray according to your will by meditating more on your word. It is a joy to have sufficient time to ponder on Scripture and then pray about my reflections. In the busyness of the day, mold my prayers according to your word. Amen.

November 13   Psalm 119:154-60

154 Defend my cause and redeem me; preserve my life according to your promise. 155 Salvation is far from the wicked, for they do not seek out your decrees. 156 Your compassion, LORD, is great; preserve my life according to your laws. 157 Many are the foes who persecute me, but I have not turned from your statutes. 158 I look on the faithless with loathing, for they do not obey your word. 159 See how I love your precepts; preserve my life, LORD, in accordance with your love. 160 All your words are true; all your righteous laws are eternal. (NIV)

"Because God is love he will give us life."

His word offers an enriched life. The psalmist faces persecution (v. 157) by those who reject God and his word (v. 158). He has, not surprisingly, prayed for deliverance (v. 153). Three times he asks for God to preserve him (vv. 154, 156, 159). There is more to the request than asking God to spare his physical life. He is asking God to "quicken" (KJV) or to renew him. This prayer to revitalize his life is founded on God's promise (v. 154) of love for him (v. 159). This rich inner soul life would sustain him even with his enemies surrounding him. Centuries later, the apostle Paul was persecuted but through the painful experience, Jesus' life was revealed through him (2 Cor 4:10). Jesus Christ, the eternal Word (John 1:1), offers himself to us (John 11:25) so we can be strengthened by his resurrection life.

Prayer. Father, I am so thankful for your life which brought me into a personal relationship through your Son, Jesus. I am also thankful for the many times I have experienced your revitalizing power when I have felt depleted by overwhelming circumstances. Amen.

November 14   Psalm 119:161–68

161 Rulers persecute me without cause, but my heart trembles at your word. 162 I rejoice in your promise like one who finds great spoil. 163 I hate and detest falsehood but I love your law. 164 Seven times a day I praise you for your righteous laws. 165 Great peace have those who love your law, and nothing can make them stumble. 166 I wait for your salvation, LORD, and I follow your commands. 167 I obey your statutes, for I love them greatly. 168 I obey your precepts and your statutes, for all my ways are known to you. (NIV)

"He trembled at the word of the Lord, and yet he rejoiced in it."

His word is awesome. The psalmist declares he trembles before God's word (v. 161). With awe he searches the truths in Scripture and is greatly rewarded (v. 162). His wonder for God's word shapes what he loves and hates (v. 163). In turn, he obeys God's truth (v. 167). This high respect for God's word is reflected by the manner in which he carefully crafts this entire psalm. Every section corresponds to a different Hebrew letter, starting from the first and ending with the last of the twenty-two letters in the Hebrew alphabet. Within each section, every verse is grouped together using the identical Hebrew letter that serves as the section header. In addition, each section contains eight verses and, with a few exceptions, eight distinct Hebrew words describing God's word. The creative and symmetrical structure points to the psalmist's awe for the word and an even greater reverence for God himself. It is no wonder we should stand in awe of God's word!

Prayer. Lord Almighty, like the man who found a hidden treasure in the field, may I appropriately respond with joy, obedience, and greater love and reverence for you, the Author of the word. Amen.

November 15   Psalm 119:169-76

169 May my cry come before you, LORD; give me understanding according to your word. 170 May my supplication come before you; deliver me according to your promise. 171 May my lips overflow with praise, for you teach me your decrees. 172 May my tongue sing of your word, for all your commands are righteous. 173 May your hand be ready to help me, for I have chosen your precepts. 174 I long for your salvation, LORD, and your law gives me delight. 175 Let me live that I may praise you, and may your laws sustain me. 176 I have strayed like a lost sheep. Seek your servant, for I have not forgotten your commands. (NIV)

"Even now I am apt to wander, and, in fact, have roamed already; therefore, restore me."

His word is for me. Until now, it is tempting to read this entire psalm as a testimony of one who continually loves, delights in, and meditates on God's word. We may think, "This is *his* testimony, but certainly not *mine*." As he does throughout the psalm, in verse 168 the psalmist reiterates his desire to obey God's commands. When we arrive at verse 176, it shocks us as it departs from the general tenor of this psalm. He now confesses his sin of wandering away, like a lost sheep, from the Lord. His confession becomes our confession. We are prone to wander from loving God and his written revelation. This is not the end story though. We, like the writer, belong to the Lord and are precious to him. We join with the psalmist, who "hopes to be not only sought, but forgiven, accepted, and taken into work again by his gracious Master." We know the truth (v. 176) and now it is a matter of being restored to Jesus, our Shepherd. The process of restoration begins by humbly praying with both the publican ("God be merciful to me, a sinner") and with the psalmist ("Seek your servant").

Prayer. Lord, I am thankful that this psalm was written for individuals who long for you but still fall far short. Thank you for your word, which expresses, shapes, and strengthens my heart so I may increasingly love and follow you. Amen.

1 I took my troubles to the LORD; I cried out to him, and he answered my prayer. 2 Rescue me, O LORD, from liars and from all deceitful people. 3 O deceptive tongue, what will God do to you? How will he increase your punishment? 4 You will be pierced with sharp arrows and burned with glowing coals. 5 How I suffer in far-off Meshech. It pains me to live in distant Kedar. 6 I am tired of living among people who hate peace. 7 I search for peace; but when I speak of peace, they want war! (NLT)

"Long, long enough, too long had he been an exile among
such barbarians."

Not my home. This is the first of fifteen psalms entitled the psalms of ascent, or pilgrim songs. In this first song, David is far from home and surrounded by deceitful people (vv. 2, 3), which distresses him (v. 1). This may refer to the specific time when Doeg the Edomite betrayed David (1 Sam 22:9). David does not respond with violence (v. 6). His love for living in peace with others stands in sharp contrast to their love for war (v. 7). In keeping with his character, David asks God to deal with them (vv. 3–4). While he was only a sojourner in Meshech, he feared settling down and living among these people (v. 5). He could not afford to risk becoming like them. As Christ-followers in our society, we need to remember and maintain our distinctive character. We face the continual danger of adopting our culture's values and practices. This is not our true world because we are foreigners with citizenship in heaven (1 Pet 2:11; Phil 3:20).

Prayer. Lord, it is not easy to live with different standards in today's society. I am tired of the negative labels this culture attaches to those who love Jesus. It would be easier just to fit in with everyone else. But this would displease you! I need your Holy Spirit to change me, and your word to instruct me, so that I do not conform to this culture's values. Amen.

November 17   Psalm 121

1 I look up to the mountains—does my help come from there? 2 My help comes from the LORD, who made heaven and earth! 3 He will not let you stumble; the one who watches over you will not slumber. 4 Indeed, he who watches over Israel never slumbers or sleeps. 5 The LORD himself watches over you! The LORD stands beside you as your protective shade. 6 The sun will not harm you by day, nor the moon at night. 7 The LORD keeps you from all harm and watches over your life. 8 The LORD keeps watch over you as you come and go, both now and forever. (NLT)

"None are so safe as those whom God keeps; none so much in danger as the self-secure."

Our keeper. The psalmist, a wise pilgrim, realizes God does not sleep (v. 5) but is engaged with his people. We are told five times that the Lord continually "watches" over us (vv. 3–5, 7–8). This word conveys more than a passive observance. He actively guards us, individually (v. 3) and collectively, as a community of faith (v. 4). He protects us from slipping and falling, whereby we would spiritually hurt ourselves (v. 3) "Soul keeping is the soul of keeping. If the soul be kept all is kept . . . God is the sole keeper of the soul. Our soul is kept from the dominion of sin, the infection of error, the crush of despondency the puffing up of pride." With confidence in his watchful eye, we can rely on him throughout the day. Therefore, "we may go on pilgrimage without trembling, and venture into battle without dread . . . since our growing sense of weakness makes us feel more deeply than ever our need of being kept."

Prayer. Loving Father, life can be very difficult and ruthless. I am so grateful that you are not oblivious to my situation. Thank you for watching and protecting me throughout my spiritual journey. Amen.

November 18   Psalm 122

1 I was glad when they said to me, "Let us go to the house of the
LORD." 2 And now here we are, standing inside your gates, O Jerusalem. 3 Jerusalem is a well-built city; its seamless walls cannot
be breached. 4 All the tribes of Israel—the LORD's people—make
their pilgrimage here. They come to give thanks to the name of
the LORD, as the law requires of Israel. 5 Here stand the thrones
where judgment is given, the thrones of the dynasty of David. 6
Pray for peace in Jerusalem. May all who love this city prosper. 7
Jerusalem, may there be peace within your walls and prosperity
in your palaces. 8 For the sake of my family and friends, I will say,
"May you have peace." 9 For the sake of the house of the LORD
our God, I will seek what is best for you, O Jerusalem. (NLT)

"He was glad to go into the house of the Lord, glad to go in holy company,
glad to find good men and women willing to have him in their society."

Journeying with God's people. We cannot do well on our spiritual journey
if we venture out on our own. We need others who are headed in the same
direction. This psalm portrays David and his people anticipating their arrival
in Jerusalem, or else they are already in the city. No matter how arduous the
journey, God watched over them (Ps 121:8) and brought them together to
joyfully worship him (vv. 1, 4). When we meet with other believers to worship the Lord, we are more than a collection of individuals. We are "closely
compacted" with each other (v. 3). In other words, we are "one in creed and
one in heart, one in testimony and one in service, one in aspiration and one
in sympathy." When the congregation is culturally and ethnically hetero-
geneous (v. 4), there must be respectful recognition of the diversity, with
fair treatment of one another (v. 5). We must be people of peace, which is
mentioned three times (vv. 6–8). For David's people, this is an appropriate
way to live in Jerusalem, the city of *shalom*. To live in unity with diversity
is to experience a wholesome, prosperous community life (v. 9). "Peace is
prosperity; there can be no prosperity which is not based on peace."

Prayer. Lord, I need other followers of Jesus to come alongside in my spiritual journey. Forgive me for thinking I can lead a solo Christian life. Help me
to be an encouragement to others by mutually directing our hearts to follow
and worship you. Amen.

November 19   Psalm 123

1 I lift my eyes to you, O God, enthroned in heaven. 2 We keep looking to the LORD our God for his mercy, just as servants keep their eyes on their master, as a slave girl watches her mistress for the slightest signal. 3 Have mercy on us, LORD, have mercy, for we have had our fill of contempt. 4 We have had more than our fill of the scoffing of the proud and the contempt of the arrogant. (NLT)

"[H]ere we look to the Lord himself, and this is the highest ascent of all by many degrees."

The looking eye. In Psalm 121, the writer looked to the hills for security. Now, he looks above them to the Lord himself (v. 1) in the face of ridicule from arrogant people (vv. 3–4). Spurgeon reminds us we must resolve to direct our focus on the Lord because our natural instinct is to look everywhere else for a quick solution. Looking to our heavenly Master, we may carefully observe his hands, which provide indications of his kindness (v. 2). By doing this, we "learn the divine will from every one of the signs which the Lord is pleased to use. Creation, providence, grace; these are all the motions of Jehovah's hand . . . Believers desire to be attentive to each and all of the directions of the Lord." When we are attentive to the ways God reveals himself, we see his mercy to us (v. 3).

Prayer. Lord, on this spiritual journey it is so tempting to look at other options to solve my problems. By your Spirit, strengthen my resolve to notice carefully the many ways you signal your love to me. Open my eyes to see them! Amen.

November 20   Psalm 124

1 What if the Lord had not been on our side? Let all Israel repeat: 2 What if the Lord had not been on our side when people attacked us? 3 They would have swallowed us alive in their burning anger. 4 The waters would have engulfed us; a torrent would have overwhelmed us. 5 Yes, the raging waters of their fury would have overwhelmed our very lives. 6 Praise the Lord, who did not let their teeth tear us apart! 7 We escaped like a bird from a hunter's trap. The trap is broken, and we are free! 8 Our help is from the Lord, who made heaven and earth. (NLT)

"From all confidence in people may we be rescued by a holy reliance upon our God."

Our supreme help. If we believe the spiritual journey is an easy one, this psalm paints a more realistic view. David uses several analogies to remind us that we will experience difficulties (vv. 3–7). Fires, floods, wild beasts, and traps are destructive, offering very little hope of survival. Nevertheless, there is hope because God is on our side (vv. 1–2). As he preserves the world he created (v. 8), he does likewise with us. "Did he create all that we see, and can he not preserve us from evils which we cannot see? Blessed be his name, he that has fashioned us will watch over us." He is also the Lord (vv. 1, 2, 6, 8) who, by his very name, has eternally pledged his love to us. No destructive forces can separate us from our Creator's covenant love (Rom 8:31, 35–39).

Prayer. Lord, it is alarming to see corrosive values and philosophies eroding many people's faith in you. Enable me to resist these destructive forces. I need your insight to see how I am influenced, your courage to repel these caustic effects, and wisdom to respond with your Spirit's power. I look to you in great dependence on your resources! Amen.

November 21   Psalm 125

1 Those who trust in the LORD are as secure as Mount Zion; they will not be defeated but will endure forever. 2 Just as the mountains surround Jerusalem, so the LORD surrounds his people, both now and forever. 3 The wicked will not rule the land of the godly, for then the godly might be tempted to do wrong. 4 O LORD, do good to those who are good, whose hearts are in tune with you. 5 But banish those who turn to crooked ways, O LORD. Take them away with those who do evil. May Israel have peace! (NLT)

"There is no conceivable reason why we should not trust in Jehovah, and there is every possible argument for doing so."

Trust God. Trials in our spiritual journey can dissipate our confidence in God. To counter this risk, the psalmist dwells on Mount Zion where God will rule as king one day (Ps 2:6; 110:2). Considering Zion's enduring quality, we are encouraged to trust in the Lord (v. 1) who is eternally King. Around Mount Zion are the mountains protecting Jerusalem's residents. The Lord envelops and protects us with his presence (v. 2), giving us confidence in him, especially when our faith is tested. "The people of God are not to expect immunity from trial because the Lord surrounds them, for they may feel the power and persecution of the ungodly." God will deal with the perpetrators of evil and those who are influenced by them (vv. 3, 5). At the same time, he will do good to those who love him (v. 4). Those who trust in God (vv. 1–2) and his actions (vv. 3–5a) will experience genuine peace (v. 5b).

Prayer. Gracious Father, you know my faith is sometimes shaken by circumstances. Strengthen my faith as I ponder on your presence and faithfulness to your people. Rather than living in fear I want to experience your peace, which exceeds human understanding. Amen.

November 22   Psalm 126

1 When the LORD brought back his exiles to Jerusalem, it was like a dream! 2 We were filled with laughter, and we sang for joy. And the other nations said, "What amazing things the LORD has done for them." 3 Yes, the LORD has done amazing things for us! What joy! 4 Restore our fortunes, LORD, as streams renew the desert. 5 Those who plant in tears will harvest with shouts of joy. 6 They weep as they go to plant their seed, but they sing as they return with the harvest. (NLT)

"If there were no sowing in tears there would be no reaping in joy."

Spiritual life cycles. During our spiritual pilgrimage we experience both the "highs" and the "lows." When this happens, too often we feel like spiritual failures. We naïvely expected the Christian life to be a steady upward climb without any stumbling and falling. The psalmist reminds us that we will encounter vibrant and dry times in our spiritual lives. It was so with the nation Israel (vv. 1–3). "Being in trouble, the gracious pilgrims remember for their comfort times of national woe which were succeeded by remarkable deliverances. Then sorrow was gone like a dream, and the joy which followed was so great that it seemed too good to be true . . . The captivity had been great, and great was the deliverance." When we feel we are in the spiritual wilderness (v. 4), sometimes God floods us with his presence. However, at other times, we experience trials for a season (vv. 5–6). We can be encouraged though. "[P]resent distress must not be viewed as if it would last forever: it is not the end, by any means, but only a means to the end." We will bear the fruit of joy in due season (vv. 5–6).

Prayer. Father, sometimes I forget that the Christian life is not a continual upward trajectory of spiritual growth. You are with me through the hard times, accomplishing your purposes. Draw me closer to you while I allow you to do your work in my life. Amen.

November 23   Psalm 127

1 Unless the LORD builds a house, the work of the builders is wasted. Unless the LORD protects a city, guarding it with sentries will do no good. 2 It is useless for you to work so hard from early morning until late at night, anxiously working for food to eat; for God gives rest to his loved ones. 3 Children are a gift from the LORD; they are a reward from him. 4 Children born to a young man are like arrows in a warrior's hands. 5 How joyful is the man whose quiver is full of them! He will not be put to shame when he confronts his accusers at the city gates. (NLT)

"He will undertake for us and prosper our trustful endeavours, and we shall enjoy a tranquil life, and prove ourselves to be our Lord's beloved by the calm and quiet of our spirit."

Futility or rest? Spurgeon reminds us that each of the pslams of ascent commence with a focus on God. If we do not depend on him and seek his divine favor in our activities, our efforts will be futile (vv. 1–3). To emphasize his point, the psalmist uses the word "vain" three times. We have a choice: to be exhausted by self-effort or to live contently by resting in God (v. 2). By depending on him, we are not only delivered from constant restlessness but we experience God's blessing. The psalmist uses the example of raising a godly family (vv. 3–5). "Let the Lord favor us with loyal, obedient, affectionate offspring, and we shall find in them our best helpers." Commenting on these verses, Spurgeon gives us a rare glimpse into his family life. He was "most grateful for two of the best sons." They were close to thirty years old when he penned his personal thoughts, "[A]s they have both grown up, and he has no child at home, he has without a tinge of murmuring . . . felt it might have been a blessing to have had a more numerous family." His sons are a witness of a father who did not live in vain because he sought God's favor in his life.

Prayer. Lord, many times I feel exhausted. This is not always due to the amount of work facing me, but because I have failed to depend on you. This is not the way to live! I want to rely on you more often in order that I may experience your favor. Then I will find true rest in you and my work will be used by you for your purposes. Amen.

November 24   Psalm 128

1 Blessed is everyone who fears the LORD, who walks in his ways!
2 you shall eat the fruit of the labor of your hands; you shall be
blessed, and it shall be well with you. 3 Your wife will be like a
fruitful vine within your house; your children will be like olive
shoots around your table. 4 Behold, thus shall the man be blessed
who fears the LORD. 5 The LORD bless you from Zion! May you
see the prosperity of Jerusalem all the days of your life! 6 May you
see your children's children! Peace be upon Israel! (ESV)

"He is happy now, for he is the child of the happy God, the ever living
Jehovah; and he is even here a joint heir with Jesus Christ, whose heritage
is not misery, but joy."

True happiness. Those who revere God are blessed (v. 1). "The fear of God is
the cornerstone of all blessedness. We must reverence the ever blessed God
before we can be blessed ourselves." According to Spurgeon, to be blessed
means to be happy as God's children. Enjoying the fruit of our labor is one
tangible expression of divine blessing (v. 2). We are happy when we are rewarded for our hard work. Healthy relationships are another blessing from
God (vv. 3–4). A fruitful ministry and a loving relationship are both evident
in Charles and Susannah Spurgeon's thirty-six years of marriage. People
knew they enjoyed a happy relationship. In addition to her husband's successful ministry, Susannah authored two books and impacted people's lives
by collecting money, clothing, and blankets for poor pastors.* These ministries were often conducted during times of severe illness for the Spurgeons.
The psalmist also mentions the blessing among the community of believers
("Zion," v. 5). The Spurgeons' ministries were a joyful blessing to their congregation and many others around the world.

Prayer. Lord, I want to experience true happiness in my life. Deepen my
reverence for you. I humbly ask you to give me a fruitful ministry which will
honor you and bless others. Extend my circle of healthy relationships and use
me to bring joy in them. Amen.

* Dallimore, *Spurgeon*, 146–50.

November 25   Psalm 129

1 "Greatly have they afflicted me from my youth"—let Israel now say—2 "Greatly have they afflicted me from my youth, yet they have not prevailed against me. 3 The plowers plowed upon my back; they made long their furrows." 4 The LORD is righteous; he has cut the cords of the wicked. 5 May all who hate Zion be put to shame and turned backward! 6 Let them be like the grass on the housetops, which withers before it grows up, 7 with which the reaper does not fill his hand nor the binder of sheaves his arms, 8 nor do those who pass by say, "The blessing of the LORD be upon you! We bless you in the name of the LORD!" (ESV)

"Lord, number me with thy saints. Let me share their grief if I may also partake of their glory."

Deliverance from oppression. Based on the previous psalm, one might assume every waking hour of the Christian life to be filled with bliss. This pain-filled psalm rudely awakens us to the harsh reality. The writer repeats the unpleasant phrase "they have afflicted me from my youth" for a purpose (vv. 1–2). Spiritual pilgrimage includes excruciating experiences at the hands of those who despise the Lord. In the midst of an awful situation, God fortunately intervenes by cutting the whips of those who are evil (v. 4). They are defeated and do not enjoy God's blessing (v. 8). Meanwhile, God delivers his people but only after they have gone through a lot of pain. Spurgeon mentions the apostle Paul, who acknowledged that he was "struck down, but not destroyed" (2 Cor 4:9). God may bring relief by some practical means or by providing us the spiritual resources to withstand afflictions. Our journey with Christ will not always be easy, but he walks with us every step of the way.

Prayer. Loving Father, I can relate to others who have gone through extremely difficult events. Those times were painful and have left scars on my life. When I have been beaten down by these adversities, you supplied me with your strength through the word and your Spirit. Thank you for sustaining me. Amen.

November 26   Psalm 130

1 From the depths of despair, O LORD, I call for your help. 2 Hear my cry, O Lord. Pay attention to my prayer. 3 LORD, if you kept a record of our sins, who, O Lord, could ever survive? 4 But you offer forgiveness, that we might learn to fear you. 5 I am counting on the LORD; yes, I am counting on him. I have put my hope in his word. 6 I long for the Lord more than sentries long for the dawn, yes, more than sentries long for the dawn. 7 O Israel, hope in the LORD; for with the LORD there is unfailing love. His redemption overflows. 8 He himself will redeem Israel from every kind of sin. (NLT)

"Deep places beget deep devotion."

Out of the depths. From the recesses of his soul, the psalmist cries out to the Lord (v. 1). In anguish, he is keenly aware of his sin and guilt (vv. 1–3). He ascends from the depths because he acknowledges the Lord forgives anyone who confesses. We are told three times that the psalmist waits, with every fiber of his being, on God (vv. 5–6). He no longer despairs and he drives home this point with an illustration. As the watchman on the night shift looks forward to the morning light, the psalmist eagerly anticipates God's wonderful forgiveness (vv. 5–6). With this expectation, the psalmist, who had once despaired, turns his focus from himself to his people. With joy, he encourages them to place their hope in the Lord (v. 7). God will show his unfailing love by redeeming them from their sin (vv. 7–8). When people experience God's forgiveness, they worship him with reverence (v. 4). "Gratitude for pardon produces far more fear and reverence of God than all the dread which is inspired by punishment." This psalm highlights the joy of forgiveness. "Prayer *de profundis* gives to God *gloria in excelsis*"—prayer from the depths gives glory to God in the highest.

Prayer. Lord, I am so thankful that it is you who lifts me from despair to assured hope through your forgiveness. Use me to tell others of your willingness to forgive them so that they, in their despair, may be encouraged. I give you all the praise and glory for your forgiving love. Amen.

November 27   Psalm 131

1 O LORD, my heart is not lifted up; my eyes are not raised too high; I do not occupy myself with things too great and too marvelous for me. 2 But I have calmed and quieted my soul, like a weaned child with its mother; like a weaned child is my soul within me. 3 O Israel, hope in the LORD from this time forth and forevermore. (ESV)

"It is one of the shortest Psalms to read, but one of the longest to learn."

True humility. Addressing our pride puts us in a conundrum. If we say we are not proud, we may be proud by doing so. However, the psalmist claims he is not proud (v. 1). How can we claim at least a measure of humility? He pictures a child being weaned (v. 2). After fussing and crying, the child finally learns to be satisfied with solid food and with the mother. True humility is measured by a contented, calm, and quiet heart (vv. 1b–2). We know we have grown in humility when we can "forgo the joys which once appeared to be essential, and can find our solace in him who denies them to us." In fact, "we find delight in giving up our delight" because afflictions "subdue our affections, which wean us from self-sufficiency . . . which teach us to love God not merely when he comforts us, but even when he tries us." Freed from self-preoccupation, we can turn to encouraging others to trust in the Lord (v. 3).

Prayer. Heavenly Father, nourish my soul to be thoroughly content with you. I want to move from making demands to submitting to your desires and growing in humility. Amen.

November 28   Psalm 132:1–10

1 Remember, O LORD, in David's favor, all the hardships he endured, 2 how he swore to the LORD and vowed to the Mighty One of Jacob, 3 "I will not enter my house or get into my bed, 4 I will not give sleep to my eyes or slumber to my eyelids, 5 until I find a place for the LORD, a dwelling place for the Mighty One of Jacob." 6 Behold, we heard of it in Ephrathah; we found it in the fields of Jaar. 7 "Let us go to his dwelling place; let us worship at his footstool!" 8 Arise, O LORD, and go to your resting place, you and the ark of your might. 9 Let your priests be clothed with righteousness, and let your saints shout for joy. 10 For the sake of your servant David, do not turn away the face of your anointed one. (ESV)

> "He resolved to find a place where Jehovah would allow his worship to be celebrated, a house where God would fix the symbol of his presence, and commune with his people."

Seeking God's presence. In this psalm Solomon is praying and remembering his father, David. The latter had a fine palace (v. 3) but wanted to build a suitable home for the ark of the covenant. He was committed to this project and would not quit until the mission was accomplished (v. 4). This involved putting real effort into the search for the ark and eventually bringing it back to Jerusalem. The time and energy spent on this task was well worth it when they found the "symbol of his presence" (v. 6). They celebrated (v. 7)! David, a man after God's heart, had resolved to find the place where God would meet with him. His example encourages us to spend time consciously and deliberately in the presence of God, who dwells within us through the Holy Spirit. However, there is a warning for us. The people pray that their king, Solomon, would not turn away from seeking God in the temple (v. 10). Similarly, we must pursue our relationship with God, not take his indwelling presence for granted. Their prayer must be our prayer.

Prayer. Father, I cannot earn my way into your presence, but I should make an effort to set aside time to seek you in prayer. Thank you that I can come before you anytime and anywhere. I am concerned that I might eventually lose my passion to pursue you. Remind me that I need people to pray for my spiritual well-being. Amen.

November 29   Psalm 132:11–18

11 The LORD swore to David a sure oath from which he will not turn back: "One of the sons of your body I will set on your throne. 12 If your Sons keep my covenant and my testimonies that I shall teach them, their sons also forever shall sit on your throne." 13 For the LORD has chosen Zion; he has desired it for his dwelling place: 14 "This is my resting place forever; here I will dwell, for I have desired it. 15 I will abundantly bless her provisions; I will satisfy her poor with bread. 16 Her priests I will clothe with salvation, and her saints will shout for joy. 17 There I will make a horn to sprout for David; I have prepared a lamp for my anointed. 18 His enemies I will clothe with shame, but on him his crown will shine." (ESV)

"The desire of God to dwell among the people whom he has chosen for himself is very gracious and very natural . . . God desires to abide with those whom he has loved with an everlasting love."

God's presence among us. In the first section (vv. 1–10), David made an oath to God; in this second section, God makes an oath to David (v. 11). David had seemingly initiated the move of the ark of the covenant to Zion. In actuality, it was God who chose Zion for his dwelling place among his people (v. 13). David is told that one of his descendants will be placed on the throne; this is none other than Jesus Christ. He initially lived on earth, revealing God's power through signs and miracles (John 1:14). A few years later, God revealed himself through the coming of the Holy Spirit, who resides with his followers (Acts 2:1–4). He indwells all believers who collectively form a spiritual temple (1 Cor 3:16). God is no longer restricted to one place (the ark) but now dwells within Jesus-followers around the world. In this new relationship, God reveals his presence by supplying all that we need for the Christian life (vv. 15–16). We should be filled with joyful praise, for he is our eternal King (v. 18)!

Prayer. Father, I am filled with gratitude that you chose me and that you dwell in my life through the Holy Spirit so that I may experience your presence. Thank you for giving me the divine resources to live for you, my Savior and eternal King. Amen.

339

November 30   Psalm 133

1 How wonderful and pleasant it is when brothers live together in harmony! 2 For harmony is as precious as the anointing oil that was poured over Aaron's head, that ran down his beard and onto the border of his robe. 3 Harmony is as refreshing as the dew from Mount Hermon that falls on the mountains of Zion. And there the LORD has pronounced his blessing, even life everlasting. (NLT)

"Christian unity is good in itself, good for ourselves, good for the brethren, good for our converts, good for the outside world."

Loving unity. Unity among God's people is best expressed by loving one another. Two word pictures (vv. 2–3) describe genuine love. Like precious oil flowing down one's face and clothes (v. 2), pure love spreads to everyone, regardless of their social and economic standing. "Christian affection knows no limits of parish, nation, sect or age." Our love should also be like the morning dew that extends from Mount Hermon to distant Zion (v. 2). Genuine love refreshes us and extends far beyond our own borders. As a pastor, Spurgeon knew the realities of division in churches and the need to be of "one heart and of one spirit." He extended love to others who held a different theological position. This love and commitment to unity enabled him to associate and work with D. L. Moody and the Quakers.* Christ's love enables us to unite with fellow believers when differences could cause division.

Prayer. Lord, how your people need to be united in love, regardless of the color of their skin or their economic and social status. Help your people to be a model, in a divided and hateful society, by truly loving another. Let those we mingle with be aware of the refreshing fragrance of Jesus in us. Amen.

* Nettles, *Living by Revealed Truth*, 49, 199, 272.

December 1   Psalm 134

1 Oh, praise the LORD, all you servants of the LORD, you who
serve at night in the house of the LORD. 2 Lift your hands toward
the sanctuary, and praise the LORD. 3 May the LORD, who made
heaven and earth, bless you from Jerusalem. (NLT)

"May *blessed* and *blessing* be the two words which describe our lives."

Blessings. After spending time in Jerusalem to worship God, the pilgrims
prepare to return home. This psalm, the last of the psalms of ascent, appropriately concludes their visit to the city. With their imminent morning
departure, they exhort the "servants"—the Levitical singers—to bless the
Lord even in the middle of the night (v. 1). We want God to bless our lives,
but it seems peculiar for us to bless him. "Think well of Jehovah, and speak
well of him. Adore him with reverence, draw near to him with love, delight
in him with exultation." We worship enthusiastically with hands and heart
"upraised, elevated, and consecrated to the adoring service of the Lord" (v.
2). While we are expected to bless God, he will bless his people (v. 3). Using
the ancient blessing given by the high priest, God blesses us "through his
church, his gospel, and the ordinances of this house [church]."

Prayer. Lord, I joyfully bless you for your majesty and holiness, your love
and justice, your compassion and discipline. You are worthy of my blessing
of praise. I humbly ask you to bless me. I covet your good gifts so that I may
serve and glorify you. Amen.

December 2   Psalm 135:1-7

1 Praise the LORD! Praise the name of the LORD! Praise him, you
who serve the LORD, 2 you who serve in the house of the LORD,
in the courts of the house of our God. 3 Praise the LORD, for
the LORD is good; celebrate his lovely name with music. 4 For
the LORD has chosen Jacob for himself, Israel for his own special
treasure. 5 I know the greatness of the LORD—that our Lord is
greater than any other god. 6 The LORD does whatever pleases
him throughout all heaven and earth, and on the seas and in their
depths. 7 He causes the clouds to rise over the whole earth. He
sends the lightning with the rain and releases the wind from his
storehouses. (NLT)

"Do not only magnify the Lord because he is God; but study his character
and his doings, and thus render intelligent, appreciative praise."

Praise God for his goodness and love. Three times the psalmist exhorts the
people to praise God (v. 1) for four outstanding reasons (vv. 3, 4, 5, 14). First,
God is good (v. 3). God is "so good that there is none good in the same sense
or degree. He is so good that all good is found in him, flows from him, and is
rewarded by him . . . truly God is the essence of goodness." Second, God, in
his love, chose people to be his special treasure (v. 4). In the Old Testament,
God chose the Israelites based not on their assets (they had none) but on his
love for them (Deut 7:7). He "gave no reason for his love except that he chose
to love . . . No, it was sovereign grace which dictated the choice." The apostle
Paul tells us, "For he [God] chose us in him before the creation of the world"
(Eph 1:4). We are his possession whom he loves. Our God deserves to receive
our hallelujahs!

Prayer. Lord, I praise you for your goodness, which surrounds me throughout the day. I am deeply grateful for your love, which chose me to be your
child and allows me to belong to your spiritual family. I love you because you
first loved me. Amen.

December 3   Psalm 135:8-14

8 He destroyed the firstborn in each Egyptian home, both people and animals. 9 He performed miraculous signs and wonders in Egypt against Pharaoh and all his people. 10 He struck down great nations and slaughtered mighty kings—11 Sihon king of the Amorites, Og king of Bashan, and all the kings of Canaan. 12 He gave their land as an inheritance, a special possession to his people Israel. 13 Your name, O LORD, endures forever; your fame, O LORD, is known to every generation. 14 For the LORD will give justice to his people and have compassion on his servants. (NLT)

"He may seem to forget his people, but it is not so; he will undertake their cause and deliver them."

Praise God for his saving deliverance. The psalmist gives us the third reason for praising God. Over the course of time, he frequently vindicated or delivered his people from oppressive, evil powers (vv. 8-11, 14). He did this to let them receive their inheritance (v. 12). God has delivered us through Jesus Christ, who defeated Satan on the cross (Col 2:15) and through the power of the Holy Spirit (Eph 6:10-18). One day, we will receive our full inheritance (1 Pet 1:4). His eternal nature is the fourth reason to praise God (v. 13). Since he is eternal, his compassion never ends (v. 14). Our salvation is totally undeserved apart from God's enduring compassion for us. This great salvation is for God's fame (v. 13). He gets all the praise and honor for what he has accomplished.

Prayer. Father, I praise you for changing my heart and drawing me to yourself. I am thankful for your Holy Spirit, who empowers me to resist the destructive schemes of the Evil One. I am thankful for your great power and for your continued love. Amen.

December 4   Psalm 135:15-21

15 The idols of the nations are merely things of silver and gold, shaped by human hands. 16 They have mouths but cannot speak, and eyes but cannot see. 17 They have ears but cannot hear, and mouths but cannot breathe. 18 And those who make idols are just like them, as are all who trust in them. 19 O Israel, praise the LORD! O priests—descendants of Aaron—praise the LORD! 20 O Levites, praise the LORD! All you who fear the LORD, praise the LORD! 21 The LORD be praised from Zion, for he lives here in Jerusalem. Praise the LORD! (NLT)

"Gracious men can see the absurdity of forsaking the true God and setting up rivals in his place."

Praise God for his supremacy. Spurgeon reminds us that verses 15–18 echo Psalm 115:4-6, 8. Nevertheless, it is worthwhile to ponder the foolishness of chasing idols. We can allow them to become substitutes for God, robbing him of his rightful place as our first love. The very thought of making and worshipping lifeless idols or gods is incredulous to Spurgeon—and should be to us. "It is the height of insanity to worship metallic manufactures . . . there is nothing about them which can entitle them to reverence and worship . . . it would seem to be impossible that intelligent beings could bow down before substances which they must themselves refine from ore, and fashion into form." What is most alarming about idolatry is the striking resemblance between the gods and those who worship them (v. 18). These people are "spiritually dead . . . their eyes do not see the truth, their ears hear not the voice of the Lord, and the life of God is not in them." In light of the lifeless idols, the psalmist concludes that the one true God is "greater than any other god" (v. 5). He alone lives and dwells, through the Holy Spirit, among his people (v. 21). Only our living God deserves to receive hallelujahs from his people (vv. 19–21)!

Prayer. Lord, I know how inclined I am to allow other things to take first place in my heart's attention and adoration. Forgive me and allow me to see again how great you are and how you deserve to be my first love. Amen.

December 5   Psalm 136:1–9

1 Give thanks to the LORD, for he is good, for his steadfast love endures forever. 2 Give thanks to the God of gods, for his steadfast love endures forever. 3 Give thanks to the LORD of Lords, for his steadfast love endures forever; 4 to him who alone does great wonders, for his steadfast love endures forever; 5 to him who by understanding made the heavens, for his steadfast love endures forever; 6 to him who spread out the earth above the waters, for his steadfast love endures forever; 7 to him who made the great lights, for his steadfast love endures forever; 8 the sun to rule over the day, for his steadfast love endures forever; 9 the moon and stars to rule over the night, for his steadfast love endures forever. (ESV)

"What joy that there is mercy, mercy with Jehovah, enduring mercy, mercy enduring forever. We are ever needing it, trying it, praying for it, receiving it."

The love of the Creator. The phrase "his steadfast love endures forever" is mentioned twenty-six times in this psalm. While we are apt to skim over this frequently repeated phrase, Spurgeon tells us, "We have this repeated in every verse of this song, but not once too often." Believing this phrase is important, and wanting us to grow in our adoration of the Lord, Spurgeon elaborates on it after every statement on God and his actions. After giving thanks to God for his love (vv. 1–3), the psalmist describes God's great wonders (v. 4). His creative work reveals his love for us (v. 5). By raising the land above the waters (v. 6), his love guarantees that no flood will destroy the human race. By creating the sun and moon (v. 7), his love provides us with the predictable orderliness of days, months, and years. During the day, the sun (v. 8) reflects God's love because without it we would "sit in doleful darkness, and find earth a hell." The moon and stars (v. 9) also reveal God's love, guiding ships and giving light to those on land. These creative acts are a witness of God's grace to humanity. Of course, the greatest light for our world is "Jesus, the Sun of Righteousness."

Prayer. Father, I am filled with awe as I reflect on your created world, with its splendor, vastness, design, and regularity. These, your expressions of love, serve as daily reminders of your care and provision for all I need. Thank you, for your enduring love. Amen.

December 6 Psalm 136:10-16

10 [T]o him who struck down the firstborn of Egypt, for his steadfast love endures forever; 11 and brought Israel out from among them, for his steadfast love endures forever; 12 with a strong hand and an outstretched arm, for his steadfast love endures forever; 13 to him who divided the Red Sea in two, for his steadfast love endures forever; 14 and made Israel pass through the midst of it, for his steadfast love endures forever; 15 but overthrew Pharaoh and his host in the Red Sea, for his steadfast love endures forever; 16 to him who led his people through the wilderness, for his steadfast love endures forever. (ESV)

"To the Israelites as they sung this song their one thought would be of the rescue of their fathers from the fierce oppressor."

The love of the Deliverer. The Israelites' epic deliverance from Egyptian oppression reveals God's love (v. 10). He displayed his love for his people through the plagues that contributed to their ultimate escape from Egypt (vv. 11–12). He showed his love by separating the waters of the Red Sea (v. 13). Not by any ingenuity, but by God's love did the Israelites pass through the Red Sea (v. 14). "Mercy cleared the road . . . mercy led them down, and mercy brought them up again." While the death of Pharaoh and his army is a tragic loss of life (v. 15), God's love protected his people, allowing them to exit Egypt and enter the wilderness (v. 16). Whether in the past or present, God works through world events to accomplish his eternal purposes and to reveal his everlasting love.

Prayer. Lord, stories of a turbulent world fill the daily news. With such chaos, I am left wondering if you are really in control. Thank you for your word, which reminds me that you are actively involved in the world's affairs. You do love your people, who are oppressed in various regions of the world. Help me to trust you more. Amen.

December 7   Psalm 136:17-26

17 [T]o him who struck down great kings, for his steadfast love endures forever; 18 and killed mighty kings, for his steadfast love endures forever; 19 Sihon, king of the Amorites, for his steadfast love endures forever; 20 and Og, king of Bashan, for his steadfast love endures forever; 21 and gave their land as a heritage, for his steadfast love endures forever; 22 a heritage to Israel his servant, for his steadfast love endures forever. 23 It is he who remembered us in our low estate, for his steadfast love endures forever; 24 and rescued us from our foes, for his steadfast love endures forever; 25 he who gives food to all flesh, for his steadfast love endures forever. 26 Give thanks to the God of heaven, for his steadfast love endures forever. (ESV)

"It is memorable mercy to remember us in our low estate."

The love of the Conqueror. The defeat of Israel's enemies by God allowed his people to move into the land he promised to them (vv. 17–22). His victory teaches us that his love is both powerful and tender. He remembered them in their low estate (v. 23). "We thought ourselves too small and too worthless for his memory to burden itself about us, yet he remembered us." God showed his love to the poor and the outcasts by sending Jesus Christ, who came to earth (v. 23). The Lord also delivered us from our enemies (v. 24), including sin, Satan, and the ways of the world. Seeing these displays of God's love, we rightly ask, "What more can be desired? What more can be imagined?" We might conclude that there are no other possible ways for God to exhibit his love. God surprises us by loving not only his people but by extending his love to every living creature (v. 25). There are no boundaries to God's stupendous love!

Prayer. Father, I praise you for your love shown to the human race through Jesus, who died on the cross. I am thankful you defeated Satan and the power of sin. Thank you for expressing your love for me in so many ways. I am filled with gratitude! Amen.

1 Beside the rivers of Babylon, we sat and wept as we thought of Jerusalem. 2 We put away our harps, hanging them on the branches of poplar trees. 3 For our captors demanded a song from us. Our tormentors insisted on a joyful hymn: "Sing us one of those songs of Jerusalem!" 4 But how can we sing the songs of the LORD while in a pagan land? 5 If I forget you, O Jerusalem, let my right hand forget how to play the harp. 6 May my tongue stick to the roof of my mouth if I fail to remember you, if I don't make Jerusalem my greatest joy. 7 O LORD, remember what the Edomites did on the day the armies of Babylon captured Jerusalem. "Destroy it!" they yelled. "Level it to the ground!" 8 O Babylon, you will be destroyed. Happy is the one who pays you back for what you have done to us. 9 Happy is the one who takes your babies and smashes them against the rocks! (NLT)

"The daughter of Babylon seemed determined to fill up her cup of iniquity by torturing the Lord's people."

A time to weep. The exiled Jews in Babylon wept by its rivers (v. 1). They lamented the earlier destruction of Jerusalem and more recent cruelties experienced in this foreign country. Their grief was so profound that they stopped playing and singing their cherished music (v. 2). There will be times when it is natural to grieve; it is important that we do not deny these deep emotions. Nevertheless, we cannot allow them to cloud our decisions and responses. When asked to sing music dedicated to God, they made a principled decision by refusing to go along with their captors' mocking demands (vv. 3–6). The exiles "had not so hardened their hearts as to be willing to please them at such a fearful cost." We must hold firm with biblical convictions if we do not want to compromise our standards in order to please others. With their refusal, the Israelites passionately pleaded with God to deal with their captors (vv. 7–9). The language is strong, but not vengeful. The plea is based on the Old Testament principle of immediate retribution and God's justice.

Prayer. Lord, I grieve at how your people have greatly suffered in many parts of the world. I ask you to sustain those who are imprisoned and tortured for their faith in you. In light of the gospel, I pray for the persecutors to come to know Jesus Christ as their Savior. Amen.

December 9   Psalm 138

1 I give you thanks, O LORD, with my whole heart; before the gods I sing your praise; 2 I bow down toward your holy temple and give thanks to your name for your steadfast love and your faithfulness, for you have exalted above all things your name and your word. 3 On the day I called, you answered me; my strength of soul you increased. 4 All the kings of the earth shall give you thanks, O LORD, for they have heard the words of your mouth, 5 and they shall sing of the ways of the LORD, for great is the glory of the LORD. 6 For though the LORD is high, he regards the lowly, but the haughty he knows from afar. 7 Though I walk in the midst of trouble, you preserve my life; you stretch out your hand against the wrath of my enemies, and your right hand delivers me. 8 The LORD will fulfill his purpose for me; your steadfast love, O LORD, endures forever. Do not forsake the work of your hands. (ESV)

"There is a time to be silent . . . and there is a time to speak openly."

A time to sing. In the previous psalm the people chose not to sing before their captors. In today's devotional, David chooses to sing to God before his foes and their gods (vv. 1, 7). This is not our natural response and it requires God's grace to respond this way. When Spurgeon completed his writing on this psalm, many of the clergy did not hold to the authority of Scripture. Though their low view of Scripture grieved Spurgeon, he knew it was important to sing to the Lord. "Praising and singing are . . . our comfort under the depression caused by insolent attacks upon the truth, and our weapons for defending the gospel." We can praise God because he knows the hearts of all people (v. 6) and he gives strength to those who honor him (v. 7). God will fulfill their faithful work (v. 8). This truth encourages us as it did Spurgeon. "Therefore we do praise him with our whole heart, even in the presence of those who depart from his Holy Word, and set up another God and another gospel."

Prayer. Lord, I am weighed down by others' inappropriate decisions. My heart is heavy as I bemoan their choices. I ask for a joyful outlook to reflect my trust in you. Move me from groaning to praising you. I know you fulfill the efforts of those who seek to honor you. Amen.

December 10   Psalm 139:1–6

1 You have searched me, Lord, and you know me. 2 You know when I sit and when I rise; you perceive my thoughts from afar. 3 You discern my going out and my lying down; you are familiar with all my ways. 4 Before a word is on my tongue you, Lord, know it completely. 5 You hem me in behind and before, and you lay your hand upon me. 6 Such knowledge is too wonderful for me, too lofty for me to attain. (NIV)

"How well it is for us to know the God who knows us!"

The all-knowing God. David declares that God's knowledge is unfathomable (v. 6). It includes knowing everything about the psalmist whom he has searched (v. 1). Spurgeon says God's searching is not analogous to a police officer looking for stolen goods in one's possession. Nor is God searching for something that he does not know about us. He certainly knows our behavior (vv. 2–3) and is intimately familiar with our thoughts (v. 2) even before we put them into words (v. 4). The "Lord knows us as thoroughly as if he had examined us minutely, and had pried into the most secret corners of our being." It is no wonder David feels surrounded by God (v. 5). We can feel the same. "We cannot turn back and so escape him, for he is behind; we cannot go forward and outmarch him, for he is before." If we think we can escape from him, he will put his hand on us (v. 5)! This action may feel threatening. Realizing this, Spurgeon changes the imagery to our heavenly Father putting his arm around us and lovingly stroking us with a gentle hand.

Prayer. Lord, I confess I feel, at times, threatened that you know every detail of my life. When I realize how much you love me then I am willing to enter into this kind of intimate relationship with you. Thank you for knowing me better than I know myself. Amen.

December 11   Psalm 139:7-12

7 Where can I go from your Spirit? Where can I flee from your presence? 8 If I go up to the heavens, you are there; if I make my bed in the depths, you are there. 9 If I rise on the wings of the dawn, if I settle on the far side of the sea, 10 even there your hand will guide me, your right hand will hold me fast. 11 If I say, "Surely the darkness will hide me and the light become night around me," 12 even the darkness will not be dark to you; the night will shine like the day, for darkness is as light to you. (NIV)

"Assuredly God is in all places, at all times, and nothing can by any possibility be kept away from his all-observing, all-comprehending mind."

The all-present God. We may want to run away from God, but this is impossible (v. 7). "Not that the psalmist wished to go from God, or to avoid the power of the divine life; but he asks this question to set forth the fact that no one can escape from the all-pervading being and observation of the Great Invisible Spirit." One can go from the heights to the depths of earth (v. 8); from the east to the west (v. 9); from the light to darkness (vv. 11–12)—but in each case God is there. His omnipresence has moral implications for us. First, when we choose to sin we are doing it in God's presence, even if the act is done in the dark. Second, God is always there to lead us in the way we should live (v. 10). Third, God is great and we dare not minimize it by embracing some "groveling notions of God." Fourth, his presence encourages and comforts us when we feel downcast and lonely. It is wise for us to say, "The spirit of the Lord is around *me;* Jehovah is omnipresent to *me.*" I am never all alone.

Prayer. Lord, I want to grow in my awareness that your presence is everywhere. I know this will contribute to my spiritual growth when I am tempted to sin. I also need your presence to calm my fearful heart wherever I go. Remind me of your all-encompassing presence to correct my thinking when I assume you have abandoned me. I am thankful you are a great God! Amen.

December 12   Psalm 139:13-18

13 For you created my inmost being; you knit me together in
my mother's womb. 14 I praise you because I am fearfully and
wonderfully made; your works are wonderful, I know that full
well. 15 My frame was not hidden from you when I was made in
the secret place, when I was woven together in the depths of the
earth. 16 Your eyes saw my unformed body; all the days ordained
for me were written in your book before one of them came to be.
17 How precious to me are your thoughts, God! How vast is the
sum of them! 18 Were I to count them, they would outnumber
the grains of sand—when I awake, I am still with you. (NIV)

"Most chastely and beautifully is here described the formation of our
being before the time of our birth."

The all-creative God. The psalmist describes, in intimate detail, God's creative work in shaping his life before birth (v. 13). In the womb, his body was
woven together (v. 15) or "embroidered with great skill [which] is an accurate
description of the creation of veins, sinews, muscles, nerves, etc. What tapes-
try can equal the human fabric?" The Hebrew word for "days" (v. 16) has also
been translated as "members" (KJV). Like an architect who draws plans and
specifications, God designed the body parts and then wrote them down in
his book. "[H]e wrote about us when there was nothing of us to write about
. . . all those members were before the eye of God in the sketchbook of his
foreknowledge and predestination." How should this passage affect our lives?
The fetus that reveals God's handiwork should fill us with awe. We have been
wonderfully made (v. 14). The thought that God continues to think about us
should also humble us (v. 17). His thoughts on each of us are innumerable,
far surpassing all the earth's grains of sand (v. 18). "The task of counting
God's thoughts of love would be a never-ending one . . . God thinks upon us
infinitely."

Prayer. Father, you know me intimately and think of me continuously. I am
humbled, knowing that I do not think of you enough throughout the day. I
also feel unworthy that you think about me, until I stop and remember that
I am your child. Thank you for creating me according to your design. Please
use my life to fulfill your divine purposes. Amen.

December 13   Psalm 139:19-24

19 If only you, God, would slay the wicked! Away from me, you who are bloodthirsty! 20 They speak of you with evil intent; your adversaries misuse your name. 21 Do I not hate those who hate you, LORD, and abhor those who are in rebellion against you? 22 I have nothing but hatred for them; I count them my enemies. 23 Search me, God, and know my heart; test me and know my anxious thoughts. 24 See if there is any offensive way in me, and lead me in the way everlasting. (NIV)

"We cannot hide our sin; salvation lies the other way, in a plain discovery of evil, and an effectual severance from it."

The all-examining God. Since God knows all things, exists everywhere, and forms us in the womb, he certainly has the right to search into the interior regions of our lives (v. 23). Based on an intimate relationship between God and himself (vv. 17–18), David wants God to explore his heart because he wants to be pure before the Lord (v. 24). He has just reason for his request! After mentioning people hating God (vv. 19–20), David honestly confesses he has nothing but hatred for his enemies (v. 22). Feeling this raw emotion, David asks God to search his interior life so as to expose any sin (v. 23). "Read not alone the desires of my heart, but the fugitive thoughts of my head." God, who loves and knows us, wants to reveal those areas that need to be confessed and changed. When we willingly open our hearts to God, he is able to expose sin in the dark recesses and bring about much-needed healing.

Prayer. Loving Father, before, I was hesitant and fearful to open my heart to you. Now, seeing how much you love me, come as the divine physician to do your soul work in my life. I know you want to reveal wrong attitudes, thoughts, and motives which I have tried to hide from myself. I am willing to have you reveal them to me so that I may live the way you want me to. Amen.

December 14   Psalm 140:1–5

1 Deliver me, O LORD, from evil men; preserve me from violent men, 2 who plan evil things in their heart and stir up wars continually. 3 They make their tongue sharp as a serpent's, and under their lips is the venom of asps. *Selah* 4 Guard me, O LORD, from the hands of the wicked; preserve me from violent men, who have planned to trip up my feet. 5 The arrogant have hidden a trap for me, and with cords they have spread a net; beside the way they have set snares for me. *Selah* (ESV)

"Evil in the heart simmers in malice, and at last boils in passion."

Malignant malice. With a seamless connection to the previous psalm's reference to the wicked (139:19–22), David now describes them in graphic language. They are evil people (v. 1) who are violent and stir up war (v. 2). Their malicious slander harms others (v. 3). They are deceitful because they want to ensnare those who follow God (v. 5). This is the appropriate time to pause (*selah*) and consider our own lives. We so often see the malice in others, but tragically fail to see it in ourselves. Spurgeon refers to Romans 1:29–30, reminding us that the "old serpent . . . has caused us to be ourselves producers of the like poison; it lies under our lips, ready for use, and, alas, it is all too freely used when we grow angry, and desire to take vengeance upon any who have caused us vexation." We need humility to examine ourselves honestly and to confess that we are not as good as we think we are, for "by nature we have as great a store of venomous words as a cobra has of poison."

Prayer. Lord, it is easy to see the meanness and cruelty in society. But I can be blind to my own nastiness and spitefulness. Reveal to me the speck in my own eye; make me more understanding and loving toward others. Amen.

December 15   Psalm 140:6-13

6 I say to the LORD, you are my God; give ear to the voice of my pleas for mercy, O LORD! 7 O LORD, my Lord, the strength of my salvation, you have covered my head in the day of battle. 8 Grant not, O LORD, the desires of the wicked; do not further their evil plot, or they will be exalted! *Selah* 9 As for the head of those who surround me, let the mischief of their lips overwhelm them! 10 Let burning coals fall upon them! Let them be cast into fire, into miry pits, no more to rise! 11 Let not the slanderer be established in the land; let evil hunt down the violent man speedily! 12 I know that the LORD will maintain the cause of the afflicted, and will execute justice for the needy. 13 Surely the righteous shall give thanks to your name; the upright shall dwell in your presence. (ESV)

"Do not permit their malicious schemes to succeed."

Addressing the malignancy. David responds to his foes' malevolent actions. With confidence, he turns to God with whom he has a personal ("my") relationship (vv. 6–7). He asks his powerful God to thwart those who are malicious (vv. 7–8). "Assuredly the Lord Jehovah will be no accomplice with the malevolent; their desires shall never be his desires" because he opposes the proud. A *selah* is rightfully located here. "The more they rise in conceit the higher let us rise in confidence." David asks God not only to thwart the ill intentions of the wicked but to punish them (vv. 9–11). He will act justly by letting them be "covered with the reward of their own malice." The tone of David's prayer is strong and we are tempted to soften it with the desire to be more forgiving like Christ. However, Spurgeon reminds us that David's prayer addresses a moral issue of right and wrong requiring God's justice. This same quality of God is also revealed by him caring for the afflicted (v. 12). "God helps those who cannot help themselves." Such a posture allows us to praise the Lord who is with us (v. 13). Like David, we can live in a world of malice while we experience God's love.

Prayer. Lord, grant me rest, knowing that you will deal justly with those who love hatred. Teach me how to hate the many forms of malice while praying for and loving those who commit these acts. May they come to know Jesus as their personal Savior. Enable me to praise you while you accomplish your purposes. Amen.

December 16   Psalm 141

1 O Lord, I am calling to you. Please hurry! Listen when I cry to
you for help! 2 Accept my prayer as incense offered to you, and
my upraised hands as an evening offering. 3 Take control of what
I say, O Lord, and guard my lips. 4 Don't let me drift toward evil
or take part in acts of wickedness. Don't let me share in the deli-
cacies of those who do wrong. 5 Let the godly strike me! It will be
a kindness! If they correct me, it is soothing medicine. Don't let
me refuse it. But I pray constantly against the wicked and their
deeds. 6 When their leaders are thrown down from a cliff, the
wicked will listen to my words and find them true. 7 Like rocks
brought up by a plow, the bones of the wicked will lie scattered
without burial. 8 I look to you for help, O Sovereign Lord. You
are my refuge; don't let them kill me. 9 Keep me from the traps
they have set for me, from the snares of those who do wrong. 10
Let the wicked fall into their own nets, but let me escape. (NLT)

"David feels that with all his own watchfulness he may be surprised into
sin, and so he bets the Lord himself to keep him."

An uncompromising life. David asks for God's help not to compromise with
sin in his speech, heart, and relationships (vv. 3–5). Since he wants his words
to honor God, David asks him to guard his mouth from saying the wrong
things (v. 3). Knowing the heart governs one's life, he asks not to be drawn
to evil so he can avoid acting wickedly (v. 4). He knows that some seek to
trap him by appealing to his human nature (vv. 4, 9). Yielding to them would
ensnare him in sin. To avoid compromise, he keeps his eyes fixed on God (v.
8) and lets him deal with the wicked (v. 10). "Nobody could preserve David
but the Omniscient and Omnipotent One; he will also preserve us." We can
live without compromising our commitment to Jesus Christ.

Prayer. Lord, I need to be wise in order to be faithful to you in our secular
society. Guard my heart against the appeal of sin. Strengthen my resolve not
to compromise what I know to be true. Reassure my mind that you will deal
with all forms of evil one day. Amen.

December 17   Psalm 142

1 I cry out to the LORD; I plead for the LORD's mercy. 2 I pour out my complaints before him and tell him all my troubles. 3 When I am overwhelmed, you alone know the way I should turn. Wherever I go, my enemies have set traps for me. 4 I look for someone to come and help me, but no one gives me a passing thought! No one will help me; no one cares a bit what happens to me. 5 Then I pray to you, O LORD. I say, "You are my place of refuge. You are all I really want in life. 6 Hear my cry, for I am very low. Rescue me from my persecutors, for they are too strong for me. 7 Bring me out of prison so I can thank you. The godly will crowd around me, for you are good to me." (NLT)

"The cave was not half such a dungeon to David's body as persecution and temptation made for his soul."

Desperate prayers. While David has previously hid in caves for protection (Ps 57), he feels very differently in this situation. He desperately and unashamedly cries out to God three times in this passage (vv. 1, 5, 6). He is in anguish because the cave now feels like a prison (v. 7). He is trapped by enemies who are far more powerful than him (v. 6). Moreover, he is deserted by his friends in his time of need (v. 4). No wonder he is so discouraged. We are wise to remember that God's people "may not only be low, but very low" for which they should not be stigmatized. Fortunately, there is hope! David declares that God is his refuge and portion (v. 5). When he perceives that he has lost everything and everyone, he knows God is still with him. He looks forward to the day when he will be surrounded by people who love him (v. 7). We are encouraged when we realize God is with us and when we are with his people who faithfully stand by us in difficult times. "When we can begin a Psalm with crying, we may hope to close it with singing."

Prayer. Father, I am truly grateful you are with me even in the most discouraging times. I also need others around me who can encourage and strengthen my walk with you. Help me to be attentive to the cries of those going through dark days and to stand with them. Amen.

December 18   Psalm 143:1-6

1 Hear my prayer, O LORD; give ear to my pleas for mercy! In your faithfulness answer me, in your righteousness! 2 Enter not into judgment with your servant, for no one living is righteous before you. 3 For the enemy has pursued my soul; he has crushed my life to the ground; he has made me sit in darkness like those long dead. 4 Therefore my spirit faints within me; my heart within me is appalled. 5 I remember the days of old; I meditate on all that you have done; I ponder the work of your hands. 6 I stretch out my hands to you; my soul thirsts for you like a parched land. *Selah* (ESV)

"He felt perplexed and overturned, lonely and afflicted."

Despondency. We may have twinges of guilt when we are overwhelmingly discouraged. On such occasions, we benefit by remembering David did not adopt a stoic approach to life. He repeatedly expresses his painful emotions (v. 4). His despondency is due largely to *external* circumstances (v. 3). His adversaries cruelly attack him, leaving him in an emotionally dark place. Unsurprisingly, he feels alone and like giving up (v. 4). He turns to God, who is faithful and righteous (v. 1), which surprisingly creates an *internal* angst for him. He acknowledges that he is not innocent before a perfect God who could bring judgment on him (v. 2). How do we start to move out of the deep, dark hole of despondency (vv. 3-4)? David remembers what God has done in the past (v. 5), which is an assurance that God will rescue him again in his present crisis. Beyond deliverance, he desires a satisfying encounter with God because his soul is thirsty (v. 6). The Lord, who has been faithful to us in the past, will continue to be faithful in the present.

Prayer. Lord, I confess I have for too long neglected my interior life by denying many of my emotions. This has hurt me and others. I am thankful that you are teaching me to express my deepest emotions to you. Remind me of your past faithfulness so I can turn to you on my bleakest days. It is really you I want more than anything else in those times. Amen.

December 19   Psalm 143:7-12

7 Answer me quickly, O LORD! My spirit fails! Hide not your face from me, lest I be like those who go down to the pit. 8 Let me hear in the morning of your steadfast love, for in you I trust. Make me know the way I should go, for to you I lift up my soul. 9 Deliver me from my enemies, O LORD! I have fled to you for refuge. 10 Teach me to do your will, for you are my God! Let your good Spirit lead me on level ground! 11 For your name's sake, O LORD, preserve my life! In your righteousness bring my soul out of trouble! 12 And in your steadfast love you will cut off my enemies, and you will destroy all the adversaries of my soul, for I am your servant. (ESV)

"The way is long, and steep, and he who goes without a divine leader will faint on that journey; but with Jehovah to lead, it is delightful to follow, and there is neither stumbling nor wandering."

A pilgrim's progress. When God does not respond to our needs, we assume God has withdrawn his presence. We feel drained of all strength and are filled with despair (v. 7). Although we may feel God is not with us, we do not proceed alone on our spiritual journey. The Lord, with his unfailing love, will lead and instruct us on the way we must travel (v. 8). Since this long trip through life is arduous, it is necessary for God to preserve or refresh us (v. 11). Along this life pilgrimage, we who are servants of God (v. 12) will encounter people who will oppose us because of our relationship with him. We can ask God our Master to deal with these people (v. 12). As followers of Jesus Christ, we also know that we are to love and pray for those who are hostile to the gospel (Matt 5:44). Through his Spirit, he will lead us eventually to level ground (v. 10). The land is a metaphor for spiritual maturity. When we reach this stage in our Christian life, we have entered the "country of holiness" which is filled with God's grace and peace.

Prayer. Lord, I know you do not promise a problem-free life even though you are with me. However, with you as my faithful companion, I can face my present and future days with confidence. I know you will continue to guide me because of your love. Amen.

1 Blessed be the LORD, my rock, who trains my hands for war, and my fingers for battle; 2 he is my steadfast love and my fortress, my stronghold and my deliverer, my shield and he in whom I take refuge, who subdues peoples under me. 3 O LORD, what is man that you regard him, or the son of man that you think of him? 4 Man is like a breath; his days are like a passing shadow. 5 Bow your heavens, O LORD, and come down! Touch the mountains so that they smoke! 6 Flash forth the lightning and scatter them; send out your arrows and rout them! 7 Stretch out your hand from on high; rescue me and deliver me from the many waters, from the hand of foreigners, 8 whose mouths speak lies and whose right hand is a right hand of falsehood. (ESV)

"He is so short lived that he scarcely attains to years, but exists by the day."

The warrior's life ends. Commenting on today's passage, Spurgeon refers to David as the "believing warrior" who faced many battles. David depended on God, who prepared and defended him in his military campaigns (vv. 1–2). Like the psalmist, Spurgeon knew he needed God's power (vv. 5–7) to fight the battles in his ministry. After many years of suffering with several debilitating diseases, Charles Haddon Spurgeon passed away on January 31, 1892, at the age of fifty-seven. His brief life was like a breath (v. 4). But he also knew God's amazing grace had redeemed and used him throughout his brief years. His comments on David's life in verses 3–4 held true for his own life and for anyone who has experienced salvation through Jesus Christ.

> The psalmist's wonder is that God should stoop to know him . . . God knows his people with a tender intimacy, a constant, careful observation; he knew them in love, he knows them by care, he will know them is acceptance at last . . . That he should make man the subject of election, the object of redemption, the child of eternal love, the darling of infallible providence, the next of kin to Deity.

Prayer. Lord, my life is going by so quickly and it is brief compared to eternity. Nevertheless, it is significant because you, by your grace, reached down and brought me into a personal relationship with you. Thank you for walking with me through this journey of life. Amen.

December 21   Psalm 144:9-15

9 I will sing a new song to you, O God; upon a ten-stringed harp I will play to you, 10 who gives victory to kings, who rescues David his servant from the cruel sword. 11 Rescue me and deliver me from the hand of foreigners, whose mouths speak lies and whose right hand is a right hand of falsehood. 12 May our sons in their youth be like plants full grown, our daughters like corner pillars cut for the structure of a palace; 13 may our granaries be full, providing all kinds of produce; may our sheep bring forth thousands and ten thousands in our fields; 14 may our cattle be heavy with young, suffering no mishap or failure in bearing; may there be no cry of distress in our streets! 15 Blessed are the people to whom such blessings fall! Blessed are the people whose God is the LORD! (ESV)

"We can scarcely judge how much of happiness may hang upon the Lord's favor to one man."

A blessed life. Reflecting on Spurgeon's life, we clearly recognize God's favor on him. His wife, Susannah, had been an encouragement and assistance in his ministry. His sons, Thomas and Charles, became pastors. Spurgeon's heart resonated with David's comments about sons (v. 12): "O the joys which we may have through our sons!" Like a prosperous farmer (vv. 13–14), Spurgeon's pastoral ministry at the metropolitan Tabernacle and his many other ministries bore much fruit.* How was this possible? Commenting on verse 15, he writes, "[A]ll these temporal gifts are a part of happiness, but still the heart and soul of happiness lies in the people being right with God, and having a full possession of him." Spurgeon wholeheartedly loved and obeyed his Lord. Will his devotion to his Savior be an example for us to encourage our walk with Jesus?

Prayer. Lord, thank you for the godly examples you give us. By your Spirit and word, enable me to love and obey you, and use my life for your glory and honor. Amen.

---

* Lawson, *Gospel Focus,* 14–17. Spurgeon's other ministries include: Bible distribution, orphanage ministry, and international sales of his sermons and books.

December 22   Psalm 145:1-7

1 I will exalt you, my God and King, and praise your name forever and ever. 2 I will praise you every day; yes, I will praise you forever. 3 Great is the LORD! He is most worthy of praise! No one can measure his greatness. 4 Let each generation tell its children of your mighty acts; let them proclaim your power. 5 I will meditate on your majestic, glorious splendour and your wonderful miracles. 6 Your awe-inspiring deeds will be on every tongue; I will proclaim your greatness. 7 Everyone will share the story of your wonderful goodness; they will sing with joy about your righteousness. (NLT)

"The best adoration of the Unsearchable is to own him to be so, and close the eyes in reverence before the excessive light of his glory."

His glory revealed. This psalm is the last of a group of eight (138–145) written by David. Today's passage centers on God's glory revealed throughout nature and human history. The psalmist praises God for his glorious actions (vv. 4–6). The readers of David's day would think of the events surrounding the Israelites' deliverance from Egypt. God's actions continue to reveal his glory, which grandparents and parents should make known to the younger generations (v. 4). "God's works of goodness and acts of power make up a subject which all the eras of human story can never exhaust." God's greatest act was announced by an angel to the shepherds "and the glory of the Lord shone around them" (Luke 2:9). Jesus came to earth in human form and "made his dwelling among us. We have seen his glory, the glory of the one and only son, who came from the Father, full of grace and truth" (John 1:14). This is good reason to celebrate God's goodness shown to us (v. 7), and to tell others of God's great act of salvation through Christ (v. 6).

Prayer. Father, I celebrate your act of sending your Son, Jesus Christ, to earth 2,000 years ago. Thank you for revealing your glory by the miracles he performed on earth, including conquering death through the resurrection. Amen.

December 23   Psalm 145:8-13

8 The LORD is merciful and compassionate, slow to get angry and filled with unfailing love. 9 The LORD is good to everyone. He showers compassion on all his creation. 10 All of your works will thank you, LORD, and your faithful followers will praise you. 11 They will speak of the glory of your kingdom; they will give examples of your power. 12 They will tell about your mighty deeds and about the majesty and glory of your reign. 13 For your kingdom is an everlasting kingdom. You rule throughout all generations. The LORD always keeps his promises; he is gracious in all he does. (NLT)

"Those who bless God from their hearts rejoice to see him enthroned, glorified, and magnified in power."

His glory described. The passage mentions God's people praising him for his glorious kingdom (vv. 11–12). When we think of God's glory, his splendor often comes to mind (v. 12). However, his glory extends beyond his brilliance. When Moses wanted to see his glory (Exod 33:18), God responded with words that are echoed in verse 8. His compassionate and loving actions reveal God's glory, which is his character. The psalmist adds that God's powerful acts further reveal who he really is (vv. 11–12). Years later, Jesus revealed his Father's glory in various ways. When he turned water into wine at a wedding feast, John testified, "He thus revealed his glory" (John 2:11). When Jesus fed the hungry, healed the sick, and restored sight to the blind, he revealed God's character of compassion and love. Jesus also demonstrated his power by casting out demons, calming a stormy lake, and rising from the dead. During this Christmas season we do well to reflect on the many ways Jesus revealed his glory. We have the joyful privilege of telling others about him who is both the Savior and King (vv. 12–13).

Prayer. Jesus, I am filled with praise and adoration for the compassion and divine power you revealed during your earthly ministry. You continue to do this as you extend the offer of salvation to us and your Spirit's power to make us more like you. Amen.

December 24   Psalm 145:14–21

14 The LORD helps the fallen and lifts those bent beneath their loads. 15 The eyes of all look to you in hope; you give them their food as they need it. 16 When you open your hand, you satisfy the hunger and thirst of every living thing. 17 The LORD is righteous in everything he does; he is filled with kindness. 18 The LORD is close to all who call on him, yes, to all who call on him in truth. 19 He grants the desires of those who fear him; he hears their cries for help and rescues them. 20 The LORD protects all those who love him, but he destroys the wicked. 21 I will praise the LORD, and may everyone on earth bless his holy name forever and ever. (NLT)

"He does not leave praying men, and men who confess his name, to battle with the world alone, but he is ever at their side."

His glory is near. God reveals his goodness to all people (known as "common grace") by providing what they need (vv. 15–16). He shows his compassion by lifting up those who are beaten down by the adversities of life (v. 14). He comes close to them (v. 18) to fulfill their deepest desires and to save them (v. 19). During this season, we think of Mary, who, upon hearing that she would bear Jesus, spoke of her "humble state" and God who "lifted up the humble" (Luke 1:48, 52). The baby she carried would be called Immanuel, meaning "God with us" (Matt 1:23). Jesus, who is both God and human, entered the world and lived among the populace. He told people that he had come to satisfy their longings (John 4:13–14) and to save them from their sin (Luke 1:68–75). In response to God stirring in our hearts, we call on him (v. 18) to be our personal Savior and he will then be with us through the indwelling Holy Spirit (John 14:17).

Prayer. Lord, I am filled with gratitude for your love in giving your Son, Jesus, to be born into this world. I am thankful that you came to provide salvation and to meet my greatest spiritual need—to know you personally. Thank you for your nearness through your indwelling Spirit. Amen.

December 25   Psalm 146

1 Praise the LORD. Praise the LORD, my soul. 2 I will praise the LORD all my life; I will sing praise to my God as long as I live. 3 Do not put your trust in princes, in human beings, who cannot save. 4 When their spirit departs, they return to the ground; on that very day their plans come to nothing. 5 Blessed are those whose help is the God of Jacob, whose hope is in the LORD their God. 6 He is the Maker of heaven and earth, the sea, and everything in them—he remains faithful forever. 7 He upholds the cause of the oppressed and gives food to the hungry. The LORD sets prisoners free, 8 the LORD gives sight to the blind, the LORD lifts up those who are bowed down, the LORD loves the righteous. 9 The LORD watches over the foreigner and sustains the fatherless and the widow, but he frustrates the ways of the wicked. 10 The LORD reigns forever, your God, O Zion, for all generations. Praise the LORD. (NIV)

"Princes are only men, and men with greater needs than others; why, then, should we look to them for aid?"

Praise for Jesus' coming. The psalmist warns us not to put our ultimate trust in princes, because as humans they are unable to save us (v. 3). "People are always far too apt to depend upon the great ones of earth, and forget the Great One above; and this habit is the fruitful source of disappointment." Rather, we are to trust another Prince, who is God (v. 5). He has the power to be the Creator of the universe (v. 6; Col 1:16), and compassion for the oppressed (vv. 7–9). Jesus began his ministry publicly reading from Isaiah 61:1–2. He told people that he had come to bring good news to the poor, proclaim freedom for the prisoners, give sight to the blind, and release the oppressed (Luke 4:18–19). Jesus entered this world to bring salvation and hope to a very needy human race. Fittingly, this is the first of five Psalms starting and ending with hallelujah, which means "Praise the Lord" (vv. 1, 10).

Prayer. Lord, I praise you for Jesus' coming to earth to demonstrate your love for humanity. How can I not place my faith in you, the true Prince and Savior, who loves me so much? Amen.

December 26   Psalm 147:1–11

1 Praise the LORD! For it is good to sing praises to our God; for it is pleasant, and a song of praise is fitting. 2 The LORD builds up Jerusalem; he gathers the outcasts of Israel. 3 He heals the brokenhearted and binds up their wounds. 4 He determines the number of the stars; he gives to all of them their names. 5 Great is our Lord, and abundant in power; his understanding is beyond measure. 6 The LORD lifts up the humble; he casts the wicked to the ground. 7 Sing to the LORD with thanksgiving; make melody to our God on the lyre! 8 He covers the heavens with clouds; he prepares rain for the earth; he makes grass grow on the hills. 9 He gives to the beasts their food, and to the young ravens that cry. 10 His delight is not in the strength of the horse, nor his pleasure in the legs of a man, 11 but the LORD takes pleasure in those who fear him, in those who hope in his steadfast love. (ESV)

"Come, broken hearts, come to the Physician who never fails to heal; uncover your wounds to him who so tenderly binds them up."

Praise for God's healing. God providentially cares for nature (vv. 8–9) and for people (vv. 2–6). By his power (v. 5), the exiles return to Jerusalem (v. 2). While we might expect them to be excited to see their home city, they come back as broken people (v. 3). "The Lord is not only a Builder, but a healer; he restores broken hearts as well as broken walls . . . he deigns to handle and heal broken hearts: he himself lays on the ointment of grace, and the soft bandages of love, and thus binds up the bleeding wounds of those convinced of sin." We can be confident of God's ceaseless love for us (v. 11). He delights in our trust and we have good reason to praise him (v. 1). Hallelujah!

Prayer. Father, I am thankful that you are the healer of my soul. You know I have been wounded and broken throughout my life. I am grateful to you for tenderly nursing me back to a greater measure of spiritual and emotional health. It is wonderful to move from brokenness to an enjoyment of life! I praise you for your restoration! Amen.

December 27   Psalm 147:12–20

12 Praise the LORD, O Jerusalem! Praise your God, O Zion! 13
For he strengthens the bars of your gates; he blesses your children within you. 14 He makes peace in your borders; he fills you with the finest of the wheat. 15 He sends out his command to the earth; his word runs swiftly. 16 He gives snow like wool; he scatters frost like ashes. 17 He hurls down his crystals of ice like crumbs; who can stand before his cold? 18 He sends out his word, and melts them; he makes his wind blow and the waters flow. 19 He declares his word to Jacob, his statutes and rules to Israel. 20 He has not dealt thus with any other nation; they do not know his rules. Praise the LORD! (ESV)

"[I]t is a still greater joy to see that the inhabitants are blessed with all good gifts."

Praise for God's gifts. The call to exalt God typically occurs at the opening and closing of this song. Near its halfway point, we discover a further call to praise him (v. 12). God is a benefactor to his people. He fortifies the city, thereby giving security for the residents' happiness (v. 13). Spurgeon suggested that churches should provide security from "false doctrine and unholy living." God also grants his people gifts of peace and prosperity (v. 14). Perhaps speaking of his own church, Spurgeon comments, "[I]t is a work of God when in large churches unbroken peace is found year after year." Finally, we have the gift of God's commands in two areas. First, he reveals his power over nature by giving us what we need (vv. 15–18). Second, he reveals himself through the commands of his word (v. 19). Regarding those who do not know his commands, we have a responsibility to tell them about the revealed incarnate Word of God—Jesus Christ (v. 20). God's generous gifts are worthy of one more hallelujah.

Prayer. Lord, this is the season for giving presents to loved ones. You, our heavenly Father, have given your spiritual children so many gifts for our good and for your honor. I feel undeserving to receive these extravagant expressions of your love, but I accept them with gratitude and praise. Amen.

December 28   Psalm 148:1–6

1 Praise the LORD! Praise the LORD from the heavens; praise him in the heights! 2 Praise him, all his angels; praise him, all his hosts! 3 Praise him, sun and moon, praise him, all you shining stars! 4 Praise him, you highest heavens, and you waters above the heavens! 5 Let them praise the name of the LORD! For he commanded and they were created. 6 And he established them forever and ever; he gave a decree, and it shall not pass away. (ESV)

"[T]he doctrine of creation logically demands worship."

Praise from the created order. Within these first six verses, the psalmist gives nine exhortations for everything in the universe to praise the Lord. There is no place above earth which should not give praise to him. "If we could climb as much above the heavens as the heavens are above the earth, we could still cry out to all around us, 'Praise the Lord'. There can be none so great and high as to be above praising Jehovah." One reason for giving praise to God is based on his command to create the heavenly host (v. 5). "The Maker should have honour from his works, they should tell forth *his* praise; and thus they should praise his *name*—by which his character is intended . . . Those who were created by command are under command to adore their Creator." God is not only the Creator but also the Sustainer who enables the heavenly creation to exist for as long as he wills (v. 6). This created order submits to the commands of God. Their obedience expresses their homage to God. We praise God with our mouths and with adoring obedience to the One who rules over all. Hallelujah!

Prayer. Lord, all the heavenly bodies praise you by their continued existence and submission to your will. I acknowledge that every breath I have ultimately comes from you. Continue to work in my life to produce further praise and obedience to you. Amen.

December 29   Psalm 148:7-14

7 Praise the LORD from the earth, you great sea creatures and all deeps, 8 fire and hail, snow and mist, stormy wind fulfilling his word! 9 Mountains and all hills, fruit trees and all cedars! 10 Beasts and all livestock, creeping things and flying birds! 11 Kings of the earth and all peoples, princes and all rulers of the earth! 12 Young men and maidens together, old men and children! 13 Let them praise the name of the LORD, for his name alone is exalted; his majesty is above earth and heaven. 14 He has raised up a horn for his people, praise for all his saints, for the people of Israel who are near to him. Praise the LORD! (ESV)

"[S]ongs coming down from heaven are to blend in with those going up from earth."

Praise of global magnitude. The psalmist employs several examples to announce that *everything* exists to praise God. The wide range of depth and height (vv. 7, 9), temperature (v. 8), temperament and abilities (v. 10), social status (v. 11), and age (v. 12) serve this supreme purpose. The focus of this praise is on God whose "name" is twice mentioned in verse 13. "His unique name should have a monopoly of praise . . . There is more glory in him personally than in all his works united." Nations are called to praise the Lord (v. 11), as are those who enjoy his affectionate love (v. 14). It is appropriate for these "faithful servants" to praise him. "He is their glory: to him they render praise; and by his mercy to them evermore gives them further reasons for praise, and higher motives for adoration . . . he exalts them, and they exalt him. The Holy One is praised by holy ones." Praise the Lord. Hallelujah!

Prayer. Father, if the entirety of this world should give you praise, then I should certainly give you all my praise. As one of your children, I want to draw closer to you and enjoy your affection and love. Amen.

December 30   Psalm 149

1 Praise the LORD! Sing to the LORD a new song, his praise in the assembly of the godly! 2 Let Israel be glad in his Maker; let the children of Zion rejoice in their King! 3 Let them praise his name with dancing, making melody to him with tambourine and lyre! 4 For the LORD takes pleasure in his people; he adorns the humble with salvation. 5 Let the godly exult in glory; let them sing for joy on their beds. 6 Let the high praises of God be in their throats and two-edged swords in their hands, 7 to execute vengeance on the nations and punishments on the peoples, 8 to bind their kings with chains and their nobles with fetters of iron, 9 to execute on them the judgment written! This is honor for all his godly ones. Praise the LORD! (ESV)

"God has honoured them, and put a rare glory on them; therefore let them exalt therein."

Praise of God's people. We are called on to praise the Lord all the time. We may be with others (vv. 1, 3), by ourselves (v. 5), or in the heat of a spiritual battle (vv. 6–9). Wherever we are, there are solid reasons to praise God unceasingly. He is our Creator and King who has made us his people (v. 2). God delights in us (v. 4). "Herein is grand argument for worshipping the Lord with the utmost exaltation: he who takes such a pleasure in us must be approached with every token of exceeding joy." In addition to his word ("double-edged sword"), God employs his people's praise (v. 6) to defeat his enemies (vv. 4, 7–9). Being in the midst of a spiritual battle should not stop us from praising God. Spurgeon comments, "If we do not praise, we shall grow sad in our conflict." There will be victory because God gives us the honor of participating with him in it (v. 9). We dare not fail to give God the glory (v. 5)! "Surely in this we have the best argument for glorying the Lord." Hallelujah!

Prayer. Lord, knowing your delight in me is unfathomable. For this alone, I give you praise. Then, you tell me that you honor me with the joy of victory over spiritual enemies. How can I fail to praise you my Creator, Savior, and King? You are worthy of all my continual worship. Amen.

December 31   Psalm 150*

1 Praise the LORD! Praise God in his sanctuary; praise him in his mighty heavens! 2 Praise him for his mighty deeds; praise him according to his excellent greatness! 3 Praise him with trumpet sound; praise him with lute and harp! 4 Praise him with tambourine and dance; praise him with strings and pipe! 5 Praise him with sounding cymbals; praise him with loud clashing cymbals! 6 Let everything that has breath praise the LORD! Praise the LORD! (ESV)

"Should they not all declare the glory of him for whose glory they are, and were created?"

The hallelujah song. We have arrived at the last of the five hallelujah psalms and the last of the psalter. The climactic conclusion is a crescendo of praise to God, who is the sole object of our worship (v. 1). This joyful song commences with "Praise the Lord" or hallelujah, followed by a groundswell of five "praise" shouts to the Lord, and concludes with a resounding hallelujah. "The exhortation is to all things in earth or in heaven . . . Let it all be filled with praise." The Lord is worthy of praise for his display of power (v. 2). "Here is the reason for praise. In these deeds of power we see himself . . . they are his acts, and his acts of might, therefore let him be praised for them." The thought of what he has done stirs us to offer exuberant praise to the Lord (vv. 3–5), and this should rouse even "the most heavy of slumberers" from their spiritual apathy. The point is clear: everyone should praise God (v. 6). "He gave them breath, let them breathe his praise." Spurgeon closes his commentary on this psalm and the psalter with a fitting challenge, "Reader, will you not at this moment pause a while, and worship the Lord your God? Hallelujah!"

Praise. Sovereign Lord, you have been with me through times of praise and accusations, intimacy and isolation, confidence and fears, refreshment and dryness, victories and defeats, crying and singing. You faithfully loved me throughout this past year. To you all the praise goes. Hallelujah! Amen!

* With the completion of this last psalm, Spurgeon writes, "And now the colossal work is done! To God be all glory. More than twenty years have glided away while this pleasant labour has been in the doing; but the wealth of mercy which has been lavished upon me during that time my grateful heart is unable to measure. Surely goodness and mercy have followed me all those years, and made my heart to sing new Psalms for new mercies" (*Treasury of David*, 6:vi).

Bibliography

Bacon, Ernest W. *Spurgeon: Heir of the Puritans.* Arlington Heights, IL: Christian Liberty, 1967.

Dallimore, Arnold A. *Spurgeon: A Biography.* 1985. Reprint, Carlisle, PA: Banner of Truth Trust, 2018.

Keller, Timothy, and Kathy Keller. *The Songs of Jesus: A Year of Daily Devotions in the Psalms.* New York: Viking, 2015.

Lawson, Steven. *The Gospel Focus of Charles Spurgeon.* Sanford, FL: Reformation Trust, 2012.

Morden, Peter. *C.H. Spurgeon: The People's Preacher.* Surrey, UK: CWR, 2009.

Nettles, Tom. *Living by Revealed Truth: The Life and Pastoral Theology of Charles Haddon Spurgeon.* 2013. Reprint, Ross-shire, Scotland: Mentor, 2015.

Spurgeon, Charles Haddon. *The Treasury of David: Containing An Original Exposition Of The Book Of Psalms; A Collection of Illustrative Extracts From The Whole Range Of Literature; A Series of Homiletical Hints Upon Almost Every Verse; And Lists Of Writers Upon Each Psalm.* 6 vols. London: Marshall Brothers, n.d. ca.1869–1885.

Made in the USA
Las Vegas, NV
12 July 2021